Chicago in the Age of Capital

CHICAGO IN THE AGE OF CAPITAL

Class, Politics,
and Democracy
during the Civil War
and Reconstruction

*John B. Jentz and
Richard Schneirov*

UNIVERSITY OF ILLINOIS PRESS
URBANA, CHICAGO, AND SPRINGFIELD

First Illinois paperback, 2015
© 2012 by the Board of Trustees
of the University of Illinois
Manufactured in the United States of America

1 2 3 4 5 C P 5 4 3 2 1
∞ This book is printed on acid-free paper.

The Library of Congress cataloged the cloth edition as follows:
Jentz, John B., 1944–
Chicago in the age of capital : class, politics,
and democracy during the Civil War and Reconstruction /
John B. Jentz and Richard Schneirov.
p. cm. — (The working class in American history)
Includes bibliographical references and index.
ISBN 978-0-252-03683-5 (hbk. : alk. paper)
1. Labor—Chicago—Illinois—History—19th century.
2. Working class—Chicago—Illinois—History—19th century.
3. Capitalism—Illinois—Chicago—History—19th century.
4. Industrialization—Chicago—Illinois—History—19th century.
5. Chicago (Ill.)—Social conditions—19th century.
6. Chicago (Ill.)—Economic conditions—19th century.
I. Schneirov, Richard. II. Title.
HD8085.C53J46   2012
331.09773'1109034—dc23   2011039506

Paperback ISBN 978-0-252-08105-7

*John Jentz dedicates this book
to the memory of his parents,
Ralph C. Jentz and June S. Jentz.
Richard Schneirov dedicates the work
to his wife, Silvia, and his two sons,
Zachary and Nathan.*

Contents

List of Illustrations

TABLES

Preface

In its conception and its writing, this book has been a collaborative project with continuous and systematic interaction between the authors. Over time, we have developed a bond, based on a common understanding and shared interpretive outlook. We have both learned enormously from each other throughout the long course of this joint project, which has been in gestation since the early 1980s.

John Jentz and Richard Schneirov came out of similar scholarly networks in the 1970s and '80s. Jentz worked closely with Eric Foner and Herbert G. Gutman at the Graduate Center of the City University of New York, while Schneirov owes intellectual debts to Alfred F. Young and Martin J. Sklar at Northern Illinois University. Their scholarly collaboration originated in the research project led by Professor Hartmut Keil of the America Institute of the University of Munich and funded by the Volkswagen Foundation, which studied German workers in Chicago in the late nineteenth and early twentieth centuries. This project, which ran from 1979 to 1983, also maintained vital links to German scholars, among whom was Dirk Hoerder, a scholar of labor and migration history, who was also a colleague and collaborator with Alfred Young.

The Chicago Project led to the grant funded by the National Endowment for the Humanities (RS-20393–83) entitled "Origins of Chicago's Industrial Working Class" and based at the Family and Community History Center of the Newberry Library in Chicago. Jentz was principal investigator, while Schneirov was the other investigator for the project; later, Robin L. Einhorn served as a research associate, providing critical help in processing and evaluating the census data. Kathleen Neils Conzen and Eric Foner gave advice at critical junctures in the research. This project provided the resources necessary for most of the basic research used in this book in both newspapers and the manuscript censuses. The community of scholars at the Newberry created a supportive environment for discussing the import of our work, with special thanks going to the Chicago Area Labor History Group, whose critical readings of works in progress helped us digest evidence and frame issues.

In the period since the decade of the 1980s, the manuscript has undergone enormous changes and several drafts. Most important, we decided to jettison the thick description of events and adopt a new conceptualization focusing on the rise of capitalism during the Civil War and Reconstruction, which provided the context for the emergence of a class-based urban politics and new social movements. We presented the basic theoretical framework of the book to scholars and critics at meetings of the Social Science History Association—November 2007—and the Labor and Working-Class History Association—May 2009—both held in Chicago. There we received thoughtful comments from Susan E. Hirsch, Rima Schultz, and others at the conference.

Throughout the course of the writing of the book, we have incurred numerous intellectual debts from scholars, including Eric Foner, Mary O. Furner, Rima L. Schultz, David R. Roediger, and Alan Lessoff. The comments of Mary Furner, James R. Barrett, and an anonymous reviewer for the University of Illinois Press were particularly helpful.

In addition to intellectual debts, we have many personal and financial ones. We would like to thank the community of archivists and librarians, particularly those at the Chicago Historical Society, now the Chicago Historical Museum, and the Newberry Library, for their ready responses to our endless requests. To the Indiana State University we owe special thanks for contributing to the subvention that helped make publication of this book possible. We want to thank the University of Illinois Press for permission to use parts of Richard Schneirov's essay "Chicago's Great Upheaval of 1877: Class Polarization and Democratic Politics" published in *The Great Strikes of 1877*, edited by David O. Stowell (2008), 76–104. Sections of this article appeared earlier in "Chicago's Great Upheaval of 1877" by Schneirov published in the March 1980 edition of *Chicago History* (vol. 9, no. 1, pp. 2–17). We thank the Chicago Historical Museum for permission to use these sections. Selections from these two essays appear in chapter 6 of this work.

John Jentz owes thanks to the deans and department heads of Marquette University's Raynor Memorial Libraries for their support of his historical projects as well as his career as a librarian. Special acknowledgement goes to colleagues Valerie Beech and Brian Evans for their help in producing the figures and maps for the book. Richard Schneirov would like to thank Indiana State University's College of Arts and Sciences and the History Department for their financial support of this project.

We both owe debts beyond measure to family and friends who have supported and sustained us over the years. We could not begin to name all of them. Thanks to everyone.

Introduction

IN 1821, JAMES MADISON PREDICTED that, with the exhaustion of the country's reservoir of open land, Americans would face the prospect of rising inequality, including "a dependence of an increasing number on the wealth of a few." Madison thought the main form of dependency would arise from "the connection between the great Capitalists in Manufactures and Commerce and the members employed by them." Like other founders, he believed that wage labor promoted servility and dependence and that a balanced distribution of landed property and the independence it provided was necessary for a viable republic. It was hardly conceivable that a republic composed of a permanent wage-worker class could survive. Nonetheless, as the proportion of wage earners in the labor force overtook the self-employed in midcentury, it became impossible to ignore the question of wage labor.[1]

The three decades from the 1850s through the 1870s—what Eric Hobsbawm called the "Age of Capital"—witnessed a dramatic capitalist transition in which the country shifted from being a nation predominantly of small producers and slaves to one in which a majority were wage earners (fig. 1). Chapter 1 explores this topic in Chicago. As the proportion of those working for wages grew ever larger, many Americans, particularly in the Northern states, scrambled to reconcile republican theory with wage labor.[2]

This book examines the further evolution of the wage-labor question during the Civil War and Reconstruction in Chicago, the most dynamic industrial city of the Northern states. In doing so, one of its organizing concepts is what political theorists have called "the public sphere," the arena of public communication in which a body of citizens develops public opinion. The public sphere consists of all those venues, such as newspapers, pamphlets, and other printed media, along with saloons, clubs, and other meeting places for associational gatherings, where political communication occurred. Though some contemporary thinkers narrow the definition of the public sphere to the body of *private* persons outside the government, there

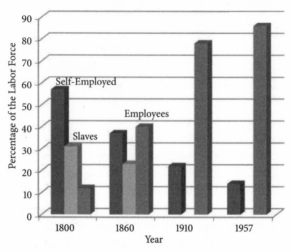

Figure 1
United States Labor Force: 1800–1957

Source: Stanley Lebergott, "The Pattern of Employment since
1800," in *American Economic History*, ed. Seymour E. Harris
(New York: McGraw-Hill, 1961), 292.

is considerable warrant in American history for including the legislative
branch of government as well.[3]

To James Madison and his allies, the public sphere was central because
they believed that public opinion was sovereign in a genuine republic. Unlike conservatives such as John Adams, who despaired of the people's virtue
and relied instead on the separation of powers and checks and balances in
government, Madison believed that a wise and just public opinion was possible and necessary to restrain a would-be tyrannical majority or minority
faction from dominating the republic. But how could such a public opinion
be achieved in the face of the ephemeral passions and narrow interests so
pervasive in the public sphere?[4]

Until the early decades of the nineteenth century, Americans answered that
question by refusing to grant legal privileges to business corporations and
other organized interests in civil society unless they served a manifest public
purpose. In practice, Americans limited the public sphere to those white
males with sufficient property and moral standing to confer independence
of judgment and a stake in the outcomes of public policy. Only at the end of
the period in question, when wage labor and a civil society independent of
the state became widely accepted, was it possible to take seriously the modern

notion that the public sphere consisted of a plurality of competing publics. In the emerging vision, each public, including that of wageworkers, reflected a legitimate interest in civil society and the public sphere.[5]

The story of how Chicago wageworkers and the labor question achieved legitimacy in the public sphere begins with the formation of the Republican Party. The Republican Party of the 1850s had an ambiguous attitude toward wage labor. On the one hand, Republicans wanted to reserve the western lands for white settlers and maintain their access to landed property and personal independence. Thus, they opposed the expansion of slavery into the territories and supported a homestead law for those with little capital. But Republicans were also the first party to offer an ideology and set of policy prescriptions that accepted and even glorified wage labor as an important element in the Northern social order. Thus, leaders of the new party substituted for propertied independence the free-labor values associated with social mobility; wage labor was acceptable in this formulation because, for those with suitable character, it served as a launching pad into the competitive struggle for wealth and self-improvement. Republicans left open the question of whether, or how much, social mobility was necessary for wage labor to be "free."

Just as significantly, Republicans developed a direct appeal to wage laborers by advocating a protective tariff to shield workers from low-wage international competition rather than merely as a stimulus to the growth of manufacturing, as the old Whig Party had viewed it. The Republican Party's support for a protective tariff as the foundation for the American standard of living remained the core of its electoral appeal to workers until the 1930s. In its array of responses to what came to be called "the labor question," the Republican Party straddled two eras: the old producers' republic and the new republic with its class-divided capitalist social order.[6]

With the election of Republican President Abraham Lincoln and the advent of the Civil War, the labor question received renewed attention in the public sphere. Even before emancipation, Republicans argued that the war was being fought for the "dignity of free labor," with the role of wage labor left ambiguous. After the issuance of the Emancipation Proclamation, the goal of the war became the abolition of slavery, rather than simply the reservation of the territories for free white labor and the maintenance of a safety valve for wage labor. Dignifying labor now referred simultaneously, but also ambiguously, to three labor systems at once: slave labor, which was to be abolished; freehold farming, which was to be encouraged; and wage labor, whose future status was uncertain.

More important, the issuance of the proclamation shifted the entire context of the labor question in the North. If the goal of the war was no longer the preservation of a white man's republic and the question of free versus slave labor was politically resolved—even as the outcome of the war remained in question—then it was no longer possible to simply subsume the wage-labor question in the metaphor of "free (white) labor." In Chicago and other Northern cities, the changed political context not only opened up the public sphere to issues of concern to wageworkers, but it also allowed the two most important segments of the immigrant working class, its Irish and German wings, to find new common ground and constitute themselves as a distinct public with a legitimate voice. When the goal of the war was no longer returning the nation to its status quo ante, a large segment of the city's Irish, which had strongly resisted abolition, broke away from its moorings in the Democratic Party with its racist appeals and fell into line with German radicals, who were to the left of Lincoln. Together with Anglo American activists, they joined forces in multiethnic unions, formed a citywide labor federation, and briefly constituted themselves as a distinct interest and party in local politics. In investigating the basis for unity among Irish, Anglo American, and German labor activists, we invoke the new understanding among historians that social processes like state formation, political ideologies, and social movements transcend national boundaries and must be investigated from that perspective. In chapter 2 and subsequent chapters, we discuss the ideology of "transnational social republicanism" and its successors, which served as the common ideological and cultural ground for multiethnic political action.

The transformation of the question of free labor into that of wage labor was not immediately evident in the public sphere. Through 1867, the Republican Party dominated the nation and the city. An uneasy coalition of Republicans, spearheaded by the party's radical wing, found common ground in opposition to Southern intransigence and President Andrew Johnson's encouragement of former Confederates. The Republican Radicals spoke on behalf of a liberal nationalist vision of America grounded in its producing classes. That stratum consisted of small farmers and artisans, but also emergent manufacturers and industrial wageworkers. Missing from the vision were wealthy eastern merchants and bankers and Southern planters. Led by the Radicals, in Chicago, Boston, and elsewhere, the Republican Party maintained its broad appeal to the producing classes by supporting the movement for an eight-hour working day—the topic of chapter 3. Even those Radicals like E. L. Godkin of *The Nation,* who would later become conspicuous opponents, were at this time sympathetic to unions, viewing them as temporary means to enable workers to pass from a state of ignorance and servility to one of dignity and equality more suited to the "age of contract."[7]

The local Republican Party fractured during the course of the struggle for an Illinois eight-hour-day law and its enforcement by a general strike of Chicago's trade unions. One issue was whether the state could violate freedom of contract in the interest of limiting work time without becoming oppressive. Intertwined with that question, however, was the one of class power for Republican manufacturers united in defense of the right to control and profit from the labor they employed. As local Republicans became more conservative in the four years after 1867, the party's Radicals in Chicago and elsewhere split into two factions. Liberals sustained the Radicals' reform ethos but shifted to new targets of opposition: tariff protection and machine politics. The bulk of the former prolabor faction withdrew support for the labor movement and substituted the protective tariff as its main appeal to working-class voters. Under the name of Stalwarts, it became the mainstream Republican Party organization.

Labor also began a transition. The 1867 eight-hour-day strike represented the high point for the legitimacy and leadership of producers' radicals like British-born Andrew Cameron and his German counterparts who idealized a republic of small producers and opposed wage labor as a kind of oppression. They had also relied on the fast-declining Republican Radicals. With the eclipse of the producers' radicals after the eight-hour defeat, Chicago labor lost its citywide unity. A new labor leadership arose in the German and Irish communities that broke with the social republican politics that had provided a common framework for the interethnic Civil War labor movement. More portentously, the riot of the unskilled workers during the strike paved the way for entrance of this new and growing segment of the working class into politics.[8]

In chapter 4, we examine the next stage of the labor question, which took shape in the years immediately following the Great Fire of 1871. Late that year, the Republican publisher of the *Chicago Tribune,* Joseph Medill, was elected mayor on a Liberal reform ticket. Liberalism had emerged after the Civil War among Republicans who advocated classical political economy and local municipal reform. When Medill attempted to enforce a new fire code restricting the building of wood homes and then appeased the city's evangelicals by attempting to enforce the state Sunday closing law, a major opposition movement arose among German workers and small businessmen. Mobilizing immigrant workers against the ruling "Yankee Puritans," this political rebellion was led by one of the last remaining prolabor Republicans, Anton Hesing, a German publisher and entrepreneur, who also maintained close ties to German artisan manufacturers. Hesing was an architect of a new urban populist ideology that updated, while preserving the core spirit of, free-labor ideology. The movement defended home ownership and the high wages required by it, along with ethnic cultural values like drinking on Sunday.

For ethnic workers, these parts of their lives represented bulwarks against being reduced to "European proletarians." As Hesing put it, "In our great West the population is still equivalent in wealth and our energetic workers are not poverty-stricken proletarians, who are dependent on the mercy of capital, rather they are the creators of capital."[9] In 1873, Hesing led his constituency of German property-holding workers and small businessmen out of the Republican Party and into coalition with rebellious Irish Democrats to produce the People's Party. The new party swept aside Medill's Liberals and claimed the mayor's seat as well as a majority on the city council. But the new party had scarcely ascended to power when it was confronted with a crushing depression. While the People's Party did not survive the depression of the 1870s, urban populism did, becoming a part of the city's ethnic culture and subsequently of urban liberalism.

In chapters 5 and 6, we examine the complicated events surrounding the depression of 1873 to 1878, which sparked the transformation of the labor question in the public sphere. More than four decades ago, in his pathbreaking work *Beyond Equality*, David Montgomery pointed to the eight-hour-day issue—the contemporary form taken by class conflict—as the "submerged shoal" on which foundered the Radical Republican project of reconstructing the South.[10] In our study, however, we argue that the 1870s depression was the event that raised the wage-labor question to political salience and, together with ethnoreligious issues, decisively shattered the Republican Party coalition—at least in Chicago. Up until that time, discussions in the public sphere, including those promoted by the People's Party, still gave precedence to the goal of restoring or reconstructing a producers' society of small property owners; wage labor was a *problem* rather than a fully legitimate feature of democratic society. The defection of German-speaking immigrant workers from the Republican coalition and the creation of an electoral alliance with working-class Irish voters not only ended local Republican hopes of maintaining their electoral supremacy, but also served as the pathway by which the wage-labor or class question moved to the center of the public sphere. The critical moment came at the start of the depression, when thousands of unemployed immigrants, representing part of the constituency of the People's Party, marched on the Relief and Aid Society under Socialist leadership, demanding "bread and work." The emergence of this new public with a straightforward working-class political demand undermined the People's Party's claim to protect wageworkers from proletarianization. It also frightened into self-awareness the new class of capitalists that had been taking root in the city's economy throughout the decade of the 1860s.

Until this moment, the city's capitalists viewed themselves as part of the broader producers' stratum, as had the leaders of the eight-hour movement. Three developments in 1873–74 catalyzed a new class-consciousness among the upper orders. First, a crime wave hit the city when large numbers of laborers were thrown out of work by the depression. They had been attracted to the city by the rebuilding following the Great Fire. Second, the Socialist-led marches of the unemployed raised the prospect of a violent upheaval on the model of the Paris Commune two years earlier. Third, another major fire in 1874 led eastern insurance companies to withdraw their coverage from the city, which occasioned an investment crisis. Just as the Irish and Germans had overcome ethnoreligious tensions to form a class alliance, so did Chicago's capitalists. They formed the Citizens Association, which had as its objectives the ousting from city government of the People's Party, the circumscribing of working-class electoral power, and the professionalizing of municipal administration.

In the several years after the formation of the Citizens Association, upper-class leaders shifted uneasily between two strategies for ruling the city: coercion and consent. The coercive response stemmed from the fear that workers could not be trusted to participate in the public sphere or vote in local politics, where they constituted a majority of citizens. As the first president of the Citizens Association put it, "How can you be sure of finding a set of men severely anxious about the protection of property who themselves have no property to protect?"[11] These leaders viewed immigrant unskilled laborers as a mob—the new "dangerous classes"—threatening the old republic. Beginning in 1872, they took steps to form a businessmen's militia to overawe and intimidate this new social class, while simultaneously attacking the machine politicians who built their power by appealing to working-class voters.

At the same time, some upper-class leaders like Medill felt that workers could be transformed into loyal citizens of the republic as well as reliable workers. They supported measures to extend property ownership to workers to give them a stake in society, either in the form of the old Republican Party solution of a homestead in the West or the newer urban solution of home ownership. They also appealed to workers' desire for a high-wage economy by trumpeting their support for a protective tariff that would insulate American workers from low-wage competition abroad. In all cases, men like Medill continued to extol the free-labor values of self-improvement, social mobility, and personal independence, though in new ways that would avoid antagonizing the culture of the new immigrants.

These two poles, coercion and consent, correspond to the social theory of hegemony developed by the Italian Marxist Antonio Gramsci. Hegemony is the process of rule in modern capitalist societies in which an upper class, or bloc of class segments, wins the active consent of subaltern groups or classes to its dominance. Though the ruling bloc may resort at times to physical coercion to maintain its power, the need to employ it signals the breakdown of hegemony. The theory of hegemony avoids two theoretical pitfalls in studying modern societies. One is the pluralistic view that politics consists of competing and associating interest groups, abstracted from existing social relations that create disparities in wealth, power, and authority. By contrast, hegemony starts with the assumption that class differences exist and that the power of one class over the other is embedded to some degree in all social institutions, not only the economy. The other pitfall sees subaltern groups as passive objects of "social control," regarding class rule as essentially one of domination or manipulation. Hegemony, on the other hand, understands that class relations are fluid, problematic, and evolve over time and that "consent" in a modern democratic society must be active. Therefore, hegemony remains at risk of breaking down and must be constantly reproduced.

The theory of hegemony is particularly relevant to studying the period of the Civil War and the Reconstruction era because Gramsci argued that the 1870s represented a turning point in the politics of Western societies. Beginning in that decade, the ruling classes shifted their strategy for governing from reliance on "domination" or coercion to leadership in civil society achieved through persuasion and accommodation—what Gramsci called active as opposed to passive consent. It is important to understand that for Gramsci civil society was not limited to the sphere of noneconomic voluntary associations, which served as a check on the power of the state, but rather consisted of an expansion of political society into both state and society. According to Joseph Buttigieg, Gramsci saw civil society as virtually coterminous with the public sphere, which included those elements of the state involved in shaping public opinion. It was the "space that is, or appears to be, free of coercion. It is within this space, the sphere of civil society, that ideas circulate and worldviews are formed 'freely,' so that when these views and ideas reaffirm or endorse the basic principles underlying existing social, economic, and political arrangements, they do so (or are seen as doing so) more or less spontaneously and thus legitimize them."[12]

According to Gramsci, the shift from domination to consent achieved through class leadership in civil society made working-class insurrection and revolution—what he called "war of maneuver"—obsolete. Instead, to defeat hegemony, workers need to contest it politically in the public sphere, using what he called "war of position." The shift to contesting upper-class power in the public sphere and in electoral politics created a new debate within the Socialist movement between advocates of reform and revolution, with the former position normally in the ascendancy.[13]

In our view, the 1873 depression constituted the city's first great crisis of hegemony. A growing segment of the immigrant working class in Chicago (and in other cities) no longer accepted the Republican free-labor compromise between producers' society and a new capitalist society. At the same time, the emerging class of capitalists recognized their inability to exercise class leadership through the cultural medium of evangelical Protestantism; nor could they accept the machine politicians, whose electoral base rested on immigrant votes and whose corruption undermined capital investment from outside the city. The Citizens Association, which attempted to rectify these problems, was the first great attempt of the Chicago upper class to exercise hegemony. Leaders of the new class cut loose from the politics of Sabbatarianism and temperance and even backed a new non-evangelical church led by a heretical liberal Presbyterian minister. Nonetheless, they were unable to gain the working class's active consent to their rule, a circumstance highlighted by the widespread strikes and quasi-insurrectionary rebellion of the immigrant working class during the 1877 railroad strikes.

In the aftermath of the 1877 upheaval, working-class organization proliferated in civil society, and the Socialist Party rose to prominence in the public sphere, developments we cover in chapter 6. The new cultural and political power of the Socialists prompted an accommodation by the Democrats, led by a creative and dynamic political leader, Mayor Carter Harrison. In chapter 7, we discuss how Harrison reconstituted the brief rule of the People's Party, but on a new and more durable basis. The new mayor forged a new regime that would dominate the city for the rest of the Gilded Age.

Regimes, another critical concept used in this study, form constellations of political power linking political party and state to the institutions of civil society and extend beyond any particular administration or election. In this book, we distinguish three regimes: the segmented regime during the Jacksonian period, the short-lived Republican regime during the Civil War and Reconstruction period, and the Harrisonian regime that characterized Chicago's Gilded Age.

The Republican regime relied on the evangelical Protestant churches and private class-run institutions, such as the Relief and Aid Society and Citizens Association. In contrast, Harrison incorporated the immigrant working class into the power structure by accepting reform Socialists, Irish and German ethnoreligious institutions, and eventually trade unionists. More important, the new regime represented a class compromise in which the local bourgeoisie won broad immunity from taxation of their newly accumulated wealth, restrained public spending by local government, and won control, through nonpartisan professionals, of key posts in municipal government. Among them were the city comptroller, public works and health directors, and fire department chief. These gains came at a price, which included the broadened participation of the immigrant working class in the public sphere, electoral politics, and local government. The price for the bourgeoisie also required tolerance for working-class associations in civil society. These accommodations produced a tenuous class peace. The active consent necessary for a lasting hegemony had been at last achieved in Chicago, but not through the Republican Party, its free-labor ideology, or its associated institutions in civil society.

The local resolution of the problem of hegemony returns us to the question of the overall character of the Civil War and Reconstruction. Since the days of Charles and Mary Beard, many historians have viewed the war and its aftermath as effecting a fundamental transformation, amounting to a "second American Revolution." The Beards viewed the war as a triumph of industrial capitalists over agrarians and Southern landowners. But since the 1960s, that simple view has become untenable. Historians have demonstrated that slavery-related issues, rather than the economic ones identified by the Beards, were central to the appeal and goals of the Republican Party and that Northern business was fractured over the issues of slavery and sectionalism. Since the publication of Eric Foner's *Free Soil, Free Labor, Free Men,* the argument that the war and subsequent efforts at reconstruction constituted a revolution has rested in large part on an interpretation of party ideology.[14]

Barrington Moore Jr. argued that the period was revolutionary on different grounds in his comprehensive comparative study, *The Social Origins of Dictatorship and Democracy.* To Moore, the Civil War was the world's "last capitalist revolution" because it forestalled the classic reactionary ruling coalition of a relatively weak commercial and industrial bourgeoisie aligned with aristocratic and repressive landlords, as exemplified in the development of Germany and Japan. The reactionary Prussian Road led to fascism, and Japan experienced a revolution from above that led to an aggressive militarist regime. Only in England, France, and the United States, where a revolution from below resulted in the defeat of an aristocracy and where market relations eliminated peasant agriculture, could democratic development proceed relatively unobstructed. Moore acknowledged that the failure of the federal government to confiscate and redistribute land in the South left the second American Revolution incomplete and ambiguous. Indeed, subsequent scholars continue to debate whether Gilded Age Southern sharecroppers were wage laborers, quasi peasants, or a hybrid of the two. Nonetheless, for Moore the results of the Civil War in the nation as a whole justify terming its outcome revolutionary: the war cleared the way, in both politics and the economy, for the full development of capitalism and the expansion of democracy.[15]

While scholarship in many ways has advanced beyond the specifics of Moore's arguments, the question of whether and to what degree capitalism triumphed and its relationship to democracy continues to be central in Reconstruction historiography. With some notable exceptions, however, historians have treated Reconstruction as a Southern question. Yet much scholarship focusing on the Gilded Age North implicitly addresses these issues as well. For example, labor historians who debate pure and simple unionism, Socialism, and "American exceptionalism" are at bottom discussing the extent to which American democracy sufficiently accommodated labor and Socialist movements to make its development roughly similar to that of Europe by the turn of the century. Similarly, scholars of the Gilded Age party machine debate whether its practices advanced or limited urban democratic development.

The best example of a scholar who has explicitly addressed the Moore question in the North has been Theda Skocpol, a student of Moore's. Skocpol argued that the postwar system of Civil War pensions that flourished in the context of Gilded Age patronage politics amounted to a "little bit of 'social democracy,'" which supports Moore's thesis that the war furthered democracy. Also addressing these issues, three political scientists and sociologists—Dietrich Rueschemeyer, Evelyne Huber Stephens, and John D. Stephens—produced a major international comparative study of the relation of capitalism and democracy. Their main conclusion was that "capitalist development is associated with democracy because it transforms the class structure, strengthening the working and middle classes and weakening the landed upper class."[16]

This book contributes to the argument over the relation of capitalism and democracy in this critical era by examining the transformation of society and politics in Chicago, one of the most important industrial cities in the North.

The argument touches on four questions: (1) whether the socioeconomic system of the city underwent a fundamental transformation as a result of the war, (2) whether a capitalist class with its own politics was able to establish its hegemony, (3) whether the city's organized workers underwent a shift in consciousness from a producer to a wage-earner orientation, and (4) whether workers were able to establish themselves as a political force in sufficient strength to sideline existing antidemocratic forces and make the city's politics and government substantially more democratic than before the war. This book answers these questions with a qualified, but still conclusive, yes.

1 The City

DURING THE WINTER OF 1869, an article in the *Chicago Daily Tribune* found that "in our principal thoroughfares the richly-dressed lady of the avenue magnificently sweeps by her thinly-clad sister of the alley who, with scanty clothing, hurries from her fireless garret to perform her daily fourteen hours labor for a pittance too small to pay rent and purchase sufficient food, much less comfortable raiment, for this inclement season. Worse than this, there are houseless wanderers in our streets who in vain seek for employment, and whose mode of existence is a mystery. Worst of all, there are many among us to whose dire poverty is added sickness, or, may be, they are crippled from accident, and who are entirely dependent on the charity of the public." The writer was experiencing the shock of a new social order that had emerged with amazing rapidity during the 1860s, while the country was fighting the Civil War and trying to reconstruct the South. The new social world was rooted in the transformation of the city from a commercial center into a dynamo of industrial capitalism. Ironically, it was this new Chicago that burned down two years later in October 1871, only to be rebuilt with the same amazing rapidity with which it had emerged. Despite all this change, the sense of social distance and cultural crisis communicated by this author remained.[1]

The social order being replaced in the 1860s was that of a preindustrial commercial city. Up through the 1850s, Chicago was a gateway for the exchange of eastern manufactured goods and western primary products. Its elite were composed of merchants who were boosters, promoters, and real estate speculators; they reinvested relatively little of their profits in manufacturing or the employment of labor. Instead they invested in land and then lobbied all levels of government to build the infrastructure that would turn it into profitable real estate. In the manufacturing sector, traditional craft labor practices remained, even as more advanced production techniques, such as stationary steam engines, made inroads. The shops in which the railroads repaired their cars were the city's most advanced manufacturing establishments, and they were funded by capital from outside the city, not by local entrepreneurs. Rather than invest in industrial pursuits, Chicago's merchant trading houses focused their energies on inventing and institutionalizing the modern commercial practices, such as grain futures and standard measures of quality, which permitted them to participate in an impersonal national, and even international, market.

The preindustrial outlook of the boosters had its counterpart in the way political leaders minimized the significance of wage labor. Abraham Lincoln famously described the antebellum North as a free labor society in which no man needed to be a wage earner for his whole life: "The prudent, penniless beginner in the world, labors for wages a while, saves a surplus with which to buy tools or land, for himself; then labors on his own account another while, and at length hires another new beginner to help him. This . . . is *free* labor—the just and generous, and prosperous system, which opens the way for all." Lincoln exaggerated the extent of social mobility, while underestimating the permanence of wage labor within the larger free labor North.[2]

Lincoln and his fellow Republican leaders knew that wage labor posed problems for their vision of the good and prosperous society, and they sought to reconcile the two. There were two major Republican factions. In the view of those like Lincoln, who believed that ownership of productive property was vital for an independent citizenry, wage labor became a phase in an individual's life dedicated to social mobility. The other large element of opinion among Republicans stressed wage labor's dignity and freedom, even if it was a permanent condition. Countering taunts from slaveholders that northern workers were "wage slaves," they stressed the choices workers had in selecting their employers, the products they bought, and their political leaders. They also stressed the dignified family life they led.[3]

The fast-disappearing society that Lincoln mythologized was rooted in a mode of production in which households were the prevalent economic unit, and these households were led by men who owned productive property, most commonly land but also a shop or tools. To Lincoln such men, who were neither capitalists nor laborers, constituted the "large majority" of the population in the North: "Men, with their families—wives, sons and daughters—work for themselves, on their farms, in their houses and in their shops, taking the whole product to themselves, and asking no favors of capital on the one hand, nor of hirelings or slaves on the other." Although such productive households strove to make a profit, they were not organized to accumulate capital before all other objectives, just as they occasionally hired laborers but did not derive their wealth from them. This mode of production and the social order it sustained survived the Civil War in the rural North.[4]

But in some rural areas and especially in the cities, another mode of production began to displace this producers' order from the center of national economic life. A capitalist economy based in wage labor became predominant in Chicago during and after the Civil War, and a new bourgeoisie organized it to produce capital accumulation, reinvesting profits in transforming the production process as well as the nature of work. Compared to large eastern cities, Chicago experienced these changes somewhat later and in a more compressed period of time, accentuating their impact. The system required a permanent wage-earning working class, and the mere existence of this class posed a challenge for men of Lincoln's social vision. The working class was also a social issue for those who found permanent wage earning to be legitimate, for their justification of it presupposed a standard of living that could support a dignified family life and considerable choice in purchasing products in the market.[5]

THE COMMERCIAL CITY, BOOSTERS, AND IMMIGRANTS

Starting as a trading post and fort, Chicago's growth accelerated in the 1830s as the national economy boomed and construction began on the Illinois and Michigan Canal. By connecting the Chicago and Illinois Rivers, the canal linked the Great Lakes and Mississippi River systems and opened much of frontier Illinois to a regional and even national market. With access to Lake Michigan, the produce of the Illinois prairie could reach the East Coast through the Erie Canal.

The Illinois and Michigan Canal also marked the beginning of massive investment in infrastructure that culminated in Chicago's becoming the railroad hub of the midcontinent. Construction on Chicago's first railroad began the year the canal was completed—1848. During the mid-1850s, investment in Chicago's railroad network profited as violence over slavery in Missouri and Kansas diverted Yankee capital from St. Louis to the Windy City. Within fifteen years, Chicago's railroads pulled both the midwestern prairie and the Great Plains into the city's economic orbit, creating the transportation infrastructure and markets for Chicago's nation-leading grain, lumber, and meatpacking industries.[6]

The trading village of five thousand in 1840 became a significant town of thirty thousand in 1850 and a substantial city of over one hundred thousand by 1860. Within the next twenty years, Chicago literally rose from the ashes of the Great Fire of 1871 to surpass its rivals St. Louis and Cincinnati, becoming the predominant city in the Midwest and one of the leading manufacturing centers of the country. In 1880 it had a population of half a million, making it the nation's fourth largest city, and it ranked third among America's manufacturing centers, after New York and Philadelphia. America's "shock city," a sort of New World Manchester producing meat and metal instead of textiles, Chicago came to symbolize in the popular and literary imagination the fascinating and frightening future of urban industrial America.[7]

Chicago's explosive growth presupposed the emergence of a large and prosperous rural market for the city's products and services. Based in the Midwest's family farms, this market reflected an extraordinary increase in land brought under cultivation, the emergence of profitable commercial agriculture, and the national economy's robust recovery from the depression that had begun in the late 1830s. The sheer amount of land brought under the plow in the 1850s dwarfed pervious decades, as the expansion of the railroad network carried people and the market to formerly isolated and underpopulated areas.[8]

Even more important, however, was the contemporaneous emergence of commercial agriculture—that is, production for sale. Douglass North illustrated this change using four counties in central Illinois that the railroad made accessible in the 1850s. In that decade, their population grew by 178 percent while their production of wheat exploded by 655 percent. (The comparative figures for the whole state were 101 percent and 114 percent, respectively.) Wheat was primarily a crop for the market, which meant that the settlement of the land and the growth of commercial agriculture took place together in this decade. New uses for corn illustrated the same phenomenon: Huge amounts of corn were consumed locally to feed livestock, which presupposed the farmers' ability to ship cattle to the East on the railroad. Formerly, Illinois cattle had been driven to Ohio for fattening and shipment east. This was the economic context that fired Lincoln's enthusiasm for a free labor society rooted in productive households.[9]

The emergence of commercial agriculture produced the income that created a huge market. Jeremy Atack and Fred Bateman calculated that in 1859 and 1860 owner-occupied farms in the Midwest earned an average of $113 per capita, with Illinois far in the lead at $165. Chicago not only transshipped and marketed the products of these farmers but also produced many of the products on which they spent their income, most obviously farm implements, such as Cyrus McCormick's famous reaper. Chicago firms were leaders in building the tools for the mechanization of agriculture that contributed the most to increasing agricultural productivity.[10]

The import of commercial agriculture for both rural life and the history of Chicago was complex. Just because farmers produced a surplus for the market did not mean that their main economic goals were the same as meat-packers and other manufacturing capitalists in Chicago. Farming was a way of life as well as a commercial enterprise, and farmers commonly made decisions that preserved and enhanced their life on the land rather than brought them the most possible return on their investment. As Allan Kulikoff has written, farmers "attended to market demand for their products but ultimately chose to produce grain or raise hogs or cattle that could be used for family subsistence as well." One of their most important decisions was to stay in farming. Atack and Bateman's quantitative analysis of northern agriculture reinforces the findings of other historians that there was "some sort of agrarian bias among Americans that led them to become and remain farmers despite potentially better opportunities in nonfarm occupations." Capital invested elsewhere would likely have been more profitable as well: Throughout most of the nineteenth century, returns from investment in manufacturing were consistently better than in farming. Nonetheless, the substantial attractions of agrarian life compared to the city, the availability of land, and the real, though uncertain, promise of profit in the commodity markets helped keep people in agriculture.[11]

One result was to create an enormous labor shortage in Chicago's booming economy that could only be met by immigrants. Daniel Nelson considers this phenomenon characteristic of the whole Midwest: "The classic transfer of labor from farm to factory, common to New England in the nineteenth century and the South in the twentieth, did not occur in the Midwest until the post–World War II years. As a result industrialists had to seek workers elsewhere. Midwestern factories, mines, and lumber camps became enclaves of European immigrants and their children." Another result of the rural population remaining on the land was a politics shaped by frequently disgruntled agricultural producers, who remained, in Kulikoff's terms, "janus-faced, looking backward to subsistence and the perpetuation of their farms and forward to the market exchange that made agriculture possible." Living and working in a sector of the economy still organized around households, farmers in the North often opposed and misunderstood urban workers, not only because immigrants constituted so high a proportion of the industrial working class, but also because urban laborers had different interests as full participants in a labor market. Similarly, while trying to get the highest prices for their goods in the Chicago markets, farmers resented the rewards and attractions of urban life and particularly the capital accumulators in Chicago who made so much money from them by selling their grain or slaughtering their livestock. Thus commercial farmers in the rural Midwest often entered politics wearing a populist face, shaping the political environment in which Chicago's labor movement, rooted in immigrant workers, maneuvered.[12]

To take advantage of this huge rural market, the city needed workers, entrepreneurs, and capital, and it imported all three in great quantities. Only a minority of workers came from Chicago's hinterland; the overwhelming majority arrived from abroad. Figure 2 illustrates the trends in nativity among Chicago's workers. Between 1850 and 1860 the percentage of the foreign-born in Chicago's working class rose from 70 to 80 percent, although over the next two decades it declined somewhat. The reduction in the percentage of the foreign-born and increase of native-born workers derived largely from the growth in the numbers of children of immigrants born in America. In 1880, almost 60 percent of native-born skilled workers had foreign-born fathers; among the unskilled, the figure was 65 percent. Chicago's working class was therefore overwhelmingly of foreign stock, and the proportion of foreign-born would rise again when the next wave of European immigration peaked in the 1880s. Immigrants from Germany, Ireland, and Great Britain met most of Chicago's demand for labor between 1850 and 1880, although Scandinavians made up a substantial share beginning in the mid-1860s.[13]

Manufacturing in Chicago can be divided into a declining artisan or producer sector and an emerging capitalist one, which was characterized most

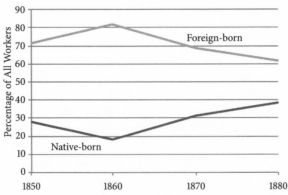

Figure 2
Workers in Chicago by Native- and Foreign-born:
1850–80

Source: Samples of the federal manuscript population censuses; smallest N = 1,472.

prominently by sustained capital investment in the production process and in hiring new wageworkers. Though it is difficult to draw precise boundaries between the two sectors, we focus on five major indices: the degree of concentration of capital, the transformation of production illustrated by the use of steam power, the increasing scale and sophistication of firms, the growth and transformation of the wage-earning workforce, and the emergence of a more unified and sophisticated market for labor. The development of wage earners and the bourgeoisie as social classes underlay the phenomena measured by these indices, and the emergence of all of them together, which can be summarized as class formation and capital accumulation, constituted capitalism as a mode of production.

The growing proportion of capital invested by the largest firms was a precondition for the transformation of production and the growth of the workforce. The increasing use of steam power was a marker for a much larger transformation of production. A firm might use a stationary steam engine but not organize all or most of its production around it. The systematic use of inanimate power throughout a plant was a sophisticated managerial project that involved reorganizing and sometimes eliminating craft labor. The capital needed to obtain steam engines and the managerial ability to systemically use them increased with the size of the firm. The larger firms, of course, needed more workers, who performed different kinds of semi- and unskilled labor than had been done by the dockhands and day laborers familiar in antebellum American cities. The larger firms obtained these workers in a labor market that integrated boardinghouses, saloons, and immigrant aid societies into a communications system linking the city to the East Coast and even abroad.

Perhaps the most prominent feature of Chicago's new economy was the growth in the scale and investment among the biggest firms. While the total number of manufacturing firms increased dramatically—from 246 in 1850 to 1,355 in 1870—a relatively small set of the largest companies began to predominate in most branches of industry. In 1850, the top 5 percent of Chicago's manufacturing firms accounted for 6 percent of all capital investment in industry; in 1870, the same group accounted for 39 percent. Yet the process was complex, as opportunities for modest-size firms brought new entrepreneurs into the economy. Even as the top 5 percent of firms expanded dramatically, the proportion of capital invested by the top 20 percent of firms remained the same at around three-fifths. And, of course, even the smallest firms multiplied amid the boom of the 1860s and early 1870s, creating opportunities for Irish and particularly German entrepreneurs. Overall capital invested in Chicago manufacturing multiplied by five times in the 1850s and by over seven times in the 1860s, increasing from about one million in 1850 to over thirty-eight million by 1870. Figure 3 illustrates these trends in capital investment.

The large firms invested more heavily in the production process, such as by employing steam power. The increase in use of steam after 1850 mirrored the concentration of capital. Out of twenty branches of manufacturing in 1850, six had at least some firms with steam power. In only two of those branches, however, did firms with steam employ over half of the workforce. In 1870 all twenty branches of manufacturing had some firms with steam power, and in fourteen of them, firms with steam employed over half of the workers.[14]

Figure 4 illustrates how larger manufacturing firms began to employ most of Chicago's industrial workers by 1870. These were the same companies typically using steam power. More generally, figure 4 shows the transformation of an urban producer economy rooted in craft manufacturing into a capitalist one based in industrial production. The firms employing more than fifty workers marked an operational dividing line between the two, even when it was not a hard and fast division.

As the size of the top firms increased, the number of workers grew exponentially. The number of Chicagoans employed in manufacturing jumped from about 3,775 in 1850 to 91,857 thirty years later, a multiple of over twenty-four. During the same years, the population grew by a multiple of almost seventeen. At the same time, the composition of the workforce changed dramatically, with the increase of women being one striking example. Rely-

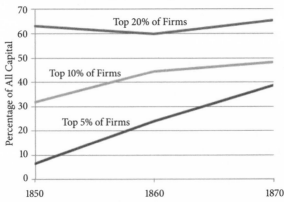

Figure 3
Proportion of Capital Invested in Chicago
Manufacturing by the Largest Firms: 1850–70

Source: Federal manuscript manufacturing censuses
for Chicago, 1850, 1860, and 1870.

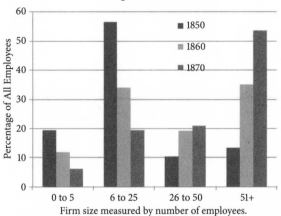

Figure 4
Employees in Manufacturing by Size of Firm:
Chicago, 1850, 1860, 1870

Firm size measured by number of employees.

Source: Federal manuscript manufacturing censuses.

ing primarily on the daughters of immigrants, Chicago's clothing makers were chiefly responsible for the growth of women in the manufacturing workforce between 1860 and 1870. The number employed grew from just over 258 to almost 4,664, an increase of 1,708 percent. Typically employed at sewing machines, these young women illustrated the transformation of work that accompanied the expansion of the manufacturing labor force. Manufacturers used semiskilled workers operating machines to increase production, lower costs, and circumscribe the central role of skilled craftsmen in production. The employment of women was an integral part of the formation of a wage-earning working class in Chicago. One illustration was the fact that in the early 1870s the proportion of females employed outside of domestic service equaled and then surpassed those remaining within that traditional occupation.[15]

An analogous change took place in some of the largest categories of unskilled labor typically performed by men (fig. 5). The term *laborer* certainly predated the mid-nineteenth century; the *Oxford English Dictionary* finds its origins in the Middle Ages. As the number of workers in Chicago grew explosively in the 1860s and 1870s, the proportion of people designated in the manuscript census by this term declined, similar to the category of *servant* among women. At the same time, a new designation appeared: *works in*. . . . Typically the term applied to people working in the city's burgeoning large enterprises, whether railroad yards and grain elevators, or rolling mills and

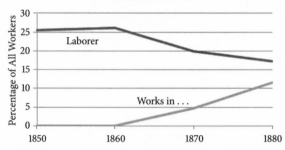

Figure 5
Two Categories of Unskilled among All Chicago
Workers: 1850–80

Source: Samples of the federal manuscript population censuses.

packinghouses. It constituted a new category of unskilled labor appropriate to a wage-earning working class in an industrial capitalist economy.

At the same time, the growth of the capitalist sector of the manufacturing economy transformed the nature of traditional craft labor. Within that sector, craft labor became more specialized as manufacturers hired unskilled workers to perform simpler tasks, perhaps tending a power-driven saw cutting pieces used by a skilled worker when he assembled the final product at the last stage of production. The growth of large-scale enterprises also put intense pressure on skilled workers remaining in small artisan shops, primarily through lowering prices. Artisans in traditional shops had to work harder while receiving less for their products. Masters felt pressure to lower costs, and their journeymen fought back, demanding higher prices for the goods they produced. Yet both masters and journeymen resisted their common decline in status as their industries were engulfed by a rising tide of unskilled wage earners working in larger and highly capitalized firms.[16]

The expansion and increasing sophistication of the Chicago labor market was an integral part of the emergence of a capitalist economy. By the mid-1860s, the labor market had grown to the point where the city government felt the need to regulate employment agencies, then called "intelligence offices." Major eastern cities had passed such ordinances somewhat earlier in the late 1850s and 1860s. Since the license in Chicago cost $52 annually, people immediately petitioned the city government for a waiver of the fee. Most of these petitioners were women, who were likely boardinghouse keepers.[17]

Boardinghouses served as convenient places where employers could find workers, and some even specialized. In the 1860s, a German journeyman baker could stay at the Bäckerherberge, a boardinghouse catering to German bakery workers. Other institutions also emerged as conduits of information about jobs, becoming part of a communications network at the base of the labor market. The Swedish Emigrant Society of Chicago was an early applicant for a license to operate an intelligence office. Similarly, Chicago's German Aid Society was under pressure to become a welfare agency and employment bureau, rather than just helping new arrivals get oriented and settled. These immigrant societies and boardinghouses were joined by saloon owners, policemen, and ward politicians—all of them sharing information about jobs. The Chicago labor market also developed broader connections, not only through letters sent to friends and family in other cities or abroad, but also utilizing the latest technology. Castle Garden in New York City, the nation's main immigrant portal, had the Intelligence Office and Labour Exchange by the mid-1860s, and Castle Garden boasted "its direct connection by telegraph with every part of the United States and the British Provinces." The head of Chicago's German Aid Society advocated cooperating with Castle Garden as early as the late 1850s, and his counterpart in New York was an ex officio member of the board that ran the immigrant reception center.[18]

Despite the transformation of both work and the workforce, the attractions of the Chicago labor market were considerable between 1850 and 1880, and not only because demand was high. For most of this period, wages were usually higher in the Midwest than in the East. According to Joshua L. Rosenbloom, in the mid-nineteenth century, real wages in the North Central states, including Illinois, were 20 to 30 percent higher than in the Middle Atlantic region. Nonetheless, wage rates rapidly converged in the 1870s as the nation's labor markets became more closely integrated. Jeffrey G. Williamson has developed statistics on wages that place Rosenbloom's data in an international context. Analyzing the four decades between 1830 and 1869, Williamson found a wage boom in the United States that by 1855 made real wages 98 percent higher than in Great Britain. Nonetheless, at about midcentury the differential began to shrink, with the Civil War producing a sharp reduction in American real wages. Although wage rates increased after the Civil War, the depression of the 1870s shrank these gains. American workers never regained the advantage they enjoyed in the 1850s.[19]

Together, Williamson and Rosenbloom's figures help explain why European immigrants, and particularly British workers, found both America and Chicago so attractive before the Civil War. The attractions of relocating in the Midwest remained substantial through the 1870s. Philip Coelho and James

Shepherd found that the midwestern cost of living was significantly lower than in the East, and the gap remained about the same between 1851 and 1880. The cost of living in the East North Central states, including Illinois, was about 15 percent lower than in New England, which was the highest of the various regions. The main exception to this long-term trend was caused by inflation during the Civil War, when prices across the North became more similar. The declining but still real regional premium in wages and prices gave Chicago's largely immigrant workers standards against which they judged threats to their social and economic position, which they perceived making their situation more like the East, or even similar to the cities of Europe.[20]

CHICAGO'S UPPER CLASS: MERCHANTS AND MANUFACTURERS

In sharp contrast to the European origins of its workers, Chicago imported its economic and political leaders from New York and New England. In 1848, when the Chicago Board of Trade was founded, its membership was composed of 87 percent New Englanders and New Yorkers, and this pattern continued into the early 1870s and beyond. In the mid-1850s, a resident of St. Louis, Chicago's western rival, complained that "Chicago [is] the pampered child of a rich and indulgent East."[21]

This antebellum period may be appropriately called the "booster" phase of Chicago's development, when building and investing in the city itself—its commercial facilities, transportation network, and real estate—preoccupied the city's leaders and created great profits for them in turn. Appropriately, Chicago's history as an incorporated town began with a "land craze" in the mid-1830s as its population growth created a boom in real estate values. As the city's largest land owners, members of Chicago's elite were the city's most enthusiastic boosters, for they had the most to gain from the increased value of real estate. The booster's bold imperial vision of the city's future could only be realized with large inflows of public and private capital. The federal government was the boosters' greatest benefactor, granting immense swaths of land to the State of Illinois to fund the Illinois and Michigan Canal, and subsequently the Illinois Central Railroad. "Chicago," according to Michael Conzen, "was born as a government program, in which land was sold at auction with liberal credit provisions to all comers." Huge amounts of private capital were needed as well, and boosting Chicago helped attract this capital, while giving the city a reputation for bombastic self-promotion. The same boosting, aimed at different audiences, attracted the immigrants necessary to build the city and make it work.[22]

Most of Chicago's first upper class—the boosters—arrived in the city before 1843, that is, before a long midcentury economic expansion that ended in 1857. They arrived by following the lines of trade and migration from New England and New York along the Erie Canal and the Great Lakes. In this antebellum period, family ties, business connections, and routes of migration were inseparable for commercial men. The banking system was chaotic and reliable currency practically nonexistent. The easiest and best means for obtaining the credit essential for trade was through prominent northeastern business families, who extended it to trusted members acting as agents, jobbers, and commission men in newly settled regions. Credit was also essential for manufacturing, and the boosters provided it to the manufacturers whose products they marketed. Yet the credit system was designed for commerce, not industry, since real estate and grain always beckoned with opportunities for quick profits. As late as 1871, the *Tribune* complained that banks habitually issued loans "only on grain certificates and similar negotiable securities," and thus it was "easier to raise $5,000 in cash on $6,000 in warehouse certificates, than to raise the same sum on $50,000 worth of useful machinery and fixed capital." The financial dependence of manufacturers on merchants helped underpin the dominant role of the boosters in Chicago's economy and politics, at least up until the Civil War. At this time, according to Bessie Pierce, "An overweening eagerness to get rich motivated most Chicagoans to embark upon enterprises from which a quick return could be expected," and these were primarily in real estate and trade in agricultural products.[23]

By the 1860s, a new generation of leaders began to emerge, men like George Pullman, Cyrus McCormick, Philip Armour, and Marshall Field, who had arrived in the late 1840s and 1850s and profited from the city's extraordinary economic growth in the Civil War decade.[24] They were also typically from New York and New England, although a significant number of these Yankees made a secondary move from St. Louis. These new leaders played a different role in the economy than the boosters. Although the new leaders had wide-ranging economic interests, including in real estate and commerce, their strongest roots were in Chicago's booming manufacturing sector. In the mid-1860s, they began to supplant the boosters, who had arrived in the 1830s and early 1840s and made fortunes in real estate and commerce. One key to their rise was access to capital from other sources than the boosters. The Civil War and the federal government provided the opportunity. The demand and inflation created by the war economy arrived as a positive boon for manufacturers. So did the protective tariff passed as part of the Republican Party's sweeping domestic program in 1862 and 1863. In addition, the rise of the New York Stock Exchange created a national capital market to which the largest manufacturers, like McCormick, had access.[25]

During the Civil War, manufacturers could repay their accumulated prewar debts in inflated currency, the new greenbacks issued by the federal government, and thus save considerable money. Freed of debt, manufacturers made higher rates of profit, which they could reinvest in their businesses. Chicago's explosively growing garment industry was a good example. The government's need for uniforms and footwear led numerous Chicago wholesalers to directly enter into the manufacture of these goods, while cutting down on imports from the East. An 1864 survey by the *Chicago Times* found that local dry-goods merchants, who had gone into manufacturing cloaks, were paying cash instead of using credit for their purchases in the East. Most of these merchants were completely out of debt by 1864, and some had doubled their capital: "War was the magic wand that changed these conditions in a season," said the report. The magic wand of the war helped transform some merchants into manufacturers, who constituted the core of the new bourgeoisie.[26]

Meatpacking provided the best example of the war's stimulus to Chicago's manufacturing. Prompted by union army contracts, the Chicago meatpacking industry tripled in size between 1861 and 1863. According to Glenn Porter and Harold C. Livesay, the "combination of Civil War finance and purchasing effected the first significant transfer of capital from the general public into the manufacturing sector," and this took place without the mediation of merchants. Just as the federal government had aided the boosters with its harbor improvements and land grants for canal and railroad construction, so it also nurtured the rise of the city's Gilded Age bourgeoisie through its system for financing the war economy.[27]

To succeed, the leaders of the new manufacturing economy needed more than capital and demand. They had to effectively manage larger numbers of workers than ever before, and they had to utilize new technology in ways that increased production and lowered costs. Both initiatives engaged them in competition with other manufacturers and conflict with workers. The extent to which they succeeded in these complex tasks is indicated in table 1, which compares the manufacturing economies of Chicago, Cincinnati, and Philadelphia in 1870—Cincinnati because it was Chicago's chief manufacturing competitor in the West and Philadelphia because it vied with New York for national manufacturing preeminence.

Table 1. Manufacturing in Chicago, Cincinnati, and Philadelphia Compared: 1870

	Chicago	Cincinnati	Philadelphia
Number of manufacturing workers	26,332	37,344	134,501
Number of manufacturing firms	1,355	2,469	8,366
Percentage of firms with more than 50 workers	7.5	6.4	6.5
Percentage of workforce in firms with more than 50 workers	53.6	49.4*	57.7

Source: Federal manuscript manufacturing census for Chicago, 1870; Steven J. Ross, *Workers on the Edge: Work, Leisure, and Politics in Industrializing Cincinnati, 1788-1890* (New York: Columbia University Press, 1985), 80; Bruce Laurie and Mark Schmitz, "Manufacture and Productivity: The Making of an Industrial Base, Philadelphia, 1850-1880," in *Philadelphia: Work, Space, Family, and Group Experience in the Nineteenth Century: Essays toward an Interdisciplinary History of the City,* ed. Theodore Hershberg (New York: Oxford University Press, 1981), 52.

* The percentages for Cincinnati are for firms with fifty employees or more, not more than fifty.

The scale of Chicago's firms and the influence of the larger ones compared favorably with the economies of its older and bigger competitors. Arriving relatively late in the field, Chicago's manufacturers took advantage of all the latest technology, as indicated by the high level of capital investment in their firms. In 1860, for example, Chicago's sash, door, and blind manufacturers invested less than half as much capital per firm as the national average in their industry, but by 1880 they invested almost three times the national norm. This industry was not idiosyncratic: In 1890, the average capital investment per firm in Chicago was double the average of the nation's 164 largest cities. Nevertheless, the Civil War decade was decisive for the city and the whole Midwest: Chicago's manufacturing workforce multiplied fivefold in those ten years, and midwestern manufacturing increased more as a share of the nation's industry in the 1860s than in any decade before 1920.[28]

THE SOCIAL RELATIONS
OF THE SEGMENTED REGIME

The boosters were merchants of a particular type characteristic of the mid-nineteenth century. Unlike the general-purpose merchants of the eighteenth century, Chicago's boosters typically specialized in one aspect of commerce, such as wholesaling, or in one type of product, like grain or livestock. Specialization was profitable because of the increased volume of trade made possible by population growth, prosperous commercial agriculture, and transportation improvements. Thus a booster specializing in grain might not only buy and sell wheat but also store it in his own grain elevators before shipping it to the

East, and he might also branch out into manufacturing by milling some of it into flour. Such processing typically involved high levels of capital investment in facilities like flour mills but did not require hiring many workers. In 1860, for example, the Chicago flour industry invested over $2,300 per worker but employed only eighty-five people. Foundries invested about $630 per worker and employed 321.[29]

The first labor historians, John R. Commons and his associates, would have called the boosters "middlemen" or "merchant-jobbers," who performed a critical function in the mid-nineteenth century by linking widely dispersed producers with poorly coordinated markets. Such middlemen were able to turn their control over access to the market into "intangible capital," such as the grain futures that were more creditworthy than fixed capital like machinery. According to Commons, "this intangible capital was the effective security for banking and loan credits, through which the merchant could command the products of labor and physical capital. Thus it was that the fundamental question for farmers and wage-laborers in the period following the Civil War was the control of capital and credit by middlemen; and the remedies sought were designed to give control of both to the producers of tangible goods." This social and political outlook has been termed *producers' republicanism*.[30]

Since the boosters, as merchants, made most of their profits from trading, transporting, and processing agricultural products, their relations with farmers were frequently hostile. Holding the producer republican outlook, farmers articulated their hostility through the Jacksonian political rhetoric so common in Illinois. Illinois farmers and their commercial allies downstate repeatedly used the state government to lower transportation costs and break the Chicago boosters' control over access to the market. Contesting one of these so-called Granger laws, Ira Munn, a Chicago merchant, went to court to fight the Illinois legislature's limiting of his power to determine prices in his grain elevators. The result was the most famous of the Granger cases, *Munn v. Illinois*, in which the U.S. Supreme Court defended the regulatory authority of state governments, at least over businesses "affected with a public interest," such as Munn's grain elevators or the railroads. Decided as a group in 1877, the Granger cases indicated that the court battles to establish legal protection of capitalist property from state control were still ongoing; they would not be decisively won for at least another fifteen to twenty years.[31]

In contrast to their relations with farmers, the boosters' relations with the city's residents were comparatively harmonious, mainly because they were not taking a substantial share of their profits from their dealings with them. The boosters dealt directly with the city's residents, including its immigrant workers, and their attitudes were even characterized by noblesse oblige. Of course, noblesse oblige presupposed that the "lower orders" reciprocated by acknowledging the boosters' economic, political, and cultural authority, which they did not always do. When open conflict over the boosters' power broke into the open, the causes usually had less to do with class conflict than with ethnic passions and political ideology, both of which abounded in a city whose population was about one-half foreign-born in the Civil War era. Typical of mercantile cities of the eighteenth and early-nineteenth centuries, this style of class relations in the boosters' Chicago was facilitated by the city's relatively small geographic size and its intermixture of commercial, manufacturing, and residential functions characteristic of compact "walking cities."[32]

Chicago's most prominent booster was William Butler Ogden, the city's first mayor and wealthiest citizen. He lived in an appropriately gracious estate on the North Side within walking distance of rich compatriots, German and Irish neighborhoods, the McCormick Reaper Works, and docks and warehouses on the Chicago River. The son of a prominent New York manufacturer and lumber dealer, Ogden came to Chicago in the 1830s to oversee the extensive real estate holdings of his brother-in-law. He re-created on the urban frontier the role his family played so well in New York, where his brother-in-law was a prominent philanthropist and law partner of Martin Van Buren. Ogden helped found numerous societies, from Rush Medical College to the Astronomical Society. Any project that he saw as benefiting Chicago received his support, whether it was the city's first railroad, the Galena and Chicago Union, or the Presbyterian Theological Seminary, to which he donated twenty acres of land despite the fact that he himself was an Episcopalian. Catholic projects likewise received his largesse. Also reflective of antebellum Chicago's social order were his regular visits to the homes of the poor, on which he always took along "the choicest product of his fruit and green-houses" as well as Christian tracts.[33]

Just as boosters like Ogden dealt directly with people of lower stations, so they also served directly as leaders in politics and society. According to Frederic Jaher's study of America's "urban establishment," between 1837 and 1868 only two of the city's nineteen mayors were not prominent businessmen, and "Chicago party leaders, congressmen, state legislators, aldermen, municipal and county commissioners, and other key public servants also came from the elite." Such personal involvement in all aspects of urban life had been typical of the boosters' elite counterparts in eastern cities before the depression of the 1840s. Afterward, the direct engagement of the eastern upper class slackened as its members exerted their influence through institutions they controlled but did not necessarily manage themselves. Similar patterns of upper-class power emerged in Chicago after the Civil War.[34]

Underlying the Chicago boosters' direct social and political involvement were the relative lack of class tensions and the weakness of civil society—the voluntary associations and contractual networks constituting economic, social, and cultural life. The difficulty of building these networks, and the necessity for them, was underlined by the short length of stay of most residents in the city. In 1857, the average length of stay in Chicago was about 3.5 years, while the median stay was considerably less—1.6 years. The difference in those figures was probably caused by the huge migration to the city during the boom years of the 1850s. There were a large number of recent arrivals as well as a significant minority of "old-timers." Despite the difficulties, the process of building a dense civil society increased substantially in the 1850s amid the prosperity preceding the Panic of 1857, and Ogden's efforts were just one example. Religious organizations of all confessions and immigrant groups of every variety energetically worked on the institutional foundations of Chicago society. Labor organizations founded in the 1850s were organized largely along ethnic and craft lines. Despite considerable advances, however, Chicago's civil society remained modest before the Civil War.[35]

Local government had to be built from the ground up as well, and the boosters' regime reflected their interests in attracting outside capital and building the city's infrastructure quickly. During the city's first fifteen years, booster rule combined Jacksonian politics with decision making about infrastructure on a citywide basis. In the late 1840s, the boosters initiated a new form of municipal politics, the "segmented" regime that has been analyzed by Robin Einhorn. The segmented system practically eliminated political conflict over infrastructure spending and prevented any redistribution of wealth through the city's general taxing powers. The essence of the system was the use of special assessments to fund city improvements. Elaborate procedures isolated—or segmented—decisions about improvements from the political control of the Common Council. The property owners who wanted a street paved petitioned the city council for the improvement; then the city clerk and relevant alderman went through a complicated process to gain the consent of the affected property owners. The elaborate paperwork required by these procedures constituted over half the public documents passing through the Common Council during a building boom in the late 1850s. The city council rarely overruled these procedures because little or no public money was involved. Those most affected by the improvement paid the cost, and those who paid largely decided how things were done.[36]

Ward boundaries illustrated the nature of the system. They did not conform to city neighborhoods but rather to groups of property owners defined by their relation to the city's infrastructure—for example, the property owners along the whole length of major thoroughfares (map 1). Councilmen were primarily managers of complicated special assessment procedures. Important property owners, of course, had a great stake in public improvements, and they made a point of serving as councilmen to oversee the process. The process took the politics out of decision making and the costs out of the general budget, and thus it helped prevent the redistribution of wealth through the government's taxing power.[37]

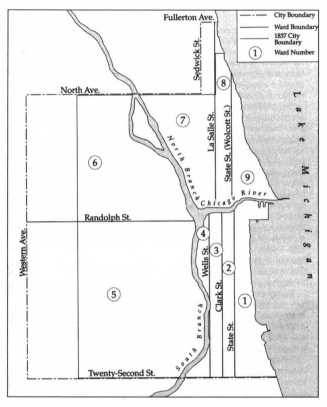

Map 1. Chicago wards in 1847. The ward boundaries were drawn according to the segmented system. Reproduced from Robin L. Einhorn, *Property Rules: Political Economy in Chicago, 1833–1872*, 81. Copyright 1991 by the University of Chicago. Used with permission of the University of Chicago Press.

To Einhorn, the segmented system solved a central problem of the ante-bellum political system: "How could government promote economic growth without redistributing wealth toward a favored class, party, or section?" This distinctively Jacksonian solution made Chicago's local political regime a species of the predominant national model in which, according to Richard L. McCormick, "government's most pervasive role was that of promoting development by distributing resources and privileges to individuals and groups." On a national level, distributive decisions did not threaten the existing distribution of property within the U.S. market. Instead, they doled out resources originating from outside the market, in particular western lands, tariffs on imports of goods, and government patronage jobs. Distributive policies, according to Theodore Lowi, are distinguished by "the ease with which they can be disaggregated and dispensed unit by small unit, each unit more or less in isolation from other units and from any general rule." With such isolated and idiosyncratic decisions, it is difficult or impossible to define winners and losers. This was exactly the way infrastructure decisions were made under Chicago's segmented system.[38]

In contrast, according to Lowi, *redistributive* governmental policies not only created winners and losers in conflicts over limited resources, but also treated the contenders in wider terms: "The categories of impact are much broader, approaching social classes. They are, crudely speaking, haves and have-nots, bigness and smallness, bourgeoisie and proletariat." By institutionalizing distributive politics, and preventing redistribution, the segmented regime precisely met the needs of the boosters as leaders of a producer republican society built around widely dispersed property ownership. Neither their property nor that of other producers could be taxed for someone else's benefit, while at the same time the boosters got the infrastructure improvements they needed to advance their innumerable projects. The boosters were willing to contribute substantially to the price for improvements in exchange for the control it gave them over decisions and for the protection it gave them against redistribution of their wealth downward. Severely constricting the government's ability to make redistributive decisions also appealed to small property owners, who typically feared that their wealth would be used to aid either a parasitic aristocracy or the undeserving poor. Nonetheless, with enthusiasm and skill, the boosters advocated redistribution of wealth nationally from the wealthier East to the developing West through federal internal improvements that would benefit their city and their investments in it.[39]

The segmented system insured that public improvements went to those willing and able to pay, which helps explain the city's notorious unimproved, muddy, pothole-pocked streets, particularly in poorer neighborhoods. The system likewise helped keep the era's intense political and ethnic conflicts from spilling over into municipal affairs, since the role of local government was so tightly circumscribed around building infrastructure through an apolitical procedure. When such conflicts did erupt into politics, they constituted a major crisis. The clearest example of such a case was the Lager Beer Riot of 1855, when a largely German but nonetheless multiethnic crowd marched on the courthouse to free saloon keepers accused of violating the local liquor ordinances. A recently elected protemperance and nativist administration had made the ordinances more stringent and enforced them more efficiently. The riot resulted in at least one death, the calling out of the militia, and the declaration of martial law. Notably, the temperance issue instigated the Beer Riot that broke the nonpartisan mold of municipal politics, mainly because it provided a basis for immigrants to unite against the native-born and the city's current evangelical Yankee leaders. In other words, it allowed local politics to be organized around the broad categories such as ethnicity and class so alien to distributive politics. The segmented system that had failed to prevent the Beer Riot was more effective in containing the class conflict during the unemployment crisis of 1857.[40]

THE UNEMPLOYMENT CRISIS OF 1857

The economic crisis of 1857 was a national phenomenon with profound local impact. In November 1857, Nikolaus Schwenck, a German coppersmith in Chicago, wrote his brother in Germany: "The worst of all bad times, this is what you hear everywhere, and it actually is! . . . No work, and why?—because business is bad. Thousands of workers are unemployed and look with fearful hearts towards the approaching winter. And what is worst, most criminal of all, what little they had put aside with the sweat of their brows and invested in saving banks—is gone! Most banks are bankrupt, or at least have *suspended* their payments."[41]

The economic crisis that had begun in the East had reached Chicago. Throughout November, Chicago papers reported crowds of workingmen in New York, Philadelphia, and Baltimore demanding "Bread or Work." New York City's workers had raised this same demand in 1854. Calling for bread or work was the clearest expression of the politics of the propertyless laborers of America's cities, the "dependent" workers who lacked the productive property in real estate, shops, tools, and skill possessed by craftsmen like Schwenck, who was the kind of worker who fit well into Lincoln's free-labor vision of republican society. Demanding "Bread or Work" assumed that the government had both the responsibility and authority to provide for the basic social and economic needs of citizens. In the late 1850s, however, Chicagoans were not ready to concede that wage labor was a permanent state or that the city government should intervene in the economy to aid the unemployed. Currently running the city, Republicans thought that such public works programs violated the authority and exceeded the resources of local government, and they considered charity destructive of the independence required of citizens. Most important, the use of government funds to provide work for the unemployed would be the kind of redistributive policy the segmented system was designed to prevent. Yet something needed to be done, for the crisis was extreme and the boosters felt a paternal responsibility for city affairs.[42]

In November, the same month that Schwenck wrote his anguished letter to his relatives in Germany, a prestigious committee met at P. W. Gates's foundry and machine shop to discuss means of providing employment to needy men. One of the largest manufacturers in the city, Gates played a significant role in Republican affairs throughout the era. One of Gates's associates, A. G. Throop, a prominent booster, came up with an ingenious solution to the unemployment crisis. Throop had run on temperance tickets in municipal elections in the early 1850s, and he had helped organize Chicago's opposition to the Fugitive Slave Law. Throop's company had planned to build docking facilities on the north side of the South Branch of the Chicago River in the "Hardscrabble" area of the South West Side. Then the financial panic left the company without enough money to pay large numbers of workers. As an alternative, he was willing to use the land his company owned along the river to either raise the money from wealthy citizens or compensate the individual laborers. If charitable societies or wealthy individuals would contribute money to pay the unemployed for their work on the docks, he would deed land over to the contributors. In the near future, the land would surely be worth much more than they had given, because the area around the new docks would boom. Thus philanthropy would also turn a profit. He was also willing to contract with individual workers, who could purchase lots by making payments in labor. The value of the lots was from $400 to $500.[43]

Stephen A. Douglas's *Chicago Times* cried, "Philanthropic speculation!" Instead it proposed using the city government to provide both work and bread, and it even considered whether landlords should be prevented from evicting people during the crisis. The city government would provide work building much-needed streets and sewers. The *Times* would admit to only two objections to its plan—that there was not enough money and that outdoor work was unprofitable in the winter—but the paper thought that the crisis of the moment overrode them. To solve the problem of funding, the *Times* argued that the city should buy flour, meat, firewood, coal, and clothing on credit now and pay in the spring when business and tax revenue picked up. It even proposed city soup kitchens and bakeries in each division of the city to supply the indigent.[44]

The approach of the *Times* was an assertion of governmental responsibility and power that went far beyond the system of nonpartisan, segmented government that all political groups, including the Democrats, had previously supported. Now, however, economic crisis and the political challenge of the Republicans pushed the Democrats toward a new more interventionist concept of local government and toward a redistributive politics. This development had gone further in the East, where, according to Amy Bridges, "in Newark, Philadelphia, and Baltimore, as well as New York, the depression of the 1850s brought demands for public works and public relief, demands that would have been 'inconceivable sixty years before.' . . . [T]hese demands won concessions from city governments and pressured politicians into a kind of primitive welfare-state-ism." The Douglas Democrats advanced this process in Chicago.[45]

On November 15—two days after the *Times* called for the city government to provide bread and work—about three hundred to four hundred Germans met to address the economic crisis. The editor of the *National Demokrat,* Douglas's German Democratic paper, made a challenging and politically volatile proposal: He urged that a committee of five laborers call on the city council and demand bread or work. Challenging the editor of the *Demokrat* was Hermann Kreismann, who had recently been appointed city clerk by Chicago's first Republican mayor. He was also part of the circle of German forty-eighters, refugees from the failed Revolution of 1848, who spoke through the *Illinois Staats-Zeitung,* which they had used to aid the Republican Party. Kreismann was also one of the directors of the Chicago Relief and Aid Society, which was central to Throop's plan. Appealing to American legal traditions, Kreismann said that the city government had no authority to provide work or relief. Unlike the European despotisms they had fled, the government here "does not interfere by unequal taxation, unjust laws and the establishment of favored classes, in times of prosperity," and thus, "it cannot be expected to act as the nursing mother in times of distress." Appealing to German ethnic pride, Kreismann acknowledged that something had to be done and called on his countrymen to take care of their own through voluntary associations. In this way, the already high reputation of the Germans among the Americans would increase even more.[46]

The new Republican administration was saved from political embarrassment when the German meeting decided not to make demands on the city council. Similarly, the Chicago city council rejected a Democratic-sponsored resolution to provide work on public improvements. Within a week of the German meeting, the Republican forty-eighters followed Kreismann's call for voluntary efforts to aid the needy and unemployed by founding of the Arbeiterverein, or Workers' Association, a social and mutual benefit organization. The Arbeiterverein was the Chicago German community's main organized response to the economic crisis, as well as one of the key institutions founded by the forty-eighters to build a constituency among German workers. The acceptance of Kreismann's plan reflected the strength of both the forty-eighters and the Republican Party in German Chicago and the correlative weakness of more radical forty-eighters and German Marxists, who were not yet strong enough to influence the debate.[47]

With the Democrats neutralized, the Republicans put the Throop plan into effect. In December, the scheme was well under way, with the largest contributor of funds being the Chicago Relief and Aid Society, the semipublic official steward of the city's poor. The laborers were paid in food and fuel at a value of about fifty cents per day. Nine-tenths of the company's reimbursement of the Society was in the form of real estate, one-tenth in cash. Throughout the winter employment crisis, the agreement between Throop and the Relief Society provided 2,495 days of labor to men certified by the Society as worthy recipients. The agreement also turned a profit for the Society. Some individual laborers also took advantage of Throop's proposal, using their labor to buy lots in the Tenth Ward, which included the area of the dock construction. Although there is no way of knowing exactly how many men worked for Throop, he claimed that he could employ two thousand throughout the winter. Throop's ingenious plan addressed the crisis without either providing charity or involving the Republican-controlled city government in redistributing resources, in this case downward.[48]

Throop's plan reflected the economic position of the boosters and their relations to Chicago's immigrant workers. Merchants and land speculators, the boosters used anticipated increases in land values to finance work on Throop's docks and aid the unemployed at the same time. Basically, this was the same method used by the federal government and the boosters, in their role as canal commissioners, to finance the building of the Illinois and Michigan Canal. It was also the key to the boosters' use of special assessments to fund infrastructure in Chicago. Similar distribution of land would finance the construction of railroads. Land of little value was given to builders of internal improvements or sold to raise capital for the construction. The land proved attractive because of the anticipated increase in value that would come with the canal or railroad and with the settlers who would follow. Although Throop's plan was distinctive in its use of land as money to pay day laborers, this use was analogous to the boosters' sale of inexpensive land to settlers: The more settlers in an area, the more the value of the boosters' remaining holdings increased.[49]

The laborers who built on land near Throop's docks were settling an urban frontier that, as predicted, soon became a vital and dense urban working-class district, much of which remained property of the boosters, despite the high rate of real estate ownership among workers. Land rich and capital poor, the boosters tried throughout the era to attract settlers to raise the value of their holdings, whether in the countryside or in the city. Although Throop did not give away land for free, as William Butler Ogden did his fruit and tracts, he dealt directly with workers in a hierarchical relationship that, in the depression of 1857, was both economic and philanthropic. Class relations would change dramatically by the depression of 1873, when crowds of unemployed workers led by the Central European left marched on City Hall and the Chicago Relief and Aid Society.

THE MANUFACTURING CITY
AND ITS WORKERS

During the booster era, manufacturing was subordinate to commerce and city building. Although there had been considerable investment in manufacturing between 1852 and 1856, especially in the railroad car shops and in the metalwork firms supplying them, the Panic of 1857 so interrupted this growth that the value of Chicago's manufactured products was probably less in 1860 than in 1856. The 1860 census found fewer employed in manufacturing than estimated by the *Democratic Press* in 1854. Subsequently, the demand created by the Civil War proved catalytic for a wave of investment and innovation. As a result, in a mere seven years between 1864 and 1871, Chicago moved from being a net importer of goods, as befitted a commercial trading center, to being a net merchandise exporter, as its manufacturing economy boomed.[50]

The city was undergoing a fundamental change in its mode of production—that is, in the way goods were made, wealth accumulated, capital invested, labor expended, and classes organized. Because the nature of classes changed, the relations between them altered, and this transformation affected Chicago's culture and politics. The change in mode of production expanded and transformed the city at the same time, and seeing both processes together illuminates the whole.

The amount of capital needed to build the new manufacturing economy was so enormous that most of it could only come from outside the city. This was nothing new to Chicagoans. The boosters had worked tirelessly to attract outside investment, particularly from the federal government, which also contributed mightily to the manufacturing economy through its purchases during the Civil War. Nonetheless, the huge investments of the railroads came earlier and had a distinctive transformative effect that was apparent to contemporaries.[51]

Railroad investment also transformed Chicago by building a new sector of the local economy making producers' goods: those needed by industry to mechanize and expand production. The railroads not only laid their track and built their depots, they also invested directly in manufacturing, constructing, for example, huge car shops where they built and repaired equipment. The demand for sophisticated and precision-built producers' goods—machinery, engines, brakes, wheels, axles—stimulated by the growth of the railroads, and to a lesser extent by the shipping industry, helped initiate Chicago into the next phase of the American industrial revolution in which making consumer products took second place. Advances in the production of consumer goods—most famously cotton cloth—had initiated the American industrial revolution.[52]

The connection to the railroads made the manufacture of producers' goods distinct from the city's commercial economy, and the local capital market that serviced it, and thus freed it from control by the boosters. The demand for railroad products was only indirectly tied to that for grain and other agricultural commodities, and the railroads had access to capital beyond the reach and control of local merchants. The railroads used this access to provide 90 percent of the capital needed to construct the Union Stock Yards in 1865. The stockyards improved the transportation infrastructure that made Chicago the country's largest transshipment center for livestock, which in turn attracted the packinghouses, major customers of the railroads.[53]

The railroads' huge investment had a ripple effect in Chicago's manufacturing economy. Before 1870, the railroad car shops were the largest metal-fabrication firms in the city, and demand by the railroads for a range of products attracted other firms. In the 1850s, E. B. Ward from Detroit built a rolling mill on the North Side to make iron products for the railroads from ingots produced elsewhere. Within a decade, ingots were made in Chicago as well. Charles Kellogg and Co., another Detroit firm, built a diversified iron plant near Ward's on the North Branch of the Chicago River, also to supply the railroads. Local metal-fabrication firms profited from railroad contracts, just as a local shipbuilding industry grew up to supply vessels for trade on both the Great Lakes and the Illinois and Michigan Canal.[54]

Unlike later mass production, these metal-fabrication firms, including the car shops, were typically "manufactories," employing large numbers of craft workers, often in specialized departments, while semiskilled and unskilled workers performed the simpler tasks. Gates's Eagle Works had departments organized to produce particular products, such as steam engines, and others to perform specialized tasks, like making castings for all other departments. The firm had eleven departments in all, and a workforce of 395, making it one of the largest businesses in the city. Manufactories used machinery here and there, but machines did not define the whole production process. According to Bruce Laurie and Mark Schmitz, few employers "mechanized the production process from end to end. . . . Their establishments hosted a mix of new, middle range, and old technologies and were a far cry from the paradigms of modernization depicted in conventional historiography. Pockets of hand techniques and labor-intensive work, survivals of the past and creations of the industrial revolution, could be found in the most advanced work settings."[55]

More dramatically than the Eagle Works, the car shops illustrated this mixture of technique in their physical layout. In the mid-1850s, the Illinois Central Car Works south of the city consisted of twelve large buildings "occupied by the various purposes of wood work, blacksmith forges, finishing and painting shops, upholstery rooms, etc., all alive with workmen, and teeming with the busy hum of industry." Tracks connected the various buildings so that the cars being built and repaired could be easily moved about to the different groups of craftsmen, many of whom still owned their own tools. During the 1860s, five of the railroads entering the city maintained shops there, employing over 1,100 men, who constituted about 20 percent of Chicago's manufacturing workforce in 1860. The metal-fabricating sector of Chicago's economy, in which manufactories predominated, grew extensively in the next decade: Employment in Chicago's machine shops, foundries, agricultural implement works, rolling mills, and steam forges increased by over 300 percent to 4,346, a rate of growth double that of their considerable expansion during the 1850s. Manufactories were also common in woodworking, particularly in Chicago's booming furniture plants, as well as in wagon-making.[56]

The expansion in manufacturing, especially in metal and wood fabrication, created opportunities for master artisans, such P. W. Gates and Nikolaus Schwenck, to turn themselves into manufacturers, even if on a small scale compared to the railroad car shops. These artisan entrepreneurs were able to increase production and lower labor costs by subdividing work into numerous small tasks, employing unskilled workers to perform them, and, in some cases, introducing some labor-saving tools and machinery. At the same time, they aggregated skilled craftsmen into specialized departments of their manufactories, where they performed more sophisticated tasks, including assembling the final product out of parts made by the less skilled. This transformation of production was particularly important to artisan entrepreneurs as a way of earning the capital that they had difficulty raising in any other way. To raise capital, the artisan entrepreneurs also relied heavily on partnerships, marriage, and kin networks.[57]

Chicago's manufacturing boom in the 1860s was so extensive that it created opportunities for the city's large number of immigrant craftsmen to become manufacturers, alongside their usually larger Yankee counterparts. Strikingly, by 1870 foreign-born men owned 64 percent of Chicago's manufacturing enterprises, although the Yankee manufacturers predominated through the scale of their firms. In general, the national origins of Chicago's manufacturers correlated with both the scale of the enterprise and their backgrounds in either commerce or the crafts. With a few exceptions, Yankees, or Yankee-dominated corporations, such as the railroads, owned the larger enterprises employing the most workers. On the other hand, Chicago's artisan entrepreneurs were disproportionately foreign-born, as were the smaller manufacturers in any branch of industry. The Germans and the British supplied the main competition for the Yankees (table 2). Although German firms were present in every branch of Chicago manufacturing, they dominated the tobacco, alcoholic beverage, and furniture industries, where Germans owned over 50 percent of the firms and hired over 50 percent of all workers. No other foreign-born group, including the British, so dominated any one branch of Chicago industry. The British firms were particularly concentrated in the wearing apparel and metal industries, which together included almost half the British businesses. The smaller number of Irish entrepreneurs tended to emerge in construction and related branches of manufacturing.[58]

No matter what their national origins, artisan entrepreneurs transformed themselves into employers, not masters of a craft, and their employees became permanent wage earners, not journeymen and apprentices on their way to independence. Often concentrated in large groups in manufactories, these craftsmen became "factory artisans," in Steven J. Ross's terms, conscious both of their traditions and their loss of status. Their considerable organizational and cultural resources made them both difficult to manage and leaders in the

Table 2. Manufacturers in Chicago by Birthplace and Selected Measures of Firm Size: 1870

Birthplace	% All Firms	Average Capital (in dollars)	Average No. Employees	% All Employed
United States	36.3	51,360	46	66.4
Germany	37.9	13,870	15	22.4
Great Britain	10.3	24,851	16	6.7
Ireland	5.6	7,064	7	1.6
Scandinavia	4.4	1,567	5	0.8
Other	5.5	7,346	10	2.1
	100			100

Source: Federal manuscript manufacturing census for Chicago, 1870.
Note: Total firms = 659.

mid-nineteenth-century labor movement. When a reporter toured the new American Car Manufactory in 1853, he saw a new Congregational church near the plant and anticipated a Methodist one soon. Both denominations represented the British Protestant tradition that appealed to Yankees and English immigrants, who were attracted by the unusually high wages in the Midwest during the 1850s. In that decade, about two-fifths of Chicago's machinists were Americans and another fifth British. Near Chicago, in what had recently been an empty prairie, these workers created cultural institutions typical of craft workers since the Jacksonian era, including churches, libraries, and debating societies. Such institutions supported a producers' culture of self-help, moral uplift, patriotism, solidarity, and popular rationalism—not the rationalism of the freethinker, but rather of the inventor. The workers of the car shops were proudly patriotic during the secession crisis, provided a ready audience for schemes of cooperation, and staunchly supported the movement for the eight-hour workday. When German and Scandinavian workers found jobs in the car shops—and built Lutheran and Catholic churches next to the Congregational and Methodist ones—the American and British metalworkers still remained leaders in the shops. Yankee and British craft workers of all types were critical leaders of the first Chicago labor movement that emerged during the Civil War.[59]

Manufactories and railroad capital were only one part of Chicago's new manufacturing economy. The demand created by the war, and particularly by the federal government's purchasing, stimulated increased production of an array of goods in Chicago, including packed meat. These products were similar to the simple consumer goods, which typified the first phase of the American industrial revolution, and their manufacture in Chicago created

the city's closest equivalents to mass production in which the whole manufacturing process was subdivided, systematized, and coordinated. Meatpacking
exemplified the type and set the pace. So profitable was the business that local
merchants, including major players on the Board of Trade, invested their
capital in meatpacking, along with capitalists from the East and even Great
Britain. The new capital that moved into Chicago's slaughtering and meatpacking industry transformed it into one of the most efficiently organized
manufacturing complexes in the country. Between 1859 and 1865, the output
of Chicago pork packers increased sixfold; in 1862 alone, the capacity of the
packing industry practically doubled. During the war, Chicago overtook
Cincinnati as the nation's leading meatpacking center, and by 1870 more
capital had been invested in meatpacking than in any other branch of local
industry, including iron and steel.[60]

Taking the lead in restructuring the industry were the new packers from
outside the city who had moved in during the war. They built their efficient
new plants on the South Branch of the Chicago River, where they took advantage of both water and rail transportation. The Chicago packers also initiated
the organization of the Union Stock Yards, which, upon their opening in 1865
adjacent to the packing district, rationalized even further the transshipment of
livestock into the slaughterhouses and packing plants. Befitting men attuned
to the needs of commerce, the packers also worked out a uniform system for
inspecting and grading meat and regulating brands in 1865.[61]

This transformation of the industry included the organization of work. The
new plants of the 1860s included "all the improvements that have been made
in the business anywhere during the past quarter of a century." Packing meat
for sale in a regional and national market had emerged in Cincinnati during
the 1830s. From the beginning, it depended on largely unskilled, seasonal labor performing minutely defined repetitive tasks. The Chicago entrepreneurs
pushed the extreme subdivision of labor even further than in the Cincinnati
plants, and, by constantly increasing investment in plant and equipment, they
built greater capacity and increased productivity more than their Cincinnati
rivals. In 1870, one-quarter of all Chicago firms used steam, compared to 13
percent of the larger Cincinnati establishments. The steam-powered Chicago
packers employed 93 percent of the industry's workforce.[62]

The firm of Tobey and Booth on East Eighteenth Street and the South
Branch was one of the new efficiently organized packinghouses. During the
peak of the season in the winter, Tobey and Both employed about 150 men in
a two-story stone building measuring about 100 by 150 feet. They slaughtered

between fifteen hundred and two thousand hogs per day. Arriving by train, the hogs were driven up a ramp to the second floor, where "the hangman" hung them by one leg to an overhead pulley apparatus and pushed them along to "the sticker," who slit their throats and pushed them to the scalding vat. Fed by the company's boiler, the vat held up to five hogs at a time. After a short bath, the "scalder" lifted them out with a mechanical scoop and dropped them on the scraping bench, where the bristles were removed. It was "a table between thirty and forty feet long, sloping gradually to the end, to facilitate the forward movement of the body." About a dozen men stood on either side of the table, each working on a particular part. "The men engaged at this bench work like beavers. From morning (with the exception of noon) until dark they have not one moment of breathing time." The *Tribune* reporter found these men, who were "all wet and bristle-covered," to be "about as uninviting in external appearance as can be imagined, and with their long knives and sharp scrapers [they] make the vicinity dangerous ground." That vicinity also supported them with work on the docks and construction sites, in the lumberyards and canal boats, when the packing industry slowed down and then stopped altogether in the spring and summer.[63]

From the scraping bench, the hog was once again hung up, this time on a wheeled device that ran on a track to different parts of the huge room. The "gutter" took out the entrails, separating the different parts into receptacles for further processing, and shoved the carcass along to a "washer," who cleaned the carcass with hot water before sending it along to the "splitter," who expertly cut the hog in half. The gutter and splitter were experts among the packing workers, performing repetitive but precise tasks. The splitter, for example, had to make a clean cut down the backbone to exactly divide the animal; a miss could ruin a considerable portion of the meat. At this point—about five minutes after it was first hung by its hind leg—the hog could be sold fresh for eating, but most hogs were cured and packed, a process that took considerably longer and involved packing and repacking the cuts of meat in salt. Tobey and Booth also did rendering in the same plant on the second floor. There a dozen men and boys tended eight huge copper vats, dividing the fat from the entrails, cooking it down, and drawing it off through a system of pipes to make lard, which was used in manufacturing lard oil, candles, and soap.

Production in the packing industry could be so quickly and dramatically subdivided and rationalized in part because the processes were basically simple. The same was the case in the manufacture of slaughtering by-products, such as hides, soap, oil, candles, and lard. Like the men and boys rendering lard at Tobey and Booth's, the workers in these industries performed simple sorting and stirring tasks under the direction of foremen amid vats, pipes, heat, and noxious fumes.[64]

Producing similarly simple products, the lumber and flour milling, brewing, and distilling industries functioned with moderate-size workforces directed by a few experts or masters. Workers in them performed physically demanding unskilled labor. In 1870, for example, the average Chicago flour mill employed ten men, while the average brewery, soap, or candle firm hired nineteen. That is considerably more than in an artisan shop, but still of middling size in comparison to the average pork packer, who employed sixty-eight. Like the makers of slaughtering by-products, distillers, millers, and sawmill operators required substantial investment in storage facilities, vats, piping, boilers, steam engines, and machinery. In 1870, the five industries with the highest capital investment per worker were, in descending order, brewing and malt production, distilling, flour and feed milling, soap and candle making, and pork packing.[65]

Pork packing was distinctive on this list for employing large numbers of laborers per firm, but not so much for the unskilled work they performed. Men and boys laboring in Chicago's highly mechanized sawmills performed routine and dangerous tasks at high speeds for long hours. The long hours usually coincided with the seasonal high point of production in industries working up products of the land. The sawmills closed when the winter ice shut down the lumber schooners plying the shores of the Great Lakes. In contrast, the packinghouses had their peak season from the late fall into the early spring; by the summer, they usually shut down. In the spring and summer, their workers sawed or stacked lumber, unloaded ships and railroad cars, or carried hod on construction sites. Some of them moved to the countryside and labored on farms. That is, most of them became the casual laborers who made up almost one-quarter of Chicago's workforce in 1860.[66]

Working outdoors, like seaport workers since the eighteenth century, they were accustomed to laboring in gangs performing specific tasks and then remaining idle until the next ship came in or the next construction job started. The varying nature and pace of outdoor work contrasted sharply with the fast-paced, subdivided, and regimented labor of the factories. The same workers frequently performed both kinds of labor in different seasons. Experiencing two contrasting worlds of labor, they often became supporters of the eight-hour movement in the 1860s to gain more control over their workday in the factories and manufactories. At the same time, these men were accustomed to working in close-knit groups, often defined by their regional and national origins. Thus, when they rebelled, as in the eight-hour strike of May 1867, they formed crowds and shut down plants, using violence when necessary. Tobey and Booth's, and the other packinghouses, were already down, given the season. These crowds of eight-hour supporters represented the largest part of the Gilded Age working class in the making, that is, propertyless wage laborers solely dependent on the labor market for their survival. Often they listened to the craftsmen leading the organized labor movement, but sometimes they did not.[67]

Chicago's craftsmen came in great variety, and they worked in a wide range of firms, not just in substantial manufactories such as the car shops or Gates's Eagle Works. Artisan shops, such as most bakeries in Chicago, typically had five or fewer workers and tried to maintain traditional relations of production between masters, journeymen, and apprentices. Artisan shops did not disappear in the mid-nineteenth century; they even increased in number in some branches of industry, although their relative importance declined. The growth in number of small businesses tended to mask a significant increase in the share of total output contributed by a much smaller number of larger, more efficient factories, which utilized inanimate sources of power to run machinery.[68]

Baking provides a good example of the impact new capital had on craft manufacturing. Bakers were typically master artisans owning small neighborhood shops where they baked bread, perhaps with the help of a few journeymen and apprentices. The 1870 manufacturing census, for example, counted twenty-six bakeries in the city, and it certainly missed quite a few of the smaller ones. Eighty percent of them employed five or fewer men, and two-thirds of the owners were foreign-born. Towering over this world of small ethnic shops was C. L. Woodman, a Yankee whose two plants together employed almost one-third of the city's bakery workers. Woodman had learned the baking trade in his native New Hampshire before arriving in Chicago in the mid-1850s, ahead of the manufacturing boom of the '60s but well after the entrance of the founding generation of boosters. He quickly rose in the social and political worlds of Chicago, becoming a Free Mason in the early 1860s, then an alderman and a member of the Board of Trade. In 1869, he was able to raise the capital—probably through his contacts at the Board of Trade—to build a two-story mechanized bakery with machinery for mixing the dough and an oven with a steam-powered system for circulating baked goods through the heating chamber. In the early 1870s, his plant had an annual production of over 1.5 million loaves of bread and seventy-five thousand pounds of crackers, which he shipped in barrels throughout the Northwest.[69]

When plants like Woodman's intruded upon a traditional craft industry, they restructured it, even when, as in baking, they did not eliminate the classic artisan shop. Their competition forced cost-cutting measures on the small producers, who sought cheaper quarters in sheds and dank basements, making cleanliness in the bakeries one of the public health issues of later decades. The small bakers also cut wages, which helped make them, along with the big bakeries, the target of union organization. The entry of large-scale plants into an industry of formerly small producers resulted in what Sean Wilentz has called "bastardized" craft production—his characterization of manufacturing in New York City at midcentury. It continued for decades; in 1872, when other workers in New York struck for the eight-hour workday, the bakers struck for a twelve-hour workday—and lost.[70]

Indicative of these trends in the Midwest, Chicago's first significant bakers' strike took place in 1864 and directly involved one of the largest firms, the Chicago Mechanical Bakery, in a conflict over wages, hours, and hiring practices. The strikers contended not with a master baker or even the owner of the bakery, but rather with its "superintendents." After they lost the strike, some returned to work, while other bakery workers tried to form a cooperative. Whether they worked for Woodman or a small master, these bakery workers represented the debased artisans who had figured prominently in American and European labor unrest since the origins of the industrial revolution in the eighteenth century. While the bakery workers' experience of long hours and low wages gave them common cause with workers in factories and manufactories, their work settings and the remnants of their crafts often divided them from the main concerns of Chicago labor. Thus, well into the 1880s, Chicago bakers were still opposing the craft practice of having part of their wages paid in room and board supplied by their masters.[71]

The most dramatic transformation and expansion of manufacturing in Chicago came not from the railroads or the packing plants, but rather from another branch of artisan production: garment making. The new garment workers, because they were young females, also provided the most obvious example of the new working class. Before the Civil War, the trade was overwhelmingly male, structured like a craft, and small. In 1854, the German journeymen tailors, joined by their compatriots of other nationalities, devised a common price list that most employers accepted until the early 1860s. The fact that the agreement pertained to prices for goods produced by the journeymen, rather than wages, indicated that both parties to it thought in craft terms. At the same time, employing a few hundred, the garment-making trade was tiny, particularly compared to Chicago's rival Cincinnati. At midcentury, Cincinnati's ready-to-wear garment industry led the nation and employed over five thousand people.[72]

Chicago soon challenged Cincinnati's preeminence. Pushing the master tailors and journeymen aside during the Civil War, Chicago's dry-goods merchants entered the garment industry and, like the meat-packers, took advantage of all the latest technological and managerial developments in the industry. Sewing machines became available for modest prices in the 1850s and '60s, and they produced more uniform results and enlarged the labor pool, since less skill was needed to operate one than to hand stitch. The entry of Chicago merchants into manufacturing was so dramatic and decisive that, by 1870, Chicago's clothing industry employed 5,306 workers, over two-thirds of them women. Over half of these women were foreign-born, and their average age was in the early twenties. The predominance of large firms in Chicago's clothing industry is just as striking as the increase in employment: Firms with more than fifty hands employed 87 percent of all the workers. Chicago's large dry-goods merchants set up clothing manufacturing departments in the same buildings where they carried on their retail and wholesale trade. During the busy season, each of these large houses employed from 150 to 250 women, who made dresses, cloaks, shirts, and children's clothing.[73]

In one sense, these women were comparable to the dockworkers and day laborers who worked in the packinghouses, planing mills, breweries, and other establishments of Chicago's agricultural-processing industries: Both the clothing workers and the casual laborers were new to industrial work, and their involvement was frequently short or episodic. The entrance of these new workers—whether they were male or female—into the Chicago manufacturing workforce was stunning, and the contrast between the lives they had previously lived—or the lives they lived during another part of the year—and the realities on the shop floor heightened their awareness of the rapid changes taking place in their lives. How they reacted to these changes varied widely and included simply moving frequently from place to place or job to job. In the process, they contributed to the growing bodies of unemployed in American cities, which disturbed more established citizens. Respectable society usually experienced the impact of the emerging manufacturing economy on civil society as disorder from below. Nonetheless, the main source of change, and disorder, came from the top down, through new capital being invested in production processes.[74]

THE GILDED AGE UPPER CLASS
AND ITS NEW REGIME

The new upper class that came to prominence in the mid-1860s had many similarities with the boosters, such as its origins in the Northeast and a Protestant religious heritage. But it was profoundly different in the way it accumulated its wealth. As merchants, the boosters bought low, sold high, and speculated in land and other commodities. The Gilded Age upper class made a substantial portion of its profits by directly or indirectly controlling manufacturing production, particularly the people integral to it. Profits were increased not only by investment in machinery but also by the subdivision and regimentation of work, a process most obvious in the packinghouses but pervasive throughout the manufacturing economy. Controlling production required a new stratum of supervisory personnel: the foremen, bookkeepers, clerks, and timekeepers who began to form a new urban middle class distinct from the traditional doctors, lawyers, and ministers. The new forms of control over production created a greater distance between the classes in Chicago, as well as previously unheard of amounts of wealth. The two developments were mutually reinforcing. With the distance came a greater hostility and tension between classes than had been typical during the booster era.[75]

An incident from 1871 in a German brewery provides an extreme case of a work environment where the unskilled and often transient worker met the expert manager or master under the stress of brutally long work hours. Martin Scheller was the engineer at Busch and Brand's Brewery, an average-size establishment employing nineteen men. He insisted on the strictest cleanliness and care in the brewery's machine room, where Charles Feodore, a recently arrived immigrant, worked. Despite engineer Scheller's warnings, Feodore repeatedly spilled kerosene on the floor when he lit the lamp. One evening, as Feodore was leaving the room carrying the lamp, Scheller discovered more spilled kerosene, and a violent argument ensued. When Scheller grabbed Feodore by the neck and tried to throw him out the door, Feodore hit him with the lamp, fracturing his skull and killing him. Feodore was arrested shortly afterward at the boardinghouse where he stayed. This incident pitted a hired professional against an operative, both of them Germans, in a highly capitalized manufacturing establishment in a branch of industry that attracted commercial capital. It was also a branch of industry undergoing enormous expansion, mechanization, and concentration throughout the country. As an ever greater proportion of Chicago's workers became concentrated in fewer and fewer large-scale enterprises, the distance between workers and their employers grew even more.[76]

The greater distance and tension evident in the workplace correlated with growing disparities in civil society that Chicago's leaders experienced as new social problems, such as prostitution, crime, and unemployment. In response, the new leaders of Chicago reformed the mechanisms for dispensing charity, which also constituted one of the means for managing the rapidly growing propertyless working class. Their reforms represented the application to organizations in civil society of the new techniques of management and control applied in the economy. They also show how the new upper class ruled through new, or transformed, mediating institutions, rather than through their own personal involvement in politics and social life, as did the boosters.

Founded in 1850, the Chicago Relief and Aid Society (originally the Chicago Relief Society) was one of the many charitable and cultural institutions sustained by the boosters serving as volunteers. During the unemployment crisis in the winter of 1857–58, the Society had supported the unemployed with food and coal in exchange for work on Throop's docks, and it had received land from Throop in exchange. In 1867, the Society was practically founded anew and put on a permanent basis by Chicago's new leaders. The historian of the Society, Kathleen McCarthy, found "surprisingly little continuity between the rejuvenated board and its predecessors," noting that "most of Chicago's Gilded Age millionaires would serve on the board at some point in their careers." One distinguishing feature of the new board was the presence of a substantial number of manufacturers, whereas they had been absent from the old one. Most important, the members of the new board gave the Society a staff, consolidated its operations, and dedicated it to promoting self-help and the "efficient management of the chronic poor." The Society's central role in the relief efforts after the Great Fire of 1871 helped it advance its new institutional objectives: After the fire, the "CRA trustees translated their newly acquired prerogatives into a system which was elitist, aloof, and tightly centralized under masculine control." The emerging class divisions foreshadowed in the reorganization of the Relief and Aid Society—and in conflicts between labor and management on the shop floor—emerged more clearly after the fire, as the rebuilding sorted out the city geographically into districts and neighborhoods characterized more by class and function than the boosters' old walking city.[77]

Chicago's new upper class transformed politics as it did civil society, first when the new manufacturers began to act as interest groups and then as they subverted the boosters' segmented system. By the time of the fire and its after-math, Chicago's Gilded Age upper class acted politically through a variety of institutions, including the Relief and Aid Society, civic reform organizations, and the English-language press.[78]

Whether artisan entrepreneurs or former merchants, local manufactur-ers started to become politically self-conscious during the 1860s, as they organized to protect their interests and develop their markets. The rise of a substantial labor movement in the midst of the Civil War pushed them in the same direction. Machine makers organized in 1862, followed by the pork packers. Chicago manufacturers met as a group to complain about a federal value-added tax during the Civil War and to promote a tariff to protect their products afterward. More dramatic than any of these developments was the eight-hour strike of 1867, during which many artisan entrepreneurs realized that their interests lay more with their fellow manufacturers than with their crafts. Their sense of independence increased when they were able to use their wartime profits to pay off debts, many of them to commercial capitalists. The new wealth of Chicago's Gilded Age leaders reduced their needs from the city government. Since their wealth derived from controlling the process of production and selling in wide markets rather than on transshipping and processing products of the land, they were less dependent on the provision of local infrastructure, and thus they needed the city government less. Rather than compete with one another over the spoils of local urban growth, as had the boosters, the new leaders competed with other producers in regional and national markets. Thus they had less of a need for the apolitical segmented system to preserve the peace among them. When the segmented system got in their way, they simply subverted it.[79]

As in so many things, the meat-packers led the way by refusing to abide by an 1862 city ordinance requiring them to pay the cost of cleaning up their pollution of the Chicago River. The ordinance applied a traditional segmented solution to the provision of a public good by making those directly involved supply the funds. The packers and their spokesmen in the press agreed that a cleaner river was in the public interest but argued that the city, in other words all property owners, should pay the cost. To make their point crudely clear, the packers organized a boycott of the ordinance, and then they threatened to leave the city if they did not get their way. Their new economic power made this threat decisive: They were in fact central to the city's new economic pros-perity—which was also in the public interest—and they could move outside its boundaries. The city capitulated by paying for dredging that helped abate the pollution problem.[80]

In the process, the packers and their allies had taken the lead in initiating a new form of urban politics in which the public interest was defined through partisan and interest group conflict. This public interest legitimated a redistributive politics in which the rewards of public funding went to the winners of political and interest group combat. In Chicago, that meant interests defined by nationality as well as class, and the political parties became vehicles for articulating and managing the politics of both. Since the new Chicago upper class had enormous advantages in the competition to define the public interest, the rewards typically went to them, as in the solution to the pollution of the Chicago River. This was the republican nightmare of redistribution upward to the moneyed aristocracy, precisely what the segmented system—which abolished all redistributive policies in any direction—was designed to prevent. A new city ward map passed in 1863 (map 2) both symbolized and helped initiate the new political order, since it more accurately reflected the city's geographical divisions by class and nationality and the interests they represented.[81]

The politics of redistribution emerged out of a rapidly industrializing, class-divided city, and it characterized a new ruling regime that emerged in Chicago during the Civil War and Reconstruction era. By the end of the 1860s, the regime linked the dominant Republican Party to both the upper class and the city's broader civil society through the Protestant churches, the bulk of the English-language press, businessmen's associations, and ethnic organizations, notably the German Arbeiterverein. Top members of the new upper class also controlled citywide associations such as the Relief and Aid Society and Citizens' Association, which afforded them the means to reform and rationalize class relations. One critical element of civil society lay outside the new regime: organized workers. The struggles of the Republican Party to integrate labor into its regime are the topic of the following chapter.

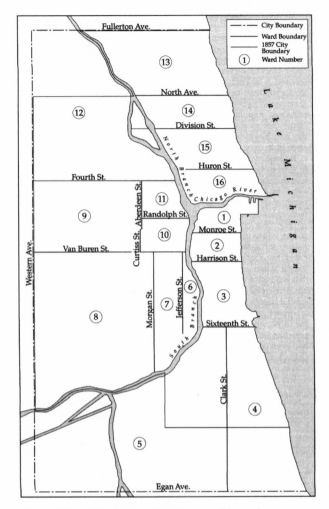

Map 2. Chicago wards in 1863. These ward boundaries
are more appropriate to the city's functional divisions
and residential districts than were those of the segmented
system. Reproduced from Robin L. Einhorn, *Property Rules:
Political Economy in Chicago, 1833–1872*, 184. Copyright 1991
by the University of Chicago. Used with permission of the
University of Chicago Press.

2 The *Internationale* of the Citizen Workers
From Slavery to the Labor Question

REFLECTING ON THE IMMINENT Fourth of July celebration in 1865, the *Chicago Tribune* felt that a bridge had been built between the two great revolutionary periods of American history, 1776–88 and 1860–65. During both periods, "the American people have risen to the grandeur of the recognition of the right of all to freedom and political equality." Now, in 1865, the truths of the Founding Fathers as expressed in the Declaration of Independence— that "irrepressible argument for radicalism"—were real and vital again: "The Gospel which they uttered we are fulfilling. What on their lips was prophecy, from ours is history. We have employed the powers of the Union which they formed for us, to overthrow that system of slavery which they denounced, and to vindicate the principles which they bequeathed to us."[1]

This was not merely Fourth of July rhetoric. Chicago's first labor movement emerged in the midst of a bourgeois revolution in which an alliance of northern farmers, artisans, manufacturers, and merchants used the "powers of the Union" to reunite the country and transform its society and economy. While the destruction of slavery was the most obvious change, the revolution also created the economic and political conditions for the emergence of capitalism as the predominant mode of production within the Union, replacing the antebellum mix of capitalism, chattel slavery, and freehold agriculture and artisanship. Cities like Chicago were at the center of this profound and sustained transformation, which was the theme of our first chapter.

The destruction of slavery as a national economic and political interest cleared the ground for the rise of a new working class of wage earners, in part by creating a space within the public sphere for working-class issues. Organized in April 1864 by eighteen unions, the General Trades Assembly served as the most important vehicle for articulating a class outlook. Labor's citywide organization was a political interest group representing workers of all skills and backgrounds in Chicago's public life. Workers' awareness of themselves as a class developed further as ethnic and political leaders began to appeal publicly to the new labor interest. The creation of such an enduring organized interest in the public sphere was a critical element in the formation of a new kind of urban politics appropriate to the new capitalist order.[2]

THE AMERICAN REPUBLIC
AND LIBERAL REPUBLICANISM

Chicago's new working class had its political heritage in an international political culture that scholars have called *republicanism*. Though as a theory and practice it dated to ancient times, republicanism was reborn as a modern social movement in the eighteenth century. Its central project was the overthrow of rule by monarchs and aristocrats and the establishment of a republic in which "the people," rather than the monarch or the state, was sovereign. American republicanism was not incompatible with liberalism, the belief that society was self-regulating and that the state should be limited to protecting the individual's pursuit of happiness in the market. The two developed in the course of American history as an intertwining set of languages and ideologies. Though sometimes in tension, they generally reinforced each other, each compensating for what the other lacked.

At first, despite the creation of the American and French republics, republican advocates continued to express grave concern about the prospects of republican government. Given ancient and early modern experience, the republic seemed to be a fragile entity, ever at risk of corruption stemming from new historical developments, most prominent among them the spread of market relations with its liberal ethic of self-interested action, known to the founders as "the spirit of faction." But, rather than attempt to circumscribe the market, American liberal republicans relied less on civic virtue to tame self-interest and more on checking, balancing, diluting, and filtering the influence of factions through a deliberative public opinion.[3]

Scholars now recognize that the republican political tradition continued to provide American politics with a key element of its ideological framework throughout most of the nineteenth century. The sine qua non to the continued vitality of the republic was a balanced—though not an equal—distribution of property in which the producers of that wealth retained the fruits of their labor through property ownership. Thus the yeomanry and artisan classes were the bedrock of the republic. Because Americans believed that the egalitarian social basis of the American republic was already established, they thought only bad government policies, rather than an autonomous economic sphere, could produce the inequality that would allow a self-interested faction to reintroduce aristocracy or monarchy. Such policies included onerous taxation, an unproductive bureaucracy, a large permanent national debt, state-sponsored monopolistic enterprises, and the manipulation of the currency. Each or some combination of these government actions could undermine the republic by unduly accommodating self-aggrandizement and undermining social equity. This did not mean that republicans had no use for government. While the Jeffersonian-Jacksonian wing of republicanism emphasized a weaker central government and stronger states, the Hamiltonian-Whig wing of republicanism came to terms with market development by arguing that government at all levels could sponsor commercial and industrial enterprise, as long as its fruits were broadly distributed.[4]

A distinctive variant of this larger political culture, artisan republicanism arose during the American Revolution but flowered fully only in the first half of the nineteenth century, when many journeymen confronted the dilution of their skill, grinding poverty, and the degradation of their crafts. Entrepreneurial masters and merchant capitalists transformed production in the crafts to seize opportunities created by new markets, undermining traditional craft practices in the process. Republicanism was a way of winning legitimacy among the broader public for the journeymen's attempt to maintain the integrity of their trade in the workshop, their independence in society, and their status as part of the producing classes in the republic. The journeymen's republican outlook distinguished them not only from the "parasitic" elements who threatened their independence from above, but also from those below like African American slaves, indentured servants, Chinese immigrants, and women. Journeymen feared that they, too, would become dependent like these groups, as a result of being undersold in the labor market. Thus artisan republicans at first used the term *wage-slavery* to describe the wage labor they performed. Beginning in the 1830s, however, many had redefined wage labor as a potentially honorable status, if only workers received adequate wages and exercised some control over their work through their protective and benevolent societies and mechanics institutes.[5]

As journeymen developed their critique and partial acceptance of wage labor, they moved toward a social interpretation of republicanism. Rather than viewing equality as a social given and inequality as a political imposition, they began to understand politics and government action as a way of confronting and even transforming a social inequality that arose from the workings of the market itself. That understanding was the working-class response to the emerging recognition in law and social thought that the market had become "disembedded" from society and that it was an autonomous realm governed by its own natural logic, manifested in the laws of political economy. The use of the state to ameliorate the unequal distribution of wealth created by the market stretched American republicanism to its breaking point and proved to be a major line of fracture between American and European social republicans. Europeans were much more inclined than Americans to use the state to intervene in civil society and the market.[6]

In recent years, scholars have begun to view historical developments like revolutions, political ideologies, class formation, and state building as processes transcending national boundaries. *Transnational* is the new term used to describe processes and patterns that can be understood in this international context. It has long been recognized that republicanism was transatlantic in its origins and development. We need only recall that the ideas of the American Revolution were British and French in their immediate origin and that the writings and personal actions of leading figures like Tom Paine had a reciprocal influence on the French and English movements. The same may be said of social republicanism. In Europe, that new variant of republicanism originated in the leading actions of the workers in the 1848 revolutions that briefly swept away the monarchies of Old Europe. But, in America, where social republicanism was weaker, it took until the Civil War and Reconstruction for a social reinterpretation of republicanism to gain traction.[7]

During the Civil War, the federal government greatly expanded its size, functions, authority, and reach into all areas of life, making the United States a modern nation-state. Not only did it set precedents in taxing internally, conscripting citizens, and suppressing dissent, but it also actively redistributed property and income. The most dramatic example was the expropriation of the wealth of the Southern slaveholders; however, after the war the federal government continued to provide welfare in the form of an expanding system of military pensions in the North, and in the South it funded the Freedman's Bureau, which provided education, basic welfare, and supervised the labor contracts of the emancipated slaves. During the war and in the decade after it, the issuance of greenbacks, cost-plus government contracts, a protective tariff, removal of the economy from the gold standard, and the retirement of the war debt resulted in a massive transference of wealth from Southern slave owners and the northeastern merchant and banking elite to rising manufacturers and other entrepreneurs. Meanwhile, land grants for transcontinental railroads and state colleges and universities subsidized the infrastructure and human capital necessary for a modern industrial society. More long term, the Fourteenth Amendment federalized protection of a national market. Defining corporations as persons, subsequent court decisions authorized the government to intervene in the regulation of that market, usually in ways that protected large national business enterprises.[8]

Although not as dramatically, local governments also executed policies that redistributed wealth. The most important example was the Chicago municipal government's paying of bounties for enlistment to attract volunteers to serve in the army, a practice pursued by many localities in the North. One goal of the policy was to avoid having to execute a draft to meet unfilled quotas. Using the draft carried a stigma for the city as well as the threat of unrest, which became a nightmare after the New York City draft riots of 1863. The city and particularly the county government also paid stipends to the families of volunteers to help offset the lower pay that recruits earned as soldiers. Both social pressure and several legal stipulations ensured that the large proportion of this money went to people at the lower end of the economic scale. While these programs were modest in size, they were significant for their break with the segmented system of government and for setting precedents in the use of public authority. A direct payment of city tax revenue for the benefit of largely poorer people, the bounties and subsidies constituted downward redistribution of wealth. Given such examples of government intervention in civil society, it is small wonder that dispossessed journeymen began to imagine ways that republican government might be used to aid them.[9]

TRANSNATIONAL REPUBLICANISM IN THE URBAN WEST

During this period, the influence of European immigrants came to be deeply felt in the public sphere. Bringing with them a more fully developed social republicanism, they played a major role in bringing the labor question into public life and in creating a distinct working-class consciousness. Transnational social republicanism drew on high rates of population movement across borders. Historians now recognize the mid-nineteenth century as the midpoint of the first phase of globalization, which lasted until World War I. In addition to high rates of capital flows and commodity trade, the movement of individuals across borders was at its highest tide. Pushed out by population increases and economic change, while attracted by access to land and high wages, approximately sixty million Europeans left their homes after 1820 to settle in the New World. This massive population shift brought a diverse international leadership to America's labor movement that was able to draw on the European experiences of popular democratic republican revolutions.

The first evidence of this transnational influence came in the romantic nationalism of the antebellum era, exemplified in Illinois by the Young America movement promoted by Senator Stephen A. Douglas. That precedent made the American public receptive to the midcentury revolutionary ferment and visiting émigrés into heroes of the moment. The wartime expansion of the public sphere made importing these ideas into politics easier, since they became part of the rhetoric of labor leaders at union meetings, ethnic publicists in the foreign-language press, and mainstream politicians addressing crowds at picnics.[10]

Chicago's first labor movement had links to a transnational culture of émigrés from the failed revolutions of the late 1840s centered in Paris and London, with outposts in American cities, including Chicago. In these cities, men from Ireland and Great Britain met journeymen from central Europe, fostering a common political idiom despite different languages. Thus, a left-wing German republican like Eduard Schläger used some of the same ideas as Fenians advocating both Irish independence and land reform. At the same time, Fenians began to articulate their nationalist cause in the terms of republican revolution and social reform. These men were social republicans who stressed the transformation of society necessary to support a republican political order, in contrast to more moderate adherents of transnational republicanism, who concentrated on political change, most notably the overthrow of unlimited monarchy and the establishment of some form of republic. Social republicans typically had a positive view of the state, seeing it as a potential instrument to effect the transformation of society. Associated with the Jacobin heritage of the eighteenth-century revolutions, the social republican tradition had resonance in an era when the federal government tried to reconstruct the South in a way that would sustain popular government and loyalty to the Union. Practically every political émigré honored the ideals of the American republic, if not their contemporary actualization, and viewed the destruction of the aristocratic South as part of a revolutionary enterprise not only freeing the United States to fulfill its ideals but also advancing the cause of international republican revolution.[11]

The prominence of foreign-born labor leaders in Chicago made the task of the transnational republicans easier. Foreign-born craftsmen were largely, but not exclusively, responsible for organizing the first Chicago labor movement during the Civil War. This is not surprising since in 1860 over 80 percent of Chicago's workers were born abroad (see fig. 2, chap. 1).

Similarly, about 80 percent of the leadership was foreign-born, and among them English-speaking immigrants—British and Irish—predominated, although the Germans were a very substantial minority (table 3). The British had influence beyond their numbers because they came from the world's first industrial nation. The British working class was already several generations old, whereas the Irish, Germans, and native-born Americans were new to modern industrial economies. The British had had practice in assuming the dual roles of worker and citizen. Hence the British brought with them experience, sophistication, and models of labor organization that made them natural leaders of the movement.

The same international connections made British dissenting Protestantism a powerful presence, and this tradition, too, had deep roots in the popular radical traditions of the Atlantic world, including the abolitionist movement. The prominence of British leaders in the Chicago labor movement meant that the rhetorical cadences and political ideas of evangelical Protestantism emanated from union meetings and the labor press. Evangelical Protestantism also provided a direct link to native-born workers as well as to the prevailing reform and political milieu in the wartime North. The antislavery movement had drawn energy, ideas, and personnel from the revivalism of the Second Great Awakening, and the predominantly Protestant culture of the North profoundly shaped the language and rhetoric in which the Abraham Lincoln administration articulated the significance of the war effort. The close fit between the ideas and rhetorical style of evangelical labor leaders and the administration's articulation of the war's goals and meaning enhanced the prestige of Protestants, and particularly the British, in the labor movement. Less obvious than evangelical rhetorical style were liberal ideas of limited government and constitutionalism associated with the dissenting Protestant

Table 3. Union Leaders by Birthplace: Chicago 1864

Office	United States	Great Britain	Ireland	Germany	Other
President	22.7%	18.1%	36.4%	13.6%	9.0%
(N = 22)	(5)	(4)	(8)	(3)	(2)
All	19.6%	21.7%	23.9%	28.3%	6.5%
Officers	(9)	(10)	(11)	(13)	(3)
(N = 46)					

Source: Reports of labor activity in the *Workingman's Advocate, Chicago Tribune,* and *Illinois Staats-Zeitung.*

Note: The birthplaces were found in the 1860s federal manuscript census and in Richard Edwards, *Chicago Census Report and Statistical Review, Embracing a Complete Directory of the City* (Chicago: Richard Edwards, 1871).

tradition. Although this Anglo American tradition of limited government was potentially in conflict with the Jacobin ideas of the continental social republicans, the tension was contained within the political environment of the Civil War era.[12]

EMANCIPATION, TRANSNATIONAL SOCIAL REPUBLICANISM, AND THE PUBLIC SPHERE

For America's founders, the health of the republic rested on the ability of citizens and their representatives to rise above the influence of faction, which was the political form of self-interest. For this to occur, a deliberative democracy required a vibrant public sphere in which wise public opinion would take form. In earlier years, membership in the public sphere required the values of the producer above all: propertied independence, good character, and civic virtue. This was evident in the segmented public sphere in the city's antebellum era in which privatized public decision making protected property by keeping it out of politics. Thus segmentation protected the basis of liberty, while at the same time it excluded from politics the most common source of faction: different types and amounts of property. According to Robin Einhorn, "A strong democratic government in which an array of factions make unpredictable demands remained terrifying, in Chicago and elsewhere." But with the spread of market relations by the Civil War, the emergence of voluntary associations, and the crumbling of legal obstacles to full political participation, membership in the public sphere came to be based on market position and included those without property. As interest and class became legitimate public identities, even while being articulated in the old republican terms, the weak and narrowly bounded public sphere of the antebellum era collapsed. A new modernized public sphere arose, based on the natural rights principle of universal access to the market and government.[13]

The Emancipation Proclamation accelerated this reverberating process of change that extended through the Reconstruction era and affected all dimensions of American life, including the social life of northern cities. Not only workers, but women, blacks, and formerly excluded immigrant groups became politicized and constructed their interests in the public sphere. The two most important immigrant groups were the Irish and the Germans.

Most German immigrants mobilized under the political leadership of the German forty-eighters. In the 1850s, political refugees from the failed German Revolution of 1848 had taken over leadership of Chicago's German immigrant community by founding institutions such as the *Illinois Staats-Zeitung* and

Deutsches Haus, a central meeting hall, by organizing opposition to the local temperance movement and by participating in the formation of the Republican Party after the passage of the Kansas-Nebraska Act in 1854. True to their liberal ideals, the forty-eighters were left-wing Republicans who supported a stronger antislavery position than the party's mainstream and candidates, particularly John C. Frémont, who agreed with them.

As both Republicans and liberals, the forty-eighters founded the Arbeiterverein, or Workers' Association, to combat unemployment during the economic crisis that began in 1857 and to spare the new Republican city administration the embarrassment of protests by unemployed workers demanding work or bread. Through the summer of 1864, the forty-eighters used their control of the Arbeiterverein to shape public opinion in German Chicago and to push the Lincoln administration toward more advanced or "radical" positions on slavery and the shape of a reconstructed South. The forty-eighters also recruited troops for the conflict, giving several Illinois regiments a distinct German and radical republican coloring, the most famous being the 82nd Illinois led by Frederich Hecker. The Arbeiterverein scoffed at predictions of massive numbers of freed blacks competing with white labor in the North, and it strove for "the equality and emancipation of all workers without reference to birth or skin color."[14]

On January 1, 1863, the Emancipation Proclamation changed the forty-eighters' political position. With emancipation now mainstream Republican policy, more moderate Germans, including some forty-eighters, could comfortably support the Lincoln administration, while more radical elements kept pushing further left. Moderate and conservative Germans began to coalesce around different political leadership exemplified by Anton Hesing, a moderate and antislavery Republican who drew on his political connections and entrepreneurial talents to turn himself into Chicago's most prominent German political leader by the late 1860s. His purchase of the *Illinois Staats-Zeitung* after the Civil War attested to his status and influence. At the same time, the more radical forty-eighters continued to oppose the Lincoln administration for being too conservative on emancipation—the proclamation did not free slaves in areas controlled by the Union army—and on the reconstructed South. The radicals' strongest institutional base of support was the Tenth Ward Sozialer Arbeiterverein (SAV), the largest of the affiliates of the central organization. The term *social* in the organization's name signified its participation in the transnational social republican tradition. The Tenth Ward had the largest concentration of unskilled workers in the city and included the area where A. G. Throop had built his docks in the recession winter of 1857–58.[15]

As the radicals staked out their ideological position after the Emancipation Proclamation, they drew more and more on the social republican parts of their tradition, that is, on those elements of the 1848 revolutions that advocated a social revolution to accompany the political revolution that all forty-eighters supported. Exemplifying this trend was the "Address to the Liberal Germans in the Union," published in October 1863 as Germans on the left of the Republican Party organized nationally in opposition to Lincoln's renomination in 1864. They found his positions on slavery and reconstruction too moderate. Coauthored by Theodore Hielscher, a leader in Chicago's SAV, the address appealed in particular to "the great number of workers" who were the "truly productive population" and who "can only count on strong unity in consideration of their just demands." The address held out the hope that only "in this free land" could the fissure between capital and labor be "peaceably overcome," thus solving the problem commonly known as "the social question." This position on labor was an updating of a similar statement in the forty-eighters' "Louisville platform" adopted in 1854.[16]

The address illustrated the radicals' need for a new constituency, after the Emancipation Proclamation made it easier for more moderate Germans to support Lincoln's Republican Party. The more successfully the radicals articulated their position, the further away they moved from mainstream opinion in German Chicago and the closer they came to rebellious journeymen of any nationality. By the summer of 1864, the Arbeiterverein split into radical and moderate organizations, and the radicals joined the ideological leaders of the Chicago labor movement, linking it directly to the currents of international democratic radicalism coursing through the Atlantic world.[17]

The Emancipation Proclamation affected the Irish in Chicago as profoundly as the Germans, though in different ways. Central to the story were the politics of race and the rise of Irish nationalism. After Fort Sumter, like Chicago's other ethnic groups, the Irish rallied to the flag with patriotic enthusiasm. After religious and political leaders called for troops, James A. Mulligan, an Irish lawyer and publisher, recruited and trained the Irish Brigade, the 23rd Illinois. Colonel Mulligan led the Brigade off to war in July 1861, not long after it had marched in Stephen A. Douglas's funeral. Yet within a year, Irish enthusiasm for the war waned amid military reverses and increasing public debate about emancipation as an aim of the war. Also affecting the mood of the Irish community was a divided and, in some cases, weak leadership. Neither as numerous or prosperous as their German counterparts, the Irish forty-eighters did not have the same central role as their German compatriots in shaping the public culture of their ethnic group. Just as important, the Roman Catholic Church did not yet play the predominant role in the Irish community that it would in the 1870s and 1880s after it achieved a modus vivendi with Irish nationalism. In the 1860s, the church and the nationalists battled each other as ideological enemies. At the same time, the politics of the war weakened the Democratic Party as it struggled to redefine its ambivalent position on the war and emancipation. The Irish nationalists, on the other hand, prospered in the wartime environment, particularly when the Fenians, their most prominent group, abandoned their secrecy and began meeting and recruiting publicly in 1863. Like the German forty-eighters, the Fenians recruited troops for the war, seeing in it an opportunity to fulfill their revolutionary aspiration to free Ireland.[18]

Fenian wartime activities, both before and after 1863, had a complex and close relation to agitation about race and the meaning of whiteness. As the question of emancipation became a burning public issue during the summer and fall of 1862, the question of the status of white men began to agitate the public and particularly workingmen on the street, in the factory, on the docks, and in the army. The Irish immigrants of the famine generation were particularly affected because of their low status and desperate economic condition. In addition, Protestants attacked their Catholicism as a threat to the republic, and these were some of the same people leading the Republican Party as well as local temperance and Sabbatarian societies. Feeling under assault, Irish workingmen found in "whiteness" an opportunity for prestige, respect, and inclusion in the white man's republic.

In antebellum culture, according to David Roediger, Eric Lott, Alexander Saxton, and others, whiteness was defined by a constant and ritualized contrast with stereotypes of blackness—the Sambos, Zip Coons, and Uncle Toms of the antebellum minstrel stage. Whiteness was a desperately sought badge, distinguishing its bearers from those in the perdition of bondage while providing them a ticket to enter a political society of free white men. Then emancipation challenged the whiteness so crucial to Irish workingmen by transforming its black opposite: If blacks were not slaves and dependents anymore, what did it mean to be white? To question whiteness was to question some of the most cherished values of the producers' republic: access to property, independence, and manliness. At this critical juncture, the Fenians offered one new definition of what it meant to be male, white, and Irish.[19]

In 1862, violent conflicts freighted with ethnic, racial, and political overtones took place in eastern cities as well as in Chicago. These ethnic and racial encounters were a continuation of the politicized social conflicts that had marked the 1850s as national political issues started to color local divisions over neighborhood turf, religion, partisan affiliation, and national traditions.

These tensions increased in 1862, when Confederate generals Robert E. Lee and Thomas "Stonewall" Jackson derailed the large federal military offensive and discussion of emancipation picked up speed in Republican political circles. In July 1862, an Irish teamster refused to serve a black citizen in the stockyard district near Bridgeport. During the ensuing altercation, the black man was supported by Sheriff Anton Hesing and a German-Jewish officer in the Hecker regiment, who happened to be in town on a recruiting drive. The Irish teamster was aided by an Irish crowd, which later in the day attacked several blacks in the area. During the teamster's trial, his lawyer delivered a diatribe against abolition, and the case resulted in a hung jury. In that same month, a serious brawl broke out between German picnickers from the Tenth Ward Sozialer Arbeiterverein and an Irish crowd. Similar conflicts between Germans and the Irish and between Irish and blacks occurred shortly afterward. In August, for example, a riot began when blacks underbid a gang of white laborers for work unloading a ship. In early 1863, several officers of the largely Irish 90th Illinois regiment resigned in protest over emancipation, and military authorities isolated the regiment and charged it with mutiny.[20]

A year later, dramatic military and political events significantly changed Irish attitudes toward the war effort, beginning with the troops in the field. The victories at Gettysburg and Vicksburg in July 1863 made success in a war for both union and emancipation more likely. The proven viability of a war for emancipation plus the experience of fighting in it solidified opinion among the soldiers, including the Irish, behind Lincoln's war aims. The efforts of Fenian organizers contributed to the same effect. Through 1862, the Fenians' main activity had been raising and sending relief funds to Ireland, an effort identical to that of an older fraternal group, the Sons of Erin. In 1863, however, under pressure from their leaders in Ireland, the American Fenians began a drive, particularly among Union army soldiers, for funds and new recruits for the Irish revolution. The Lincoln administration condoned this Fenian recruiting in the hopes that it would build up political support among the Irish for both the war effort and the Republican Party.[21]

The Fenians' recruiting efforts were aided by attitudes among Irish soldiers, some of whom dreamed that the conflict with the South would develop into an American war with Britain, the oppressor of Ireland. Proslavery sentiment in the 90th Illinois changed. In early 1864, an officer of that regiment wrote, "We believe in a thorough prosecution and speedy termination of this unholy warfare—unholy so far only as one side can be concerned, and that side can be no other than the one that espouses slavery and seeks to destroy our glorious temple of Liberty and Justice." He concluded that the majority of the regiment supported Lincoln for reelection. These Irish soldiers were a significant alternative to Irish crowds attacking black laborers because they offered a new definition of what it meant to be a white man that appealed to masses of Irish workers.[22]

The rise of Irish nationalism under the aegis of the Fenians had a wider import than making racial categories more elastic and creating a constituency for the Lincoln administration's war aims among Irish immigrants. According to Lawrence McCaffrey, the Fenian movement represented "the first tough, hard-nosed commitment to revolution" among the Irish American nationalists. Their growth during the Civil War represented a break from the liberalism and cultural nationalism of the Young Irelanders, romantic revolutionaries of the previous generation, and marked the initial convergence of Irish revolutionary nationalism with the masses of Irish workingmen.[23]

Fenianism had close affinities with the continental secular radical republicanism of the 1850s. Two Fenian leaders of international repute, James Stephens and John O'Mahoney, were social republicans committed to land redistribution. These two viewed their nationalism in an international context, derived from their experience in the community of exiles in Paris after the revolutions of 1848. In 1863, O'Mahoney could charge that "the papacy has made common cause with the tyrants of Europe to put down republican propagandism, and that even Catholic Ireland must be sacrificed to Protestant England, lest the recoil of her resurrection might shake the despotisms of the old continent and among them Rome." This kind of republicanism made American Fenians into enemies of the Catholic hierarchy and ideological allies of the German radicals of the Arbeiterverein. Chicago's main Roman Catholic newspaper, the *Western Tablet,* roundly criticized such "foreign radicals." The Fenians actively competed with the Democratic Party and the Roman Catholic Church to shape the politics and culture of Irish Chicago. This fluid environment made it easier for labor organizers to find an audience and propose a new organizational initiative that cut across the lines of national origin, religious affiliation, and partisan allegiance.[24]

The Fenians' impact on the Irish community was analogous to that of the forty-eighter radicals on the German community. While not mainly concerned with labor, the ethnic politics of both groups were sympathetic to it, helping to open up new opportunities for organization and influence by the labor movement. Both groups provided the new labor unions with additional leadership talent. Both advocated issues, particularly the creation of independent republics in their homelands, which had wide appeal in their ethnic communities.[25]

The Fenians and the Arbeiterverein radicals were also conduits through which social republicanism entered the labor movement. Both raised issues like land distribution and made them vital questions for their countrymen in the United States. Both led workers to see themselves as part of a revolutionary international enterprise of which the American Civil War was a part. Themselves representatives of a transnational political culture, they helped make communication and cooperation between German and Irish labor leaders possible. Most important, their own histories illustrated how the Civil War transformed their ethnic communities, redefining political affiliations, cultural attitudes, and even the meaning of liberty.

LABOR'S AWAKENING IN 1863 AND 1864

The wartime initiatives of the federal government had a decisive impact on Chicago's distinctive social and economic order, creating the conditions for a vibrant labor movement. During the war, Cook County contributed almost 22,500 men to the Union army, of whom about 15,000 came from Chicago. The 15,000 constituted approximately 42 percent of Chicago's workforce in 1860 and 38 percent of an estimated workforce of 40,000 in 1864. All of these men did not leave at once, of course, and the economic impact of their military service was mitigated by underutilized labor and excess manufacturing capacity left from the Panic of 1857.[26]

Yet after a year, the war began to affect all families and businesses, altering the way they organized their daily activities. The combination of enlistments and wartime demand created a labor shortage that became pervasive by 1863. In that year, the *Tribune* reported that "manufacturers are crowded with work—have orders ahead for weeks and cannot get enough hands or increase their facilities to keep pace with the increasing demand. . . . Mechanics too, of every trade, are busy as bees." As this labor shortage intensified wartime inflation, working people became aware of their vulnerability in a labor market over which they had no control. By expanding the market for wage labor and widening perception of it, this wartime economic boom helped make workers more conscious of their shared class position as wage earners.[27]

Confronted by wartime inflation and emboldened by the labor shortage, rebellious journeymen initiated a new pattern of organizing. Beginning in the spring of 1863, the carpenters, painters, coopers, tailors, and bakers conducted strikes, which usually resulted in the founding of unions. Earlier labor organizations had been almost exclusively mutual benefit societies, not unions, and strikes had been relatively few. In 1863, the construction carpenters conducted the most notable strike. A group of three hundred carpenters employed at building a new grain elevator went on strike, took up a collection for a flag and a band, and then marched throughout the city, calling carpenters off the job. Altogether five hundred to six hundred men of several nationalities joined the carpenters' walkout. The same labor shortage drew women into the workforce. In 1863, the first women sales clerks appeared in downtown dry-goods stores, joining the swelling numbers of female garment workers.[28]

These rebellious journeymen and women workers stepped out of their normal lives into new social roles. The sheer fact of women working for wages outside the home raised issues of sex, family, and the place of women in the social order. At the same time, the wartime organization of journeymen into multiethnic unions violated their social role in the crafts and their ethnic groups. By forming unions, the journeymen were rejecting the claims of their ethnic and religious leaders to speak for them in public. They were assuming a new role in society just as other men did when they became soldiers.

Labor organizing in 1863 anticipated the upheaval in 1864 when Chicago's workers turned numerous new unions into a genuine movement with a central organization and vital newspaper. The year workers organized their movement was one of extraordinary political volatility. When Ulysses S. Grant's spring offensive against Robert E. Lee in 1864 produced staggering casualties and then an apparent stalemate in the trenches around Petersburg, Northern public support for the war effort almost crumbled. In the late summer, Lincoln doubted his chances for reelection, and party competition reached a fever pitch. Any significant group whose political affiliations appeared malleable, such as the forty-eighter radicals, the Fenians, or the labor movement, received intense appeals from the major parties.

The situation in Chicago was not unusual. Throughout the Northern industrial states, workers organized unions, labor federations, newspapers, and lobbying efforts. These labor movements enlisted the sympathies and energies of Northern workingmen more than any other cause, with the exception of the preservation of the Union itself. At the height of the national organizing effort in 1864, the number of trade unions in the United States multiplied almost three-and-one-half times. In Chicago, alliances of German, Irish, British, and American journeymen formed most of the unions that served as the constituent parts of the city's labor movement. Key strikes in 1864, one at the *Chicago Times* and the other at the Illinois Central Car Shops, solidified the support of both British and native-born craftsmen, who predominated in the elite trade of printing and in the sophisticated metal crafts, especially as practiced in the railroad car shops. To unite their disparate forces and win political influence, the printers led local labor to form the General Trades Assembly. The Assembly supported one of the nation's most important labor journals, the *Workingman's Advocate,* run by Andrew Cameron, whom John R. Commons called "the greatest labor editor of his time."[29]

Higher compensation was the most prominent issue for all workers in 1864 because wartime inflation had shrunk their purchasing power. Amid several strikes in January 1864, the *Tribune* concluded that, while "mechanics" wages had risen 55 percent over those of 1861, prices of the necessities of life had increased an average of 82 percent. Modern scholarship confirms this basic finding.[30] By March 1864, the *Times* noted, "The employees witness every necessity of life increasing daily in price. House rents are going up to a figure that compels many married couples to seek the unfriendly shelter of boarding houses." Most boardinghouses were in the city center where labor's organizing efforts could take advantage of the communications network provided by a vibrant street life.[31]

The higher compensation demanded by workers came in the form of both wages and higher prices for piecework. Journeymen, as opposed to laborers, were commonly paid by the piece for their work, so they fought for a higher "bill of prices" as well as for their right to establish prices. Eric Hobsbawm has argued that in the mid-nineteenth century, custom more than the market determined what craftsmen asked for their labor as well as how much production their employers expected of them. Neither journeymen nor their employers had fully learned the "rules of the game," that is, each side asking for as much as it could get, the result determined by the market. The war economy speeded the education of both sides by undermining custom and mutual expectations conditioned by membership in the craft community. As a result, journeymen began to recognize that they were wageworkers dependent on the labor market. The coopers and bakers illustrated this process. Both were crafts in which Germans and Irish together composed at least half the members.[32]

The coopers represented a classic craft severely affected by wartime inflation and mechanization. Before 1864, the only coopers' labor organization was the Kueferverein, a German mutual benefit society illustrative of the Germans' prominence in the trade. In January 1864, sixteen hundred coopers held a meeting at Deutsches Haus to found a union. A substantial representation from Bridgeport attended, and speeches were given in English and German. The journeymen coopers fought to raise prices for their work and to limit the workday to ten hours. They also tried to uphold the traditional skills of their craft by limiting their membership to men who had served an apprenticeship of three years. Upholding their skills was daunting in the face of the drive to mechanize their craft, which in Chicago was led by Hurlbut Bros. and Company.[33]

The Hurlbut brothers—one of whom was a machinist and the other a member of the Board of Trade—had invented a machine to make barrel staves. With access to capital through the Board of Trade, they were able to construct a plant along the railroad tracks in northwestern Indiana, where in 1864 two of their machines turned out six to eight thousand barrel staves a day. At the terminus of the railroad near the packing district in Chicago, the enterprising brothers constructed another plant in which fifty coopers made the barrels using the machine-produced staves. The coopers union fought the Hurlbut machine along with their employers, but to little effect: In the 1850s, the number of workers in cooperage firms grew by over 230 percent, whereas in the 1860s, a decade of explosive manufacturing growth in Chicago, the cooperage workforce expanded by only 6 percent. Although the craft also faced competition from prison labor, this flat performance was primarily the result of the rapid mechanization of the production process.[34]

The organization of Chicago's bakery workers followed the pattern of the journeymen coopers, with the exception that the bakers' market was divided ethnically and regionally. Since practically every national group had its distinctive tastes in baked goods catered to by their countrymen, the bakers' national origins were more evenly distributed than among the coopers. In addition to the many small neighborhood shops, Chicago also had a few highly capitalized bakeries owned by Yankees producing crackers and biscuits that could be packed in barrels and shipped to a regional market. As in so many other trades, journeymen bakers began organizing in the spring of 1864. The Journeyman Bakers Protective Union held several of its early meetings at the Hall of the Sons of Erin in the heart of the central business district, while the bakers also threw a ball at Deutsches Haus to promote their organizing activities. The union's leadership reflected this Irish and German cooperation.[35]

During their strike in June, the journeyman bakers asked for and received support from bakers in Cincinnati and Milwaukee, who assured them that no journeymen would go to Chicago. The strike began after the employers rejected the union's demands for a 25 percent wage increase, the establishment of a uniform and viable apprenticeship system, and shorter hours. There was no talk of a traditional "scale of prices." Central to the employers' resistance was the Chicago Mechanical Bakery, the largest employer of bakery workers in the city, where the union dealt with superintendents, not master bakers. The superintendents threatened to replace the striking journeymen with Irish and German women. Despite support from the recently founded General Trades Assembly and from other unions in Chicago and several other cities, the journeymen bakers lost their strike, returning to work under their former conditions.[36]

The construction carpenters differed from the workers in the crafts just discussed. In the 1860s, there were seven times more carpenters than coopers and eleven times more carpenters than bakers. Because the carpenters labored in a booming industry in a boomtown, workers of all nationalities were attracted to their ranks, including the native-born and the British. Thus, even though German and Irish workers composed half their ranks, the carpenters included a rather even distribution of nationalities. In addition, despite being affected by machine-produced doors and windows, the carpenters were less threatened by mechanization than craftsmen like the coopers. Thus there existed a substantial number of skilled workers who could serve as the foundation of a union. In the 1860s, Chicago's construction carpenters drew on the model of the furniture workers, who had founded a state-chartered mutual benefit society in 1855, as well as on the craft and ethnic traditions of their German and British compatriots.[37]

The Carpenters and Joiners Protective Union had organized in March 1863. Amid the labor unrest of 1864, the carpenters met to demand wage increases but apparently did not need to strike to achieve them, a clear indication of their strength compared to the coopers and bakers. At the same time German carpenters organized a cooperative building society to construct inexpensive homes for its members; inflation had put home ownership beyond the means of even the best-paid carpenters.[38]

The journeymen coopers, bakers, and carpenters were similar to the craftsmen at the core of the first American labor movements founded during the Jacksonian era in the eastern seaport cities. (In the 1830s, Chicago was too small to support a labor movement.) In both eras, craftsmen making light consumer goods and in construction formed the base of the movement. However, by the Civil War, the journeymen in these Chicago trades were predominantly foreign-born rather than native-born, as they had been in cities such as Philadelphia. Culturally, Chicago's rebellious journeymen in the 1860s were closer to their contemporary counterparts in Europe than to the trade unionists of the Jacksonian era. By the 1860s, Chicago's journeymen also faced more challenging threats to their crafts from the likes of the Hurlbut barrel stave machine and the Mechanical Bakery.[39]

The labor movement of the Civil War era was also distinct because it reflected the concerns of workers in the most advanced sector of the economy. The railroads maintained the largest and most sophisticated manufacturing establishments in the city: the car shops where they serviced and repaired their equipment. The workforce at the car shops included high proportions of the city's metal craftsmen, who along with their counterparts in construction constituted the largest groupings of skilled workers in the city (table 4). The railroads also hired huge numbers of laborers to lay track, unload cars, and perform unskilled work in the car shops. In addition, they created whole new occupations, including low-level white-collar jobs for agents, clerks, timekeepers, and stationmasters. Similarly, they developed new skilled occupations, such as locomotive engineers, which were of high status in the new economic order. Whether of white-collar or blue-collar status, the jobs operating the trains were typically held by native-born Americans. The craftsmen working in the car shops were more often foreign-born. All types of railroad workers, except white-collar employees, participated in the labor unrest of 1864, usually without success. Nonetheless, the railroad labor initiatives and their defeat were especially significant for bringing American and British workers in high-status crafts into the movement.[40]

Table 4. Male Skilled Workers in Selected Groups of Industry by National Origin: Chicago 1860

	Industry[1]					
	Construction	Metal	Apparel	Wood	Food	Other
National Origin (%)						
American	21.6	24.3	5.1	25.4	24.1	32.8[2]
British	15.7	18.1	6.2	1.7	14.8	5.1
Irish	23.1	23.6	19.6	11.9	11.1	16.5
German	31.4	24.3	52.6	47.5	40.7	36.1[3]
Other	8.2	9.7	16.5	13.5	9.3	9.5
	100	100	100	100	100	100
% of All Skilled Workers	33.2	18.8	12.6	7.7	7.0	20.7

Source: Sample of the 1860 federal manuscript population census for Chicago; N = 767.

1. The construction, metal, wood, apparel, and food industries together employed 79.2 percent of all male skilled workers in 1860. The groups were defined with the aid of the industry codes of the Philadelphia Social History Project.

2. Over half of these American skilled workers were in transportation and printing and publishing, which were dominated by the native-born (see table 5).

3. The German skilled workers were more widely scattered across the economy than the other major national groups, often in small traditional crafts (see table 5).

When the Brotherhood of Locomotive Engineers opened 1864 with a demand for higher wages, most railroads gave in, except for the Galena and Chicago Union. The Brotherhood tried to force the Galena and Chicago Union into line with pressure and then strikes against the other companies, but this strategy failed, in part because it interfered with the transport of military supplies. By March, engineers at several Chicago lines repudiated the Brotherhood, and there were reports that the organization was crumbling. Railroad laborers struck for higher wages soon after the engineers' strike disintegrated. This strike began at one railroad and spread to others as groups of workers marched from freight yard to freight yard. The striking railroad laborers refused to allow reporters into their meetings because they said all newspapers were biased against them.[41]

In the late summer, when the Illinois Central Railroad imported sixty Belgian machinists to work at less than standard wages, workers in the car shops were outraged. Speaking to a large political meeting of workers in late August, Eduard Schläger, a prominent member of the forty-eighter left, condemned the action as the beginning of the "war between Capital and Labor," a conflict the newspapers were afraid to acknowledge. According to George Hazlitt, leader of the recently founded Trades Assembly, the company had received millions of acres of government land to benefit the people; it had "grown rich on that land," and now it used its power against "the people who *par excellence* are the working men." The importation of the Belgians was particularly enflaming because it revealed the power of the Illinois Central Railroad to reach outside the local labor market, even across the ocean, to undermine the position of "native" machinists. Despite their high status and large proportions of native-born Americans, the engineers and machinists were no match for the Illinois Central. They realized that they, too, needed a labor movement, even one largely composed of the foreign-born.[42]

The crafts discussed so far illustrate the origins of the unions that provided the organizational base of the first Chicago labor movement. Altogether, leaders of eighteen unions signed the call published in April 1864 for the formation of the General Trades Assembly. In most of these unions, German and Irish journeymen constituted the core constituency, complemented by Britons, Scandinavians, and in some cases native-born Americans. English-speaking immigrants, supplemented by critically important native-born workers, predominated in the leadership, particularly in the top positions. Germans were substantially represented, especially in the lower leadership echelons (see table 3).[43]

The energy and will to organize these unions originated in a familiar complex of factors accentuated by the war economy: a declining standard of living rooted in wartime inflation, crafts undermined by mechanization and the reorganization of production, and the deteriorating social and political status of workers as a new class structure emerged. Yet the way these unions acted in the public sphere cannot fully be explained by these factors. The decision to found the General Trades Assembly in April 1864—essentially a political interest group representing labor in the public sphere—was not immediately obvious. Why did the unions need one? Where did they get the organizational and political skills to actually form it? What were the Assembly's politics and how did it maneuver in the political minefield of 1864 when the course of the war and the fate of the country saturated local politics?

FROM PARTISAN POLITICS TO LABOR POLITICS

When a significant union movement emerged in the spring of 1864, the Fenians, the German forty-eighter left, and the Democrats all took special notice, in part because all three were trying to broaden their constituencies.

The Fenians abandoned their secrecy during the previous fall, meeting openly for the first time in Chicago, and recruited actively in the Union army. Heartened by a strong local base of support, the Fenians called for a National Fair to be held in Chicago in late March of 1864 to publicize their cause and raise funds. They also agitated within the city for both their organization and Irish liberation, provoking a strong reaction from the Roman Catholic Church. On January 29, 1864, as union organizing among journeymen increased, Chicago's Bishop James Duggan formally denounced the Fenians for advocating violent revolution and refused church sacraments not only to the Fenians but also to those who aided them. But his actions did little to dampen Irish enthusiasm for the Fenians in Chicago or in the regiments it sent to the war.[44]

In early February, Colonel Mulligan, the leading organizer of the Irish Brigade, sent a public letter supporting the National Fair with a $100 donation. Mulligan, who may have been a Fenian, avowed that once the struggle for the Union had been successful, he would "devote all I possess to aid in establishing and maintaining the cause of Irish nationality." Other substantially Irish regiments recruited in Chicago reported pro-Fenian sentiment in early 1864, and the Fenian appeal was not limited to the army. The Sons of Erin passed a pro-Fenian resolution, and their president, John Comiskey, included the Fenians in the St. Patrick's Day parade, over Bishop Duggan's opposition.[45]

Taking place a week and a half later, the Fenian National Fair was an immense popular success for Irish nationalism. Like the contemporary "sanitary" fairs to raise money for aid to wounded soldiers, the Fenian event involved women at all levels of its organization, drawing them into new institutional and political roles. Chicago labor leaders strongly supported the fair, despite the demands of contemporaneous labor union struggles. Representatives of six unions attended an organizational meeting. The unions of tailors, iron molders, and horseshoers marched in the grand procession opening the fair, as did leading officers of municipal government, the fire department, numerous Irish societies, several army units, and the German Turners. During the march, the Iron Molder's Union presented the fair with a McCormick reaper, and the Fenian band played the international anthem of republican revolution "La Marseillaise." At the terminus of the procession, two prominent Republicans addressed the marchers: Mayor John Wentworth and Lieutenant Governor Francis Hoffmann, one of the leading members of the German community in Chicago.[46]

At the same time that the Fenians were building a constituency in the labor movement, the German left found itself in need of supporters, in part because of its opposition to the Lincoln administration. Between the fall of 1863 and the spring of 1864, prominent liberal to radical Chicago Germans spoke out against the renomination of Lincoln and in favor of Frémont. It was at this time that the Arbeiterverein's Theodore Hielscher coauthored the "Address to the Liberal Germans of the Union," which called for the unconditional surrender of the South, the complete abolition of slavery, vigorous support for European revolutions, and opposition to Napoleon III's Mexican adventure. This same address said that their emerging "German Organization" of liberals wanted to be known as "the representative of the 'great number of the workers.'"[47]

The Democrats were as anxious to appeal to the labor unions as the Fenians and the German left, since they hoped to capitalize on the dissatisfaction with the war effort to overcome their minority status. When eighteen unions met to organize the General Trades Assembly on April 26, the Democrats sent Edward W. McComas, former lieutenant governor of Virginia, Jacksonian Democrat, and ex-editor of the *Chicago Times*. McComas spoke to the meeting and continued to play a role in the politics of the General Trades Assembly through the fall electoral campaign.[48]

The founding meeting took place at Bryan Hall, site of the Fenian Fair one month previously. George K. Hazlitt, president of the typographers' union, sounded the keynote of the meeting by arguing that Chicago workingmen needed a Trades Assembly like those that had been established in other cities, "to protect ourselves against the present aggressive attitude of capital." Echoing the Dred Scott decision, Hazlitt said that mechanics had to demonstrate to capitalists that they had "some rights which they were bound to respect." James Tracy, also of the Typographical Union, seconded Hazlitt in referring to "lock-outs" and the need to "resist the encroachments of arbitrary capitalists" that threatened to reduce workingmen "to a condition of servitude." Such comparisons of white labor to slavery had been revived late in the war and intensified as the labor issue became more prominent. The active support of workingmen in a war to emancipate the slaves freed up labor leaders to use the volatile and powerful imagery of servitude to describe labor's plight. The implication was that white labor should be freed, too.[49]

The founding meeting concluded with a resolution to form both a Trades Assembly and a workingman's newspaper, with each union taking a share in its stock. The subsequent founding of the *Workingman's Advocate,* with Scotland-born printer Andrew Cameron as editor, was probably the greatest achievement of the Assembly. Cameron quickly brought in Eduard Schläger to edit the paper's German edition, and Schläger insured that the forty-eighter left played a significant role in the Assembly for the rest of the year, including sending representatives to its meetings. Six weeks later, the Trades Assembly elected a board of officers, three out six of whom were typographers. The prominence of the typographers—who were overwhelmingly American and British—reflected both their early leading role in the Chicago labor movement and the recent mobilization of the printing trade during a bitter strike against the *Chicago Post* in April, the same month in which the General Trades Assembly been founded.[50]

The General Trades Assembly was a new political force in the city based on an alliance of Anglo American, German, and Irish workingmen. On August 20, four months after its founding, it burst into politics with a mass meeting of two thousand, organized in preparation for the presidential campaign of 1864. Though the meeting occurred in the midst of ongoing strikes of the coopers, stonecutters, and German printers, the immediate spark for the turn toward politics was the importation of nonunion machinists from Belgium by the Illinois Central Railroad, an affront to the Machinists and Blacksmiths Union. The active involvement of the sophisticated metalworkers in the huge Illinois Central car shops added substantially to the size and talents of the labor movement and marked a shift in its base of strength from the traditional crafts to one of the city's most advanced large-scale industries. Dissatisfaction with the conduct of the war also motivated the workers attending the meeting.

Many workingmen there believed that they were being asked to bear most of the burdens of the war in the form of inflated consumer prices, inequitable taxes, and a draft law that permitted the purchase of substitutes for $300. The August 20 labor meeting took place at a low point in Northern morale as Grant's drive against Richmond ground on inconclusively while consuming soldiers in unheard-of numbers. General William Tecumseh Sherman's campaign against Atlanta also appeared to be going nowhere. During this gloomy late summer of 1864, Lincoln discussed with his cabinet the problems of a possible transition to a new administration. The August 20 labor meeting amounted, therefore, to a protest against both capital and the policies of the Lincoln administration, and the Democrats helped organize and hoped to profit from it.[51]

The meeting made a gesture toward bipartisanship but tilted Democratic. There were three major speakers: George K. Hazlitt, president of the Trades Assembly, who was a Republican and member of the loyalist Union League; Edward W. McComas, the prolabor "copperhead" Democrat; and Eduard Schläger, the pro-Frémont leader of the German forty-eighter left. Hazlitt opened the proceedings by accentuating the "war against capital, which the working men of the city are now waging." To prosecute this local war, Chicago's laboring men needed to form a political party and "place the exponents of their principles in office." Begging the question of what those principles were, Hazlitt deferred the task to "men of mind," who had drafted resolutions and a platform. Two of these "men of mind" were Schläger and McComas.[52]

In his address, Schläger concentrated his fire on more narrow labor questions, although he was no stranger to the big issues. A radical on slavery since his arrival in the early 1850s, he would soon advocate a Reconstruction plan to redistribute rebel estates to former slaves and soldiers. Schläger knew that opposing the war effort directly would alienate too many in his German constituency. Except for the debt question, he entirely ignored war issues in his speech and focused attention on "the war between capital and labor [that] has already begun in this city though the papers were afraid to state it. The battle commenced with the importation of sixty Belgian machinists by the Illinois Central Railroad Company." Schläger put no faith in either the major parties or the established newspapers in helping resolve this conflict for the betterment of labor.[53]

McComas concentrated more on the issues of the war and race, advocating the war position of the Peace Democrats and updating the racism of the Douglas Democracy by accepting emancipation while reaffirming the privileged status of whites. The resolutions of the meeting on the war reflected the thinking of McComas, who served on the drafting committee. The resolutions condemned it as "a war which no sincere and peaceful effort had been made to arrest . . . and which bids fair to finally end, even if we triumph, in common bankruptcy and ruin of both sections of the country; and the probable overthrow of our common liberties." This was not a laboring man's war, said the resolutions: "The present war was not caused by the laboring men of the North, nor fought under their direction, nor continued for their interest—their only part being to bear its burdens and shed their blood in its ranks." Like the Democratic Party, the resolutions called for "an armistice and the call of a national convention whose duty it shall be to peaceably recognize the union and re-establish the rights of the states and people in such a manner as shall be consistent with the rights, honor, interest, and happiness of the whole people." This untenable position on the war refused to acknowledge that there was no way to restore the Union through a negotiated peace that recognized the rights of the states as the South defined them. For the Confederacy, states' rights still meant Southern independence. But, within a week and a half, the Northern Democratic Party met in Chicago and adopted a similar call for a negotiated peace.[54]

Other resolutions of the August 20 labor meeting focused on the war debt question. In producers' republican thinking, prevalent since the American Revolution, a high public debt was feared as a means of siphoning off the earnings of labor, overturning a balanced distribution of wealth, and fastening a tyranny on the people. The resolutions charged that the national bonds had been engrossed by the rich at low values and that the people should not be taxed to pay for them. They proposed the enactment of a progressive tax, with the farmlands, humble estates, and income of the poor exempt from taxation. Finally, the resolutions implied that since labor was fighting the war, "capital should pay its money." To these demands the meeting appended a more traditional labor platform, which endorsed the establishment of free polytechnic schools, a return to a gold basis for wages, opposition to the competition of convict labor with free labor, shorter hours, and a mechanic lien law. The resolutions concluded by vowing that labor would nominate no candidates on its presidential ticket but would run on its own platform and nominate candidates for other offices "until we can ascertain who will prove most loyal to our interest." The fundamental flaw in this seemingly reasonable strategy was that there was no definable labor interest on the conduct of the war, the overriding issue of the presidential election. In the absence of a labor position, the Trades Assembly had allowed itself to be captured by the Peace Democrats, a "fusion" tactic, typical of third parties in this era.[55]

The progress of the war short-circuited Chicago labor's initial foray into the political arena. On September 2—two days after the Democratic convention closed in Chicago and two weeks after labor's August 22 political meeting—the fortunes of war altered dramatically when Atlanta fell to the Union army. General Sherman's victory dramatically altered public opinion in the North about the war's prospects and ensured Lincoln's victory in November. Chicago labor's platform went down with the Democrats.

Labor's first political initiative tainted it with disloyalty and made it vulnerable to attack within Chicago's ethnic communities. The ethnic enemies of labor's German and Irish allies tarred them with the brush of treason, wrapped themselves in the American flag, and proclaimed that they were the true representatives of their national cultures. The clearest case was in the Irish community, which had buried its hero James A. Mulligan, organizer of the Irish Brigade, in early August. When the mourners passed the casket, they saw a banner with his dying words on the battlefield, "Lay me down and save the flag." The Fenians were conspicuously absent from the huge procession that accompanied him to his grave, having boycotted it in protest of their handling by Bishop Duggan. After Atlanta fell, the bishop used the opportunity to make the Fenians and their allies look even more like traitors, not only to the Northern war effort but also to Irish pride.[56]

If the Chicago labor movement had any remaining questions about the high costs of alliance with the Democrats, they were answered by a bitter strike against the *Chicago Times* in September. The *Times* was the voice of the Douglas Democrats in Chicago, and its editor, Wilbur Storey, was on the National Democratic Executive Committee. The strike added to labor disaffection from the Democracy, as the Trades Assembly called for the expulsion of Storey from the Executive Committee and the designation of a new official Democratic paper in the city. The *Tribune*'s support of the *Times* in the strike reinforced the alienation of the labor movement from the established powers behind the city's major parties and confirmed labor's desire for its own newspaper voice and its own politics. Storey added to the union's hostility against him by using women as compositors to help break the strike, and then cynically replaced the women with nonunion men after his victory. The strike appeared as an assault on the strikers' "manhood," defined both by their gender and their status as independent craftsmen. Overall, the strike substantiated the conviction of Chicago trade unionists that they faced an all-out assault on their new unions, their manhood, and their rights as Americans.[57]

Alienation from the two major political parties pushed Chicago workers to independently lobby the larger political organizations. In the fall election campaign, the Trades Assembly called on candidates to respond to a questionnaire enumerating labor's program. The meeting also called for workers to "lay aside our party ties and predilections, in our municipal and county elections, and vote only for the known friends of the laboring man." When Republican congressional candidate John Wentworth refused to reply and Democratic candidate Cyrus McCormick gave an affirmative answer, the Trades Assembly endorsed Chicago's conservative reaper magnate. Republican workingmen formed an association of "loyal" workers and condemned the *Workingman's Advocate* for its support of the "copperhead" McCormick, who lost by a substantial margin. For the first time in Chicago politics, both Democrats and Republicans appealed to an organized labor interest. Although labor's endorsement had no discernible impact amid Lincoln's sweeping victory, the fall campaign showed that independent labor politics drew attention that labor would otherwise not receive.[58]

The missed steps, embarrassments, and modest results of labor's first entry into Chicago politics obscure its significance. Karl Marx, then covering the Civil War for the *New York Herald Tribune,* observed that "in the United States of North America, every independent movement of the workers was paralyzed so long as slavery disfigured a part of the Republic. Labour cannot emancipate itself in the white skin where in the black it is branded. But out of the death of slavery a new life at once arose."[59] Beginning in the spring of 1864, an independent labor coalition had formed in the wake of emancipation linking the new unions, their Trades Assembly, and friendly ethnic organizations like the Fenians and German forty-eighter left.

The dramatic politicization of American life by the war both aided the mobilization of this labor coalition and made its entry into the public sphere extraordinarily treacherous. Meanwhile, the federal government's wartime initiatives transformed the public sphere in Chicago, making categories of gender, ethnicity, and race open to redefinition by people acting out new roles as soldiers, workers, immigrants, and citizens. Immigrants became patriotic American citizens fighting for their new country, women became garment workers working and living outside of male-led households, craftsmen became wageworkers struggling to support their families in an expanded labor market, and soldiers became emancipators whose success on the battlefield ended slavery in America and might lead to destroying oppression in Europe. The transformation of the public sphere occasioned by the end of slavery made the cooperation of foreign-born workers in the labor movement possible, and this interethnic movement brought the labor question and labor interest into Chicago politics for the first time.

In the immediate aftermath of the war, labor would mount a demand for an eight-hour workday—the subject of the next chapter—which sanctioned state intervention in civil society as a precondition for the preservation of the republic that had so recently been saved from slavery. This was a social republican agenda promoted primarily by Anglo American and German labor leaders at a millennial moment in American history, when the revolutionary changes instituted during the Civil War made the social order appear malleable.

3 The Eight-Hour Day and the Legitimacy of Wage Labor

ON A SUNNY WEDNESDAY, May 1, 1867, over five thousand workers marched to the lakefront in Chicago to support the eight-hour working day recently written into Illinois law. The sidewalks were thronged with workingmen, who "loudly cheered" the procession at several points, but "in general a strict silence prevailed, if indeed that can be called silence which is marked by the low, ceaseless murmur of a multitude as restless as a bag of fleas." At the end of the march, Mayor John B. Rice addressed the crowd. His sympathy was mixed with anxiety about disorder.[1]

The mayor noted that proponents of the law "argued that in the great change in the world's economy, by the invention of the steam engine and by the thousand different kinds of labor-saving machines that have been brought into use, which are all, or perhaps nearly all, of them operated by steam with great rapidity, that every man's mind and body is impelled—is necessarily compelled to greater and more rapid action . . . and that eight hours' labor in those surroundings are more exhaustive than ten or twelve hours' in earlier times. [A voice—'That is so.'] This is my understanding of the matter. [A voice—'Right,' and cheers] Now, if this be true, . . . then it is right that a man should insist that eight hours should be the length of his day's work. [A voice, 'Bully for you,' and much applause.] But, gentlemen, remember that great changes in the body politic or economy cannot be brought about on a sudden without great trouble and serious loss." He recommended caution and calm reflection, including discussions with wives, before the workers took action.[2]

The mayor was right to emphasize the magnitude of the change involved in the eight-hour workday, but by highlighting mechanization he emphasized only one vivid component of the political and economic change out of which the eight-hour movement arose. National in scope, the movement for an eight-hour workday prompted the first public recognition of how capitalism—commonly called the "wages system" after its most obvious aspect—was affecting American social life. This public recognition came amid a generation-long national debate about slavery, free labor, and the roles of both in defining the social and economic order desired by Americans. Beginning at least in the 1820s and lasting into the 1890s, the evolution of capitalism in the North was characterized above all by the expansion of a market in labor and the emergence of a permanent wage-earning working class. By 1850, the number of wage earners in the United States surpassed the number of slaves, and ten years later the number of workers exceeded that of the self-employed (see fig. 1, introduction). In what Eric Hobsbawm has termed "The Age of Capital" from 1848 to 1875, America became a republic of primarily wage earners, rather than one of small producers in the North and slaves in the South. Neither social thought nor public policy fully recognized this fact at the time.[3]

As property in one's labor or self-employment gave way to wagework, the ability to work, or labor power, became a commodity measured by units of time and valued at the going price in the market. In the words of labor reformer George E. McNeill, workers became "merchants of their time." According to David Brody, the journeymen carpenters in the antebellum era observed their masters using calculations of time to measure and value their work, and they "became themselves calculating." In a larger sense, they saw new economic "rules of the game" and insisted on equality in defining them. Struggling to control their work lives, the carpenters achieved a rise in their "level of popular intelligence" that put them in the forefront of the fight for a shorter working day in the antebellum era.[4]

When workers no longer made whole products, much less sold them, it became apparent that they were selling their time and, thus, part of themselves in the labor market for the going price. They were wage-slaves in the eyes of a producers' republican society that rooted independence and liberty in the ownership of productive property. A wage-slave could not be an independent citizen of a producers' republic. Reflecting this view, some leaders of the labor movement saw capitalism as threatening the political order. Many of the craftsmen and labor reformers who organized the eight-hour movement saw their goal as restricting—and for some overthrowing—the "wages system," particularly because it destroyed liberty and thus the republic as well.[5]

On the other hand, labor spokespersons less dedicated to the ideals of the producers' republic gave a different answer to the crucial issue put by historian Amy Dru Stanley: "whether time was a property that could be alienated from the self."[6] Those who answered "Yes" accepted the legitimacy of the labor market, at least to the point of trying to organize institutions and social life within it. People who answered "No" rejected the legitimacy of the labor market, even if they struggled to survive within it until they established an alternative to it. The typical basis for rejecting the legitimacy of the labor market was the producers' concept of liberty as rooted in property owner-ship. Advocates of democracy, cooperation, and a shorter working day could answer the question either way, but their answer profoundly influenced how they viewed the reform they advocated.

Ambivalent about their new status, wageworkers nonetheless strongly re-jected the conclusion that they could not be citizens because they lacked property. Instead they insisted on full and equal political rights, forming a key constituency for a democratic suffrage, which separated voting rights from property ownership. Their insistence on democracy presupposed that one could sell labor time in the market without creating bondage. Politically free, workers now found it more difficult to claim that wage labor put them in bondage to their employers. If they were in bondage, how could they be citizens in a democracy? Was not the wage bargain they made with their em-ployers a contract freely arrived at in the economic sphere and thus outside the bounds of public scrutiny? This appeal to a separate and independent economic sphere was itself a part of the ideological transformation occasioned by the development of capitalism. To counter these new arguments, the more advanced labor leaders both fought for workers' democratic rights and sought to use the political power created by democracy to rectify the inequalities rooted in workers' lack of economic power.[7]

Intervening politically in the economy required intellectual justification, and labor leaders sought it in producers' cooperation as well as the shorter working day. Cooperation was an effort at collective control of the new means of production, in some plans through outright worker ownership and in others through less radical means, such as profit sharing. Cooperation ac-cepted, and even celebrated, the rapid expansion of productive capacity by capitalism while trying to control it for the advantage of workers. The advo-cates of producers' cooperation wanted the workers in a plant to own and manage it outright. Committed to property as the ultimate basis of liberty and rejecting the sale of time in the labor market, they saw cooperation as a means for abolishing the "wages system" altogether. Others staked out a more moderate position, based on the assumption that there were degrees of freedom and not a simple dichotomy between liberty and the bondage of selling oneself. One could increase one's freedom by sharing in the earnings of a productive enterprise through profit sharing—a conservative form of cooperation that assumed the legitimacy of wage labor—or by lessening the amount of time one sold in the market. Pursuing both enhanced the time at one's own disposal while increasing the means to use it, making one freer in the process.

Cooperation had its core constituency among craftsmen who had enough savings to imagine investing in the enterprises where they worked. But the primary constituency of the eight-hour movement was among less-prosperous wage earners, who were typically not craftsmen and who had no capital to invest in a business. They were the people who marched on May 1, 1867, and cheered on Mayor Rice. The eight-hour movement was a working-class effort to control time and thus increase liberty in the face of a labor market that was defining more and more of people's lives. Nonetheless, as with cooperation, some working-class advocates—often the craftsmen who typically led the labor movement—saw the demand as a fulcrum for lifting a new cooperative order into place. Speaking for those who did not accept the legitimacy of selling labor in the market, Chicago's Andrew Cameron wrote that "labor reform aims to restore this lost ownership of self," that is, the ownership of self lost in the wage bargain. Stressing the efficacy of politics, Cameron saw the eight-hour workday as creating the leisure time necessary for workers to predominate in the republic. Workers could then use their power to overcome the "wages system."[8]

Others, such as Boston's Ira Steward, combined the two labor positions. Steward accepted the wage-labor relation as a starting point for future action and portrayed shorter hours as a means of increasing workers' standard of living. Rejecting the wages-fund theory of orthodox political economy, which held that workers' wages were strictly limited by the available pool of capital, Steward argued the wages were determined by the standard of living. Increased leisure stemming from shorter hours would allow less-skilled workers the time to observe the standard of living of those above them and stimulate in them new wants and desires. Over time, increased ambitions would lead them to demand and win higher wages. Rather than increasing prices as predicted by the wages-fund theory, higher wages would boost consumer purchasing power, which would allow manufacturers to take advantage of economies of scale to introduce the latest labor-saving machinery, thus actually lowering prices. Steward's theory was the foundation and starting point for subsequent arguments by the American labor movement that a "high wage economy" was viable and in the interest of both labor and capital.[9]

Chicago's Andrew Cameron disagreed with Steward, staying within the ideological world of producers' republicanism. Rivaling Steward in influence, if not in ideological leadership, Cameron never accepted the legitimacy of selling labor in the market. On the fundamental issue of wage labor, Cameron was closer to Abraham Lincoln, for whom wage labor was compatible with liberty only if it was a temporary stage on the way to independence.[10]

Most labor leaders saw the eight-hour workday simply as a way to increase the realm of freedom for workers by lessening the amount of time one sold. Redefining liberty was essential because the spread of wage labor was undermining the viability of liberty based on owning productive property. Eight hours had a wider constituency than cooperation because of the large numbers of new unskilled wageworkers experiencing the transformation of production, particularly by the subdivision of tasks and mechanization. As they sought to control the amount of time they worked, and as they participated in the debates about slavery and free labor in the Civil War era, these workers developed a new politics for American labor.

THE EIGHT-HOUR WORKDAY DURING THE CIVIL WAR

Journeymen's unions emerged during the Civil War in cities across the North, seeking to control the price of labor in the newly pervasive labor market. They combined their unions into local labor movements, and then a national one, by linking up with labor reformers. Labor reform was part of a transatlantic political culture that antedated the Civil War but that received new impetus from it. Illustrative of labor reform in the United States was *Fincher's Trades Review,* labor's most important national voice during the Civil War. Jonathan C. Fincher, a native-born machinist, published his weekly paper in Philadelphia with the institutional support of the Machinists' and Blacksmiths' Union and other organized trades. The machinists and blacksmiths were members of prestigious trades that promoted a culture of science, moral uplift, and the independence cherished by all craftsmen, especially by the Yankee inventor types attracted to the sophisticated metal trades. Such metalworkers also gave the culture a Protestant tone. By the Civil War, the immigration waves of the 1840s and 1850s had diluted the Yankee presence among metalworkers, but the antebellum culture of science, uplift, and independence continued, often with the active support of British immigrant craftsmen who were both dissenting Protestants and participants in the transatlantic reform culture.[11]

Although the original prospectus for Fincher's paper did not mention the eight-hour workday, the issue appeared on the paper's masthead in the fall of 1863 as "Eight Hours for a Day's Labor." His paper saw the reform simply as a means to counteract anticipated massive unemployment, when the end of the war would bring huge numbers of men into the labor market at the same time that the suspension of government contracts shrank demand. He repeated the argument in March 1864 but called for immediate agitation on the issue so that the policy might be instituted in time to make a difference when the war ended. This call resonated in northern cities, including midwestern centers of labor activity like St. Louis, Detroit, and Chicago. At this time, the Chicago labor movement was in the midst of the strike wave that produced the Trades Assembly in April.[12]

In Chicago, the eight-hour issue emerged in English-speaking labor reform circles, where British-born skilled workers exercised unusual influence. By far the two most influential organizers of the Chicago eight-hour movement were Andrew Cameron and Richard Trevellick, two British immigrants. Cameron was the Scottish printer who helped organize the Chicago labor movement during the Civil War and who edited the Chicago *Workingman's Advocate*. Although based in Detroit, Trevellick came to Chicago so frequently on his trips as an organizer that he was a regular part of the Chicago labor scene. He subsequently moved to Chicago as an organizer for the Trades Assembly. At the time of the eight-hour agitation, Trevellick was the president of the International Association of Ship Carpenters and Caulkers. More widely traveled than Cameron, he had promoted labor reform, including shorter hours, in Australia and New Zealand before settling in the United States. Looking to Britain for reform ideas and models, both men commonly made references to British precedent, such as the repeal of the Corn Laws or the Rochdale model of cooperative stores. Both also drew inspiration from the British shortening of the working day in the 1850s.[13]

Like the other Protestant labor reformers who dominated the leadership of the eight-hour movement in the mid-1860s, Cameron and Trevellick were deeply influenced by evangelical religion, especially Methodism. Religious metaphors and images appeared repeatedly in their speeches and writings. David R. Roediger has argued that the Wesleyan doctrine of "free agency" helped the evangelical leaders of the eight-hour movement justify the increase of leisure that would come with the shorter working day. In opposition to orthodox concepts of the bondage of the will, the doctrine asserted that men were free to accept or reject Christ. Applied to increased leisure, the doctrine meant that men must be given the chance to exercise their freedom to choose better lives or not. There was no guarantee that they would choose well at first, but these leaders had faith that progress and moral growth would eventually result. Such an argument was indispensable in opposing the repeated accusation that workers would simply use their free time for dissipation, especially drunkenness. These evangelical Protestant connections linked the eight-hour movement to the middle-class Anglo American reform tradition that achieved a culmination with emancipation brought by the Northern victory in the Civil War. Both the links to Anglo American reform and the prominence of evangelical British advocates lent the eight-hour movement a millennial tone and driving energy that pushed well beyond the utilitarian argument with which Jonathan Fincher originally justified the reform in his paper in 1863.[14]

Steward, Cameron, and Trevellick appealed first of all to Chicago's narrow stratum of Anglo American Protestant skilled workers. In Chicago and elsewhere, these men spoke a language of cultural uplift, attended lectures at Mechanics Institutes, frequented reading rooms, subscribed to labor newspapers, cherished respectability, advocated temperance, and built craft unions. They were the "factory artisans" who built Methodist churches near the Illinois Central car shops and celebrated the glories of "mechanism" in large-scale enterprise, even as they resisted some of the new conditions of work. Many of them built the machinery and kept it running. Trevellick spoke to such workers in Chicago when he said that "this was the great object of the movement, to enable laborers to read, study and acquire knowledge. Were this reduction of toil obtained, laboring men would encourage the establishment of, and patronize when established, reading rooms and libraries, instead of drinking shops and low places of amusement." It is not surprising that in a city with so many Germans and Irish, as well as Catholics, a movement centered among these Protestant skilled workers originally had the character of a narrow faction. What is astonishing is that their movement developed a mass base well beyond its origins.[15]

One reason for this wider appeal among workers was the existence of a German counterpart—minus temperance—to the culture of Anglo American skilled workers. In Chicago, it was represented by the Arbeiterverein, which from its beginnings in the winter of 1857 promoted education and moral uplift. In 1861, when it had two hundred and fifty members, the Arbeiterverein had a library, debating society, and singing club, and it offered classes for learning English and drawing. The Arbeiterverein also marched in eight-hour workday parades and called for the federal government to make eight hours a legal day's work in its own workshops as well as for all its contractors.[16]

Yet the main reason for the wider working-class appeal of eight hours was that it appealed to the deeply felt needs of Chicago workers experiencing the rapid, even frenetic, growth of the city's manufacturing economy. Craft workers witnessed the transformation of their traditional tasks at the same time that people new to industrial work were entering the manufacturing labor force in unprecedented numbers. The eight-hour workday demand cut across lines of skill and national origin by stressing the experience of these people with newly subdivided tasks and increasingly regimented work routines. The pace and dimensions of industrial change thus made the length of the working day a vital issue with mass support well beyond that of cooperation. "Eight hours for work, eight hours for rest, and eight hours for ourselves" became the most widely shared demand of Chicago's new industrial working class after the fateful fall of 1864, when Lincoln's resounding reelection shattered labor's temporary alliance with the Democrats and sent the movement in search of a reformulated agenda.[17]

THE EIGHT-HOUR CAMPAIGN OF 1865–67

After the fall 1864 elections, the labor movement sought a new way of exercising political influence outside the major political parties. But as long as the Irish remained within the Democratic fold, this required a coalescing of the Germans and Anglo Americans in the labor movement. The main German labor leaders had been left-wing forty-eighter Republicans who rebelled against Lincoln in the hapless John C. Frémont campaign for the presidential nomination in 1864. As this faction lost status in German American political circles, the emergent German manufacturers assumed a larger role in the local Republican Party, sending the German left in pursuit of new political audiences. The Anglo American leaders of the labor movement had been Douglas Democrats, but their frustration with the Democracy had culminated in the fall of 1864 first with the printers' strike against the Democratic *Chicago Times* and then in the election itself, in which they launched labor's ill-fated first political initiative. In late 1864, the eight-hour question provided Chicago labor leaders with a platform appropriate to independently mobilizing an interethnic coalition, because neither major party owned the issue. Starting to organize modestly in early 1865, the advocates of eight hours quickly evolved into leaders of a mass movement when the appeal of the issue carried well beyond its original constituency. Eight hours became a demand for social regeneration that drew on all the cultural and political resources the labor movement could muster.[18]

When 1865 opened, the war's end was in sight. Issues that had been subordinated to the goal of winning the conflict now came to the fore, particularly as various groups and parties maneuvered to shape the postwar order. Labor leaders foresaw an impending collision between labor and capital, given tensions that had built up during the conflict. Such foreboding was apparent when William Sylvis and Trevellick addressed the Fourth of July celebration organized by the Chicago Trades Assembly in 1865. For the first time, Chicago labor felt that it would not receive the respect it deserved in

Chicago's annual patriotic parade, arranging its own affair instead. Sylvis and Trevellick gave speeches to the assembled thirty-five hundred, in which they linked the eight-hour issue with the need to renew the republic.[19]

By the fall of that year, Andrew Cameron organized the Grand Eight Hour League with branch organizations in several wards. As part of this effort, the Trades Assembly sponsored a lecture by Trevellick in September at which he made a critical argument that he and other eight-hour advocates elaborated for the next two years: "The development of the products of the earth were and would be in exact accordance with, and proportion to, the mental development of the producers, and the material prosperity of the world would advance as the minds of the people were enlightened." Since the "great object" of the eight-hour movement was to "enable laborers to read, study and acquire knowledge" by providing them with the time to do so, achieving its goal of a shorter working day would enhance the "mental development of the producers," while leading them from saloons to reading rooms. Because the eight-hour workday increased workers' mental capacity, it would increase material prosperity as well as their moral well-being. This argument permitted the eight-hour movement to bridge attempts to segregate the economy from social and political life. It also expanded the nature and significance of the self that working people claimed to own. This ownership of the self justified not only the franchise but also economic and social reforms to enhance it, from a shorter working day to quality public education.[20]

In his speech, Trevellick also argued that workers should receive ten hours' pay for eight hours of work—in other words, no pay reduction. The *Tribune* utilized its laissez-faire Liberalism to attack this contention while disregarding the complex of arguments about the enhanced self and its import for productivity and morality. The issues of wages and hours, according to the paper, were simply beyond the legitimate authority of legislation, which could not affect them anyway. The paper's placement of the economy into a separate sphere operating under distinctive laws was part of the ideological transformation occasioned by the emergence of capitalism in Chicago and across the North. Seeking to shape this transformation, Trevellick argued that the increased productivity made possible by the enhanced mental capacities of working people would cover the cost of the wage increase. Other eight-hour advocates stressed the cultural and political renewal that would come with more leisure time, and Ira Steward argued that higher tastes, customs, and desires would produce a higher standard of living.[21]

Cameron used meetings like the one addressed by Trevellick in September 1865 to build eight-hour organizations in the city's wards as well as a citywide

Grand Eight Hour League. The League was organized independently of both the major political parties and the unions, although unions and their members were friends of the effort. This symbiotic relationship between unions and affiliated political organizations was common in nineteenth-century America and was exemplified in Chicago by the union support for the Fenians evident in their fair of 1864. Most important, however, was the fact that the Grand Eight Hour League was building a political organization based in the wards but independent of the two major parties. It was an independent labor interest in the body politic, a voice for labor in the public sphere that went well beyond a labor newspaper.[22]

This organizational strategy reflected the lesson Cameron drew from 1864: Labor needed to find ways to influence politics without capture by one of the major parties. Reformers, including the abolitionists, had faced this conundrum since mass-based democratic politics brought new problems and possibilities to American political life in the 1830s. In contrast to Cameron's advocacy of independent labor politics, Jonathan Fincher advocated the strategy followed by abolitionists in the 1830s through their petition campaign: Change public sentiment and then rely on it to affect politics without the reformers forming political organizations that ran candidates or made deals with the existing parties. He articulated this strategy in 1863 before the Chicago labor movement had organized: "'Tis not legislatures that we want, but sentiment. Let workingmen but educate themselves in that, and legislatures will follow." Despite some quarreling with Fincher, the Chicagoans continued to organize an independent labor interest in the city and the state. The structure and constituency of the eight-hour movement in Illinois was evident in the parade advocated by Cameron during December 1865, a few months after Trevellick's speech earlier in the fall.[23]

The eight-hour procession was impressive for a new organization. About fifteen hundred men marched to the light of their torches on a cold winter evening, witnessed by "a dense crowd of citizens, patiently gaping for a spectacle, and vigorously stamping upon the pavement and upon each other, in a futile attempt to keep warm." Eight-hour leagues from ten of the city's sixteen wards marched, as did ten unions plus the Arbeiterverein. At this time, there were about twenty-five unions in the Chicago Trades Assembly. Metalworkers made up the largest number of unions marching in the procession: iron molders, machinists and blacksmiths, boilermakers, brass founders and finishers. Woodworkers were a close second, represented by the ship carpenters and caulkers, the cabinetmakers, and the carpenters and joiners. The typographers, stonecutters, and cigar makers rounded out the represented union organizations. Typical of artisan parades dating from the eighteenth century, the Chicago unions built floats for the parade on which members of their crafts performed their work, hammering metal, cutting stone, and printing leaflets promoting eight hours.[24]

This was a political demonstration aimed at the municipal elections of April 1866. Cameron and his supporters proved themselves masters of local political maneuvering by getting the Common Council to take a position on eight hours just before the election. In early March, they began petitioning the Common Council for an ordinance making eight hours a legal day's work for workmen employed by the city. Although the Common Council tried to bury the issue in committee, it was brought to a vote in early April. When the council split twelve to twelve on the resolution, Republican Mayor Rice broke the tie with a negative vote. Labor speakers castigated Mayor Rice's vote the night before the April municipal election in an eight-hour rally at the courthouse featuring Cameron, Trevellick, and Sylvis. The most imposing contingent was from the Third Ward, home of the Illinois Central Railroad's car shops, which had been seedbeds of labor protest and organization since the previous fall.[25]

Since the great issues of Reconstruction were not impinging on the election, the campaign itself was unexciting and the turnout down considerably from earlier years. The Republicans maintained their control of the city government, electing the mayor and two-thirds of the aldermen. No candidates of the eight-hour movement who ran independently of the two major parties won. At the same time, the eight-hour movement had induced seven candidates to take pledges of support, and these seven won. An additional five supporters had apparently not taken the pledge but expressed sympathy.[26]

These modest successes in Chicago came amid setbacks for the national movement, as eight-hour bills were defeated in the state legislatures of New York, Pennsylvania, Wisconsin, and Ohio. In this situation, Chicago was in the limelight as a center of the national campaign, and Cameron became more insistent on the transformative consequences of shorter hours. He argued that eight hours was "not a matter of mere philanthropy, of victories easily won, of results earned without effort; ours is the ushering in of a social revolution, of a war of labor against capital, in which one or the other has to go to the wall." The fact that eight hours could not easily be enacted under the aegis of reform seemed to Cameron proof of its radical logic, since fundamental change involved the "ushering in of a new class into power." He called for "systematic action" and a "comprehensive" labor platform in evangelical tones: "We do not say that such a platform can be constructed now . . . ; nobody can say when and how the new gospel is to announce itself, but we insist on a little preparation. . . . We must create more agitation among ourselves or we shall lose ground; the waters of Shiloh only worked miracles when stirred. . . . We have no St. John to do the work for us."[27]

Although Cameron was correct in anticipating class conflict in the eight-hour reform, he was mistaken in his prediction that eight hours would become the major issue during the polarizing period of Reconstruction. In 1865 and 1866, the great issues of Reconstruction preoccupied public discussion in Chicago, as they did in the rest of the North: On what terms were the Southern states to be readmitted to the Union? What was to be the status of freed blacks? How was the war debt to be retired? Should President Andrew Johnson be impeached? These issues reached down into the political grassroots, particularly in the fall elections of 1866 as the Radical Republicans successfully sought to wrest control of Reconstruction policy from the president.

Still, this same election witnessed a surprising success for the Illinois eight-hour movement, in part because the major parties appealed to it in their bitter struggle over the larger issues of Reconstruction. Popularly based minority movements, such as Fenianism and eight hours, gained an unusual opportunity to act as the balance of power, even as the political passions of Reconstruction pushed them to the back page. The cross-ethnic constituency of the labor reformers enhanced these opportunities. A similar situation arose in Massachusetts, where, Dale Baum has argued, "the new consciousness of the workers sliced across ethnic, religious, and partisan lines, and the move of the laborites into politics threatened to sever the bonds between the Irish and the Democratic party."[28] With such a prize in the offing, it was no wonder that Radical Republicans throughout the country appealed to both labor and the Fenians as they struggled to win their climactic campaign against Andrew Johnson in the fall 1866 elections.

The Radical Republicans in Chicago were no exception. In the fall of 1866, the prisoners captured during the Fenians' disastrous invasion of Canada became a cause célèbre in Chicago politics and an opportunity for Republicans opposed to Andrew Johnson to identify themselves with a Democratic constituency in the imminent congressional elections. The prominent Republican and German-Jewish entrepreneur Henry Greenebaum chaired a meeting of ten thousand in October to oppose the execution of Fenian leaders by Canadian authorities. His rhetoric made the Fenians an heir of both the American Revolution and the revolutionary spirit of 1848.

Yet the eight-hour movement in Chicago got more substantive benefits than rhetoric. On September 10, 1866, a much broader eight-hour ordinance than had been proposed in March passed the Republican-dominated Chicago Common Council with only one negative vote. The ordinance committed the Public Works Department to the eight-hour workday and the Common Council itself to recommending to the next legislature that it pass a state eight-hour law. The Grand Eight Hour League's grassroots organizing in the wards had paid off in an independent organization that could move the local political system.[29]

The bipartisan support for the Chicago eight-hour ordinance in September 1866 prefigured party endorsement of the issue during the congressional elections the next month. The Cook County Republican Union convention committed itself not only to an eight-hour working day for Illinois but also to "all legislation which tends to alleviate the hardships, improve the condition, and shorten the hours of labor of the working classes." The Cook County Democratic Convention was less sweeping in its support of labor's goals but declined to field candidates in four state legislative districts in which eight-hour men, including Andrew Cameron, were running. The eight-hour men lost, however, along with the Democrats, amid a Radical Republican triumph in Chicago and across the North. Congress subsequently undertook the policy of Reconstruction that included military rule in the former Confederacy.[30]

Despite the defeat of its candidates, the eight-hour movement succeeded after the election, mainly because of Republican hopes of appealing to a new constituency. A bill written by Republican State Representative Henry M. Shephard of Chicago glided through the state legislature with virtually no opposition, and Governor Richard Oglesby signed it on March 5, 1867. It was the nation's first statewide eight-hour law.[31]

THE EIGHT-HOUR DEBATE IN THE SPRING OF 1867

Cameron's prediction that the eight-hour issue would arouse class divisions came true after the law was passed. The city woke up to the implications of the law after being preoccupied with national issues of Reconstruction in the fall of 1866. As the contending sides mobilized, a profound debate took place in the city over the merits, the meaning, and the possible alternatives to the eight-hour working day. Unlike the Fenians—whom Chicago's establishment perceived as an ethnic constituency temporarily loose from its political moorings—the eight-hour movement challenged the city ideologically by questioning the very organization of the economy. Representatives of all classes and points of view participated in the debate on the pages of the city's press and in public meetings. Normal political divisions blurred, and the city's public sphere divided between a center supporting the basic elements of a capitalist society and a periphery opposed to all or part of it. Key players in the debate were modest-size manufacturers and the skilled workers whom they hired; both groups included native-born and foreign-born who had profited immensely from the manufacturing boom of the 1860s. These two groups were central because their place in the new order was still indeterminate, because they were critical ingredients of both the Republican coalition and labor reform, and because they were well organized and articulate. In addition, the issue of free trade versus protection, an issue of intense interest among artisan entrepreneurs and craftsmen, intersected with the eight-hour debate.

The *Times* and the *Tribune* as well as the two major political parties in the city served as the medium for this public discussion. Both newspapers opposed the eight-hour law and supported free trade, although they used different arguments and, of course, could not acknowledge that they agreed. The *Times* opposed the law from the beginning as an impractical scheme promoted by demagogues, most of them Radical Republicans, that would render the city's industry unable to compete with other regions and thus bring economic ruin. The *Times* even argued that the eight-hour law was a plot by eastern manufacturers to stifle their emerging western competition by raising its costs: The law was a sort of protective tariff on western goods analogous to the one against European products, the kind of law upon which the easterners had grown wealthy and monopolistic. For the *Times,* free trade was the antidote to monopoly that would help both small manufacturers, by increasing the competition faced by large firms, and workers, who would profit from lower prices that competition would bring.[32]

The *Tribune* took a different path to the same positions, revealing along the way serious fissures in the Republican Party's free-labor coalition. Divisions among Republicans had ideological ramifications as well as political import, given the power of Republicans in Congress, who were attempting to impose the free-labor system on the South through military Reconstruction. Owned by Joseph Medill and William Bross and edited by Horace White, the *Tribune* had represented the local Republican establishment since the inception of the party in the mid-1850s. One of the country's leading Radical Republicans, White, in association with E. L. Godkin of *The Nation,* pioneered the reformulation of free-labor ideology into postwar Liberalism during Reconstruction.

Both White and Godkin were leading reform intellectuals of the day, seeking to transform politics from the national to the local level. Each of the three figures associated with the *Tribune*—Medill, Bross, and White—felt that, if enforced, the eight-hour law would subvert business and private property. Each turned for support to the classical political economy of Adam Smith, expounded by Edward A. Atkinson. Yet, despite their mutual opposition to eight hours, these men divided over free trade versus protectionism, with Medill advocating protection against White's free-trade Liberalism. White's views determined the position of the paper until Medill bought full ownership in 1874. They also provoked the founding of a rival paper, the *Chicago Republican*.[33]

At the beginning of the eight-hour debate in 1867, White reprinted a report from the Massachusetts legislature opposing eight hours. The Massachusetts report condemned state interference in bargaining between workers and capitalists, especially if the state favored the workers with more than the capitalists were willing to give; such state action would undermine the rights of property and establish communism. White rejected eight hours on a similar basis, arguing that the eight-hour legislation was a disastrous interference in the "elementary laws of political economy."[34]

Following passage of the eight-hour law in Illinois, White, along with Godkin, advocated profit-sharing cooperation, though not an alternative to the wage system. According to one editorial, "when the co-operative system shall have reached its fullest development there will still be as much room for the employment of capital as before, and it is not at all probable the system of hired labor will be essentially modified." The express purpose of this form of cooperation was to prevent class conflict and induce employees to take an interest in their firm and hence to work harder. White's Liberal argument presupposed that the free-labor prescription for independence—workingmen starting up small businesses either as individuals or associated with one another in producers' cooperatives—was impractical in modern industrial capitalism. This was a substantial break from the free-labor ideology that had unified the Republican coalition during the Civil War.[35]

In line with his new laissez-faire economics, White made another break with the Republican tradition by putting the *Tribune* behind free trade. Protection had been critical to the party's appeal to modest-size manufacturers and craft workers. More than anyone else, the Chicago manufacturing entrepreneurs of the 1860s fulfilled the Republican social ideal of the self-made, upwardly mobile individual. They had escaped wage labor and achieved independence making useful goods that increased the wealth of society. They represented a constituency in Chicago that identified with and hoped to perpetuate this central social and economic vision of the antebellum Republican Party.

Republican protectionist doctrine, however, was not simply probusiness; it represented a full-throated appeal to the nation's new industrial workers as well as the artisan entrepreneurs who employed so many of them. The protectionists were critical of Liberals who followed the reigning economic orthodoxy espoused by English economists David Ricardo and Thomas Malthus, which taught that wages tended toward a subsistence level—the so-called iron law of wages. In contrast, the protectionists followed the American economist Henry C. Carey. Carey, like many Republicans, worried that the looming end of free land would doom an economy of high wages. Nonetheless, he believed that America could escape the fate of a class-divided society like England's by cutting itself loose from the division of labor imposed by English free trade. By protecting its market from low-wage English manufactures, American workers could maintain their high wages.[36]

The new *Chicago Republican* faithfully reproduced Carey's views while attacking the *Tribune* for abandoning core Republican principles, particularly a protective tariff, a position that had been ratified in the Republican platforms of 1860 and 1864. To initiate their enterprise in 1865, the *Republican*'s owners brought in as editor Charles A. Dana, who had been an editor of Horace Greeley's *New York Herald Tribune* as well as assistant secretary of war in the second Lincoln administration. From 1841 to 1846, Dana had been an enthusiastic participant in the utopian Brook Farm community, which helps explain some of his radical views. The founding of the *Republican* represented a serious ideological division within the Chicago Republican movement. Under Dana, the *Republican* sought to reconcile labor and capital on the basis of a radical interpretation of the party's free-labor ideology.[37]

Drawing on the arguments of Carey, the *Republican* saw protectionism as part of a social and economic philosophy of "cooperation." In contrast, the Liberal free traders like White, according to the *Republican,* advocated "competition": "Competition in our national policy says let our workingmen compete with the untaxed paupers of the whole world and if there be any labor, capital, and machinery anywhere capable of underworking them and driving then out of employment, let them be underworked and starved. Let there be a free trade in labor—and to this end let the laborer be regarded as of secondary importance and his product as primary; let wealth be the god and man the creator of wealth be subordinate to the creature he has made." To the *Republican,* cooperation meant support for protection because "we hold the man, the creator of wealth to be of supreme importance rather than the product he creates." In this, the *Republican* closely paralleled Carey, who rejected orthodox political economy, which attributed the ability to produce increased wealth to the division of labor and economies of scale. Instead, Carey emphasized the human creativity of the worker.[38]

In sharp contrast to the *Tribune* and other papers, all of which expressed pessimism as to the viability of cooperatives started by workingmen, the *Republican* asserted that cooperatives "indicate the drift and current of the time which is undoubtedly toward the further emancipation of labor by substituting co-operative associations for employment at wages. The former is as much freer and will prove as much more productive than the latter as employment at wages is freer and more productive than slavery itself. . . . Co-operation . . . is the practical application of Christianity, liberty and true democracy to the labor question. This is the perfect emancipation of the working classes." To the *Republican,* industrialization and social progress required labor's full emancipation from wage labor through producers' cooperatives, not the profit sharing advocated by the *Tribune.*[39]

The *Republican's* philosophy of cooperation also put it behind the eight-hour law. It was the only major English-language daily in the city to support workers' eight-hour demands and the strike that followed. The *Illinois Staats-Zeitung* was also supportive, but from a less ideologically articulated position. The *Republican's* main argument in support of eight hours was that workingmen would "eventually produce more in eight as they did in ten, just as they now produce more in ten than they used to produce in twelve or fourteen hours." The *Republican* based this assertion on the idea that increased productivity derived directly from the hand and brain of the mechanic rather than capital: "The value of a man's service is in proportion to his skill, through comprehension of the work he is employed to perform, and of the natural laws employed in its performance. The best mechanics are not mere machines. They combine the motive power and the directing skill of the engineer. Knowing the philosophy of their trade, its possibilities, it becomes a fine art to them, a recreation of itself, and they learn to labor in it from a love of it, and with a deftness and elasticity which the overworked tool in the shape of the human muscle never acquires." This was basically the same argument made by Richard Trevellick in September 1865 when he asserted that increased productivity came from the mental development of workers.[40]

Labor reformers responded positively to the *Republican's* vision of social regeneration based on cooperation and the eight-hour workday, although Cameron supported free trade, not protection. That position reflected his Democratic background and, more important, the character of his constituency. Unlike the *Republican*, he did not have to hold artisan entrepreneurs in his coalition, people to whom protection had great appeal. The *Workingman's Advocate* and its associated labor reformers, including Germans, participated in the eight-hour debate during the spring of 1867 by advocating eight hours and cooperation as an alternative to wage labor, and particularly in opposition to the *Tribune*. The Arbeiterverein passed resolutions calling for the enforcement of the eight-hour law, one of which stated "that we think the eight-hour system [is] the first step toward the abolition of the system of hired labor, the entire abolition of which is only a question of time, as it formerly was with slavery." Similarly, labor reformer H. H. Marsh argued that the eight-hour movement "is in reality part of the great national upheaval which during the last few years, has through war taken the first steps toward converting human cattle into reasoning men." To Marsh, the eight-hour campaign was a continuation in the North of the revolutionary enterprise begun during the war.[41]

Nonetheless, Cameron and many of the labor reformers had problems with craftsmen, artisan entrepreneurs, and small manufacturers—the *Republican's* core constituency. And the main problem remained free trade. The issue might resonate with workers in the huge railroad car shops, because the shops could hold their own in competitive battles with imports. But workers in smaller enterprises were not so confident. German workers in P. W. Gates's machine shop had, in fact, argued in the press with Cameron about free trade versus protection, advocating the latter to protect firms like the Eagle Works and their skilled jobs. They were furious that Cameron accused them of being subservient to a tyrannical boss. What was more, many of them owned stock in the company through Gates's profit-sharing plan, and they considered Gates to be a worker like themselves. That is why, despite an accusation by Cameron to the contrary, the company accepted trade unions, as long as they kept narrowly to the issue of wages. These protectionist workers defended firms like Gates's against unfair foreign competition based on cheap and exploited labor, much of it coming, by the way, from England, the birthplace of Cameron and many of his friends.[42]

To define their relationships with workers, men like Gates used a tradition of paternalism that, according to Philip Scranton, emerged from the face-to-face contact between owners and workers in modest-size firms utilizing high proportions of skilled labor. With over four hundred workers organized in eleven departments, Gates's versatile machine shop demonstrated that such firms were not necessarily small and antiquated. Gates had numerous counterparts among the startling number of German manufacturing entrepreneurs who had recently attained an economic foothold in the Chicago industrial boom during the war (see table 2, chap. 1). These German artisan entrepreneurs were in the forefront of protectionist organizations in Chicago, working together with Charles Henry Dana and manufacturers like Gates. The eight-hour issue was so divisive because it made men like Gates and his workers choose between their cultural identity as producers and their emerging interests as employers and workers under capitalism. While their cultural identity told them they might work cooperatively for their mutual advantage, their emerging interests as capitalists and workers pushed them to organize among themselves for mutual protection, just as Gates had in 1863 when he founded an organization of Chicago's machine-shop and foundry owners to counter the initiatives of new unions.[43]

Seth Paine, a Yankee master mechanic employed by Gates, acted out the dilemmas of this constituency. Born in New Hampshire, Paine migrated to Chicago early enough to attend the Industrial Congress in 1850. He was active in the Mechanics Institute and numerous reform causes. He was a strong advocate of the interests of manufacturers, so much so that he was a leader among Chicagoans in the movement to found the National Association of Manufacturers. But he also supported the eight-hour law, speaking in its favor at a large meeting of workingmen chaired by Governor Oglesby. Paine was angered by the fact that "the pulpits, and every daily press in this city but the *Republican*, [are] struck worse than dumb at this critical moment." In a letter to the *Tribune,* Paine argued that eight hours' work with ten hours' pay was possible if it was combined with joint-stock cooperation, similar to that advocated by the *Republican.* Cooperation would give employees a proprietary stake in the firm and therefore induce them to work harder and produce more. According to Paine, cooperation would ultimately lead to "universal brotherhood," but it would also do away with unions and give Chicago the manufacturing lead in the nation.[44]

Up to the eve of the strike, Paine met secretly with Gates to support just such a course, apparently arguing that cooperation would knock the props out of the eight-hour movement. He made the same appeal to Horace White at the *Tribune* offices. Among manufacturers like Gates who had profit-sharing plans, this approach must have struck a responsive chord. But as it turned out, it was incapable of stemming the eight-hour tide. The failure of the Radical Republican position as articulated by the *Republican* was symbolized by Paine's fate. Toward the end of the strike, Paine resigned from his position at Eagle Works, declaring that Gates's scheme of profit-sharing cooperation was a "humbug."[45] The eight-hour strike had forced a class division through the sector of the Chicago manufacturing economy led by artisan entrepreneurs. It also threw into question the efforts of Chicago's Radical Republicans to use their free-labor ideology to unite their coalition behind a cooperative vision of society.

THE EIGHT-HOUR STRIKE OF MAY 1867

As the day of reckoning approached on May 1, the day the state law went into effect, the eight-hour question moved from debate to mobilization as the various contenders organized and staked out their plans of action. While leaders of the eight-hour movement organized a huge parade to inaugurate the new system, the reaction of Chicago's workers to their appeals was profoundly shaped by loopholes in the eight-hour law. The most important loophole was that the law applied to all firms, except "where there is no special contract or agreement to the contrary." In other words, any company could set up another arrangement. In addition, the law applied to non-farmworkers earning wages by the day, not to those paid by the piece or employed by the week, month, or year. The McCormick Reaper Works was not a center of strike activity, for example, because most of its workers were paid by the piece, indicating in this period that they probably maintained a status as semi-independent craft workers. Similarly, the powerful printers, who were paid by the "em," refused to endorse eight hours and did not participate in the May 1 parade or subsequent strike, a reversal from their traditional leading role in the Chicago labor movement. The law also did not apply to the mass of female garment workers who were paid by the piece, as were many boot and shoe workers, bookbinders, harness and saddle makers, and the most skilled furniture workers. The brewers and gasworkers, paid by the month, also did not participate in the movement. The furniture and brewery workers constituted critical elements of the German workforce employed in sectors of the Chicago manufacturing economy dominated by German-owned firms. In general, the more workers engaged in casual day labor or who practiced traditional craft methods, the less likely the law applied to them. The law was more likely to apply to both skilled and unskilled workers using machinery in the most advanced sectors of the economy, such as the planing mills, machine shops, foundries, and railroad car works. The varied impact of the eight-hour law reflected the uneven development of wage labor in the Chicago economy.[46]

The employers in these advanced sectors organized in opposition, particularly those from firms owned by local merchant capitalists or corporations based outside the city. These owners accepted wage labor as a natural condition, and they did not feel themselves a part of the "web of 'reciprocal obligation'" that was supposed to link all members of a craft. Most of the city's large manufacturers—the railroad car shops, planing mills, tanneries, and rolling mills—notified their employees that they would refuse to accede to eight hours under any circumstances. The railroads went a step further by reducing the hourly pay of their men by 10 percent while still demanding ten hours of labor. The railroads also threatened to move their car shops to Indiana if the eight-hour law were enforced.[47]

Chicago's artisan entrepreneurs were more ambivalent. After asserting that employers and employees had the same interests, R. T. Crane, one of the city's largest metal fabricators and an associate of P. W. Gates, gave a speech to his workers on April 30 opposing the eight-hour workday for subjecting him to ruinous competition from other cities. Crane asked his men to think the matter over. Gates posted a notice that the decision was up to his employees, but if they chose eight hours he would have to cut back on employment or perhaps shut down. On May 1, most of the employers in the West Side metal-fabrication district tried to proceed as usual under the "old system." The numerous small employers in the building trades were more accommodating, for they were largely immune from the pressures of intercity competition that so threatened the manufacturers.[48]

The political establishment of the city and state was even more ambivalent than the artisan entrepreneurs and thus sent additional contradictory messages. On May 1, the state's leading Republican officeholders—including Governor Oglesby, Attorney General Robert G. Ingersoll, and Representative Henry M. Shephard—scheduled a mass meeting of Chicago workingmen to call for obedience to the law by employers and for restraint on the part of workers in trying to enforce it. For Republican politicians, the purpose of the gathering was to circumvent "a bloody battleground" over the issue. This was a pious gesture, since the Republican Party had been instrumental in passing a law instituting profound social and economic change, which nonetheless lacked any governmental means of enforcement. The lack of an enforcement mechanism was actually in keeping with almost universal popular attitudes about state intervention in society. Typical of their era, according to David Montgomery, "workingmen demanded 'just laws.' They never requested, or even dreamed of, the establishment of bureaucratic agencies to administer such laws." Eight-hour reformers believed that passage of the law would, by itself, confer legitimacy and prestige on the movement and therefore deter employers from resisting it and encourage workers to demand it.[49]

The sense of legitimacy that workers drew from the law was as important as the gaping loopholes in its wording. The law's "spirit" combined with the lack of enforcement mechanism encouraged workers to unite and act. Minus its loopholes, the critical section of the law read, "eight hours of labor, between the rising and the setting of the sun, in all mechanical trades, arts, and employments, and other cases of labor and services by the day . . . shall constitute and be a legal day's work." This mainstream sanction for change made it clear that American politics was still revolutionized by the Civil War crisis, which was transforming the North at the same time that the federal government used its military powers to reconstruct the South. The mainstream origins of the eight-hour movement's sense of legitimacy increased the moral assertiveness of Chicago workers as they tried to get what the legislature had said was theirs.[50]

As the first step in enforcing the law, the Trades Assembly planned a mass demonstration for May 1. It was a clear, mild day in Chicago whose brilliance was marred only by clouds of dust raised by people teeming through the streets. The *Tribune* estimated that the parade was somewhat over a mile long and took about three-quarters of an hour to pass any one point. So many men were in the parade that the day was an undeclared holiday. The exhausting route of the march demonstrated visually the central purpose of the parade: to show the city that the eight-hour men were an expression of the majority will (map 3).[51]

The speeches to the assembled marchers at the conclusion of the parade revealed the same combination of class perceptions and ethnic culture sustaining labor's political independence. Richard Trevellick asked, "what was the reason that from all the nationalities of Europe people stood before him. Was it because Irishmen had forgotten their native land? Never, never. French and German citizens, had they forgotten their native land? No, nor had the sons of Scotland. They were here because their own lands denied them their rights. . . . What has disfranchised the millions of Europe? The very power that is now trying to oppose laboring men." Several speakers linked labor's current antagonists to the recent Civil War. Trevellick asked, "Who conquered the late rebellion? Was it the man who fought against them today? [Cries of 'No.'] . . . It was the laborer that had defended the country through war, and created her power through peace. Labor was the creative power of wealth." Trevellick and other speakers drew the conclusion that labor should therefore control wealth. A. J. Kuykendall, a U.S. congressman from downstate Illinois, thought that "if all the wealth is produced by labor it ought to be subservient to labor, otherwise labor is as completely the slave as the African ever was.

We must not stop with freeing the African and allow ourselves to be slaves." The eight-hour workday was the next step in labor's fight for emancipation. In his speech, Mayor Rice identified himself as a friend of the laboring men but appealed to them to try to reach a compromise with capital, if possible.[52]

Although organized skilled workers formed the bulk of the audience, the eight-hour issue had wider appeal, especially to all who worked in mechanized plants. The mechanization that made the eight-hour workday so urgent had, in fact, affected the work of some lake port laborers more decisively than even the skilled workers in the railroad car shops. Moving from job to job, port laborers were accustomed to working in gangs doing seasonal labor. Depending on the time of year, they moved from unloading ships to wielding knives and scrapers in the meatpacking industry or tending power-driven machines in the planing mills. Shipping, meatpacking, and lumber milling all shut down at various seasons during the year, and all three were concentrated along the South Branch of the Chicago River (map 3). Like seaport laborers in the East, workers in these industries had traditions of forming political crowds to enforce their perception of the will of the community. These workers made the first dramatic efforts to enforce the eight-hour law.[53]

The planing mills on the West Side were the first targets of the crowds of strikers, particularly those in or near the mammoth Red Mill on the Near West Side, which housed six firms employing a total of three hundred to four hundred men. In the early-morning hours of May 2, according to the *Times,* "a body of bad men" assembled to "enforce by intimidation or by violence, the observance of the eight-hour system. A large number of these men, armed with clubs, brick bats, stones, and a few pistols, commenced its operations in the West division of the city, causing shops where ten hour men were at work to be closed, either by threatening violence to the laborers, or forcibly ejecting them. In the meantime, a kind of committee of about 200 men, divided themselves into small squads of from half a dozen to 30 or 40, and went from shop to shop warning the workmen to lay down their tools or they would be summarily dealt with." Such "squads" shut down tanneries, lumber yards, planing mills, and railroad freight depots as they moved south, particularly along Canal Street between Madison and Twelfth. There "groups of men were early seen on almost every corner, engaged in earnest and sometimes angry discussion. At one time near the corner of Canal and Twelfth Streets at least one thousand men were thus assembled." Among those men were probably the 250 employees of the huge Palmer, Fuller and Company sash and blind manufactory, located on that corner. They had left en masse when management rejected their proposal to work eight hours for nine hours' pay. They

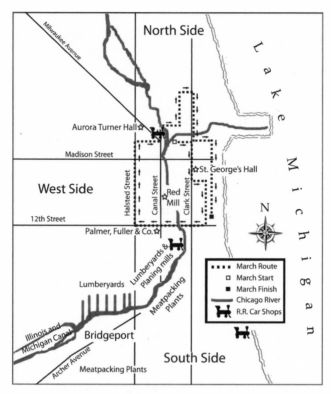

Map 3. The eight-hour strike of 1867. Redrawn from *Atlas of Whiteside Co. and the State of Illinois to Which Is Added an Atlas of the United States, Maps of the Hemispheres, &c., &c., &c.* (Chicago: Warner and Beers, 1872), 13.

became part of the "mob which subsequently ruled for a brief period that part of the city."[54]

Bridgeport and the area north of it along the South Branch of the Chicago River formed the other main locus for the strike of the unskilled. Here brickyards, coal yards, lumberyards, planing mills, and docks lined the South Branch as it swung west at Halsted Street. The area to the north had developed after A. G. Throop built his docks during the depression of 1857–58, aided by his distribution of building lots as payment to his unskilled workers. Bridgeport had been settled by Irish and German laborers who had dug the Illinois-Michigan Canal and had bought cheap land located at the canal's terminus. In 1867, the *Republican* described Bridgeport as a "thoroughly despised and neglected ward" without paved streets or sewers. On May 2, Bridgeport was "in the hands of the mob," according to the *Tribune*. The men "resorted to saloons" and were "excitable and obstinate." Crowds of such men attempted to close up whole manufacturing districts in and around their neighborhoods. One crowd leader told a reporter that in the future they would visit every business twice a day at 8 A.M. and at 5 P.M. to ensure that the eight-hour law was being followed.[55]

The crowd actions continued, despite hysterical headlines in the newspapers, calls for help from manufacturers, and the swearing in of 160 special police officers. On May 3, the second day of the strike, the *Tribune* described the "little knots of men" gathering all over Bridgeport: "There were few Americans among them, the Irish element predominating, mixed in with the German." That was a roughly accurate description of the mixed ethnic composition of those arrested during the disturbances as well as of the immigrant working-class districts from which the crowds arose. The *Tribune* was also insightful about the age and work performed by the participants in the crowds, when it noted "it is well known that numerous boys are employed [in the planing mills] to attend to the various processes and machines, it being found that in the majority of cases a boy can tend a machine or put work together almost as well as a man, and, of course at lesser wages. These composed the body of the mob." In the planing mill districts, the workers most directly affected by mechanization had taken the eight-hour issue into the streets. And they tended to be young and foreign-born, primarily German and Irish, although with some Bohemians as well. The crowds were an interethnic labor movement of their own, in which class temporarily overshadowed ethnic divisions as immigrant workers pursued a common goal of enforcing the eight-hour law.[56]

Determined to carry out their plan of twice-daily visits, about two hundred to three hundred Bridgeport men and boys visited and closed the planing mills and packinghouses along Archer Avenue on the way toward Halsted Street. But before they entered the lumber district, police with revolvers drawn dispersed them. Another South Side crowd moved on a planing mill where it met police resistance. These and other actions of the police seem to have surprised the rioters, who trusted in the efficacy of the new law and the public statements of support from Republican leaders. According to one reporter, some crowd members had wanted to petition the governor to have police drive off men working longer than eight hours. Others felt that, if arrested trying to enforce the law, the governor would pardon them.[57]

A glance at the city's press reporting on that day's events would have convinced the eight-hour crowds that Chicago's established powers did not endorse their resort to popular justice in enforcing the eight-hour law. Both the *Tribune* and the *Times* loudly condemned the violence and called for stronger action from the mayor and police force. Thinking that the city faced a revolutionary movement, the *Times* called for the use of artillery against the mob and threatened vigilante action if the mayor and police force continued to be sympathetic to the rioters. The *Times,* of course, sought as much partisan advantage as could be gained by the disorder under a Republican administration.[58]

On the other hand, while condemning the violence, the *Republican* and the *Workingman's Advocate* continued to support the strike. The *Illinois Staats-Zeitung* took the same position. These three papers were really taking the side of skilled workmen who sought to dissociate themselves from the rioters in order to legitimate their own strike. After five days and faced with more resolute police action, the crowds of unskilled workers dissolved back into the immigrant working-class communities along the South Branch from which they had arisen. The participants in the crowds constituted the kernel of the city's rapidly expanding industrial proletariat. In the 1870s, they would again form crowds that would shake the city even more than in 1867.[59]

While the crowds of striking laborers had roamed for three days, and vanished in five, the strike of the skilled lasted over a month. The politics of the crowd were succeeded by the politics of the public sphere, as committees of skilled workers sought to enforce the eight-hour law by changing public opinion in the city as well as the opinions of workers not supporting the strike. Metalworkers formed the core of the organized skilled strikers: machinists, blacksmiths, boilermakers, and iron molders. These were craftsmen whose unions had been forerunners in the eight-hour agitation during the Civil War. Men in these crafts worked in the railroad car shops as well as in foundries, machine shops, stove and boiler works, and other metal-fabricating plants. Building tradesmen, particularly stonecutters and skilled woodworkers, stood next to the metalworkers as stalwarts of the eight-hour movement. The woodworkers labored in building construction, the car shops, sash and door factories, and furniture plants. Nonetheless, the metalworkers, particularly those in the railroad car shops, made up the strike's core constituency, just as they had formed the largest component of the parade on May 1.

Reflecting this constituency, the leadership of the strike represented the Anglo American, Irish, and German coalition that had led the organization of the Chicago labor movement since 1864. The ethnic makeup of the strike's leadership was reflected in the two most frequently used meeting halls during the strike: St. George's Hall in the city center and the Aurora Turner Hall in the vicinity of the car shops on the North and West Sides. The St. George's Society was a British fraternal and friendly organization that, among other things, sponsored annual dinners and balls to celebrate their British heritage. The German Turners had been part of German labor affairs in Chicago since the 1850s, and the Aurora Turners were the most politically radical of the Chicago Turner organizations.[60]

Among the strike's leaders, British metalworkers stood out. Machinists, in turn, were prominent amid the British metal craftsmen, offering intellectual, moral, and organizational leadership. At least two of the most active strike leaders in the city—John Hayes, who chaired the largest citywide meeting of machinists and railroad men, and Jabez Ramsbottom, secretary of the Central Executive Committee—were members of the Chicago branch of the Amalgamated Society of Engineers. The Amalgamated Society was the strongest union in Britain at the time and the first and most influential of the New Model Unions, which pioneered high dues, substantial benefits, and centralized organization. Such unions set examples on both sides of the Atlantic. In Great Britain during the 1840s and 1850s, the Amalgamated Society and its predecessors had promoted a shorter workday, free trade, and cooperative schemes for both the production and distribution of goods—goals similar to those pursued by labor reformers in Chicago since the 1850s. The Amalgamated Society in Great Britain also proved adept at promoting these goals in alliance with Christian socialists and other middle-class labor reformers, just as the eight-hour men in Chicago formed a coalition with American labor reformers and elements of the Republican Party. Notably, the British society was an "amalgamation" of several types of metal craftsmen—especially machine builders, molders, and smiths—who were also prominent in Chicago's eight-hour agitation.[61]

Whether formally involved in the Amalgamated Society of Engineers or not, British metal craftsmen in Chicago participated in transnational networks of communication for labor-reform ideas. Andrew Cameron and Richard Trevellick were not alone as eight-hour agitators, as British immigrants, or as evangelical Christians. One of their most articulate compatriots was Welsh-born William D. Taylor of the Illinois Central car shops, an older man whose experiences dated back to the ten-hour movement in the 1830s. Addressing a meeting of "railroad employees and other workers" at St. George's Hall, Taylor read a "lengthy extract" from the English artisan philosopher William Cobbett on the duty of the workingmen to uphold "industry, sobriety and unity." Cobbett had been a hero of Anglo American labor reform from its origins in the early nineteenth century. In the same speech, Taylor said that "John Bright, in England, is fighting for us, and workingmen will soon rule England, as they will this country." These British craftsmen mixed well with Americans such as Seth Paine, the Yankee machinist.[62]

Drawing on their own traditions, the German forty-eighters leading the German element in the Chicago labor movement spoke a similar transnational political language, although they had difficulties with the evangelical piety of the Anglo Americans. A continental forty-eighter, Eduard Schläger, also spoke at the meetings of railroad strikers. Schläger tried to translate evangelical revivalism into secular political terms. To a gathering at St. George's Hall, Schläger stated that "this was a grand revival. He was glad that the workingmen of this city were able to carry on a revival which was of far more importance than any revival carried on by the Methodists and Baptists or any other sect." The next day at the Aurora Turner Hall, Schläger "wanted the workmen to take an enlarged view of their eight-hour movement. . . . It was essentially a revolutionary movement intended to break down the old basis of rank, power, and prerogative which capital, for centuries past had endeavored, and partly succeeded, to establish and force upon the people. The time had come when the workingmen of this nation should form a great liberal party in the interests of a common humanity." Some of his fellow speakers were, in turn, uncomfortable with him because of his talk of revolution and political parties; Mr. Jones, who followed Schläger at St. George's Hall, said workers should keep aloof from "dangerous" political and religious theories.[63]

When Schläger and the Anglo American leaders of the strike addressed these meetings at Aurora Turner Hall and St. George's Hall, the strike of the skilled was still in full swing a week and a half after May 1. The striking craftsmen held regular meetings, issued manifestos, argued with opponents through the press, and organized support committees. Such organizational techniques had become part of the cultural resources available to artisans throughout the transatlantic world since the Revolutionary era, when they struggled to organize popular unrest into sustained political movements. All these activities had two audiences—the strikers and the public—both of which the leaders hoped to use to influence the employers. The first priority was to sustain the solidarity of the strikers. In reaction to crowd violence early in the strike, the Central Executive Committee authorized the formation of "moral suasion" or "vigilance" committees to enforce discipline. Groups of strikers would visit workers on the job and try to argue them into joining the walkout, or they would visit reluctant strikers in their homes to shore up their resolve. These committees carried the solidarities of the workplace outside the plant into the streets and neighborhoods. They also had special appeal to evangelical workmen who were used to using argument, agitation, and interpersonal pressure—"moral suasion"—to win converts and stiffen the backbone of backsliders during revivals. Both the term *moral suasion* and its techniques dated from the Second Great Awakening and were used by the immediate abolitionists in the 1830s. The use of moral suasion by the eight-hour strikers exemplified both the power of abolition as a model for change and the politicization of American life by the Civil War crisis.[64]

On May 1, the Trades Assembly showed its concern with public opinion when it issued its resolutions on the relation of wages and shorter hours: "*Resolved.* That the question of wages is of secondary importance and that we have never proposed to demand ten hours' pay for eight hours' work, or any other sum which would not be *equitable.*" The link between shorter hours and wages had been one of the most hotly contested issues of the monthlong April debate about eight hours. Employers regularly claimed that shortening the working day was a strike for more pay wrapped in reform rhetoric. Andrew Cameron and the Trades Assembly wanted to disengage the two issues and let individual trades resolve the wage rate separately. With its resolution on wages, the Trades Assembly was trying to influence public opinion, just as the eight-hour law itself was designed to give the reform legitimacy before the public by giving it the sanction of the law. Jonathan Fincher had advocated this tactic during the Civil War when he called for changing public "sentiment" rather than organizing a political party. This same goal of influencing public opinion made the press coverage of the strike such a vital and volatile issue. So obnoxious did the striking skilled workers find most reporting that they began excluding reporters from the *Tribune* and *Times* from their meetings, welcoming only the reporter of the *Republican.*[65]

The eight-hour men perceived themselves as part of a great nineteenth-century popular movement that had just abolished slavery. This revolutionary change had begun with the transformation of public opinion. The public had now expressed itself on the eight-hour question through the law passed by the Illinois legislature. The eight-hour movement was more than a labor issue, and its advocates felt that they were still living amid the political and cultural momentum created by the Civil War. In England, the Liberal politician John Bright drew similar energy and lessons from the American Civil War. In 1866, he "attributed 'the revival of Reform agitation to the result of the American War. Republicanism is now looking up in the world.'"[66]

For Chicago's workers, the "revival of Reform" lasted until June 1867 when the eight-hour strike was defeated. The experience in Chicago anticipated the shift in the national mood that came with Ulysses S. Grant's victory in the presidential election of 1868 and the subsequent retrenchment in the Republican Party. By mid-June, even the machinists in the railroad car shops had given up. The only trades that had achieved the eight-hour workday were in the construction industry, and here the achievement could not be sustained.[67] The millennial mood of the time had shaped the eight-hour movement by making profound change seem within reach and by fostering—through sheer momentum and hope—the cooperation of disparate groups, from dockworkers to Radical Republicans, from pious British evangelical Christians to free-thinking German forty-eighters. When defeat altered the climate of opinion, the disparate elements separated and went in different directions. For Chicago workers, the results were profound as labor reform lost prestige and new leaders emerged with fundamentally different perspectives and ideas.

Tarnished by the strike's defeat, Chicago's labor reformers lost the ability to speak for the city's working people, who in turn lost their connections to the antebellum evangelical reform tradition. Led by Andrew Cameron, speaking through his *Workingman's Advocate,* and based in the Trades Assembly, labor reformers had been the voice of organized Chicago labor since 1864. Labor reformers did not disappear, and their national organization, the National Labor Union, even met in Chicago within two months after the end of the eight-hour strike. Cameron assumed a prominent role in this national organization and even attended international congresses in its name. But in Chicago, labor reformers no longer commanded the institutional base and allegiance they had formerly. The Trades Assembly even disbanded in 1870. Cameron and his paper continued into the 1870s, but he spoke only for one relatively small labor faction.

As the prestige and power of labor reformers shrank, so did the unusual influence of British skilled workers as well as the evangelical Protestant rhetoric they used to articulate labor's cause. Never again would the British exercise so decisive a leadership role in the Chicago labor movement. Contributing to this shift in ethnic leadership of labor was the decline in significance of the railroad car shops, where so many British metalworkers had labored. The railroads moved some of the shops out of the city and became more repressive toward labor within them, wherever they were located.[68] At the same time, other expanding industries made the shops a smaller part of the constellation of manufacturing enterprise in the city. Also weakening British influence was their lack of a strong base of ethnic community institutions rooted in Chicago neighborhoods. There simply were not enough British immigrants to provide this institutional cultural base outside the organizations of the labor movement.

When labor reform and its Anglo American leaders shrank in significance, the Irish and Germans took over the leadership of working-class institutions in Chicago. Their growing prominence in labor circles drew upon the increasing institutional and political power of their communities in the city. Irish entrepreneurs, many of them former craftsmen, asserted themselves in the construction, building materials, carriage and wagon, and alcoholic beverage industries (see table 2, chap. 1; table 4, chap. 2). The construction industry was characterized by a dense network of subcontracting to often ephemeral small firms, many of them started by the large number of skilled Irish workers in the industry's workforce. The rise of the Irish in these industries was analogous, though on a reduced scale, to the German rise in the whole Chicago manufacturing economy. It also had some of the same effects, including encouraging Irish assertiveness in politics. Several of these industries where the Irish advanced, both as entrepreneurs and as workers, involved constant contact with the local government, especially alcoholic beverages and construction. Irish political power was an economic asset, not just in dealing with fees, fines, and licenses but also in raising capital through public contracts.[69]

Irish workers sustained and profited from the Irish rise in Chicago business and politics during the 1860s. Whether skilled or unskilled, they drew strength from their high concentration in construction and in metal production and fabrication, expanding sectors of the manufacturing economy, while the Germans were dispersed more widely and often in declining traditional crafts (table 5). Possessing fewer skills to begin with, the Irish moved into expanding sectors of the economy and rose within them, often to skilled status, and these sectors tended to pay more and offer more regular work. The Irish rise in the labor movement grew out of this achievement of Irish workers.[70]

Cultural and political developments also fostered the exercise of Irish influence in labor circles after the eight-hour strike. The integration of the Irish into the local labor leadership was aided by the Irish experiences in the Civil War, the Fenian nationalist movement, and, especially for Chicago, the eight-hour agitation. According to David Montgomery, when these experiences mixed with that of trade unionism, they formed the ingredients of a "working-class consciousness, which was devoted not to success, but to sober and deliberate

Eight-Hour Day and the Legitimacy of Wage Labor 111

Table 5. Male Skilled Workers by Nationality and Selected Industry Groups: Chicago 1860

Industry	American	British	Irish	German	Other
Construction	31.3	44.4	39.1	29.3	26.6
Metal	19.9	28.9	22.5	12.8	17.7
Apparel	2.8	6.7	12.6	18.7	20.3
Wood	8.5	1.1	4.6	10.3	7.6
Food	7.4	8.9	4.0	8.1	6.3
Transportation	9.7	1.1	2.0	0	1.3
Building Materials	1.1	0	6.6	2.9	2.5
Printing	6.8	1.1	0	2.2	2.5
Tobacco	1.7	2.2	0	2.9	1.3
Wagons	0	1.1	1.3	2.2	2.5
Leather	0.6	0	0.7	2.2	1.3
Liquor	0.6	0	0.7	1.1	0
Other	9.6	4.5	5.9	7.3	10.1
	100	100	100	100	100
% All Male Skilled Workers	22.9	11.7	19.7	35.5	10.2

Source: Sample of the 1860 federal manuscript manufacturing census for Chicago; N = 767.
Note: Industry groups are listed by the proportion of all skilled workers that they employed.

group self-help." Such a consciousness was indispensable for Irish participation in unions whose constituencies reached beyond Irish ethnic lines and neighborhood institutions. Chicago was a showcase of this Irish labor initiative. Typically Democrats, Chicago's Irish labor leaders were less inclined to follow independent political initiatives, such as that proposed by labor reformers in the National Labor Union. The Irish assertiveness in labor evident in the late 1860s started a trend that put Irishmen at the center of American labor leadership by the 1880s.[71]

New and more assertive German labor leaders arose in Chicago at the same time, similarly drawing upon the rising economic and political power of their communities in the city. As noted in chapter 1, Chicago's German manufacturers profited so much from the economic boom of the 1860s that they outnumbered their native-born counterparts in 1870, although their firms were smaller (see table 2, chap. 1). Germans dominated several sectors of the Chicago economy, including furniture making and brewing. German economic power also meant that there were enough German workers in some industries to make labor organizing in the German language both feasible and advantageous. Substantially increased German immigration to the city after the Civil War added to the number of German workers while importing a new group of German labor leaders with different ideas about society and politics than those of the forty-eighter generation. Soon after the failure of the eight-hour strike, German workers, disgruntled with Anglo American labor reform, turned to their countrymen for leadership. The shabby treatment of Eduard Schläger and the Arbeiterverein at the convention of the National Labor Union in Chicago soon after the 1867 strike did not help the reputation of labor reform among Germans. Within two years of the eight-hour strike, Chicago had its own German labor movement, complete with a trades assembly and labor newspaper, which was edited by a Lassallean socialist, rather than a forty-eighter.[72]

The transformation of Chicago labor's leadership meant that Irish and Germans were among the key players in interpreting the emergence of capitalism to Chicago's workers at the beginning of the Gilded Age. Immigrants had to deal with central issues such as the new class lines in the city, state intervention in the economy, the control of large-scale enterprise, and the legitimacy of wage labor. The immediacy and significance of all these issues were heightened by labor's experience with the eight-hour movement. One notable example was how the eight-hour strike changed the meaning of cooperation as class lines cut through the critical constituency of producers, the modest-size manufacturers and craftsmen who had figured so prominently in the eight-hour debate. This was the same constituency that provided a recruiting ground for both the Radical Republicans and labor reform. The strike forced a new recognition among artisan entrepreneurs that they were capitalist employers first of all, and they redefined cooperation to meet their needs as employers and subverted labor unions. As was so often the case, P. W. Gates and R. T. Crane were leaders among their fellow manufacturers.

In a meeting during the strike with fifty of his loyal workers, Gates proposed an enhanced profit-sharing venture. Since 1862, some of his workers had owned shares in Eagle Works, although Gates was still the single largest stockholder, but now he proposed to give each workman 5 percent of the wages he earned as a bonus in the form of stock. Three days later, thirty-three of one hundred employees decided to participate, while the rest contemplated joining. The German employees who had defended Gates and his workers against the *Workingman's Advocate* in the protection versus free trade debate were likely candidates for this profit-sharing program. Similarly to Gates, Crane initiated an ambitious and well-publicized profit-sharing scheme at his Northwestern Manufacturing Company. On May 25, as the strike was winding down, Crane proposed that all profits above 10 percent return on capital be divided into two equal parts, with one to be set aside for loyal employees selected by the company's executive officers and foremen. The chosen workers would receive the profits as part of their wages, although they could also invest these profits in the company's stock. In addition to this, they would receive time and a half for overtime past ten hours, double time for Sunday work, and a guarantee of no layoffs due to lack of business. An elected committee of workers would be allowed to examine the company's books. In return, workers participating in the plan agreed to labor ten hours, to work on two lathes or planers if asked to, and not to belong to any trade union or be influenced by them. Crane also asked his employees to increase their efforts at work and to be sober and industrious. Altogether, two-thirds of Crane's 140 employees were invited to join the plan. Horace White of the *Tribune* cheered Crane's profit-sharing plan because it promised to eliminate unions and increase productivity.[73]

The popularity of profit sharing among manufacturers was not limited to Gates and Crane. On May 11, the *Tribune* reported that "a good many employers in different parts of the city are canvassing the subject with their men, and striving to arrive at some method of co-operation which will place them outside of the Trades Unions, and give to every man employed an interest in the establishment with which he is connected." Class conflict in the strike had clarified the previously ambiguous meaning of the term *cooperation*. Before the strike, artisan entrepreneurs saw profit sharing as a means of preserving an older tie of sympathy with their workers based on common interest and craft heritage. After the strike, they viewed cooperation as a means of containing unions, reconciling their employees to their status as permanent wage earners, and building a stable and loyal workforce among the skilled. The artisan entrepreneurs' redefinition of cooperation had the same goals as similar earlier efforts to "reform" workers' behavior in manufacturing cities in the East. By changing the culture and politics of Chicago's artisan entrepreneurs, the eight-hour strike contributed to the formation of the Gilded Age bourgeoisie in Chicago, pushing its development ahead of businessmen in a city like Cincinnati. During this era, Cincinnati's employers did not face a comparable political challenge from labor, and the formative social conflict of the Gilded Age—the Courthouse Riot of 1884—did not involve working-class organizations.[74]

Some former strikers sharply rejected the artisan entrepreneurs' version of cooperation as profit sharing, formulating instead a more radical version of producers' cooperation that would protect them from becoming permanent wageworkers as well as give them control of the new large-scale means of production. The change was evident in a series of reports and letters in the *Republican*. E. S. Warner offered a plan to metalworkers to begin a cooperative by buying out the Chicago Steam Works. The reformer John

Orvis, also in the *Republican,* attacked various arguments for the equality and interdependence of labor and capital. He proposed that no dividend be issued to capital and that all profits be divided among the workers and managers proportional to wages and salaries. Editorially, the *Republican* continued to support producers' cooperation, reviewing, for example, the nature and success of such endeavors in Europe and encouraging American workers to build cooperative enterprises.[75]

Union carpenters formed their own cooperative and commenced work on two buildings. The German Masons Mutual Benefit Society, which had existed for many years in the city, formed a cooperative that they viewed as the solution to the labor question. Metalworkers embraced cooperation most fervently. Like their fellows in other cities, iron molders established a foundry with an anticipated capital of $35,000, more than one-half of which was immediately subscribed. No owners were to be allowed more than ten shares. German machinists began a machine shop capitalized at $13,000. They invited fellow machinists with a capital of $100 to $1,000 to take part as a way of profitably investing their savings and guaranteeing themselves work. Striking machinists from Crane's plant also started a cooperative called the Union Manufacturing Company, located a block away from Crane's profit-sharing enterprise. On May 31, the *Republican* concluded that workers were no longer viewing cooperatives as utopian schemes but as realistic alternatives to working for wages.[76]

These cooperatives failed, most of them within a few years, and all of them when the depression of the mid-1870s struck the Chicago economy. Although cooperation as an ideal survived to become an ingredient in the social vision of subsequent protest movements, it did not provide Chicago workers with a viable alternative to wage labor or a route to self-employment. Neither did the eight-hour movement. Cooperation as profit sharing, the form defined by Gates and Crane, proved more in tune with the capitalist future of the city, in part because it accepted and reinforced the permanency of wage labor. Chicago's workers had to decide for themselves whether wage labor was legitimate and then, if it was, decide how to make the wages system into a means for their own liberation. This was the task of a whole generation, not that of any individual thinker or labor leader. At this juncture in the late 1860s, it was only clear that labor reformers and the transnational culture of social republicanism to which they belonged rejected the legitimacy of the "wages system" and, as a consequence, marginalized themselves in addressing the central questions facing most workers. As a consequence, Andrew Cameron faded as an intellectual leader of Chicago labor. By the late 1870s, Ira Steward's ideas, which accepted wage labor and sought to leverage it for transformative change, had become dominant in the city's labor circles.[77]

Samuel Gompers recognized this transition when he described Cameron and his fellows: "A very distinct type of American workingman was that to which Alexander Toup, then of New York, A. C. Cameron of Chicago, Martin A. Foran of Cleveland, Thompson Murch of Maine, and William H. Sylvis of Troy belonged. There was an intellectual quality that kept them from feeling the barriers of a wage-earning class. They looked at industrial problems from the point of view of American citizens and turned instinctively to political activity for reform." In contrast, the new leaders of Chicago labor were able to feel "the barriers of a wage-earning class," and they "looked at industrial problems from the point of view" of immigrant workers, who may or may not have been American citizens.[78]

4 Chicago's Immigrant Working Class and the Rise of Urban Populism, 1867–73

IN JANUARY 1872—THREE MONTHS after the Great Fire—Anton Hesing, Chicago's German political boss, organized a protest against the city government's effort to ban new wooden housing in the city as a fire control measure. The protesters thought that the added expense of brick housing would prevent the city's workers from building their own homes, and they marched on city hall to make their point publicly. The crowd got disruptive, creating a sensation in the English-language press, which called for a grand jury investigation.

Hesing and his allies portrayed themselves as representing the "real" working people of Chicago. He clarified this term in his arguments in defense of the crowd: "For he is no genuine American (irrespective of where he may be from) who would like to depress our working classes to the level of European proletarians by robbing them of the possibility of living under their own roof. To a large extent the rapid growth of Chicago is owed to the ease with which the industrious worker here can become an independent property owner. . . . For luckily in our great West the population is still equivalent in wealth and our energetic workers are not poverty-stricken proletarians, who are dependent on the mercy of capital, rather they are the creators of capital."[1]

For Hesing, the fight against the "fire limits" was a battle against the proletarianization of Chicago's workers, whose distinctive independent status was based on the ownership of real property and a house. He fought to preserve a particular kind of working class, loyal to its Old World traditions but also to Chicago and America, independent of large-scale capital, and free of alien radicalism, particularly socialism. In leading the movement against the fire limits, Hesing became the chief architect of urban populism in the city.

Hesing's march was an important factor in creating a period of intense political instability in Chicago running from the end of the Civil War through the 1870s. With labor reform marginalized, urban populism helped politicize the city's immigrant skilled workers and lower middle class. At the same time, the labor and socialist movements brought unskilled and semiskilled workers into the public sphere—the very proletarians who did not fit into Hesing's vision of the Chicago working class. As national partisan divisions faded in importance, these working-class political initiatives—whether led by urban populists, socialists, trade unionists, or others—posed new threats to the established parties, contributing to the party factionalism, electoral fluidity, reform initiatives, and political creativity of the era.[2]

Political turmoil was, of course, not limited to the local level during the Reconstruction era. Nationally, revolutionary change peaked in 1867 with the impeachment of President Andrew Johnson by the Republican Congress, the passage of military Reconstruction in the South, and the movement for the eight-hour workday in Northern cities. Then Republican Party dominance began to falter toward the end of the decade. By the early 1870s, the Republican revolutionary project in the South was "under siege." White Leagues proliferated throughout the once-occupied South, orchestrating a violent resistance to black participation in politics and to Republican Party rule. By the start of 1874, only three thousand federal troops remained in the South, and all but three Southern states had restored white supremacy.[3]

Republicans were also beset in the North. Liberal Republicans revolted against party corruption and promoted reconciliation with the white South. Throughout the Midwest, pietistic Protestants launched a temperance movement, which drove many "wet" German Republicans out of the party. A third group, skilled industrial workers, became dissatisfied with Republican leadership when the 1873 depression brought mass unemployment and cuts in wages. Meanwhile, many trade unionists were attracted to the Democrats because of their support for greenbacks as a supplement to the national currency. These developments came to a head in the election of 1874, which marked the return of the South to Democratic rule and ended Republican dominance, first of all in the Congress and subsequently in the nation as whole.[4]

In Chicago, events of a similar nature resulted in the Democrats establishing themselves as the dominant party by the end of the decade. Following the Great Fire of 1871, Liberal Republicans took control of city government, but, soon after, their resort to temperance reform drove large numbers of German Republicans out of the party. These political refugees coalesced with restive Irish in a new urban populist initiative known as the People's Party. Under its aegis, the city's immigrants took over the municipal government.

In 1869, the *Chicago Daily Tribune* discerned a new group of workers in the city. These people were "without trades and go where the wages are highest." By the 1860s, the labor market that served these transients had become extensive enough that the city followed the earlier example of eastern cities by licensing employment bureaus. Newly forged links between the larger employment bureaus—together with the spreading impact of the telegraph, the railroad network, and transatlantic steamship service—integrated local, national, and transatlantic labor markets. New waves of immigrants poured into the country and city after the Civil War, particularly from Scandinavia and central Europe, and these immigrants differed markedly from those in the antebellum era (fig. 6). Higher proportions of them were younger, more likely to be single or unaccompanied by family members, and more experienced than their predecessors—both before and after their arrival in the United States—with cities, labor markets, and factory work. In other

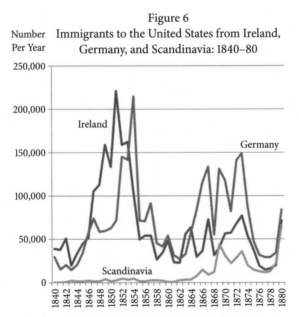

Figure 6
Immigrants to the United States from Ireland,
Germany, and Scandinavia: 1840–80

Source: Susan B. Carter et al., *Historical Statistics of the United States Earliest Times to the Present: Millennial Edition Online* (New York: Cambridge University Press, 2006), Table Ad106-120.

words, a higher proportion of the recent immigrants were workers rather than prospective farmers, and they were in pursuit of jobs, not land. Often viewing their stay as temporary, such immigrants readily moved in pursuit of more favorable circumstances.[5]

Transient workers affronted the preconceptions of mid-nineteenth-century Americans. Chicagoans, most of whom came from small-town backgrounds, had an inbred suspicion of those with no stake in local community institutions, whether it be the church, farm, business, or school. Republican theory also counseled Americans to fear those who lacked the independence to support active citizenship. Persons without a stake in society could become a mob susceptible to manipulation by power-seeking demagogues.

Yet the phenomenon of transience, far from being marginal, was a central characteristic of the industrializing urban centers of mid-nineteenth-century America. In his study of geographic mobility in Gilded Age Boston, Stephen Thernstrom showed that enormous population turnover characterized that city. Almost 800,000 people moved into and out of Boston between 1880 and 1890 to produce a population increase from 363,000 to 448,000. Turnover was probably greater in Chicago and even more dramatic and unsettling, given the city's explosive growth and the large numbers of single laborers seeking work in the city's reconstruction after the Great Fire of 1871. Under these circumstances, transience became a metaphor in the minds of many middle- and upper-class Chicagoans for the new working class and its lack of integration into the fast evolving social order.[6]

Transient districts developed in urban America during the last quarter of the nineteenth century, and they were centrally located and dense because of the rigid character of a transportation system built around the railroads. Anchored by the railroad stations, Chicago's transient district had its largest concentration on the Near West Side, which was also a boardinghouse district that accommodated the influx of workers after the Great Fire. There, factories, saloons, brothels, boardinghouses, and train stations shared the same blighted space. These institutions formed an elaborate communication network based in personal encounters, usually in the streets and saloons. That network often included the police, who directed immigrant workers to key institutions in the labor market, such as the boardinghouses, which also doubled as labor exchanges. This decrepit transient district was also the central site of late-nine-teenth-century Chicago labor history, as labor groups took advantage of the communication network and transportation system to organize meetings.[7]

Adjacent to the transient district, and then spreading outward, were vast tracts of working-class houses, typically constructed of wood. The Great

Fire began in one of these tracts on the Southwest Side. Primarily, but not exclusively, skilled, those workers who owned or leased a house, and perhaps a building lot, formed a relatively stable stratum that served as the foundation for the labor movement. Participation in civil society also linked these workers to prevailing American political traditions, particularly those of a free-labor or populist persuasion that prized the freedom and independence that came with property ownership or its equivalent. This populist persuasion was part of the complex political heritage of the producers' social order idealized by both political parties before the Civil War.[8]

When people became owners or leasers of building lots and houses, they took one of the most elemental steps in becoming active participants in civil society. This step normally involved considerable sacrifice to accumulate savings and a move outward toward cheaper land. Squatting was usually the first step for poor people settling in Chicago. Taking additional steps was by no means a given, and many of them remained squatters or left the city. If they did take the next steps toward home ownership, they made the most significant economic and symbolic decision marking their citizenship in the city. The process of transforming squatters into home owners worked for significant numbers of people, as the city's economic expansion increasingly made the purchase of a home and building lot feasible.[9]

Chicago's expanding workforce created a huge market for wooden housing affordable by workers. In September 1867, the *Workingman's Advocate* published an advertisement from the Merchants', Farmers', and Mechanics' Savings Bank calling for designs of houses that could be built for $600 to $1,000. According to the bank, "people who are drifting about seldom accumulate wealth. Every scheme for bettering the condition of men, must, if success is hoped for, be tested by men who are anchored, and, for an anchorage, home affords the best 'holding ground.'" Willing to do its part to better conditions, the bank offered to make loans for the cost of home construction, holding city lots as collateral. The bank thought that building lots were available for about $300, with a $100 down payment in cash. Such lots were "within a mile of some of our heaviest manufacturing establishments, and convenient to the river, schools and to the horse railroads." "Most industrious mechanics" could save the down payment in about eight months by depositing around $3 per week in their account at the bank.[10]

Andrew Cameron, still Chicago's most prominent labor leader, struggled to turn workers into home owners who would help build the institutions of the labor movement. In the same issue publishing the ad for the housing design contest, Cameron's *Workingman's Advocate* commented: "Men who are continually moving from place to place seldom accumulate wealth or have much influence. We have experienced this to some extent in our Trades Associations. When an officer of a Trades Union lives in his own house we always know where to find him. And a man who has his own cellar full of provisions is always in a condition to hold out on a long strike. Co-operative organizations cannot be successfully established by men who are tenants, and strangers to each other. Therefore, the first step towards improvements in the condition of men is, to get them settled in permanent and comfortable homes." Not surprisingly, such working-class property owners were older than those without real estate. They had also been in Chicago longer and were disproportionately foreign-born and overwhelmingly male. Just before the Great Fire of 1871, there were about sixty thousand buildings in the city, of which around forty thousand were wooden houses with an average value of about $1,000. That was the upper limit of what the Merchants,' Farmers,' and Mechanics' Bank thought "mechanics" could afford.[11]

But most Chicago workers could not follow this path through home ownership to stability and respectability. In 1870, 20 percent of skilled workers owned real estate, compared to 17 percent of unskilled workers. These figures constituted lower limits of the home-owning working class, however, because they did not include leasing. Nonetheless, Chicago's typical workers in the late 1860s were like the hod carrier who collapsed on a construction site in the summer of 1870. When a reporter from the *Workingman's Advocate* asked for the man's name and address, someone said, "Nobody here can tell you: almost every man on the building—eighty in number—are strangers. He only came to Chicago last Saturday, and on Monday he went to work, because he would work for $1.50 a day." The nameless, sunstruck hod carrier was one of thousands of such "strangers" who were attracted by Chicago's widespread reputation as a boomtown in the 1860s, a reputation enhanced by the previous three years of unprecedented postwar construction that had practically built a new city.[12]

Transient males were not the only "strangers" in the city's emerging industrial working class. The explosion of female employment in the 1860s was shocking, even by Chicago standards. In that decade, the population multiplied by three, the manufacturing workforce by five, and the female manufacturing workforce by eighteen. While just before the Civil War women hardly mattered in the Chicago manufacturing workforce, a decade later they constituted 18 percent of it. These women were concentrated in the apparel industry that had received such an impetus from the Civil War; almost four-fifths of the women workers in 1870 made clothing, and they constituted 60 percent of workers in the garment industry. The female garment workers were also concentrated in large firms; in 1870, 87 percent of all Chicago's clothing workers, male and female, labored in firms with more than fifty employees. Typical of women clothing workers in other cities, Chicago's sewing women had an average age of twenty-five, and they were multiethnic, with 55 percent of them foreign-born. Neither these sewing women nor the transient male workers fit into the vision of a producers' social order built around male-led households owning productive property.[13]

Commonly living and working outside of male-dominated households, sewing women transgressed the normal social boundaries for women, making them vulnerable to numerous threats, the worst of which, in the eyes of proper society, was prostitution. The link between prostitution and women living and working outside of households had been dramatically illustrated during the Civil War with the rise of the "war widow" problem, when the euphemism connoted prostitution practiced in the city's central boarding-house district by women whose husbands were dead or absent. A comparison with female servants illustrated the challenge to society posed by the sewing women (fig. 7). Although the sewing women constituted the great majority of female manufacturing workers, most females labored in other sectors of the economy, primarily domestic service. Nevertheless, although twice as many young women labored as servants in 1870 than as garment workers, the servant women were not recognized as a social problem to the same extent because they lived and worked in households, even if not led by males to

Figure 7
Females among All Chicago Workers by Servant
and Not Servant: 1860–80

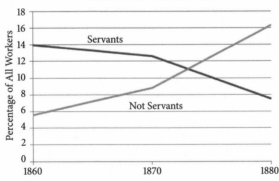

Source: Samples of the federal manuscript population censuses;
smallest N = 1,472.

whom they were related. Women wage earners living and working outside of male-dominated households did not fit into the nineteenth-century "domestic code" for women. They were the social analogue to transient males without a house and lot.[14]

It is not surprising that the groups shaping public opinion about Chicago's social problems had common responses to the new Gilded Age working class, because they shared a vision of a social order centered on patriarchal producers. Opinion leaders wanted to get the transient males out of town and the women wage earners into male-led households. *Der Westen,* the Sunday edition of the *Illinois Staats-Zeitung,* argued that the best solution to the problem of sewing women was for them to become servants. Similarly, during the winter of 1869–70, the overtaxed Chicago Relief and Aid Society tried passing out flyers to job applicants explaining the benefits of moving to the countryside where work and comfortable living arrangements in farm households awaited them, in other words, the benefits of moving into a producers' social order still composed of households owning productive property.[15]

Neither transient male workers nor the sewing women responded well to the reformers' appeals. Repeatedly, reformers complained that women preferred factory work to domestic service, and American-born women were the worst: "The 'woman of America' will not work in the kitchen. They will sew their fingers 'to the bone' at poorly paid labor; they will starve genteely [*sic*]; they will sell themselves to perdition; but they will not perform menial service, which they consider degrading to one's nature." These male and female workers recognized something the reformers did not: As a productive unit, the male-led household institutionalized its own limits, dependencies, and injustices. For some workers, wage labor offered new freedoms. Susan B. Anthony recognized these liberating possibilities when she addressed a union of Chicago sewing women in 1865: "A desire to be wealthy, to be pecuniarly [*sic*] independent of all human beings, must be planted into the soul—the very life of womanhood. She must not be content to earn just enough to live upon. She must feel it a disgrace to live at home in idleness, under any circumstances." Anthony linked independence with earning wages outside the home, and so did enough Chicago workingwomen to frustrate the efforts of reformers to promote domestic service among them. In an era when so many labor reformers fought the "wages system," these women found in the labor market a basis for the independence extolled by American political culture.[16]

The appearance of this new female working class, the middle-class fear of proletarians, especially immigrants, and the rise of organized labor framed the ideas of the first independent feminist movement. Born during the Civil War when the public sphere broadened, the movement sought to uproot the legal and social relations of the patriarchal family characteristic of the producers' mode of production. Thus in 1861, Illinois women fought for and won the right to own the property they brought into marriage and to transfer it as well. By the end of the decade, suffragists were able to win from the legislature the right of a married woman to receive, use, and possess her earnings and sue for those earnings without the interference of her husband or his creditors. But many local as well as national feminists also recognized that equality for women in the market required labor organization. These feminists shared with labor activists the belief that they needed to move "beyond equality" in the market.[17]

At first, Chicago feminists split into two camps, with one faction, the Sorosis, holding to an ideology similar to that of the labor-reform movement. These feminists were critical of the wing headed by Mary Livermore because of its support for limiting the vote to white, native-born persons. But the two factions soon reconciled. From 1870 onward, they developed a common concern with the issues of "sewing girls" and the rise of concentrated wealth, which Livermore blamed for rising class conflict. Newly organized women's clubs and the Woman's Christian Temperance Union, which would be founded in Chicago in 1874, also recognized that activist women needed to support women wageworkers and cooperate with the labor movement.[18]

For female unskilled workers, just as for males, independence through property ownership was not a realistic option, while wagework was an ambiguous status with its own pitfalls. To women, it offered freedom from an older patriarchal family and a limited form of independence, but it also brought instability, insecurity, and estrangement from the city's political culture and social institutions. To men, wage labor might provide freedom from often debased craft practices, such as the use of apprenticeship simply for cheap labor, and it did allow for the independence of earning a living without owning productive property, but such freedoms were hollow if one was unemployed. This class of unskilled workers expanded greatly in the late 1860s and 1870s, particularly as a result of the massive rebuilding after the Great Fire of 1871, setting in motion a momentous series of events.

STABLE IRISH AND GERMAN WORKERS

After the defeat of the eight-hour movement, immigrant workers concentrated on building the institutions of civil society, usually, but not always, within the framework of ethnic neighborhoods. From churches to ward political organizations, from fraternal orders to cooperatives, from saloons to labor unions, these institutions drew strength from the culture and allegiances of immigrants, even when their leaders sought to transcend the ethnic limits of their core constituencies. In their search for stability, security, and status, these workers formed shifting alliances with fellow countrymen to accumulate the resources needed for this larger institution-building project. Their allies included people near to them in status—saloon keepers, policemen, grocers, teachers—mostly low-level government employees and small entrepreneurs, particularly those selling in ethnically confined markets. As the construction of this ethnically colored civil society progressed, Chicago's Irish and German immigrants navigated two profound transitions: They developed new leadership different from the founding generation that had arrived in the late 1840s and early 1850s, and they built American ethnic communities with cultures distinct from those of both their native lands and the dominant culture of the United States. Labor unions and working-class political movements were part of this larger project of building their own civil society, which would enable immigrants to survive poverty and the rigors of the labor market.[19]

Chicago's Irish were a major force in founding this urban order, and the construction industry was unusually important to them. Among skilled Irish workers, around two-fifths labored in construction, by far their largest employer (see table 5, chap. 3). Skilled Irish construction workers profited from the thin line between craft labor and entrepreneurship, just as they seized opportunities to build trade unions in their crafts. They also utilized Irish political influence to profit from local public works projects, such as the new courthouse. Amid the construction boom of the late 1860s, the unions of bricklayers, plasterers, stonecutters, and carpenters all showed renewed activity. While the Irish dominated none of these trades, they figured largely in their unions, benefiting from their facility with English, the strength of their ethnic ties, and their organizational and political skills. The Irish were prominent trade unionists in other branches of industry, particularly metal fabrication and production.[20]

The growing strength of Irish workers was evident in a local labor convention organized by the Trades Assembly in September 1868 to draft a platform for the coming election. The Irish constituted well over a third of the delegates, making them the largest national group, including the native-born. Writing of the Irish at this same time, Andrew Cameron said they form "the bone and sinew" of the union element in Chicago, and "the truest, staunchest, most unflinching of our trade's unionists rejoice in the possession of an Irish brogue."[21]

German workers made a similar assertion of ethnic and labor power after the collapse of the eight-hour strike. One example of future trends was buried in the *Illinois Staats-Zeitung* of September 8, 1867, a few months after the upheaval. A note said that Albrecht Strehlow was the president of Chicago's recently formed Allgemeiner Deutscher Arbeiterverein (Universal German Workers Association; ADAV). Founded in Germany in 1863 by Ferdinand Lassalle, the ADAV was Germany's first political movement with a mass base among workers, and it was the predominant organization on the German left during the 1860s. A construction carpenter, Strehlow had been active in the eight-hour movement, even carrying a flag at the head of the German division of the eight-hour parade on May 1. As the strike began to falter, Strehlow organized meetings of German workers on the South and West Sides, one of which was designed to promote the founding of a German labor paper in Chicago. If German workers felt the need for their own paper, it meant that they were dissatisfied with the German community's forty-eighter leadership, which provided the editors of the existing German-language press. The effort to found a labor paper combined with the organization of the ADAV marked the earliest beginnings of an independent German labor movement in the city.[22]

Within two years of the eight-hour defeat, Germans had established their own citywide union organization and a German labor paper. Founded in 1868, the Arbeiter-Central-Verein (Workers' Central Association; ACV) was modeled after the local English-speaking Chicago Trades Assembly and similar organizations of German craft unions. Such German associations had arisen on the East Coast in the 1850s, their fates rising and falling with the business cycle. New York City had been the trendsetter then and was again after the Civil War, when German craft unions founded their Arbeiter Union in 1866. Notably, neither Chicago's ACV nor the New York organization followed the pattern of the contemporary Lassallean ADAV. In Germany at this time, trade unions faced far greater obstacles than in the United States and Great Britain, making a political party more viable there than an association of unions.[23]

Supported by ten unions, the Chicago ACV formulated political platforms for local election campaigns and sponsored social events, such as balls and picnics, to attract members and raise money. In both activities, the ACV cooperated with the English-speaking Trades Assembly, even at one point working with it in an unsuccessful attempt to build a meeting hall. In January 1869, the *Workingman's Advocate* estimated that the Trades Assembly represented five thousand workers, while its counterpart, the German ACV, spoke for another five thousand. By a conservative estimate, the two together would have encompassed about one-quarter of the skilled workers in the city. Together they represented a substantial labor presence in Chicago that mirrored a significant national labor resurgence in the late 1860s and especially during the economic expansion in the early 1870s. Between 1870 and 1873, nine new national unions formed, while the twenty-three previously existing ones grew considerably in membership.[24]

Like the Trades Assembly, the ACV supported its own paper, *Der Deutsche Arbeiter* (The German Worker), edited by Carl Klings, a recent immigrant and Lassallean who became one of the most important German labor leaders in the city during the Gilded Age. Klings and his associates made the *Deutsche Arbeiter* a conduit for the latest continental political thinking as well as a voice for German labor in Chicago. The editorship of Klings marked the new labor movement's independence from the established leadership of German Chicago, not only from the forty-eighters but also from the new German businessmen who were rising to wealth and power on the tide of the city's economic expansion. Klings and his circle of left-leaning émigrés also insured that the new German labor movement had less in common with the labor reformers around Andrew Cameron than had the radical forty-eighters, such as Eduard Schläger. This change in the leadership of German labor complemented the generational transition taking place in the larger Chicago German community, as the aging forty-eighters were displaced by the youth and the assertiveness of new leaders. Symbolic of this transition was the return of Schläger to Germany in 1872. The ideological and organizational independence of the new German labor movement provided a platform from which it negotiated with other organized powers in the city, including the English-speaking Trades Assembly.[25]

The ACV's union locals were organized in branches of industry in which German manufacturers had a significant, but not dominant, role. In 1870, nine of its ten unions were in industries in which Germans employed less than 50 percent of the workers, and six were in branches where Germans employed less than 20 percent. In contrast, there were no German locals in the tobacco, alcoholic beverage, and furniture industries where German manufacturers employed at least 50 percent of the workforce, although unions in these branches of manufacturing emerged later in the 1870s. Analogous to ethnic residential neighborhoods, the early German unions were like ethnic beachheads within an alien environment, organized among German workers in industries dominated by English-speaking employers. Within their own unions, German workers could develop their social life and culture, control their own institutions, and negotiate with the larger powers around them.[26]

Each of the two main labor federations brought together a distinct array of ethnicities. The English-speaking movement included significant numbers of British and native-born American workers, even as the Irish were emerging to prominence. In addition, unions, such as the stonecutters, which were represented in the English-speaking Trades Assembly, often had substantial numbers of German and Scandinavian members. On the other hand, the German-speaking movement became a home to Scandinavian and central European workers, who knew the German language through the wide influence of the Austro-Hungarian Empire and through the traditions of wandering journeymen. Chicago's two labor movements were ethnic constellations with the largest and most influential national groups exercising a central gravitational pull.[27]

The immigrant workers who built these two labor movements allied with traditional professionals, white-collar workers, and small shopkeepers to construct distinct civil societies segmented by ethnicity. Foreign-born skilled workers, saloon keepers, building contractors, bookkeepers, grocers, policemen, teachers, and ward politicians differed moderately in status and class position, but they occupied the same social space, living in the vicinity of one another, shopping in the same commercial districts, reading the same newspapers, and listening to the same local politicians. They also shared a common interest in building a sustaining social order within the emerging capitalist city. Thus trade unionists, as well as skilled workers in general, were drawn into social and political relationships with people of a "middling" sort. In the twenty years before 1870, the foreign-born consistently made up almost one-half of the middling stratum of employed Chicagoans, defined as small proprietors, low-level government employees, and low-status white-collar workers.[28]

The foreign-born of a middling status were more dependent on the state than their native-born counterparts. In 1870, about half of Chicago's policemen, inspectors, streetcar workers, and employees at the gasworks were foreign-born. Another significant segment of the foreign-born middle stratum worked in occupations regulated or licensed by the government. Saloon keepers were the most obvious example, of whom two-thirds in 1870 were foreign-born. Saloon keepers and government employees alone constituted over 13 percent of the city's foreign-born of middling status in 1870, in contrast to 7 percent of the native-born. Influence over local government was vital for these people.[29]

Chicago's Immigrant Working Class and Urban Populism 129

Government also offered an opportunity for accumulating capital that was particularly useful to foreign-born entrepreneurs, who had less access to the credit markets than their native-born counterparts. Both foreign-born construction entrepreneurs and the unions in the building trades wanted more public works, the source of so much building activity in the late 1860s. To men like Anton Hesing, politics and business were a seamless web. Since their origin in the Jacksonian era, American mass-based political parties had been a means to acquire power and wealth, even for the lowly. The explosive growth of the Republican Party after 1854 offered an unusual chance to get in at the ground floor for central European and Scandinavian immigrants of Protestant backgrounds. Immigrant political entrepreneurs of all nationalities and both major parties seized their chances while the country fought the Civil War, just as business entrepreneurs of all nationalities profited from the wartime boom. They transformed both political parties, but especially the Republicans, whose predominant position in the city made influence within it especially appealing and profitable.

LABOR POLITICS AND PARTISAN POLITICS: 1867 TO THE GREAT FIRE

Labor reformers were still influential in the city, and they brought their most important organization to Chicago for its national meeting soon after the eight-hour strike. The National Labor Union adopted currency reform as its main solution to the social and economic crisis following the war, and currency reform reflected its producers' vision of the American political economy. According to this vision, the equitable distribution of property required by a republican form of government would be insured by the naturally just working of the economy, unless it was disturbed by the aristocratic use of the state to unfairly redistribute wealth from the producers to society's unproductive parasites. Manipulation of the means of exchange was one of the chief aristocratic means for effecting this transfer of wealth, and the National Labor Union's currency and fiscal reforms after the Civil War were designed to address that threat. Writing in the *Workingman's Advocate,* Andrew Cameron and William Sylvis proposed replacing the existing national banking system with an "interconvertible" bond system to keep the interest rate at 3 percent, which they thought would prevent capital from accumulating in the hands of parasitic and aristocratic nonproducers. This producers' vision sought to preserve and enhance a political economy in which small manufacturers, farmers, and skilled craftsmen with their producers' cooperatives predominated in a decentralized, regionally oriented market economy. Such opinions were sure to receive considerable space in the *Workingman's Advocate,* since it had been purchased by Alexander Campbell, the nation's leading theorist of currency reform.[30]

At the same time, increasing numbers of trade unionists were gravitating toward a very different outlook from that of producers' republicanism, one that by the 1880s would crystallize into a labor ideology known as "pure and simple unionism." This perspective grew organically out of the organizing experience of workers who had to contend with employers' use of the common law's conspiracy doctrine to stymie unionization campaigns. The political platform advanced by the Chicago Trades Assembly in the fall 1868 elections included practical demands to aid such organizing, including repealing Illinois's own conspiracy law, the La Salle Black law. Passed in 1863, this law "prohibited any person from seeking to prevent, by threat, intimidation, or otherwise, any other person from working at any lawful business on any terms that he might see fit." The unions' opposition to the use of conspiracy injunctions portended a break with the old producer outlook. In contrast to producerism, unions did not fear combination within markets, including the labor market, and fought the use of the courts to restrict their power to associate for the purpose of raising wages. Trade unionists argued that their associations simply sought to counteract the concentrated power of capital with the collective power of organized labor. Rather than rejecting the new industrial system, unionists argued that through their collective power workers could shape to their benefit the supposedly immutable rules of the competitive market. Since the 1868 platform articulated much of this trade union vision, it remained a touchstone in subsequent Chicago labor politics.[31]

Despite this platform, the Trades Assembly hardly fared better in the fall 1868 elections than it had the previous spring, when its campaign stressed currency reform. The main problem was the absence of the Germans, who were organizing their own labor movement at this time. An obvious solution was to make an alliance with the Germans behind a common platform in 1869. Building a multilingual labor alliance in the fall 1869 elections appeared promising, particularly when the ACV drafted a platform similar to the one formulated by the Trades Assembly in 1868. (In 1869, a new state law moved the municipal elections to the fall.) In August, the ACV sponsored a multiethnic conference chaired by its president, Frederick Betz, but also attended by several Anglo Americans who had been delegates to the Trades Assembly's 1868 convention. Conspicuous by his absence was Andrew Cameron, who had departed the city to attend the assembly of the International

Workingmen's Association in Basel, Switzerland, as the official representative of the National Labor Union. The resolutions of this August 1869 meeting incorporated most of the issues in the 1868 platform, while adding several of its own. Among these, two stood out: the progressive income tax and the repeal of all laws infringing personal liberty, the latter a direct attack on temperance and Sabbatarian legislation that Germans found particularly obnoxious. This was a platform that could be supported by all organized Chicago labor.[32]

Nevertheless, this promising labor alliance collapsed when, upon returning to Chicago from Europe, Cameron endorsed the candidates from the Citizens reform movement instead of a joint labor slate. Although bipartisan in their appeal, the Citizens were primarily a Liberal Republican reform movement aimed at wresting control of the local Republican Party from the hands of the "Barnacles," the regular party workers and officeholders, many of whom were German, who had risen to power amid the Civil War crisis. Since such people were not limited to the Republican Party, opposing them could take on a bipartisan appeal, yet their power in the currently predominant Republican Party made the Republican Barnacles lightning rods for reformers' wrath, including that of Andrew Cameron. Cameron reacted in horror to the Barnacles and hoped the Citizens would advance antimonopoly principles for which he and the National Labor Union stood.[33]

The chief Barnacle was Anton Hesing, who had parlayed his political influence as sheriff in the late 1850s into personal wealth sufficient to buy the *Illinois-Staats-Zeitung* and one of the largest planing mills in the city. A high-tariff Republican, Hesing had close allies among the city's manufacturers, especially the powerful German brewers and distillers, who needed protection from local and state temperance and Sabbatarian laws. Possessing a common touch as well as wealth, Hesing strongly appealed to German-speaking craftsmen, government employees, proprietors, and low white-collar workers, since he presented himself as protector of their ethnic turf, their jobs, and their lifestyle, especially when it involved drinking alcoholic beverages. Hesing and the rest of the Barnacles had infiltrated the government and used it for their advantage, which, of course, the Yankee booster elite had done as well. The Barnacles were just the wrong sort of people.[34]

The Citizens' campaign against the corruptors of local government was led by Horace White, editor of the *Tribune* and an intellectual leader of the emerging Liberal wing of the national Republican Party. Long an advocate of laissez-faire economics, White also supported free trade, a policy that made him even more attractive to Andrew Cameron while at the same time rendering him especially obnoxious to local manufacturers, who were championed by Hesing and his allies. In mounting their nonpartisan campaign, the Citizens took advantage of programmatic confusion between the two national parties. The passage of the Thirteenth and Fourteenth amendments to the U.S. Constitution and the imminent adoption of the Fifteenth fashioned a peace settlement for the Civil War and thus seemed to resolve the most salient partisan issues dividing the country. It was time, argued the Citizens, to put aside national party labels and turn to neglected local issues, the most glaring of which was the control of government by unscrupulous men using it for their selfish advantage.[35]

The Citizens solutions to the supposed crisis in public authority bore several family resemblances to the reforms imposed on the contemporary Chicago Relief and Aid Society by the powerful manufacturers on its reconstituted board of directors. As with the Relief and Aid Society, centralization, efficiency, and bureaucratic organization would reduce the local government's numerous independently elected boards and commissions, professionalize the delivery of services such as police and fire protection, and make the day-to-day administration of the government less open to manipulation by minor officeholders. They would also make the government more open to the influence of elites who had access to the more powerful central authorities, such as the mayor and city council.[36]

Full-time partisans as well as officeholders, the Barnacles knew how to fight back. They formed the Chicago version of the rapidly coalescing Stalwart wing of the national Republican Party that subsequently fought so bitterly with the party's Liberals for decades. The Barnacles used their influence in the state legislature to redraw the city's ward map to more closely conform to the actual settlement patterns of the population, and thus to their own immigrant power base. They also used the same influence to move the municipal elections from the spring to the fall so that they would be contemporaneous with wider state and national contests. In this way, the Barnacles hoped to perpetuate on the local level the national partisan divisions from which they had profited. In this election, however, the Barnacles were outmatched by the Citizens bipartisan coalition, particularly because the Citizens had substantial Irish politicians on their ticket. Although the Citizens jubilantly claimed that a revolution had taken place in local affairs, scandal and corruption quickly emerged among their own officeholders. While the Barnacles would eventually regroup, organized labor proved less resourceful at recovering from defeat in 1869.[37]

Supporters of a joint labor ticket in the election felt betrayed by Cameron's support of the Citizens, and their anger was fueled by his attacks on them as tools of scheming politicians. Particularly incensed, the Germans in the ACV nursed a sense of betrayal well into the 1870s. More important, the election had weakened both the English-speaking and German trades assemblies by undermining support among workers for independent labor politics. The assemblies were essentially political bodies representing their constituent unions in the public sphere. When the unions began to doubt the feasibility and rewards of independent politics, the rationale for the trades assemblies evaporated. Both assemblies collapsed within two years.[38]

Other factors contributed to their demise. The English-speaking assembly disappeared in 1870 amid a slump in the building industry that weakened its substantial construction unions. The ACV disintegrated in a surge of German ethnic chauvinism prompted by the Prussian victory over France in 1871 and the subsequent founding of the Second Empire. The Franco-Prussian War marked a turning point in the prevailing opinion within German American communities, tilting it away from the liberal ideals of the 1848 revolutions, which until that point had defined German nationhood. More racially colored definitions of Germany prevailed, and former liberals were willing to find social virtues in a unified German empire ruled by a monarch. At the same time, the left-wing émigrés congregating around the *Deutsche Arbeiter* used the paper to oppose Otto von Bismarck's imperial designs and champion the Paris Commune, which had been crushed with Prussian support. Thus they isolated themselves from prevailing opinion in the Chicago German ethnic community, which had been a necessary ingredient in the ACV's strength. The ACV disappeared along with its newspaper in the late summer and fall of 1871.[39]

The failure of the trades assemblies, combined with the related isolation of Cameron and the labor reformers from a mass base, meant that organized Chicago labor had no effective voice in the public sphere during the crisis of the Great Fire. The field was thus open for others to speak in the name of the city's working people.

THE FIRE LIMITS CONTROVERSY
AND STABLE WORKERS

Although there is skepticism about whether Mrs. O'Leary's cow started the Great Fire of October 8, 1871, there is no doubt about where it began. It started on the Southwest Side in an area packed with wooden working-class housing. This district had been a locus of crowd actions during the eight-hour strike of 1867, and just before the fire it included the most densely settled area of the city. Driven by high winds, the blaze quickly became a firestorm, sweeping northeastward up the lower West Side, across the South Branch of the Chicago River into the central business district, and then across the main branch of the Chicago River into the North Side, where it consumed practically all of the existing housing stock, including the original German and Swedish settlements. Blackening over twenty-one hundred acres, the fire destroyed 30 percent of the city's buildings, including the most valuable ones, and left ninety thousand homeless, a third of the population. And this catastrophe took place when Chicago's notorious winter was imminent and organized labor was impotent.[40]

Rebuilding Chicago after the Great Fire marked a decisive chapter in the evolution of a capitalist social order in the city because it united and mobilized leading elements of Chicago's business community. Chicago's remaining boosters were especially vulnerable to the loss of credit from the East. Boosters aggregated capital created elsewhere by buying low and selling high in the commercial economy, by attracting federal land grants and investments in internal improvements, and by inducing eastern manufacturers to relocate to Chicago. Chicago's emergent manufacturing capitalists also required eastern credit to expand their investment and to market the products of their firms. Nevertheless, in contrast to the boosters, they accumulated substantial capital locally by reinvesting in the means of production and by managing the working class necessary to run it. Notably, the capital invested in Chicago manufacturing had jumped sevenfold between 1860 and 1870, helping put the city at the cutting edge of a national trend. Nationally, the share of capital investment in the gross national product rose from 14 to 22 percent between the 1850s and 1870s.[41]

Capital accumulation involved much more than new investment in plant and equipment; it also required a social and political transformation that undermined the producers' order of small property holders. Central to this transformation was the creation, maintenance, and expansion of a wage-earning working class. After the fire, the immediate need of local employers was to retain the services of workers who might be inclined to leave the city if no lodging or employment was available. At the same time, they were concerned that relief might be distributed too liberally, thus weakening workers' incentive to re-enter the labor market in search of work. The Relief and Aid Society was the major institution available to achieve these goals. Its restructuring in 1867 had put it under the control of leading capitalists, who used it to maintain the conditions for an efficient labor market. But before decisive action could be taken, the city's Common Council, still in the hands of the

Barnacles, had to be circumvented. Immediately following the fire, Mayor Roswell Mason, elected in the Citizens' campaign of 1869, made two key decisions. Bypassing the Board of Police and Fire Commissioners, he turned the task of insuring law and order over to the United States Army under General Philip Sheridan of Civil War fame. Then, bypassing the Common Council, he made the Relief and Aid Society responsible for collecting and disbursing the aid pouring into the city from across the nation and even from abroad. These two actions effectively distanced the rebuilding effort from political institutions close to Chicago's electorate, encouraging large capitalists to proceed with their rebuilding plans.[42]

Headed by Henry W. King, a leading clothing manufacturer, and Illinois Central Railroad attorney Wirt Dexter, the Relief and Aid Society was equal to the immense tasks of rebuilding. It immediately constructed long rows of makeshift barracks to house the homeless, thereby preventing an exodus from the city that might hinder the rebuilding. After a week of indiscriminate disbursement of aid, it began distributing its monies more cautiously, so as to maintain the incentive to work while avoiding a labor shortage that might raise wages to levels that would hinder investment. Aware that thirty-five thousand people, most of them potential laborers, were being succored by the Society, the *Tribune* repeatedly reminded its readership to distinguish between the truly destitute and "the free loaders." Only two weeks after the fire, it even asked the churches to close their soup kitchens. "All the men who can work are not at work," editorialized the paper. "Honest sufferers want employment not alms. Servant girls' conduct has been reprehensible. The Committee must cut off all deadbeats."[43]

It was also imperative to turn on the flow of capital investment to the city. The *Tribune* put it bluntly: "What the people of Chicago need in order to rebuild the burnt district and restore the matters to their former condition is the abundant use of foreign and Eastern capital." And a municipal government with Barnacles entrenched in the City Council and threatening to capture the mayor's seat was in no position to raise it. The city's leaders sought a sweeping and reassuring victory through a bipartisan "Fireproof" ticket that would demonstrate to outside investors that the city's reconstruction was in safe hands. Eventually, the *Tribune*'s part owner, Joseph Medill, ran as the Fireproof candidate for mayor and on November 7—a month after the fire—handily defeated Democratic candidate Charles C. P. Holden. Holden had earlier represented the Common Council in its fight with Mayor Roswell over the choice of the Relief and Aid Society to take possession of the relief funds.[44]

Medill's administration was really an emergency government backed by a fragile and heterogeneous interethnic alliance that included Andrew Cameron and Anton Hesing. In short order, it initiated three new policies, all of which embroiled it in deep controversy. First, to propitiate eastern investors, it proposed an extension of the fire limits, that is, the area in which only brick construction was allowed. Second, it framed a bill in the state legislature centralizing in the mayor's hands the control of appointments to the city's boards, including the all-important Board of Police and Fire Commissioners. The emergency authority would last for two years. This bill, which was necessary to secure enforcement of the new fire limits, was passed on March 9, 1872. Finally, Medill made the momentous decision in the fall of 1872 to enforce the city's Sunday closing law, a controversial temperance measure.[45]

Medill's proposal to make the fire limits coextensive with the city's borders represented the final break with the old segmented system of city government, which militated against government making decisions on the basis of the general interest of the community. It immediately ran into opposition, despite its importance in reassuring New York fire insurance companies. By banning wood-built homes, the new law would have made it too expensive for most of the city's workers to construct homes within the city; it was also against the interest of speculators in land who hoped to make a killing by buying up small lots and constructing cheap homes to sell to workers. Some large real estate holders and the city's foreign-born property owners accurately perceived the proposed fire limits as a direct threat.[46]

To the city's immigrants, the fire limits were more dangerous than the Sunday closing laws and the high liquor licenses of the nativist Levi Boone administration in 1855, the last major flashpoint between the native- and foreign-born. Chicago's Germans were hit the hardest: 44 percent of German property holders lived in wards destroyed by the fire, compared to 25 percent of the native-born and 21 percent of other immigrant groups. Anton Hesing's *Illinois Staats-Zeitung* termed the issue as "essentially a question of the ownership of capital. The ordinance currently before the Common Council is an initiative that creates advantages for big capital at the expense of small capital, that makes the rich richer and the poor poorer." Hesing spoke for the broad middling stratum of the population that was hardworking, property-owning, and largely foreign-born.[47]

While such people represented the main political constituency opposing the fire limits, they were joined by some of the wealthiest North Siders, including William Butler Ogden and M. D. Ogden. They realized that the proposed fire limits would make it difficult to sell or lease much of their extensive property holdings on the North Side. Together the Ogdens and the North Division's small property owners represented the broad spectrum of people who had built a producers' social order in Chicago before the Civil War; this order presupposed the wide distribution of land, which here meant building lots. Despite the presence of the Ogdens, the opposition's political center of gravity was among the middle levels of the immigrant population. The rage they felt at the threat to their way of life and their status in the community was palpable, even though the proposed law would not affect the large number of wooden homes already built since the fire.[48]

The mounting protest culminated in a march on City Hall on Monday, January 15, 1872. It originated on the North Side. Although the assembly attracted both Irish and Germans, Anton Hesing gave the main address. His themes were that workers had built Chicago, not capitalists, and the workers had made quite a few people rich along the way. This claim of having built the city was not idle rhetoric to the immigrants of western frontier cities, where they participated from the beginning in the construction of local society, instead of being integrated into a preexisting order. Their contribution made them feel like equal members of the community, and they reacted angrily to anyone who implied second-class citizenship. In his speech, Hesing went on to say that everyone was proud that a greater proportion of Chicago's workers were independent property owners than in any other city of comparable size, whether on the East Coast or in Europe. As independent property owners, they would not stand to live in rented barracks under the control of a monopoly of apartment owners or suffer the decline in standard of living that would come with paying rent, particularly during the winter season when work was slack. The crowd's response to Hesing was vociferous and heated: Voices from the audience threatened to lynch any policeman who tried to stop a father from building a wooden house for his family.[49]

The crowds began gathering early Monday evening in different districts, with estimates of their numbers ranging between three thousand and ten thousand. The largest crowd came from the German northern district. When the crowds joined up to march across the river, their numbers included Germans, Irish, and Scandinavians, probably in that order of magnitude. When the crowd gathered in front of city hall, a delegation that included Hesing, Peter Conlan, former alderman from the Sixteenth Ward, and bearers of banners entered the council chambers. As Hesing and Conlan attempted to give speeches, members of the crowd demanded "the rights of the poor man" and threateningly showed the aldermen a banner with a man hanging from a gallows, the fate of those supporting the fire limits. The meeting, if it could be called such, dissolved when rocks were thrown through the windows from outside, causing a panic, which increased when the lights were turned out in order to force people to leave.[50]

Hesing vigorously defended himself and the march from attacks in the English-language press. He was particularly eloquent in reacting to an open letter addressed to him from Rev. Robert Collyer, a British immigrant. Feeling that immigrants should be cognizant of their "place and station" in a land to which they owed so much, Collyer argued that they should defer to the city government's definition of the public good, which in this case meant fire limits coextensive with the city's boundaries. Dismissive of such deference, Hesing said that, as a Briton, Collyer had not experienced the prejudice of Yankees against the "d—d Dutch" and that Germans were "as good and true Americans as any born in this country." More important, the city fathers, including Mayor Medill, had not followed the "American usages" that the crowd marching on city hall were accused of violating: "Neither Mr. Medill, nor the editors of two or three newspapers, are the *people* of Chicago. The sense of the people is, according to *American* usage, evolved by meetings. Where *have* there been, up to this date, any such public meetings in which the proposition of Mr. Medill has been endorsed by the people?" Hesing and his allies rejected the notion that the public good should be defined by the city's established and largely Yankee leaders, and they insisted that it emerge in open debate in which they would participate. They were willing to take this debate to the streets. At its origins, urban populism questioned who constituted the people and how their voices should be heard. It also exposed the ethnic prejudices of the city's establishment.[51]

Hesing shared his vision of a property-holding working class and his fear of the left with other German leaders, such as Wilhelm Rapp, a forty-eighter and former editor of the *Illinois Staats-Zeitung*. In a speech against the fire limits, Rapp argued that a lawful solution to the social question of the age was only possible when "the working classes can move freely and maintain their self-determination, as they can still do now in the West. Where the working classes are subjugated and exploited, there one has a 'bloody Commune' as in Paris." For the established leadership of German Chicago, the native-born politicians who proposed the fire limits were foolishly risking the whirlwind of class insurrection by destroying the communities of the propertied working class that had built the city and preserved its social peace. The presence in the city of radicals such as Carl Klings of the *Deutsche Arbeiter* gave substance to their fears and made the ideological polarization of the German community more severe than in other national groups.[52]

After the dust settled—a grand jury brought no indictments—the city's political leaders came to terms with the crowd's main political demands by limiting the extent of the fire limits. On the North Side, this meant permitting wooden construction north of Chicago Avenue and west of Wells Street, that is, in the German and Scandinavian districts in that division of the city. This political compromise on the fire limits facilitated the construction of a vast ring of wooden working-class housing around the city's central core, housing that congregated around manufacturing plants newly relocated far from the old central city as well as near newly extended commercial streets with their horse-drawn omnibus lines.[53]

Chicago as the city of ethnic working-class neighborhoods was rapidly emerging. Aiding its development was the Relief and Aid Society, which proved solicitous of the same stable property-owning workers idealized by Hesing. In the Society's words, these were "mechanics and the better class of laboring people, thrifty, domestic, and stable, whose skill and labor were indispensable in rebuilding the city, and most of whom had accumulated enough to become the owners of their own homesteads either as proprietors or lessees of the lots. To restore them to these homes would be to raise them at once from depression and anxiety, if not despair, to hope, renewed energy, and comparative prosperity." To the Society's board, sustaining the stable working class was at least as important as reassuring outside creditors and investors, the goal of the original proposal extending the fire limits to the city's boundaries. The resolution of the fire-limits controversy—shrinking their extent but not eliminating them—represented a compromise between these two goals.[54]

The need for wooden housing became immediately evident to the Chicago Relief and Aid Society as it sought to quickly provide shelter for almost ninety thousand people before the depth of winter set in. The Society began to give away the material to construct wooden houses to "mechanics and the better class of laboring people," defined usually by whether they owned or leased a building lot. In all, the Society gave away material for 7,983 houses, providing shelter for about thirty-five thousand to forty thousand people, or almost half of those rendered homeless by the fire. The Society showed even more consideration for the needs of the middle-class Chicagoans affected by the fire, setting up a "special relief" mechanism for them. Through this array of policies, the Relief and Aid Society reproduced and reshaped the class structure of the emerging industrial city.[55]

THE GREAT FIRE AND THE GILDED AGE WORKING CLASS: THE RECONSTRUCTION LABORERS

The Great Fire attracted large numbers of laborers to participate in Chicago's rebuilding, making the sunstruck construction laborer mentioned earlier into a harbinger of thousands who, like him, were experienced as "strangers" by those more integrated into the local social order. As the reconstruction began, advertisements by companies and newspaper reports, including some from abroad, spread the news that "there is an unlimited demand for labor in this city." In late March 1872, the *Tribune* wrote, "Workmen are here from all parts of the West and Northwest. Many of them have expended all the means in transit, have sold a silver watch, a shot-gun, any small article of personal property in their possession to pay their passage. Single men are naturally the most largely represented." By mid-May 1872, between forty-five thousand and fifty-five thousand men were engaged in the reconstruction, about equally divided between craftsmen and common laborers. This number was considerably more than all those employed in Cook County's manufacturing workforce in 1870.[56]

The essential quality of these workers was their position outside the social order but inside the city's labor market, which made them indispensable to the economy while threatening to those who felt themselves a part of established society, especially to the police dedicated to protecting it. Anticipating strikes during the construction season, the superintendent of police feared that they "would be of greater magnitude than any we have had to encounter heretofore" because of the "great influx of workmen from abroad." On his recommendation, the Board of Police and Fire Commissioners asked the governor to supply the police force with three hundred muskets and ten thousand rounds of ammunition to "provide against any trouble that might arise . . . as well as for the moral effect that it would produce upon persons instigating riotous proceedings." The city's political establishment, from Mayor Medill through Hesing and his allies, were also threatened by the new workers, as were the labor unions, for the recently arrived laborers quickly overwhelmed their efforts to control the local labor market.[57]

The opening of the first construction season after the fire in the spring of 1872 raised anxiety throughout the city. Mayor Medill declared strikes economically futile and threatened the use of force. Subsequently, he would use temperance laws as a means to fight crime and disorder among the new workers. For Hesing, the recently arrived laborers were a special problem, because he had just fought extending the fire limits to the city's boundaries in the name of the city's hardworking home owners. The new workers lacked that entrance ticket to Hesing's vision of Chicago. They were also a special threat to him and his German allies because of the presence in the city of the central European left. In an article on the Paris Commune published shortly after the fire, the *Illinois Staats-Zeitung* described how "cosmopolitanism" promoted by the Paris Commune had undermined French patriotism because it "atomized" workers, leaving nothing tying them to the larger community. Yet such atomization threatened workers in all industrial cities, including some in the United States, where "the citizen threatens to disappear into the worker, and local patriotism to weaken."[58]

Most of the unions were as wary of the new workers as Hesing, although they were more concerned with controlling the labor market than with building a city of small property owners. In the spring of 1872, rumors circulated wildly about massive strikes for higher wages and a revival of the eight-hour movement. Anxiety reached a peak when an ad hoc group of mainly construction unions met to organize a march of the building trades on May 15. Significantly, when the issue of forming a permanent Trades Assembly came up at one meeting, a representative of the stonecutters roundly attacked Andrew Cameron for bringing politics into the proceedings and thus jeopardizing his union's participation. Cameron was allowed to stay, even given an honored seat, but this incident made it plain that he and the labor reformers associated with the *Workingman's Advocate* were no longer the spokesmen for Chicago's organized workers.[59]

The clearest statement of the purpose of the march came from Frank Lawler, a representative of the ship carpenters and longtime Chicago labor activist: The newspapers notwithstanding, the demonstration had nothing to do with eight hours or wages, although workers needed higher wages to pay for the exorbitant rents they were charged. Rather, the march was "merely a gala day—a day of recreation" designed to "show the strength of the Trades Unions to the strange workmen now here, and to induce them to unite with their brethren." Any discussion of strikes and higher wages in association with the march was hushed up. In notable contrast to the eight-hour demonstration of 1867, which was directed primarily at employers and the whole political structure of the city, the main audience for the building trades demonstration consisted of other workers. Uncertain about what the new men might do, Chicago's union leaders were in no mood to call a general strike on the order of 1867.[60]

Events in New York City raised fears of just such an occurrence. Starting in May, New York witnessed an eight-week strike for the eight-hour day involving approximately one hundred thousand workers, about two-thirds of the city's manufacturing workforce. For the first time, New York's large-scale employers began to organize to resist striking workers and to force into line the smaller employers whose lack of resources left them vulnerable to strikes. In Chicago, the fear of a similar strike led the city's "better sort" to prepare for the worst. Before the demonstration, Mayor Medill had asked Governor John M. Palmer to supply arms to the city in case of an uprising. When this was rejected, businessmen placed an ad in the *Tribune* stating that "Printed blanks are being circulated for the signatures of such merchants and professional men as are willing to join a regiment soon to be organized.... The projectors, men of the highest commercial standing, believe that Chicago at the present time is in peculiar need of such a military body and that every banker, merchant, and real estate owner should contribute liberally to its support."[61]

To the surprise of the press, the demonstration was orderly and without incident. It had been intended to do exactly what Frank Lawler had stated: impress the strange workers in the city with the need to join a powerful union movement. Instead of the twenty thousand to thirty thousand who were anticipated at one point, only three thousand to five thousand actually marched. The low turnout for the demonstration meant that it did not achieve its goal of impressing the nonunion workers with the power of organized labor in Chicago. Its conservative intentions also stood in stark contrast to the millennial goals of the eight-hour demonstrations only five years earlier.[62]

The speeches of the mayors to the two labor parades were also a study in contrasts. Unlike Mayor Rice in 1867, who sympathized with the eight-hour movement while pleading for calm, Mayor Medill in 1872 attacked the whole idea of strikes and threatened the use of all legal force—from the local police and the state militia to the national army and navy—to stop violence. Preaching laissez-faire political economy, Medill argued that strikes were irrational and self-destructive. To improve the condition of labor, Medill offered arbitration to settle disputes and cooperation to divide profits. Aside from these policies, for which he evidenced little enthusiasm, he could only suggest industriousness, temperance, and thrift as a way of achieving independence. Cautious and defensive, the labor leaders sharing the platform with Medill did not challenge his policies or ideology. The meeting that concluded the march adopted a set of resolutions presented by Andrew Cameron that endorsed arbitration and cooperation, recognized the "right of any workman to dispose of his labor as he deems proper," and repudiated violence. The resolutions also declared labor's readiness to repress "lawlessness."[63]

Despite the tone of the building trades march, Chicago's workers wanted higher wages, and eight hours was still a popular goal. While there was no rash of strikes immediately after the building trades march, the carpenters mounted a significant, but unsuccessful, strike in the spring. During the summer and particularly in the fall, however, there were several sizable construction strikes, the largest of which was again organized by the carpenters. The carpenters' strikes revealed that there were new labor leaders in Chicago along with new workers and that at least some of the unions had national affiliations.[64]

The new trend was suggested when a reporter from the *Illinois Staats-Zeitung* interviewed Edward Owen, leader of Union No. 1, the largest of six locals. Owen refused to answer a whole series of questions, however—among them: who was on the three-man strike committee, if the union had tried to keep carpenters from coming to Chicago, whether he himself came to Chicago after the Great Fire, and if the strike had been organized by citizens of Chicago or recent arrivals. Owen did say that of the six locals in Chicago, four spoke English, while one spoke German and the other Swedish. He also said that most of the members were single men living in boardinghouses and rented rooms. In a subsequent interview after the strike began, the *Illinois Staats-Zeitung* reporter talked to Georg Schindler, "the apparent leader of the Germans." Schindler tried to convince the reporter that "he [the reporter] was really nothing more than a worker, whose interests lay in an entirely different direction from those of the owners of the newspaper, and that therefore he should write from the perspective of the strikers, otherwise he could go to hell."[65]

This class consciousness differed markedly from the resolutions and mood of the spring building trades demonstration. These labor leaders were new to the city, as suggested by Owen's refusal to say when he arrived and by the fact that the *Illinois Staats-Zeitung* reporter did not know Schindler at all, and they appealed to the city's carpenters with the same class-based arguments and demands that they directed at the reporter. During the carpenters' strike in the spring, the union demanded, for the first time in Chicago history, a standard minimum wage that attempted to reverse the ill effects of piecework, such as specialization and deskilling. Rather than futilely trying to expel lesser-skilled men from the trade, carpenters' unions now welcomed them as equals. A standard minimum wage was a class-conscious demand that violated prevailing ideas of reward for individual performance, and it formed a cornerstone of the carpenters' successful organization in the 1880s because it linked the unskilled to the craftsmen in the trade.[66]

THE TRANSIENT WORKING CLASS, TEMPERANCE, AND THE RISE OF URBAN POPULISM

To the political leaders of Chicago, the 1872 construction strikes were not only labor disputes but also parts of a larger upsurge of lawlessness. In the summer and fall of 1872—less than a year after the fire and in the midst of the colossal reconstruction effort—the established citizens of Chicago felt as if they were under siege. According to the *Tribune*, "Life and property were greatly endangered by the prevalence of reckless law-breaking. Day after day the newspapers have chronicled the horrible deeds of the preceding night, until the community became fully aroused to a sense of the desperate condition of the city, and the utter disregard for law, and life, and property displayed by the rowdy element of the city." This rowdy element was usually associated with the new workers concentrated in boardinghouses, saloons, and makeshift barracks, the same sorts of places sheltering the men organized by Owen and Schindler's carpenters' union. The murder of a policeman contributed to the sense of disorder. As the random violence continued in the summer and fall of 1872, the police became edgy, particularly in boardinghouse districts and around crowded saloons, and the hasty use of their weapons added to the killings, sparking angry crowds that threatened them in turn. The police failed to make fine distinctions between rowdy crowds associated with construction strikes and those occurring in the saloons and boardinghouses.[67]

In the fall of 1872, frightened and outraged citizens began to coalesce into pressure groups pushing the government to act. Demanding "that murderers should be hanged," a coalition of leading citizens, the Committee of Twenty-Five, called for expeditious prosecution of those accused of murder and threatened vigilante action if nothing was done. Bipartisan, this group included substantial Democrats, among them the Irish politician Barney Caulfield, as well as German Republicans, such as Anton Hesing. Competing with the Committee of Twenty-five was the city's revived temperance movement, which viewed the suppression of liquor consumption as the key to crime control. The temperance forces viewed the Committee of Twenty-Five as an ally of the liquor industry. The temperance advocates constituted a significant portion of the powerful evangelical wing of the local Republican Party, and their numbers included the head of the Board of Police and Fire Commissioners as well as former mayor Levi Boone, whose policies had provoked the Lager Beer Riot in 1855.[68]

Medill resisted the temperance pressure, arguing that the Sunday closing laws were unenforceable in a city where three-quarters of the one hundred thousand adults were foreign-born and accustomed to drinking on Sundays: "We have entire wards in which it is scarcely possible to find one man who was born in America or is descended from Americans. The native-born men predominate in scarcely half dozen wards [out of twenty] in Chicago." Claiming that the police department was inadequate to the task, he urged the temperance forces to use the moral suasion techniques characteristic of their movement in the antebellum era. Medill had ample political reason to temporize on this volatile issue: The native-born constituted only two-fifths of the city's electorate (fig. 8).[69]

After Medill made a halfhearted attempt to enforce the Sunday closing laws in October, the temperance forces pushed harder, even organizing a special bureau with hired detectives to collect evidence against violators of the Sunday closing law. For these determined temperance advocates, more was at stake than alcohol and crime: The city's native-born citizens were claiming once again, as they had in 1855, to set the terms of public life in Chicago and define who was, and who was not, a genuine citizen. As the lawyer for the temperance forces, M. C. Kelley told an *Illinois Staats-Zeitung* reporter: "We Americans have made the laws and execute them, and whoever cannot accommodate themselves to that does not need to live here among us. We intend to close, and keep closed, all saloons and associated Sunday amusements." It was a question of whose city was it.[70]

The aggressiveness of the temperance forces split the Committee of Twenty-Five that originally had called for swift administration of justice. When even this group supported enforcing the Sunday closing law, the committee's founding leaders resigned, including Hesing. His angry resignation speech echoed those he used to mobilize the North Siders against the fire limits only ten months earlier. Defending himself against the accusation of being the associate of drunkards and sots, Hesing identified himself instead with workers, artisans, and mechanics—with seventy-five thousand

> industrious, honest, thrifty, sober men, who on Monday morning go to work with their lunch pails in their hands full of cold food, return again around six o'clock in the evening, exhausted from their work and from an often three to four mile march. . . . The worker lives in a small home with his family, in a room 7 by 9. He cannot invite anyone to visit him because the room doesn't permit it; he is not invited out either because his acquaintances are no better off. Then comes Sunday. In the morning he goes to

church . . . ; when he comes back he yearns to go out in the fresh air with his wife and child, to look up acquaintances and discuss the events of the week, politics, religion—and to seek out the one diversion that this life offers him. These people have the same right to live here as those who live in palaces, and who on Sunday stretch out on soft couch cushions, lazy and doing nothing.

Laboring to build the city was the best criterion of genuine citizenship, not the restrictive moral codes of the Yankees. Hesing provided a midwestern example of how local Stalwart Republicans and emergent machine politicians built strong constituencies amid the stable, foreign-born workers of American cities. He also demonstrated how machine politicians pioneered an urban populism to communicate with their constituents and legitimate their roles as brokers for immigrant communities.[71]

After resigning from the Committee of Twenty-Five, Hesing organized several antitemperance rallies in which enthusiastic audiences ratified his leadership of the German community. The public endorsement of Hesing's leadership blended into a celebration of the North Side, which stood like a "brand-new German city" rebuilt from the ashes by "German labor power, thriftiness, and business acumen." For Germans, the rebuilding of Chicago, and of the North Side in particular, took on mythological proportions, stemming from the severity of the fire's impact on their community. For Chicago Germans, the North Side became analogous in space to Sunday in time, a refuge sustaining what was most valuable in life amid the vagaries of a market society and the attacks of the evangelical Yankees. In this way, they made their distinct contribution to building the Chicago ethnic neighborhood, itself a substantial component of the emerging capitalist city.[72]

As the conflicts over the fire limits and the temperance laws suggest, the rebuilding of the North Side, both physically and culturally, was a political act. Other ethnic groups had to perform comparable feats of political, cultural, and social reconstruction. Given their proximity to the Germans on the North Side, the Swedes and Norwegians suffered similar losses and rebuilt their communities in similar ways. Less directly in the fire's path, the Irish were nonetheless affected. Bridgeport did not burn down, but Irish neighborhoods on the North and West Sides did. The heavy involvement of the Irish in the construction industry—from laborers and craftsmen to union leaders and entrepreneurs—meant that they were key players in the reconstruction. Similarly, the Irish influence in politics involved them in all the battles over reconstruction policy. The battles over rebuilding the city helped politicize all these ethnic communities. Through this movement, Chicago's working class acted politically for the first time after the eight-hour movement, though not under labor or socialist leadership. The political momentum continued when temperance reemerged as a public issue.[73]

Under relentless pressure from the temperance forces, the Medill administration moved decisively to enforce the Sunday closing law in the spring of 1873.[74] On April 28, Police Superintendent Elihu Washburne issued General Order No. 20, which told officers on their beats to enter any saloons where they suspected violations of the law and to immediately arrest the offending saloon keepers. General Order No. 20 expanded the temperance issue into a question of civil rights and the administration of the police, thus providing broader issues around which the opposition could rally. The use of the police had been festering in local politics for over a year because of the crime wave after the fire. The Board of Police and Fire Commissioners was one of the semi-independent governing bodies that made Chicago's government complex, cumbersome, and open to influence by neighborhood-based politicians, the men whom civic reformers had called Barnacles and Bummers since the Citizens' campaign in 1869. The crisis of the Great Fire created an opportunity for reformers through the "Mayor's Bill," the new state law that gave the mayor unusual powers to deal with the crisis of reconstruction.[75]

Medill used his new emergency powers to appoint Elihu Washburne, a temperance advocate, as superintendent of police and to remove two members of the Board of Police and Fire Commissioners who opposed Washburne's new policies. Such changes in the administration and policies of the police were analogous to the creation of New York City's Metropolitan Police in 1857. Imposed on the city by Republicans in charge of the New York State Legislature, the Metropolitan Police had native-born personnel and a more bureaucratic structure, both designed to sever their ties to local immigrant working-class neighborhoods. The "Metropolitans" immediately set out to enforce new state temperance laws, with higher license fees for saloon keepers and Sunday closing requirements. The upshot was open street battles in New York City's working-class neighborhoods between residents and the police, some of which required the state militia to intervene. Sixteen years later, Chicago's response to Medill's new police policies was more political.[76]

The politics involved the independent power of democratically elected members of independent boards and commissions. One of the three police commissioners was too powerful to remove: Mark Sheridan, who was a considerable force in the Irish community. As a young man, Sheridan had actively supported the abortive Irish rebellion in 1848, and he fled to the United States after its repression, arriving in Chicago in 1856. An Irish forty-eighter, Sheridan was one of the most important politicians in Chicago sympathetic to the interests of labor, and he led the police and fire commissioners in opposition to the extended patrol requirements. When Washburne issued General Order No. 20, Sheridan also protested that it violated the constitutional protection against unlawful searches and seizures. Sheridan also attacked the "Mayor's Bill" for being contrary to the spirit of republican institutions. Although Sheridan had not been popular with Hesing and the *Illinois Staats-Zeitung*, his opposition to police policy cast him in a different light.[77]

Hesing had been working throughout the spring of 1873 to organize political opposition to the Medill administration, and he sought to create a broad coalition well beyond the saloon keepers, distillers, and brewers who were already up in arms over the temperance issue. Special Order No. 20 provided an ideal opportunity, and the *Illinois Staats-Zeitung* attacked it for violating citizens' civil rights. The first meeting of what became the People's Party was held on May 14, 1873, in the very heart of the German North Side. Subsequent political meetings during the spring of 1873 culminated in the organization of a permanent—and overwhelmingly German—Centralverein at a meeting in late May. In addition to ward organizations, a wide range of German social and labor groups were represented at this meeting, including Turners, singing societies, German regional organizations, the Sozialer Arbeiterverein of the West Side, and the carpenters' union. The presence of these groups is one indication of the broad populist appeal of the movement. While adding some distinctive ethnic and labor themes to this tradition, Hesing's emerging coalition accentuated the heart of it: the misuse of the state against the people by parasitical elites. In the case of the fire limits, these Yankee elites would have sacrificed the wooden homes of the working class in order to satisfy the demands of bankers and insurance companies from outside the city. In the case of enforcing the temperance laws, the same aristocrats were trying to use the state to directly attack a whole way of life. When Mayor Medill ordered his administration to enforce the temperance laws, he created the ideal enemy for Hesing's urban populist coalition.[78]

While Hesing was proud of the German origins of the political rebellion, he was also anxious that Germans not alienate other groups. At this juncture, he saw the Germans properly taking the lead as they had in 1854, when they met at North Market Hall to oppose Stephen A. Douglas's Kansas-Nebraska Act, and in 1855, when they led the opposition to Mayor Boone's temperance policies that resulted in the Lager Beer Riot. Then their action had found wider resonance among other national groups. In 1873, the critically important other group was the Irish, without whom Hesing and his allies knew they could not win. He had turned to his Irish allies in the recent battle against the fire limits, which had taken place a year and a half earlier. First among them was James J. McGrath, one of the two aldermen from the Fifteenth Ward located on the Northwest Side, which contained a substantial German and Scandinavian population. Now Hesing reached out even farther.[79]

By late August, Hesing and his allies were ready to cement an alliance with Chicago's most prominent Irish politicians. The critical meeting took place in Henry Greenebaum's bank on August 31, 1873, attended by prominent Irish Democrats and German Republicans, who were also representatives of the Centralverein. Hermann Lieb, editor of the city's German Democratic paper, the *Chicago Union,* wanted to support the Democrats, but he was successfully opposed by two of the most important Irish leaders present, Daniel O'Hara and Barney Caulfield. Fearing the effects of old partisan divisions on issues like the tariff, they argued that the local questions facing Chicago had nothing to do with national party divisions; what did city finance and the administration of the police have to do with differences between Republicans and Democrats? The meeting resolved that the Democratic Party would not campaign in the fall but rather join with the Centralverein in the battle for liberty against the so-called Law and Order Party. In order to insure that the new party was not identified as German, agitation committees were set up in each ward, consisting of one representative of the Centralverein and two members from non-German groups. In the same vein, Hesing took a backseat at the proceedings. The upshot of this meeting was that the German wing of the local Republican Party and the Irish wing of the Democratic Party had formed an alliance—catalyzed by an aggressive temperance movement among the native-born—and threw the local political system into complete disarray.[80]

Leaders quickly formed a multiethnic agitation committee, drafted a platform, and organized a mass meeting at Kingsbury Hall on October 4 to kick off the campaign. The meeting adopted the platform, whose central theme was that the municipal government had been taken over by an intolerant minority and used against the majority of the people for narrow, sectarian purposes. It also issued a statement of principles for dealing with the recent bank failures that would soon give way to the nation's worst depression. Currency reform was central to this economic proposal, making the new coalition an ideological ally of labor reformers and the Greenback movement that burst into prominence nationally in the mid-1870s. The statement of principles called for the federal government to issue more currency, instead of contracting it, and—given the city's current shortage of circulating medium—asked the city authorities to issue scrip to pay workers currently engaged on city projects so that they could continue on the job. It also called for stopping foreclosures on city lots for failure of tax payment. Currency reform was part of the emerging late-nineteenth-century urban populist tradition. Currency reformers viewed themselves as resisting the aristocratic use of the government to unjustly reward bond holders who owned the Civil War debt.[81]

Although Hesing spoke at the Kingsbury Hall meeting, Barney Caulfield gave the main address. After attacking the efforts of any nationality to take over the city government, he launched into his main theme: It was time to establish "the same government for the rich as for the poor" in Chicago. During the current economic crisis, people did not even have the means to pay their taxes, but their property was being confiscated anyway. He called for the city to "hold back the arm of vengeance." He added that the plight of the delinquent small taxpayers was exacerbated by an open secret: Inequitable assessments meant that the wealthy, particularly those holding corporate property, paid little or no taxes.[82]

The People's Party threw the local Republicans and Democrats completely off balance. Supportive of the political rebellion, the Democratic Party declined to campaign, and the Republicans never mounted one, despite half-hearted efforts to develop a platform and field candidates. Declining to run on any ticket, Medill took his family on a grand tour of Europe, leaving even before the end of his term. Not surprisingly, the People's Party won the election in a landslide, taking control of both the city and county governments. The party's candidates for major city offices typically won by margins of ten thousand votes out of about forty-seven thousand ballots cast, and it won thirteen aldermanic contests compared to seven for the opposition. The People's Party had mobilized the large majority of the city's foreign-born citizens—almost three-fifths of the electorate—along with some native-born Democratic allies (fig. 8).[83]

Cast out in the Citizens' campaign of 1869, the Barnacles—now called the Bummers—had returned. Both Chicago and Cook County had governments in which their immigrant populations held a substantial proportion of offices and in which a party controlled by immigrants, and heavily influenced by Democrats, set policy. This policy was not hard to predict. The Sunday closing of saloons was a dead issue. The final resolution of the issue reinstated the modus vivendi that had existed through the fall of 1872: Saloons would remain open on Sunday but with closed doors and shuttered windows. Just

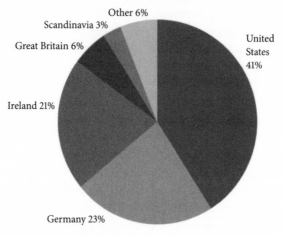

Figure 8
Male Citizens 21 Years and Older by Place of Birth:
Chicago 1870

Other 6%

Scandinavia 3%

Great Britain 6%

United
States
41%

Ireland 21%

Germany 23%

Source: Sample of male citizens with occupations in the 1870
manuscript population census for Chicago; N = 1,467.

as important, the victory of the People's Party settled the question of controlling the police: E. F. C. Klokke and C. A. Reno, the two men fired by Medill, returned to the Board of Police and Fire Commissioners. Since Mark Sheridan remained on the board, the election returned control of the police commissioners to the situation prior to the conflict with Washburne and Medill. Notably, in the first three months of the People's Party's administration, the proportion of white native-born Americans among all of those arrested increased by 30 percent over the previously reported administrative year. The governing policy of the People's Party confirmed the reactive character of the original movement. It had arisen in response to the initiatives of the temperance forces, and in many respects its victory returned the government to the status quo ante.[84]

And yet the election was less about government policy than about the status of first-generation immigrants in Chicago, including those recently arrived to rebuild the city. In a reflective editorial, Hesing looked back on the election and saw it as the end of a political era defined by the issues of the Civil War. Looking forward, he saw a city shaped by its immigrants. The election meant "that Chicago was not a pitiful Yankee village but rather a cosmopolitan, world-class city; that the foreign-born citizens, who have helped make the city what it is, are here in the majority and in power; and that they are not willing to let be forced upon them the absurdities and effronteries which their fellow New England-born citizens hold to be a requirement for morality."[85] Hesing reached too far, however, in claiming that the People's Party spoke for all immigrants, for it did not represent the immigrants of the transient working class, who would soon march on city hall to demand work or bread. Neither did he reach far enough in depicting the party's broader constituency, which extended beyond the middling sectors of the immigrant population to include some wealthy native-born Democrats, most notably Carter Harrison, who would play a pivotal role in the city's politics for two decades.

The People's Party was an urban, ethnic incarnation of American populism. Like many other nineteenth-century movements, including the contemporaneous anti-Chinese movement in California, it drew on republican concepts and language dating to the American Revolution: praise of a virtuous "people" struggling against betrayal by a parasitical elite, fear of monopoly and aristocratic privilege, belief in the labor theory of value, and advocacy of a balanced distribution of property. It used these ideas and terms to mobilize a defensive popular movement against threats by an insolent aristocracy of wealth that it saw using the power of the state to upset a more natural and egalitarian social order that was the birthright of Americans, including naturalized citizens. Whatever the basis in reality of such an order—and in Chicago that foundation was eroding quickly—populism posited a vision of a balanced distribution of wealth in a producers' society in which labor would own the fruits of its labor in the shape of small-scale property or in the form of wages high enough to allow workers to accumulate wealth.

In the 1870s and '80s, this vision was neither nostalgic nor utopian. Despite the growth of wage labor, the opportunity for self-employment was still great in the whole country, as indicated by the fact that the ratio between the number of businesses and farms to the total number of Americans employed actually rose between 1850 and 1880.[86] Similarly, in Chicago the total number of manufacturing firms grew substantially even as the largest firms hired larger proportions of the workforce. In the same vein, the top one-fifth of manufacturers maintained the same level of all capital investment even while the leading 5 percent dramatically increased their share (see figs. 3 and 4, chap. 1). The opportunities for small- and medium-size firms remained substantial in urban America, and in Chicago the People's Party found a significant constituency among them.

Nonetheless, the Peoples Party existed in an emerging urban system that was increasingly hostile to the social context of a producers' order of independent, economically productive, property-owning households. Two new phenomena of the capitalist order—a transient working class and an industrial bourgeoisie—together challenged the viability of the People's Party shortly after its electoral victory. Within two months, the new government was faced with a depression, mass unemployment, and marches of thousands of immigrant workers on the Common Council and the Relief and Aid Society. They were organized and led by the central European left—the Internationals—espousing the "cosmopolitan" ideologies that Hesing had feared would undermine his vision of a home-owning working class.

For similar reasons, the city unions were cool to the populist appeals of the People's Party. They were organizations of wage earners first of all, not property owners, and their priority was gaining government assistance in winning their strikes. The unions also posed a political threat to the People's Party—as did the Internationals—because they could speak for the city's working people, only with a different voice and goals.

The new administration was challenged from above as well. Reeling from the onset of the depression and then mobilized by the need to make the city safe for outside investors, the local bourgeoisie revolted against the rule of the People's Party. Like its counterparts in other large northern cities, the Chicago bourgeoisie also feared that mass marches led by foreign-born communists portended riots, strikes, and perhaps even a local "Commune." The outcome of this upper-class political insurgency, which will be chronicled in the next chapter, was a major upheaval in the city and state. The results included an intensification of the ethnic and class conflicts of 1871–72, the overthrow of the People's Party, a partially successful enhancement of the local government's administrative capacities, and a more successful effort to fasten on that government a new set of policies favorable to accumulating capital and containing the political influence of the city's workers.

5 Class and Politics during the Depression of the 1870s

THE ECONOMIC DEPRESSION COMBINED with Chicago's notorious cold weather to make the winter of 1873–74 especially severe. On the afternoon of December 31, 1873, a crowd of about two thousand gathered outside of C. L. Woodman's bakery factory to receive free bread donated by a local bank and an insurance company to help the families of the unemployed. "There were several policemen present, and, by much cursing and pushing, they succeeded in making a lane through the crowd, through which the men, women, and children escaped after receiving their loaves. The majority of the crowd were women, and children, and many of the latter were so jammed and crushed that there was a constant wail of distress."[1]

The distress of the people of Chicago had only begun. Aggregate wages in Chicago's manufacturing industries fell from just over $6 million in 1873 to slightly more than $4 million in 1876. Nationally, half of the nation's railways were bankrupted, all major industries experienced steep declines in revenues, and perhaps a third of the nation's workers lost their jobs. Small farmers in the South and West saw the prices for their crops fall precipitously, and many fell deep into debt. It took five years and five months for the economy to recover, while people from all walks of life struggled to understand the causes of the economic disaster.[2]

The depression was the outcome of a new development only little understood. Chicago was at the leading edge of a new political economy of capital accumulation that was becoming predominant first in the North and then throughout the country after the Civil War. In Chicago, this phenomenon was dramatically apparent in the rising share of all manufacturing investment controlled by the top 5 percent of firms; between 1850 and 1870 it grew from about 6% to almost 40 percent (see fig. 3, chap. 1). At the same time, capital accumulation required an increase in the ratio of capital invested in the form of machinery, buildings, and other equipment to capital in the form of wages, a ratio that rose continuously in the United States during the late nineteenth century. The increased importance of fixed capital investment created the infrastructure necessary for a modern industrial society—from a dense railroad network, to the plant and equipment required for mechanized production, to the industrial city itself that housed the working class necessary to run the factories.[3]

But the growth in the value ratio of capital to labor had a terrible downside. Businesses with high fixed costs had less flexibility to respond to fluctuations in demand and often resorted to cutthroat competitive practices. In turn, this increased the likelihood of overproduction, that is, the tendency to continue producing goods that were sold at below the cost of production. Although contemporary economic theory did not recognize the existence of general overproduction, some close observers began to think it was at the root of depressions by the late 1870s. Testifying before a House committee in 1879 on the origins of the 1870s depression, Chicago banker Lyman Gage argued that its cause was "the immense transfer of capital into fixed forms, such as ships, railroads, mines, and manufactories, &c." The economic theorist Arthur T. Hadley also traced the 1873 panic and subsequent depression to the much greater investment of capital in fixed forms, mainly in railroad building. Hadley argued that general overproduction not only was possible, but that it characterized the new era: "[T]he continued existence of such masses of undisposable [sic] surplus may be regarded as a leading difference between the long crisis of 1873 and the shorter one of 1857."[4]

When confronted with overproduction, businessmen of this era normally did not shut down their firms and create mass unemployment; rather, they tried to reduce costs by cutting wages, investing in labor-saving machinery, and reorganizing production. In some cases, such as meatpacking in Chicago, they even increased the scale of their operations. The prime national example of this phenomenon was Andrew Carnegie, who took advantage of the depression to buy iron and steel companies at bargain prices and then applied to his operation the advanced management techniques that he had learned working for the Pennsylvania Railroad. In the nation's manufacturing economy, the depression of the 1870s resulted in a distinctive combination of stagnation and transformation, as some industries declined while others transformed their production and sometimes increased their demand for labor. These trends in investment and technology created an anomaly for workers: *if* they had a job in the first place, their paychecks shrank but their real wages—adjusted for inflation—increased modestly. That was because prices declined, due largely to increased competition and mechanization. The depression of the 1870s witnessed the beginning of three decades of deflation and instability combined with economic growth.[5]

All types of workers opposed the wage cuts that came with cutthroat competition, while craftsmen led resistance to the transformation of production, since their status and power were under direct assault. Both skilled and unskilled workers increasingly had to travel to find work, creating the "tramp menace" or transience so prominent in the decade. The tramps compounded Chicago's problems with the reconstruction laborers who had arrived after the Great Fire of 1871. These thousands of "strangers" moving in and through the city appeared ominous, while the emerging industrial economy looked brittle and unstable.

Tramps were just one example of an extended crisis in social relations brought to a head by the depression. The city's business leaders decided that they could not continue to allow the city to be run by machine politicians who were not responsive to their interests, which led them to enter politics in earnest. In attempting to win other elements of society to their leadership, Chicago's capitalists launched their first great attempt at what theorist Antonio Gramsci called "hegemony." Leading elements of this new class attempted to forge a political coalition with an agenda through which it could win and maintain political power. To gain the consent or acquiescence of other elements of society, this project required a new politics underpinned by new cultural norms shared by groups across the social order. But the new urban agenda forged by the city's upper class was contested on several fronts and in the end found only limited success.[6]

THE WORKINGMEN'S PARTY OF ILLINOIS AND THE RISE OF THE CENTRAL EUROPEAN LABOR MOVEMENT: 1873–74

With the start of the 1873 depression, it quickly became apparent that the city's unskilled, largely immigrant working class could not be ignored. Distinctly different from the crowds during the eight-hour strike in 1867, the marches of the unemployed in December 1873 marked a new era in the history of Chicago's working class. The 1867 strike had been led by well-organized skilled workers with their own labor movement, which was an extension of the American and European republican revolutionary traditions. In 1867, the crowds of unskilled and semiskilled workers emerged after skilled workers started the strike, and the crowds' political significance derived from the eight-hour law, which was an achievement of the craftsmen's labor movement. The crowds were a popular effort to enforce the law. In 1873, the crowds of the unskilled took the initiative under new leadership that owed relatively little to antebellum American labor traditions, and the crowds themselves were closer to a classical wage-earning proletariat than to rebellious journeymen. The December 1873 marches helped push the city's upper class into new self-awareness and political action, while crystallizing divisions between Anglo Americans and central Europeans in the Chicago labor movement.

Preparations for the December marches had been going on for weeks previously, centered at the two halls of the international left on the Near West Side. Local newspapers called these left-wing leaders of the unemployed "the Internationals," a reference to their ideology of international solidarity, but the term might as well have signified their multiethnic constituency and the transnational labor market that brought them to Chicago. The three groups that organized a mass meeting on December 21—the Sozial-Politischer Arbeiterverein, the Arbeiterverein, and the furniture workers union—were overwhelmingly German. Although the Arbeiterverein had been a fixture in the labor politics of Chicago's German-speaking workers since it was organized in 1857, it now played a much more modest role. Founded in 1872, the furniture workers union had a left political cast from the beginning, and its vitality stood out in a period of labor weakness and uncertainty. The third group, the Sozial-Politischer Arbeiterverein, led the organizational activities prior to the December 21 mass meeting.[7]

The Sozial-Politischer Arbeiterverein had been founded in July 1870 from the remnants of the declining German union movement and its city central body. Its organizers included Carl Klings, editor of the old movement's *Deutsche Arbeiter,* and his associates in the local Lassallean Allgemeiner Deutscher Arbeiterverein (Universal German Workers Association; ADAV). The effort of Klings and his allies to turn the unrest during the depression into a left political party was a natural outgrowth of German precedent and recent Chicago history. Germany's first labor movement began with a national political organization, Ferdinand Lassalle's ADAV, not with local alliances of trade unions as in Great Britain and the United States. As Lassalleans, Klings and his allies saw universal male suffrage as an opportunity to build a labor party in the United States. That opportunity had recently been partially realized by the People's Party, and the Internationals concluded that they could accomplish the same feat of uniting most working people, but now under the aegis of a real labor party led by them, not charlatans like Anton Hesing. The prominence of immigrant workers in the Chicago electorate lent credence to their anticipated success. Almost 60 percent of the electorate in Chicago was foreign-born, among whom over three-quarters were either skilled or unskilled workers. These foreign-born voting workers constituted 45 percent of the eligible voters (see fig. 8, chap. 4).[8]

The huge meeting on Sunday, December 21 at the Vorwärts Turner Hall near Twelfth Street and Blue Island Avenue struck "the American portion of the population of Chicago like lightning from a clear sky." At least five thousand people showed up, overflowing the facility. The multiethnic crowd heard speakers in several languages compare Chicago's workers to slaves, suffering materially and politically at the hands of an idle and parasitic aristocracy reminiscent of Europe. The solution for workers was to found their own press and independent political party, just as the rebellious farmers in the Granger movement had recently done.[9]

The December 21 meeting called on the city government to take responsibility for relieving the plight of the workers by providing work to the unemployed and, if that was not possible, then aid. The Chicago proposals of 1873 not only echoed the political debate of 1857 but also reflected the contemporary ones put forward by workers in other cities influenced by the International, particularly New York. In Chicago, the new issue, in contrast to 1857, concerned the administration of aid for those who could not find work. The Vorwärts Turner Hall meeting did not trust the Chicago Relief and Aid Society to disperse aid to the needy. This rejection of the Relief and Aid Society implicitly challenged the stewardship of the city's native-born upper class and its policies toward workers, particularly its concern that the indiscriminate dispersal of relief would undermine the incentive to work.[10]

The Turner Hall meeting called for a march on city hall the next evening, Monday, December 22, 1873. A huge crowd of around ten thousand gathered in the Haymarket Square and divided into four separate contingents, which marched along different routes in order to confuse the police. Leading one of the contingents were members of the Sozial-Demokratische Arbeiterverein, carrying an American and a red flag. This name change from the Sozial-Politische to the Sozial-Demokratische Arbeiterverein reflected the close connection between the Chicago Internationals and the left in Germany. Marxists August Bebel and Karl Liebknecht had founded the German Sozial-Demokratische Arbeiterpartei in 1869, and it quickly became the dominant German labor party. The *Illinois Staats-Zeitung* asserted that never before had the ideas of the European left been so boldly proclaimed on American soil; now Chicago had its equivalent of Bebel and company, "demagogues" and "tempters" of the laboring man.[11]

When representatives of the marchers failed to obtain substantial concessions from their meetings with the Common Council and the Relief and Aid Society, the Internationals proceeded to found a new political party. The first step was to cut ties to the forty-eighter generation that had provided political leadership to Chicago's German workers since the 1850s, which meant rejecting Francis A. Hoffmann Jr. as their spokesman. He was both the son of one of the city's most prominent liberal German politicians and head of the Arbeiterverein. The new public spokesman for the Internationals was their own weekly newspaper, the *Vorbote,* which they soon founded. The Internationals also broke with the German democratic tradition of international republicanism that the radical forty-eighters such as Eduard Schläger had articulated in the 1860s. Schläger was no longer even in the country, having returned recently to Germany. The forty-eighter left had spoken a common idiom with the Anglo American labor republicanism of people like Andrew Cameron, Richard Trevellick, and William Sylvis. In contrast, most of the Internationals drew on a mixture of Lassallean and Marxist ideas from the contemporary European and German labor movements. The Internationals presented their platform in January 1874, naming their new organization the Workingmen's Party of Illinois. Afterward, the mainstream press called them the "Workingmen."[12]

The core of the Workingmen's program called for the public control of institutions that directly affected the lives of workers—the telegraph, savings banks, and fire insurance companies—while most of its other planks pertained to economic and social practices particularly important to people working for wages.[13] Thus it had a class-specific character, in contrast to the platform of the People's Party, the central thrust of which was the status of the foreign-born within the city. The platform promoted governmental reform by increasing democratic controls, such as recall, and by weakening of the influence of professional politicians through measures such as direct payment of governmental officials and abolishing the contract system in public works. These proposals placed the Workingmen's program in the mainstream of the broader urban reform movement after the Civil War that opposed the weak and fragmented municipal government and sought to replace it with a stronger one administered by politically independent public officials. These ideas meshed with those coming from some upper-class urban reformers, who, like the Workingmen, despised the rule of ward politicians such as Anton Hesing, who had built fiefdoms within the old, decentralized structure of power.

The *Illinois Staats-Zeitung* thought that, except for two or three planks, everything in the Workingmen's platform had been advocated for years by the German liberal press. In the eyes of the *Illinois Staats-Zeitung,* the new elements did not pertain to public control of transportation and communication—which the *Illinois Staats-Zeitung* had supported in various forms for a considerable time—but rather to state control of savings banks and building and loan associations, the elimination of the contract system for public works, and the recall of public officials. The *Illinois Staats-Zeitung's* opposition to state control of small financial institutions and to eliminating the contract system for public works reflected the interests of its constituency of ethnic businessmen and contractors. The *Illinois Staats-Zeitung* considered the recall of public officials to be a thinly disguised attempt to remove the recently elected officials of the People's Party.[14]

The *Tribune* did not react strongly against the Workingmen's proposals for public control of transportation and communication either. In the 1870s, its editorial pages advocated various forms of governmental regulation of transportation, communication, and grain elevators, and Joseph Medill even supported the public takeover of the Western Union Company, since it was a de facto monopoly. The Republican Party had initiated a vast expansion of the federal government's power over the economy during and after the Civil War, not only as a military measure but also to create a national market. The more industrialized parts of the country, and especially those in the West, strongly supported federal subsidies for infrastructure improvements and more generally federal promotion of economic development. Thus, although government ownership and management of enterprises had no significant base of support, opinions about the government's role in the economy were more fluid and varied in the 1870s than one might expect, given the prevalence of classical economics.[15]

Despite reservations among the Workingmen, Klings won the day for independent political action, aided considerably by the enthusiasm of his constituency. In early January 1874, Klings wrote, "The mood is thoroughly revolutionary. If it depended on Chicago, we could blow the building in the air any day." Not only did Klings strongly favor a labor party, but he also pressed for an alliance with the Grangers, whose organizations were growing explosively at the same time. Like the People's Party, Illinois farmers had burst into the state's political life as an independent political force in 1873, first by electing judges favorable to railroad regulation in the spring and then by winning fifty-three out of sixty-six county elections they had contested in the fall.[16]

The prospect of linking the city's workers and the Grangers in an alliance of producers contributed to the revolutionary élan of Chicago's left. Klings even hoped that workers and farmers would use the state to construct huge manufactories, reminiscent of the French national workshops of 1848, as well as storehouses for agricultural products. Farmers and workers could then exchange their products without middlemen, practically for the cost of production. Eliminating middlemen—or at least reducing their power—had long been a goal of small producers making their own products, and the contemporary effort of Illinois Grangers to use the state government to regulate grain elevators reflected this political mind-set. Even the Workingmen's most radical plank calling for state control of transportation and communication was adopted with an eye to the Grangers, who had made governmental regulation of the railroads a public issue.[17]

Such an alliance of producers also fit well with the contemporary labor movement in Germany, which was foremost a political phenomenon stemming from the Revolution of 1848 and rooted in associations whose primary constituency consisted of artisans in small-scale firms, not of wage earners in large factories. Through the early 1870s, a substantial majority of Germans labored in small enterprises with from one to five workers, a considerably higher proportion than in contemporary Chicago, where only about 5 percent of the manufacturing workforce worked in such small firms (see fig. 3, chap. 1). The voluntary associations at the base of the German labor movement were more like political clubs than unions. Although the German movement understood itself as composed of workers, that term really meant those participating in these associations, thus *worker* was fundamentally a political construction. Although craftsmen constituted the largest group of participants, the associations also included some laborers, masters, small manufacturers, and traditional professionals, such as teachers and journalists. The Workingmen's attempt to ally with the Grange and subsequent American populist coalitions fit well within this inclusive conception of labor's constituency and echoed some of the producers' republicanism of the American labor movement.[18]

The preparation of a platform and subsequent organization of the new party touched off several months of intense activity among the Internationals in early 1874. Language groups could form their own sections of the party. Within four days, they had organized eight German sections, two Irish ones, and one each for the Danes, Poles, and Bohemians. Despite the Irish sections, the center of gravity of the movement remained among German-speaking workers, including those not ethnically German but who nevertheless spoke some of the language, such as Bohemians or Poles from territories controlled by Austria-Hungary. The voice of the new party was the *Vorbote,* founded as the organ of the Workingmen's Party of Illinois in February 1874 with Klings as editor. The editorship of the *Vorbote* was the most important leadership position in the international left in Chicago. The paper and its offshoots served as conduits for the main currents of German labor thought to enter Chicago.[19]

More than its ideology, it was the Workingmen's goal of supplanting the People's Party that aroused the ire of the city's established German press. The prime voice of the People's Party, Anton Hesing's *Illinois Staats-Zeitung*, felt obliged to counter the threat. Despite dismissing the Workingmen's politics, the paper realized that it had to address "the social question" as well as celebrate American political freedoms, and it did so following the intellectual lead of Gottlieb Kellner, editor of the Philadelphia *Demokrat* and one of the minority of German forty-eighters who remained in the Democratic Party. Kellner thought that the choice of the age was between wage labor in a capitalist society and some form of cooperation or profit sharing that would form the basis for a social order rooted in independent producers. Although the *Illinois Staats-Zeitung* never took one clear position on these alternatives, it had shown sympathy for the cooperative movement. It also supported labor's right to organize but not the right to monopolize the determination of wages. This ambivalence on "the social question" reflected the constituencies of both the *Illinois Staats-Zeitung* and the People's Party among foreign-born working people and the moderate-size manufacturers so prominent in German Chicago. The issues raised by the Workingmen tended to divide this constituency, whereas urban populism could unite them in a fight for a just place in local society.[20]

The Workingmen's first electoral contest took place in the spring of 1874, when the modest offices of Chicago's three town governments on the North, South, and West Sides were at stake. But the Workingmen showed strength in only two of the North Side's wards, where their candidates received on average about 16 percent of the vote for the offices they contested. Their real opponent had been Hesing, whose base of strength was on the North Side, and he rebuffed them easily. The electoral defeat of the Workingmen in the spring of 1874 shook Klings's leadership within the Workingmen's Party of Illinois but did not dislodge him. Yet the allies that Klings needed for his political strategy were falling away.[21]

The party had failed to attract proprietors and tradesmen in the spring election, and the alliance with the Grangers never materialized. Both the *Tribune* and the party's Marxists agreed that property ownership among American farmers would keep them distant from the Workingmen's Party of Illinois. They were seconded by the *Prairie Farmer,* the Chicago-based paper in whose offices the Illinois Grange had been founded in 1868. Reacting to the marches of the unemployed in the city, the paper attacked the Internationals, asserting that "the farmers are sternly and everlastingly opposed to Communistic ideas" and would help the governor put down any attempt to "sack and plunder" the city. The Grangers lived in a threatened but still vital social order based in simple commodity production. Their mind-set was shared by small manufacturers in hinterland cities who still saw the feasibility of a free-labor society in which craftsmen could become independent producers like themselves. Besides being foreign-born, Klings and his followers represented mostly wage earners who would never be independent producers.[22]

Just as important, the Internationals failed to establish an effective alliance with the city's English-speaking labor reformers and unions. Compared to the sustained effort they put into wooing the farmers, they hardly even tried to build relationships with English-speaking labor organizations. This was partly the result of their Lassallean heritage that placed much more significance on politics than on union organization, whereas the English-speaking labor movement was an alliance of unions first of all. In addition, German labor leaders had felt betrayed when Cameron and his friends supported the Citizens' reform ticket instead of their labor candidates in the local election of 1869. But most important was the Anglo American tradition of republicanism to which Cameron and the English-speaking labor movement subscribed.[23]

ANDREW CAMERON, ANGLO AMERICAN LABOR REFORM, AND THE EMERGENCE OF TWO LABOR TRADITIONS: 1873–74

Andrew Cameron had been cordial to the Internationals up until the marches of the unemployed in December 1873 and the subsequent organization of the Workingmen's Party of Illinois. His attendance at the 1869 conference of the International in Basel, Switzerland, as the representative of the National Labor Union illustrated the prevailing mood of cooperation and interchange within the culture of international labor reform. Yet after the marches of the unemployed, Cameron began to distinguish more sharply between the reforms he advocated and the revolution he saw the Internationals promoting. He greeted the marches of the unemployed in December 1873 with an editorial entitled "Let Us Have No Appeals to Arms," in which he argued, like the *Illinois Staats-Zeitung*, that political violence was unnecessary in a republic because workingmen had the political power to peacefully redress their grievances through the ballot. They had only to pull themselves together and resolve to put their own men in power. In other words, he clung to the political strategy that Anglo American labor reformers had followed since the early nineteenth century: uniting the producers to reclaim the state, which was theirs by birthright. Actually, Klings was following a similar strategy in 1874, although the nationality of the Workingmen, their foreign rhetoric, and their tactics of mass marches obscured that fact from Cameron.[24]

Still, there were fundamental differences between Cameron and the Internationals that the unemployment crisis during the depression brought to the fore. While the Internationals were organizing the Workingmen's Party of Illinois in January 1874, Cameron published an editorial opposing the American state's responsibility for providing employment. For him, such a demand was only legitimate in a despotic government where the citizens were dependent on the state for everything else while not being able to control its actions. But in "a republican form of government the citizen is the State, therefore we insist that . . . the State is not bound to find employment for the citizen. Here we have all the incentives to industry, frugality, and perseverance. If we were to admit the correctness of the theory that the State is bound to find employment for the citizen, we would destroy the noblest ambition in man, that of independence, and he would become a simple pensioner. If the citizens of a republican government experience panics, and a suspension of business, causing general distress, it is because they have been derelict in their duty to themselves, and have tolerated bad laws and class legislation." Cameron was invoking an American tradition of political values that stressed a limited state based on an independent citizenry, and the great danger of the Internationals was that their proposals would undermine this independence.[25]

Cameron's thinking was rooted in an older Jacksonian view of the state, which contrasted with the Republicans' assertive use of it during the Civil War. The libertarian side of the American republican tradition had been rekindled in the 1850s by a revival of Democratic thinking led by Stephen A. Douglas and his allies. For Cameron, the Civil War had fulfilled his worst fears of "centralization," particularly when the Republicans established a national banking system concentrating the money power and the mammoth war debt in the hands of the bankers and allied wealth holders. Then the new railroad corporations sought and received giveaways of land for speculative purposes. To secure these nefarious goals, a centralized powerful nation-state on the federal level had been necessary. To Cameron, the victims of the centralized state were society's backbone: the producers, whose independence and civic virtue was essential to any healthy republic. True to his principles, Cameron also resisted centralization within the Anglo American wing of the labor movement, successfully opposing a proposal for state ownership of the means of transportation and communication when it arose within the

National Labor Union in 1868. State ownership would increase the patronage available to the party in power and facilitate the use of military force against the people.[26]

Up to the depression winter of 1873–74, Cameron had maintained an uneasy sympathy for the left in Europe by arguing that a centralized state and the abolition of private property may have been appropriate for conditions in the Old World but not in the New. Then the headquarters of the International moved to New York in 1871; the unemployed demanded work or bread in 1873; Carl Klings called for government-owned national workshops; and the Workingmen's Party advocated government control of transportation, communication, banking, and insurance. Even more ominously, the Internationals began celebrating the European left's politics of insurrection, symbolized by the annual commemorations in Chicago of the Paris Commune. Faced with these developments, the libertarian side of Cameron's republicanism came to the fore, leading him to openly oppose communism, revolution, and state centralization. For him, the United States needed not revolution but a revival of the people to take back control of the government and eliminate class legislation. The central raison d'être of the American labor movement, this political revival would "preserve a pure Democratic Republican form of government with distributive powers as opposed to Caesarism or monarchy with centralized powers." The clear Jeffersonian echoes in the phrase "Democratic Republican" were surely intentional. A Jacksonian Democrat who had moved left during the Civil war, Cameron returned to the center of his tradition when challenged by the depression and the Internationals.[27]

Cameron's evolving political opposition to the Internationals was reflected in the practical activities of English-speaking trade unionists, who excluded the Internationals from their organizational activities. In 1874, the Industrial Congress, successor to the National Labor Union, called on all workers of America to protest the recent undermining of the federal law mandating the eight-hour workday on public works. The Industrial Congress called for nationwide protest meetings on May 18, in preparation for which representatives of several Chicago unions met at the offices of the *Workingman's Advocate*. The group rejected a proposal by Frank Lawler to invite all workingmen's associations to the protest meetings and instead limited their appeal to fellow trade unionists. In obvious reference to the Internationals' distaste for unions, one man said that if those invited "were ashamed to come forward as Trades Unionists, then he did not want to work with them." A further resolution determined that members of any "communistic body" would be excluded. In reaction, the Internationals organized their own meeting one day before that of the trade unionists. Although the two meetings passed similar resolutions, neither acknowledged the existence of the other. When the "English-speaking workingmen"—about fifty people, mostly members of the Typographical Union—met in the fall to discuss candidates for the state legislature, they did not endorse the ticket of the Workingmen's Party of Illinois. Amid the conflicts precipitated by the depression of the 1870s, two labor political cultures had emerged within transnational republicanism, each with distinct working-class constituencies and complex ideologies containing hidden commonalities but differing views of politics and the state.[28]

THE WORKINGMEN'S ELECTORAL DEFEAT AND THE CONSTRUCTION OF A LEFT SUBCULTURE: 1874–76

Still undaunted, the Workingmen's Party of Illinois entered the 1874 fall elections, fielding practically complete slates for state, county, and city offices. Throughout the country, this election was hotly contested and of profound significance as a resurgent Democratic Party in the North challenged a Republican Party that had long been in office and that was on the defensive because of corruption and the controversies over Reconstruction. In Chicago, the People's Party maintained its separate identity, forming the main opposition to the Chicago Republican Party, while prominent Democrats of both past and future import, such as John Wentworth and Carter Harrison, worked closely with it. The politically transitional character of the election for Germans was best defined by a statement of purpose frequently reprinted in the *Illinois Staats-Zeitung* beginning in early 1874. It declared that up through 1872 it had supported the Republican Party in order to fight slavery and uphold the legal achievements of the Northern victory against forces of reaction, but now it was an independent paper trying to give expression to a popular spirit struggling for political form as well as to all liberal ideas appropriate to building a new party. Not only the *Illinois Staats-Zeitung* but also the two other German dailies in Chicago—the *Freie Presse* and the *Union*—supported the People's Party. The fall campaign was unusual by any measure, with the Democrats abstaining and the Republicans running on a local platform so weak that even the *Tribune* made fun of it. Amid a broad victory for the People's Party locally and the Democrats nationally, the vote for the Workingmen's Party of Illinois was insignificant.[29]

The meager showing of the Workingmen in the fall of 1874 emboldened the elements among the Chicago Internationals opposed to an independent labor party and skeptical of electoral politics generally. Klings's ambivalence toward labor unions and support for the Grangers had been provoking stronger opposition for a considerable time. In early 1875, Conrad Conzett took over the editorship of the *Vorbote* and made it more sympathetic to the Marxist left and less inclined to Lassallean independent political action. The Marxists also considered the alliance with the Grangers a mistake, since, according to Marxist Hermann Schlüter, the commitment of the farmers to maintaining their land meant that they would always want to save capitalism rather than abolish private property. In the eyes of Marxian socialists, the party needed to shed its petty bourgeois platform. These predominantly foreign-born radicals helped found and sustain trade unions, particularly left-leaning ones like the furniture workers, and their union connections provided them with a stronger institutional base of support than Klings's Lassallean group developed.[30]

Weak in electoral politics, the Internationals focused on building unions and a left-wing subculture rooted in a network of newspapers, Turnvereins, political groups, singing societies, theater groups, militia companies, labor-friendly saloons, and radical unions. This subculture drew upon the practices and organizational models of the larger world of associational life—the *Vereinswesen*—typical of German districts in nineteenth-century American cities. The Chicago left's ability to mix pleasure and politics in its social events probably derived from this ethnic culture. Nonetheless, the left's subculture was distinguished from the *Vereinswesen* because of its Socialist cultural and political activities and its multiethnic character. The Socialist movement in Chicago had an international cast from its origins in the marches of the unemployed in December 1873.[31]

The subculture of the left had a central European center of gravity, not only because of its large German constituency but also because of the strong presence of Bohemians and other nationalities that were part of the Austro-Hungarian Empire. There was also a large left-wing Scandinavian constituency, evidenced in Chicago through both Scandinavian leaders and labor papers published in Danish, Swedish, and Finnish. The key event in the history of this left subculture was the founding of the *Vorbote* in February 1874, a date that made it one of the earliest of numerous German labor papers founded during the 1870s in major American cities. The weekly *Vorbote* was complemented by the *Chicagoer Arbeiter-Zeitung*, which was published three times a week beginning in May 1877; it became a daily two years later, at the same time that the *Fackel*, a Sunday edition, appeared. The *Arbeiter-Zeitung* survived until 1919. The fund-raising to support these papers became one of the social and political rituals of the German left, drawing on the whole range of sympathetic associations. The associational network among left-leaning central Europeans was the envy of Andrew Cameron when he wrote in 1876 that it was "to the eternal disgrace of our American, Irish, English, and Scotch mechanics" that they lacked their own meeting halls, while the Germans had "their lyceums, their reading rooms, their lecture and music halls, their gymnasiums, where they can meet in social concourse, discuss the political situations, enjoy an intellectual treat and improve their physical conditions."[32]

The left also had its own militia companies, which were founded as a reaction to militia units founded by businessmen. Beginning in 1872, local business interests had attempted to found their own militia company to provide self-protection and to aid the police when faced with crowds and strikes. The appearance of business-friendly militia units in other cities, particularly New York, provided models for Chicago. The formation of private militia companies was normal at the time, and the units were organized and equipped by their members, even though militia duty was required by state law. Success for business-friendly militia units in Chicago came with $17,000 provided by the Citizens' Association in the fall of 1874, and Chicago's First Regiment—"the patent leather mob," in the words on one Socialist—was ready for duty in the New Year. About 60 percent of its members were bookkeepers and clerks. In February 1875, when the Chicago left planned another march on the Relief and Aid Society, it was intimidated into inaction by the police backed up by the First Regiment.[33]

This humiliating defeat prompted the founding in April 1875 of the Lehr- und Wehr-Verein, joined later by other labor-related militias, the Bohemian Sharpshooters and the Irish Labor Guard. At its peak in 1879, the organization probably had over six hundred members, primarily skilled workers. Although the Verein had antecedents among radical exiles in Switzerland following the revolutions of 1848, it was modeled as much after American militia traditions, and it even tried to join the Illinois National Guard when it was under legal attack in the late 1870s. The Verein engaged in elaborate marching drills, participated in parades, protected picnics from rowdy intruders, and supported its own band. Although it never engaged in combat, it raised fears in the broader public of an armed insurrection by foreign-born workers, especially after its ranks swelled following the railroad strike of 1877. Such fears prompted the Citizens' Association and its allies to lobby for a state law, passed in 1879, banning public military parades by private groups.

While it may appear exotic, the Lehr- und Wehr-Verein shared values and activities with the Turners, many of whose clubs in Chicago and other cities had formed the core of regiments during the Civil War. The Turners had also defended German social gatherings and political meetings from street toughs and mobs before the Lehr- und Wehr-Verein was founded. Both Turners and the Lehr- und Wehr-Verein combined physical exercise with moral uplift and political education in order to prepare their members to be citizens of the republic. In Germany, that meant the republic that was yet to be founded; in Chicago in the 1870s, it was the republic that was under attack by a new aristocracy of capital.[34]

The vitality of the immigrant left stemmed in part from its imaginative response to a unique situation for central European radicals. In Germany and Austria-Hungary, its counterparts were fighting to establish democratic republics, since workers, the clear majority, could use them for their liberation. There the fight for democracy took on the character of a broad social movement uniting a wide spectrum of the lower orders behind a party identified with labor. In Chicago during the depression of the 1870s, the Internationals discovered that they could not unite the workers so understood behind a platform that could take over the government, even though the People's Party had done so using a different program. A large part of their constituency was among the transient segment of the working class that was outside the electorate, their concept of an active state alienated potential coalition partners among farmers and Anglo American skilled workers, and their culture and language identified them as immigrants. Thus the Internationals found themselves politically isolated in a democratic republic, a state of affairs that was not supposed to happen. In response, they turned toward institution building and cultural formation, establishing connections to the transient working class that gave them considerable power in crises, although not in elections.[35]

THREE UPPER-CLASS CHICAGOANS EXPLORE THE ACCOMMODATIONS NEEDED TO RULE

In the mid-1870s, the new Chicago business elite became conscious of itself as a class in battles with both machine politicians and workers. Fighting on two fronts against the "bummers" and the "communists," the new economic elite transformed itself into the Gilded Age bourgeoisie.

The depression severely affected Chicago's businessmen, not only by lessening demand for their products but also by ending a boom in real estate. In turn, the decline in real estate highlighted a set of problems that businessmen had with the city government. The appreciating value of real estate had helped pay for infrastructure improvements by financing the cost with the anticipated increase in the value of land affected by new roads, canals, or railroads. But now that method was severely hobbled. Shrinking land values also diminished the collateral available for raising capital in the East, the major source for the city's growth. Finally, declining real estate values reduced the local tax base and sent the government in pursuit of taxable personal property. The assessment of personal property quickly became one of the central public issues of the decade and beyond. Since personal property could include new forms for investing and preserving capital, such as commodity futures, warehouse receipts, and stocks, the tax issue had direct implications for capital accumulation.[36]

The tax issue was one aspect of a larger complex of problems that Chicago's "best men" called "corruption," a term central to the whole rhetoric of municipal reform. Corruption was a set of practices outside the law—fixing elections, perverting the judicial system, raiding the city finances, destroying Chicago's credit rating, undermining police and fire protection—carried out by machine politicians usually referred to as "bummers," but also called "loafers, vagabonds, scalawags, gamblers, and thieves." Despite the menu of abuses meant by the term, the central offense of the bummers was their redistribution of wealth downward to themselves, their friends, and their constituents in order to get rich and stay in power. As the *Tribune* put it, "And now, having inflicted this blow upon the good name and fame of the city, the bummers and scalawags have commenced to devastate and destroy the property of its citizens. The present popular [municipal reform] movement is an effort of the people who work for a living to rid themselves of this dangerous class who do not work for their living, and to save their property from being stolen." The rhetoric of corruption effectively embedded this central concern for property and capital accumulation in a politically effective language of threatened republican virtue.[37]

To the sense of outrage and threat from corruption felt by the "best men," the depression added a foreboding that the new economic order was fragile and that America's industrial cities might become like the class-divided societies of the Old World. Around the country, sober observers asked whether a Paris Commune loomed in America's future, and in Chicago there were even rumors that incendiaries connected to the Commune started the Great Fire. Such stories related the fire to class conflict rather than to natural calamity.[38]

Within this milieu, the founding of the Citizens' Association in 1874 became a vital chapter in the process of upper-class formation. At the peak of its influence between 1874 and 1876, the Citizens' Association articulated a broad political program and took the lead in carrying it into effect, organizing in all parts of the city, calling mass meetings, molding public opinion through the press, and mounting repeated legal challenges to both governmental decisions and election results. This campaign aimed at restructuring city government, so that it could no longer be captured by machine politicians, while arming it sufficiently to protect the property and assert the interests of the emerging Chicago bourgeoisie. While only partially successful, the program broadened the power of the new upper class beyond its economic base, as it sought to establish its social and political authority in the wider society through creating what E. Digby Baltzell has called "a goal-integrating elite."[39]

To attain that authority, it had to embed its interests in a concept of the public good broad enough to win the allegiance or acquiescence of enough people in all strata of society to obviate the regular resort to force. Achieving society's voluntary consent to the leadership of this new class required an unremitting process of persuasion, accommodation, and compromise of diverse worldviews and interests. Such freely given consent could only be secured in the public sphere, that realm within civil and political society where conflicting interests and contrary opinions were shaped through debate into the common sense of a social order. The difficulty of achieving cultural, social, and political leadership in a city with a largely foreign-born working class taxed the abilities of Chicago's new upper class, making successes short-lived and accommodations tenuous.[40]

Just as for workers, 1873 was a turning point for Chicago's business leaders as well as for those in other northern cities. The defeat of the "Law and Order" ticket by the People's Party in Chicago's 1873 municipal election and the social impact of the depression were so shattering that it forced articulate members of the city's elite to begin reformulating their political strategies and goals.

Three influential Chicagoans illustrated the evolution of upper-class leadership within the public sphere. Two of the men, Horace White and Joseph Medill, were Republican editors of the *Tribune*. Although both owned an interest in the paper, White had the strongest hand in defining editorial policy from the mid-1860s until Medill bought a controlling interest in the fall of 1874. Up until then, White made the *Tribune* one of the leading papers in the country, while promoting Radical Republicanism in the 1860s and the Liberal Republican revolt in the early 1870s. Medill, of course, had been mayor during the critical years after the Great Fire as head of the Union Fire-Proof ticket. Although he resigned his mayoral post in August 1873 to go on a yearlong tour of Europe with his family, he took the opportunity to investigate European reform movements and send back reports to the paper. His desire to fight municipal corruption plus the threat of Democratic

political strength brought him back from Europe and induced him to purchase control of the *Tribune*. While Medill was in Europe during 1873 and
1874, Franklin MacVeagh—the third influential Chicagoan—took the lead
in founding the Citizens' Association. MacVeagh, a Democrat through the
1880s, was one of the city's largest wholesale provision dealers; legal training
supplemented his business experience. After converting to Republicanism
in the 1890s, he served as secretary of the treasury under President William
Howard Taft. Like White and Medill, MacVeagh took an active interest in
Chicago municipal affairs throughout his adult life.[41]

After the People's Party victory in November 1873, the first priority of Republican leaders was to find a new policy on the consumption of alcohol. As
a public policy in a city with a largely foreign-born electorate, temperance
had been a disaster. Under White's leadership, the *Tribune* began an extended
argument with the temperance forces, strongly opposing legal prohibition
of the use of alcoholic beverages while advocating moderation in their use.
Fearing the further fracturing of the Republican majority that had ruled the
city from 1857 to 1873, White accepted the position of the People's Party on the
consumption of alcohol, which was a victory for the city's German and Irish
voters. When Medill took over the *Tribune* in November 1874, he advocated
a similar position, rejecting temperance enforced by the state. He was well
aware of the electoral strength of those opposed or indifferent to temperance. Three years later, he noted that of the sixty-eight thousand registered
voters in the city, only twelve thousand were affiliated with "orthodox Protestant churches." They were outmatched by twelve thousand English-speaking
Catholics, three thousand German-speaking Catholics, two thousand Jews,
two thousand unorthodox Protestants, and thirty-six thousand religiously
unaffiliated voters. As a substitute, he supported voluntary temperance and
evangelical revivalism in a larger effort to build a stable urban order.[42]

Medill was looking for an alternative to temperance that would achieve
the goal of transforming the lower orders through spreading a morality of
individual self-discipline. He considered the wide acceptance of this morality
to be a precondition for a stable democracy, particularly in cities, because it
would insure that under the new social order freedom would not be abused.
In January 1874—just after the marches of the unemployed and while the
Workingmen's Party of Illinois was being organized—Medill published a
series of articles on labor in the *Tribune*'s new special Sunday section. Still on
his European tour, he analyzed cooperative enterprises in England, Ireland,
France, and Germany. He was much impressed by Franz Hermann Schulze-
Delitzsch's cooperative People's Banks in Germany, small locally controlled

institutions rooted in the artisans and small proprietors of German towns. But it was Medill's firsthand observation of cooperation in England that practically made him a convert. He came away speaking of a "miracle" produced by the reform: "'Cooperation has raised men who were worse than dead in body, mind, and soul, to keen and vigorous life.' It had worked its wonders by educating a worker both . . . 'directly and indirectly. Directly, by its schools, and reading-rooms, and libraries. Indirectly, by giving him an insight into the methods of business, and by teaching him how to guide his fellows. It discourages law-breaking. This is the universal testimony of English writers. Co-operation checks crime.'" Reducing crime was no idle matter for a man who had been mayor during the crime wave that followed the Great Fire and whose administration fractured when it used the government to enforce temperance, largely as an anticrime measure.[43]

For Medill, cooperation promised to reach foreign-born workers outside the realm of evangelical religion and to regenerate them into self-disciplined citizens of the republic. The need for regenerating the working class was dire: "In every State, the workingmen, the instant they combine, will be the strongest force, the ruling power. That combination is only a question of time. When it comes, shall we have a mob, maddened by the fear of want, blind, reckless, demagogue-ridden, rioting in our cities till musketry drives it back to its cheerless home to bide its time for future deviltry? Or shall we have an army of educated men, taught by the irresistible logic of bank-books that property is not robbery?"[44]

Medill's questions posed for his time the fundamental issue raised by James Madison in the 1780s during the debate over the ratification of the Constitution: How can a republic avoid the "tyranny of the majority," especially if that majority is composed of men with little or no property? While Madison's remedy was the constitutional system of limited, self-checking governing institutions and a refined public opinion, nineteenth-century Americans had added other institutions, including the self-disciplined citizen produced by market competition and by religion, particularly evangelical revivalism and its reform offshoots, such as temperance. As Medill recognized, the political failure of temperance in the 1870s raised the most fundamental issues about the endurance of the republic, most prominently the conflict between property and democracy.[45]

Horace White of the *Tribune* was a leader in exploring alternatives outside the traditional reform agenda of religious and social regeneration. In this task, he joined with a group of national public intellectuals, most of them based in New York, who were attempting to rethink the ideology and agenda of the

Republican Party. Less than two weeks after the march of the unemployed in December 1873, White's *Tribune* editorialized that the local labor radicals were part of a well-organized international movement that had decided that American freedoms offered the best opportunity for advancing its cause. Here they could propagate their ideas and found their organizations with impunity while, because of its freedoms, America stood vulnerable before them. It lacked a standing army, and its cities had no "military police" to put down communist aggressions. Only recently, the Civil War had found the country unprepared. Now the Internationals have given fair warning of their intentions, and the country could not fail to take action: "It is time that every State in the Union should go earnestly to work to prepare for the onset of the followers of Karl Marx, for they mean business,—not in Paris and Berlin merely, but in New York and Chicago." Like his counterparts in New York City, White advocated strengthening the militia and professionalizing the police. Transforming workers into self-disciplined citizens was not even an issue.[46]

White also moved beyond the expedient of repression to rethink his positions on universal suffrage and the nature of the state itself. During military Reconstruction in the late 1860s, he had backed the enfranchisement of former slaves, but with lingering hesitations because it set a precedent for voting without reference to "intelligence or virtue" and for including "shoals of emigrants from the Old World." While vigorously promoting the expansion of suffrage to blacks during Reconstruction, like other Republican intellectuals he never conceded the Democratic position of the natural right to the vote. The victory of the People's Party in November 1873 and subsequent marches of the unemployed forced White to formulate his assumptions more clearly. To him, the proposals put forward by the Internationals represented the dangers of enfranchising the immigrant masses congregated in large American cities.[47]

Writing a few days after the mass meeting of the unemployed in December 1873, White's *Tribune* argued that demands for jobs required a "paternal government" that was "wholly at variation with our laws and institutions." Such a government undermined the personal independence that was the foundation of freedom. For White, independence had a moral basis, not an economic one, such as productive property. The perversity of the paternal state was that it destroyed this moral foundation of individual freedom and thus ultimately republican liberty as well. White's response to Carl Klings's advocacy of national workshops in December 1873 brought out this point clearly. For White, the whole idea of state responsibility for employment originated with the French Revolution and came to an ignominious fulfillment with the national workshops during the Revolution of 1848. They proved themselves economically unsound because the government could not guarantee customers for the products. This impracticality, rather than government ownership itself, was one of the central issues. But the worst consequences of the workshops were moral: "Let the State take care of the laboring class if it can, and it takes from them all inducement to take care of themselves. The ambition they have would be extinguished. . . . All incentive to foresight and economy, and temperance would be destroyed." This was the same moral vision that kept the Chicago Relief and Aid Society from giving aid to able-bodied men. The paternal state would undermine the market incentives necessary for capital accumulation.[48]

In attacking the moral iniquity of the paternal state, White revealed the intellectual dilemmas and social pessimism of a free trader confronted with Chicago's new working class. In the mid-nineteenth century, free traders like White combined a Jeffersonian vision of the ideal political economy with the economic theories of British thinkers such as Thomas Malthus, David Ricardo, and John Stuart Mill, who thought that wages would always be at a subsistence level, due to population growth exceeding the capacity of a finite supply of land to produce adequate food. Given the presumably inevitable excessive reproduction of the lower orders, there would always be an oversupply of workers, while a limited fund available for wages and the pressures of competition would push capitalists to pay as little as possible. This theory of wages produced a dark vision of the future in which capitalist societies would be radically divided into opposing classes with little hope of improvement for workers.

In the 1850s and 1860s, Republicans, led by the *Chicago Tribune,* sought to escape the predicted impoverishment with a dual strategy. First, passage of the Homestead Act would open up free land in the West to settlement, delaying the operation of this iron law. Yet this safety valve in the West offered little consolation to someone trying to build a stable social order in Chicago during the 1870s. Republicans' second solution owed much to the influence of Henry Carey's economic theories and was more popular among workers. The *Chicago Republican,* and its successor the *Inter Ocean,* argued that a protective tariff promoting industrialization could permanently raise the standard of living of American workers. Yet, as a free trader, Horace White could offer no leadership in pursuing this second option while the depression undercut its credibility. What remained was the foreboding vision of a restive, alienated, and—for Chicago—foreign-born working class. The uncertainty led White to lurch between hope for workers through moral uplift and the despairing use of bullets and bayonets to keep them in place.[49]

There was a third threat from the paternal state. In addition to destroying the moral foundations of the republic and undermining the self-discipline of the working class, it also would take property from the capitalist and redistribute it to the workers. The levying of a tax to provide employment "is dividing the wealth of the capitalist with the laborer. It is a covert way of effecting a community of goods. Its effect is the same, so far as the owner is concerned, as if it was taken from him and divided among the laboring class. ... The doctrine of the right to employment is the negation of property."[50] More to the point, it represented the redistribution of capital downward at a time when the city's new bourgeoisie was struggling to accumulate it and even redistribute it upward by using general tax revenues for public improvements. The collapse of real estate prices and interruption of capital investment from the East made the threat of redistribution through the taxing power even more threatening. Confronted with the Internationals, White articulated a severely limited vision of the state in which the fear of want—not revivalism, temperance, or cooperation—was the great moral teacher of the working class.

Unfortunately for White, the Internationals were not the only contemporary threat to property. The Granger movement spread across the Illinois countryside, even as White tried to console himself that the wide distribution of property, particularly in rural America, would insure the defeat of the urban left and its paternal state. While at first sympathetic to the Grangers, he turned on them after the financial collapse in the fall of 1873, fearing that their attacks on railroads had contributed to the crisis. Their broader opposition to corporations and the rich also seemed to aid the left. And the Grangers were sympathetic to the ideas of the Greenbackers who advocated an inflationary monetary policy. To White, such a policy was also practically the negation of property, a kind of gambler's intoxication that would lead to financial and then political ruin. Yet he confessed to Hermann Raster, editor of the *Illinois Staats-Zeitung,* his fear "that 'inflators' are a numerical majority of this country." White doubted the people's ability to understand the complexities of finance, and he feared that their addiction to inflation demonstrated their incapacity to rule. The support for inflation by reconstructed state governments in the South added to his disillusionment.[51]

In the spring of 1874, upper-class liberals concluded that universal suffrage had become a threat to property and order in the countryside, in the Reconstruction legislatures of the South, and particularly in America's large northern cities. According to the *Tribune,* the "dangerous classes" establish "a sort of mob-law in their section of a city which defies the law of the land. In this country, when the law has given them votes, they sell themselves to the highest bidder, and eagerly follow any demagogue who will distribute among them a hundredth part of the blackmail he levies upon the rich." These were the people who elected the machines that dominated American cities, so that "in politics as in currency . . . the worse drives out the better. When the suffrage is universal, the worst classes will be best represented in the city governments." Yet White doubted the traditional American solution, which was to improve the character of the sovereign people. He advocated universal compulsory education as a means to this end, but it was only good for the young. He was left with a despairing option: "Cure the elders with club and bayonet, and force the young into schools. Drain their sewage-soaked streets. Cleanse the tenements reeking with disease, in which their minds and bodies rot. Do, in a word, what can be done to give them a fair chance at life, and then, if they still cling to their false gods of misrule and crime, let justice be swift and sharp. If the New York mob of 1863 had been shot down to the last man, the New York Ring of 1870 might never have been." White offered municipal reform as a last chance for the urban masses, but he had no political strategy for carrying reforms into effect so that the people could make the stark choice he offered them. His only viable solution to the problem of urban democracy was repressive violence.[52]

While Medill and White futilely grasped at one reform after another, often turning to the past rather than to the future, Franklin MacVeagh helped the new Citizens' Association formulate a more effective political strategy for urban reform. In March 1874, MacVeagh delivered a prescient speech in which he argued that for the first time in its history the country had become a state in the true sense, whereas before it had been a confederation, which tried to divide sovereignty between the federal government and the states with disastrous consequences. As a result of decades-long battles over sovereignty, American public life and politics drifted and degenerated. According to MacVeagh, the need of the moment was for "cultured statesmanship" to give direction, helping the nation along the way toward the ideal of politics: the replacement of interest with duty in public life and of corrupt politicians with a virtuous elite. Threatening the evolution of such leadership—and public life as a whole—was the new tendency toward "combination." (He probably had the Grange and the Workingmen's Party of Illinois in mind.) According to MacVeagh, there were three alternatives facing statesmanship in dealing with combination: limiting the extent of the suffrage, education of the people to a new higher level, and weakening the power of the vote. The last alternative—one that White had not developed—held the most promise and was already taking place. Soon afterward, MacVeagh helped found the

Citizens' Association, whose proposals for the restructuring of the city government had the effect of reducing the power of the voters over city affairs.[53]

THE CITIZENS' ASSOCIATION
AND THE STRUGGLE FOR HEGEMONY, 1874–76

The catalytic event for the formation of the Citizens' Association was a second huge fire that took place on July 14, 1874. The fire burned sixty acres on the South Side, threatening but not consuming the new business district that had been built after the conflagration of 1871. According to the *Tribune,* it began in an oil factory in a cramped industrial and residential district of wooden buildings that had emerged with the permission of "a weak Common Council and a weak Mayor." The new brick buildings of the business center had helped confine it. For Horace White's *Tribune,* the fire of 1874 heightened general anxiety about social disorder and violence in addition to highlighting the inadequacies of local government. In response to looting following the fire, White wrote that "Chicago lies at the mercy of the mob," and it needed a "drilled" militia regiment like New York's Seventh that could provide "an hour's steady work with ball-cartridge" to "drive ruffianism back to its lair." Chicago, New York, and cities across the North faced similar threats.[54]

The fire of July 14, 1874, strengthened the conviction that municipal government was incompetent and the city's "lower orders" rebellious—twin threats that would engage the Chicago bourgeoisie for the rest of the decade and beyond. Those beliefs exacerbated the unease generated by the capital accumulation crisis caused by the national depression. The city was still dependent on outside investment in the mid-1870s, a condition that did not change fundamentally until the 1880s and 1890s. The *Tribune* foresaw a loss of local and outside business confidence that "signifies the withdrawal of capital from the city, the departure of our most energetic citizens, the diversion of population, trade, wealth, and all things that go to making a great city, away from us, and the dwarfing of Chicago to the dimensions of a second or third-rate town."[55]

Many of the nation's insurance companies temporarily withdrew insurance coverage from the city after July 14, which further jeopardized the flow of investment into Chicago. Then spurring Chicago's businessmen to near panic was a substantial fire in the recently built central business district eight days after the July 14 conflagration. Rumors circulated of incendiaries loose in the city. People listened when voices like the *Tribune* said, "We must act, and act soon."[56]

Among the first to act after July 14 were the members of the Chicago Board of Insurance Underwriters. Within a few days of the fire, they presented a set of resolutions on what the city should do to protect itself from future fires, including reorganizing the fire department and extending the fire limits to the city boundaries. These resolutions framed the subsequent public discussion about how to meet the fire threat. Supporting the enactment of the underwriters' proposals was a broad multiethnic coalition of the city's business interests. A small committee, including Marshall Field and George Howe, the president of the Board of Trade, called a meeting on July 17 at McCormick's Hall that was attended by practically every leading businessman in the city. Among them were the most prominent Germans, including Anton Hesing. The meeting, including Hesing, supported the extension of the fire limits to the city boundaries and the reorganization of the fire department.[57]

Hesing argued that his new position on extending the fire limits was not inconsistent with his previous one because brick construction had become more affordable, due to lower costs for material and labor. The wooden houses of Hesing's constituency had already been built, they had not burned in 1874, and they would not be threatened by the new ordinance. He was in a position to act like a statesman in conjunction with the Board of Trade. Andrew Cameron and leaders of the Workingmen's Party of Illinois were the only champions of his old position that wooden houses were essential for the poor, but they were too weak to make a difference. Backed by the Board of Trade and the People's Party, an ordinance extending the fire limits to the city boundaries passed the Common Council on July 20. For the time being, the class interest of maintaining the preconditions for capital investment trumped class, partisan, and ethnic divisions.[58]

This was not enough for men like Franklin MacVeagh and E. A. Storrs, an evangelical temperance reformer, because they sensed a crisis that went well beyond fire prevention. To them, a government in the hands of the People's Party meant control by the bummers, who in their eyes were corrupt by definition or, more precisely, because of who they were. The bummers could never be trusted to take the actions needed to restore business confidence. To MacVeagh and Storrs, only a restructured government led by the "best men" like themselves could make the necessary changes to restore the confidence necessary to resume outside investment. By July 25, a week and a half after the 1874 fire, the Citizens' Association published its constitution.[59]

The constitution of the Citizens' Association set up committees in each ward, which were in turn represented in a permanent central executive committee. While ignoring "partisan politics altogether," according to Storrs, the

Citizens' Association was to investigate local problems, support their solution, monitor public officials, and "create such a public opinion as will secure the nomination and election of fit and proper men to the city offices." In a September speech articulating the purposes of the Citizens' Association, MacVeagh decried the "disenfranchisement" of the best citizens in the city and argued that the "better portion of the community" needed "a supplemental political organization like this, that will, to some extent, represent these disfranchised people." Its main political tactic was to systematically mold public opinion.[60]

Storrs and MacVeagh were helping invent the "nonpartisan" citizens' movement that was the immediate forerunner of the Mugwumps and the urban "good government" progressives in the late nineteenth and early twentieth centuries. This style of reform politics sought to replace the nineteenth-century party state, which depended on patronage and had an unpredictable and weak administrative apparatus, with a more modern administrative one that could create a predictable and efficient environment for a society dependent on capital accumulation for its prosperity and stability. While such a state crystallized only after the turn of the century, it had its origins in the class divisions of America's industrial cities during the Gilded Age. Contributing to the possible success of citizens' politics was a political lesson Storrs and MacVeagh had learned from the Chicago municipal election of 1873: There would be no effort to legally force temperance on everyone. As one prominent Chicagoan said, "we will have no temperance or sumptuary nonsense." This break with the nineteenth-century reform tradition was essential to uniting the native-born men of property with their counterparts among the Germans and Irish.[61]

The belief that business reformers needed to move beyond religion and temperance to act as a leading class also found expression in their support of Presbyterian minister David Swing, who helped them formulate a more flexible set of religious values than those current in mainstream evangelical Protestantism. Swing was one of the more liberal "New School" Presbyterians, many of whom had strongly opposed slavery and sympathized with the Radical Republicans. Swing himself argued in favor of a cultural relativism in religious doctrine, which allowed him to dispense with old tenets, such as infant depravity. He was also notorious for his associations with Protestants even more liberal than himself, including Unitarians. Under the leadership of "Old School" Presbyterians like Cyrus McCormick, his denomination brought him to trial in Chicago on charges of heresy. Swing withdrew from the Presbyterian Church, taking about a fourth of his congregation with him, and his new nondenominational Central Church of Chicago began services in

December 1875. Among fifty men subscribing $1,000 each for the new church were Franklin MacVeagh, Wirt Dexter, Murry Nelson, and Joseph Medill, all among the most active members of the Citizens' Association. According to the *Times*, Swing's supporters represented "three-fourths of all the brains, courage, and progress of the city of Chicago."[62]

While Swing was sympathetic to "the masses," he lauded "another class of human beings, educated, moral, often rich, and always powerful," the men who filled his church. In fact, he found such people to be a new type of human being: "Each class of mankind needs its own peculiar treatment. When a new form of human soul comes along, a new school-house, new politics, a new religion, must be made for this new soul." Swing rejected the revivalists' demand that everyone have a similar conversion experience and the millennialists' rejection of this world in anticipation of its imminent end. Instead, he called for "a religion that shall blend with these days on earth, and help it in its liberty, in its law, in its arts, its letters, its honors, its pleasures." Such a religion would appeal to a new social reality: "There is rising up a class powerful in education and in reason and in virtue, a class that does not fill our jails, but that makes our laws, that sits upon the judge's bench, that shapes our literature, that molds our social life, a class which neither clergyman nor theologian will dare pass by in his effort to plant Christ in the human soul." To this class he offered a religion that judged doctrines by experience and stressed the practice of an ethical life every day of the week. Swing's sermons also conveyed openness to social change and a tolerance for other groups and religions.[63]

What Swing did for members of the Citizens' Association in his congregation, and for the Chicago upper class more generally, was articulate a set of values that legitimated a liberal disposition toward cultural differences and a tolerance for rapid social change. His religion also called on them to demonstrate a stewardship commensurate with their elevated social position by reshaping the world around them in accord with their high ideals. Reshaping their world meant intervening in politics, and Swing aided his wealthy and powerful audience in justifying this intervention and mustering the moral courage to do so.

A founder of the Citizens' Association and active member of Swing's church, Franklin MacVeagh heeded this call to political engagement when he helped revitalize the concept of a single, nonpartisan public good. MacVeagh elaborated this idea when he addressed the Common Council on fire prevention as the Citizens' Association's representative: "We believe we represent an overwhelming sentiment in the Community and that it is the veritable voice of the people that speaks to you through these committees to-night." This conception of the public good also allowed the Citizens' Association to claim to represent groups that were obviously not part of its constituency, such as the city's poor, particularly "frugal good citizens" who own houses, however modest. Surely they had an interest in seeing that their sacrifices did not go up in flames. What was more, he noted, "are they a class with separate interests, walled about and separated . . . from the manufacturing and commercial interests of the City?" No, they were all, of course, interdependent. In the current crisis, there was a clear common good, and by expressing it the Citizens' Association spoke for everyone as the voice of the people. In this voice, it called not simply for improved fire protection but also for the structural reform that circumscribed democratic politics in local government. In short, the Citizens' Association made a strong case for equating the class interests of the new bourgeoisie with the general interests of society.[64]

MacVeagh candidly argued for these class interests when he delivered a speech before the Citizens' Association in September 1874. He asserted that universal [male] suffrage was at the root of the problems of municipal government, which really boiled down to "the mere management of property." It was absurd to apply partisan divisions deriving from national issues to local affairs and just as absurd to make these affairs subject to the universal suffrage. The result of universal suffrage for the city was pernicious, driving the people best suited to manage property out of local politics. Compounding the problems caused by universal suffrage was the decentralization of power in the local government, creating "innumerable grooves and ruts" that frustrated efficient administration. MacVeagh's arguments echoed the contemporary national disillusionment with Reconstruction, particularly with the way that the "baser elements of the people" had transformed state and local politics in the South. Nonetheless, his reaction against democracy grew primarily out of the experience of the Citizens' Association in Chicago in the decade after the July 1874 fire.[65]

In contrast to MacVeagh's vision of good government, the Common Council appeared to be more interested in spreading government largesse to the unemployed and political allies through its distribution of the contracts for the new courthouse. At the same time, the powerful Board of Police and Fire Commissioners opposed the Citizens' Association's proposed reform of the fire department. In response, the Citizens' Association and the insurance underwriters proposed the appointment of a new fire marshal to indicate to eastern interests that fundamental change was on the way. The man most frequently mentioned as a replacement was General Alexander Shaler, who had reorganized New York City's fire department. Led by the Irish politician Mark Sheridan, the Board of Police and Fire Commissioners, an elected body with powers of appointment and removal, defended its current marshal, arguing that he was being made a scapegoat. But, by late September, insurance was getting even more difficult to obtain, and those companies that could get it were paying premiums that were as much as 570 percent over those paid before the fire of 1871.[66]

Following an October 1 deadline set by the National Board of Insurance Underwriters, about forty of one hundred fifty insurance companies withdrew from Chicago, and the Citizens' Association assumed the role of the city's representative to outside capital interests. In fact, it did even more, taking on aspects of a private government, as the Relief and Aid Society had done after the Great Fire. One obvious measure was to reinforce the military power of the government against crowds, which the Citizens' Association did through its substantial funding of the new First Regiment. In another effort to reassure outside capital interests, the Citizens' Association brought Shaler to Chicago at its own expense, and he toured the city on October 5 in the company of MacVeagh. By the end of the month, the Citizens' Association announced that he would be a "consulting engineer" on the reorganization of the fire department, but informed people expected the police and fire commissioners, and Mark Sheridan in particular, to sabotage his work.[67]

The hostility between the Citizens' Association and the Board of Police and Fire Commissioners rested in part on the nature of the board's constituency. Sheridan and his fellow police and fire commissioners represented just the sort of neighborhood-based ward politicians whom the Citizens' Association detested. Sheridan was a long-standing Irish politician with a considerable following in the labor movement, gained in his support for the eight-hour workday. Two years earlier, he had defended the police against the effort following the Great Fire to have them work a twelve-hour day. Other aldermen had delayed appropriations for new water pipe—part of the fire protection reform—because they said it would benefit only the industrial and commercial sections of the city. Accordingly, the charter reform advocated by the Citizens' Association targeted the Board of Police and Fire Commissioners along with other municipal institutions.[68]

The changes envisioned by the Citizens' Association were intended to lessen the voting power of immigrants, workers, and all other groups whose political power stood in the way of implementing its vision. There would be a strong mayor, a "real Executive of the city," who would have full powers of appointment and removal. The numerous boards would be replaced by departments with heads appointed by the mayor. Not only would the town governments be abolished, but city appointees would be chosen as representatives of the interests of the whole city, not as representatives of the various geographic divisions. This streamlining and centralization of the government would lessen the opportunities for intervention by neighborhood interest groups. The number of aldermen was also to be reduced and ward representation abolished in favor of citywide elections. These electoral reforms would effectively distance the government from the local interests that came with ward representation while making an aldermanic candidacy much more expensive and dependent on citywide name recognition, which would make the office more appropriate for men of wealth and standing. The program of structural reform developed by the Citizens' Association incorporated the upper-class and antidemocratic bias that Samuel P. Hays found in later municipal reform agendas during the Progressive Era.[69]

Just before the fall 1874 election, the Citizens' Association mounted an extensive petition drive, asking the Common Council to hold a special election to determine whether to abandon the old charter and reorganize under the Illinois general incorporation law of 1872. In October, they placed before the Common Council petitions with fifteen thousand signatures. Dominated by aldermen from the People's Party and the Democrats, the council temporized on the question until after the election in November. That election would mark a turning point in local and national affairs.[70]

In the South, local elites had accepted the Civil War amendments so their states could return to the union. Yet they also sought to consolidate their power locally by using violence and intimidation to disenfranchise the freedmen and thus restore white supremacy in the South. Seeking local control and freedom from outside influence, these elites learned to speak a political language of taxpayer revolt, fiscal retrenchment, and opposition to corruption that resonated with their counterparts in the North. People like MacVeagh and Horace White likewise felt that the lower orders were undermining both their influence locally and American government generally. Sensing the depth of the crisis, Alfred Cowles, one of the major stockholders of the Tribune Company, appealed to Joseph Medill in Europe to return and take charge of matters. After some hesitation, he did, arriving in October, following which he purchased a controlling interest in the paper. Horace White departed for a yearlong tour of the continent with his new wife, leaving the local Liberal Republicans in disarray. Medill put the paper solidly behind the regular Republican Party while supporting the campaign of the Citizens' Association to reconstruct local government. This campaign developed a more imaginative way to contain the "baser elements of the people" than White's advocacy of bullets and bayonets.[71]

MUNICIPAL REFORM, EVANGELICAL REVIVALISM, AND THE STRUGGLE FOR HEGEMONY: 1874–77

In the fall of 1874, the Democratic Party regained control of Congress, initiating a period of political stalemate between the major parties on the national level that distinguished the Gilded Age. In the words of Paul Kleppner, the third American party system was moving from "realignment to equilibrium" because northern constituencies predisposed to vote Democratic became politically mobilized by the temperance issue, the depression, and the corruption of the Ulysses S. Grant administration. The Democratic revival was aided by the return of the former Confederate states, which voted solidly Democratic with their politics of white "restoration." In the North, the key swing group was the Germans, particularly those in the Midwest, where they had been predominantly Republican in the Civil War era. Now German Republicans were increasingly divided, particularly because temperance agitation revived their historic alienation from the evangelical wing of their party. This expansion of the northern Democratic base had been occurring for several years and would have manifested itself in the 1872 presidential election had the Democrats not made the disastrous decision to nominate Horace Greeley as their candidate.[72]

The Chicago election in the fall of 1874 reflected these national trends, with the addition of the tax issue. The *Tribune* published a long critical article on the subject, which noted that "many thousands" of local citizens were "in a state of war" against the system of state and county taxes. This rebellion of businessmen had enduring and profound implications for the state and city governments, dramatically reducing their tax assessments from the mid-1870s through the turn of the century. The assessed valuation of personal property in Chicago did not regain its 1873 level until 1898, despite the extraordinary expansion of the city and its economy.[73]

The businessmen's tax revolt combined economic self-interest and politics for those with high assessments. The wealthy had already suffered two blows from the depression: It reduced the value of their substantial real estate holdings—up to 50 percent by 1877—while it also shrank profits, from both slower business and increased competition. With their ability to borrow and create capital constricted, the wealthy felt threatened by a local government in the hands of politicians who might use the taxing power to take more of their wealth and, worst of all, distribute it downward to their cronies in the city's immigrant, working-class wards. The state's new constitution of 1870, which went into effect in 1872, had increased this threat by expanding taxation to the personal property of individuals and the capital stock of corporations. The wealthy fought back by not paying taxes, particularly on personal property. Withholding taxes had the double effect of protecting their wealth and starving the local government they detested.[74]

As typically reported in the press, the contest in 1874 was between the Republicans and the "Opposition," a term describing a statewide alliance between the Democrats and the People's Party, which was still in control of the Chicago municipal government. Local Republicans were on the defensive throughout the campaign because of the revived temperance issue and the taint of corruption from the Grant administration.[75]

Sensing the direction of the political winds, the Opposition was more confident, though hardly clearer on principles. Hesing was aided by anti-temperance organizations composed of his friends among the distillers and brewers as well as by German liberals disaffected by Republican corruption. The Opposition also included Carter Harrison and "Long John" Wentworth. Harrison was the Opposition's successful candidate for the U.S. Congress from the Second District in 1874. Wentworth had been a fixture in local politics since the 1840s, beginning as a Democrat but elected the city's first Republican mayor in 1857. Returning to his Democratic roots, he campaigned hard for the Opposition in 1874.[76]

In November 1874, the Opposition won a sweeping victory in congressional, state, and county offices, defeating not only the Republicans but also the Workingmen led by Karl Klings. (Chicago's municipal offices were contested in the spring.) Thus the People's Party remained in control of city and county governments, but elite reformers maintained their momentum. In January 1875, the Common Council, and thus the People's Party, acknowledged that petitioners advocating restructuring the government had met the requirements for a charter election and set the date for April 23. In choosing this date, the Common Council acted with cunning. Under the general incorporation law of 1872, municipal elections were held on the third Tuesday in April, instead of in the fall as they had been previously. In 1875, the third Tuesday fell on the 20th. Since the charter election was to be held three days later, if the new charter were adopted, incumbents could claim that they did not face reelection for another year, because they had been legally chosen under the earlier system, and the new system set the next election for the following spring. Similarly, because, under the new charter, the mayor was to be chosen in odd years for a two-year term, Harvey Doolittle Colvin, the People's Party mayor, could claim that he did not face election for two years—if the charter passed.[77]

The new incorporation referendum did pass, and the standing officials of the People's Party refused to leave their positions. Their manipulation of the election dates fueled an indignation that the Citizens' Association and its allies exploited to the fullest. Drawing on its solid grassroots organization, the municipal reform campaign took on both a bipartisan and evangelical Protestant character. The formation of "independent" reform clubs fostered bipartisan "citizen" politics. Thomas Hoyne, a Democrat and municipal reform advocate, illustrated this bipartisanship when he warned Hesing in mid-1875 about being too closely allied with "the disreputable or bummer elements" and admonished him that "he was pressing too much upon the chronic inattention of the business classes to their political interests at the local elections." Hoyne thought that "an uprising might take place."[78]

Ministers across the Protestant spectrum reacted to the manipulation of the charter election with thundering indignation. Church support helped expand the import of municipal reform beyond charter revision into a crusade for social regeneration that would reclaim the city for the native-born and Protestant values, especially temperance and Sabbath-keeping. Native-born Protestants associated the recent political corruption with immigrants, Catholics, liquor, and labor protests, all of which seemed concentrated in the city's working-class neighborhoods. This constellation of associations was reinforced on May 10, 1875, when federal agents carried out simultaneous raids in Chicago, Milwaukee, and St. Louis, arresting scores of public officials and whiskey manufacturers for evasion of the federal excise tax on liquor. Among those convicted in Chicago were officials of the People's Party, including Anton Hesing, who was accused of organizing the Whiskey Ring in the city. Hesing eventually served three months in prison, and the ongoing scandal gravely damaged the People's Party.[79]

The threat to the future of the People's Party was evident in a meeting of "merchants, tax-payers, and representative business men" on October 28, 1875. Called by a bipartisan group of municipal reformers, including Thomas Hoyne, the meeting rallied Chicago's men of property to reclaim the ballot box and the city's treasury from the manipulations of Mayor Colvin and his allies like Hesing. Hoyne told the meeting that Chicago had reached a "commercial crisis" brought on by the mismanagement of the city's finances. Actually, the fiscal crisis had begun with the tax revolt of the city's business-men the previous year and was compounded when the Colvin administration neither reformed the tax collection system nor challenged the businessmen to pay the taxes they owed. In order to stay solvent, the government resorted to heavy borrowing on the New York capital market. In response, under the leadership of men like Hoyne, the businessmen attacked the creditworthiness of the city because of the exploding debt, further undermining the detested "Ring" running the government.[80]

In the first election held under the new charter in April 1876, the municipal reform candidates for the Common Council triumphed. The office of mayor was another matter. Since Mayor Colvin of the People's Party claimed that he was not even up for reelection, he stayed in office, rejecting the claims of his opponent, Thomas Hoyne, champion of the municipal reformers, who had written in his name on their ballots. When the new Common Council declared Hoyne to be the mayor, Chicago had two claimants to the mayor's office. The circuit court declared Hoyne's election illegal but allowed the new Common Council to call a special mayoral election, which it set for July 12, 1876. Widespread indignation at blatant ballot box fraud in the recent municipal election helped the reformers mobilize their constituency. In this election, the municipal reformers abandoned Hoyne, an independent with Democratic roots, and nominated Monroe Heath for mayor. A Republican, Heath triumphed over two Democratic candidates, one nominated by the regular Democratic Party and one by the Colvin Democrats, the remnant of the People's Party. Heath began two terms as Republican mayor of Chicago, aided considerably by the energetic efforts of the Citizens' Association and by an upsurge of Protestant revivalism in the city.[81]

By mid-1876, the Citizens' Association and the English-speaking Protestant churches had reformulated the program and energized the base of the local Republican Party. The upshot was a coalition of political forces similar to the Law and Order Party that had lost badly to the People's Party in 1873. The difference was that in 1876 the divisive issues of temperance and Sabbatarianism were not prominent in the Republican political platform. Instead, the platform focused on municipal reform. The Heath administration wholeheartedly supported the key goals of the Citizens' Association: retrenchment in city finances, reform in tax assessment and collection, and centralization of local government. Both Heath and the Citizens' Association could draw on the model of New York's citizens' movement that toppled Boss Tweed in 1871 and 1872. Fearful of New York's reputation with foreign creditors, this movement "spearheaded a concerted refusal by a thousand property owners to pay municipal taxes until the books of the city were audited." After the anti-Tweed forces took control of the city government in the fall of 1872, they instituted a vigorous fiscal retrenchment policy, cutting salaries, public works projects, and future development plans.[82]

In his inaugural address, Mayor Heath told the Common Council that "our retrenchment must be thorough, searching, and comprehensive. . . . [Y]ou must dig down below the roots, and, if necessary, instead of pruning, pluck out both root and branch." That meant ending practically all projects in "a gigantic system of public improvements" initiated by the previous adminis-tration. It also meant eliminating whole divisions of government, the first of which was the Board of Public Works, which the Common Council abolished in September. Reforming the system of assessing and collecting taxes was more complicated and long-lasting because it involved actions by the state legislature and by Cook County, which was still in the hands of the bummers. Nonetheless, the rapidly instituted fiscal retrenchment provided an occasion to appeal to citizens to pay their taxes. The Citizens' Association was happy enough with the new fiscal discipline to call on its six hundred members to subscribe to a new city loan, which was quickly and fully financed. Once the city government was in the right hands, the city's prominent citizens shifted from attacking its credit to shoring up its finances.[83]

Throughout the fall and winter of 1876, the Citizens' Association acted as an arm of the Heath administration, supplying it with a political organiza-tion, legal aid, personnel, and loans. The Citizens' Association's annual report for 1876 bragged about the connection: "Many conferences of a public and private character were held upon the subject of the city finances at our rooms and between members of your committee and the Finance Committee of the new Council, and all the influences which worked together to this end finally resulted in the inauguration of a well-defined policy of retrenchment and economy in our municipal affairs." The Citizens' Association had suc-ceeded in the task of incorporating the interests of the city's new bourgeoisie in a program that provided the basis for a successful cross-class governing coalition with the "best men" at the helm.[84]

Resurgent Protestant revivalism in Chicago helps explain the wider ap-peal of that program beyond the six hundred members of the Citizens' As-sociation or those who congregated at Reverend David Swing's new church. Energized by the revival, evangelical Protestants believed that people who practiced renewed self-restraint as a sign of their conversion found it easier to understand the need for fiscal restraint in the city government. While the Heath administration transformed city politics, Dwight L. Moody led the decade's largest revival, which ran almost continuously between October 1876 and January 1877.

Prominent local businessmen contributed to the preparatory work necessary for success. They included Marshall Field, Henry Field, George Armour, John Farwell, Cyrus McCormick, William Deering, and John Crerar. The city's English-language press was practically unanimous in its favorable reporting. The preparations paid off with immense audiences in numerous halls and churches drawn from both the city and its hinterland; one estimate put the cumulative attendance at nine hundred thousand in a city with a total population of about four hundred thousand. (The attendance figures do not account for individuals attending several meetings, a common practice.) Using the rhetoric of Anglo American evangelical Protestantism and the cultural traditions of small-town America, Moody preached a message of conversion leading to renewed self-discipline in private life and temperance and Sabbath-keeping in public. Both directly and by implication, he identified the threats to this Protestant moral life as Catholics, immigrants, and the street life of the city.[85]

Moody and his allies hoped that they could convert the whole city and thus create a widespread social regeneration that would eliminate everything from drunkenness and crime to political corruption and labor unrest, including the unions associated with it. Temperance and Sabbath-keeping were to be the public manifestations of the individual conversions that would renew Chicago's social and political life. Thousands of evangelicals from the whole spectrum of English-speaking churches reached out to the city's poor and working populations through meetings in private homes and public preaching. Their successes were considerable but limited. The revivalists held one meeting aimed at the city's large German Lutheran population, but it was not successful enough for them to try again. The revival had little success reaching beyond its core constituencies of English-speaking evangelicals and the native-born middle class. Among its male converts, the low-white-collar occupations predominated, particularly clerks, bookkeepers, and salesmen.[86]

The revival contributed most to forming Chicago's native-born middle class, which accentuated its differences from the foreign-born and working-class populations. Darrel M. Robertson, the revival's main historian, summarizes its divisive effect: "The revival meetings in Chicago, thereby, probably worked to fragment the existing social structure into two loosely defined, generalized camps—the community of the righteous (middle-class, Anglo-American, and Protestant) and the community of the unrighteous (foreign-born and Catholic). While these communities possessed no formal organizational structure and were avowedly apolitical, their sense of right attitudes and behavior could and did take political forms. Each saw the other, increasingly, as the enemy of a just moral and social order." Instead of uniting and regenerating the city and sustaining the political authority of the city's "best men," the revivals had reinvigorated the cultural "common sense" of Chicago's Anglo American middle class. This ethnically and class-divided social order became the setting for the city's greatest labor upheaval to date in 1877.[87]

The evangelical revival was one of several social movements that transformed civil society and the public sphere in Chicago during the 1870s, along with municipal reform, the labor awakening, and urban populism. Revivalism helped build the cultural and political world of a new native-born middle class in Chicago, while the Citizens' Association invented a new politics for the bourgeoisie. In the same decade, an urban populist movement had taken over the city government with a coalition linking foreign-born skilled workers with elements of the city's immigrant middle class. Then central European workers founded their own independent labor party and built a dense associational network that supported a socialist labor movement. Partly in response to that initiative, Anglo American workers elaborated a labor tradition that feared the state centralization inherent in the program of immigrant radicals. Competition between these two labor traditions prevented Chicago labor from forging a united response to the challenges of the decade, at least until the 1877 railroad strike.

To rule without constant reliance on force—that is, to rule through consent—the Chicago upper class had to defeat, marginalize, co-opt, or incorporate these alternative political movements. To do so, it had to adopt some elements of them, vigorously oppose others, develop its own proposals, and then merge the mixture into a procapitalist political agenda that could span the enormous cultural, political, and class divisions in the city. In short, the achievement of capitalist hegemony was neither inevitable nor was its rule monolithic, as is commonly implied by historians who use the concept of "social control."[88] By the beginning of 1877, the Chicago bourgeoisie had begun to make substantial progress in this complex and difficult task. It did so by mobilizing the evangelical fervor of the Anglo American middle class, but without making temperance a governmental policy; by uniting most business interests through the Citizens' Association to meet the interrelated crises in local government and capital accumulation; and by defeating or marginalizing both urban populism and working-class politics, whether in the central European or Anglo American versions.

The achievement of Chicago's capitalists was fragile, however. The Anglo American evangelical culture congenial to the bourgeoisie could never unite the city. Without a common culture, or even language, the process of conflict and accommodation within civil society and the public sphere was even harder to manage. The cross-class appeal of the upper class's liberal politics was almost as narrow as that of the revival. These limits became obvious to everyone when the great railroad strike of 1877 arrived in Chicago, and force rather than consent once again became the means of maintaining order.

6 Combat in the Streets
The Railroad Strike of 1877 and Its Consequences

IN THE SUMMER OF 1877, the United States experienced its first national strike, an unorganized, spontaneous rebellion of working people in cities from Baltimore and Pittsburgh to St. Louis and Chicago. The Great Strike produced a fundamental change in public awareness. Beforehand, according to George Schilling, a Socialist and labor leader, "the labor question was of little or no importance to the average citizen. The large mass of our people contented themselves with the belief that in this great and free Republic there was no room for real complaint. The idea that all Americans were on an equal footing seemed to be recognized as an incontrovertible fact in the halls of legislation, in the press, and the pulpit." The 1877 strike "was the calcium light that il-lumined the skies of our social and industrial life, and revealed the pinched faces of the workers and the opulence, arrogance, and unscrupulousness of the rich." The *New York Times* drew a similar conclusion: "The workmen have . . . attracted popular attention to their grievances, real or alleged, to an extent that will render future indifference impossible." After the strike, no one could deny that there was a "labor question" or a working class that did not feel on an "equal footing" with the rest of society. In the new climate of opinion, the Socialists prospered, according to Schilling, because they had answers to the new labor question, whereas others had denied its existence.[1]

On the eve of the strike, the political situation in Chicago contrasted with many eastern cities where the German component of the working class was smaller and machine politicians were able to offer inducements to workers to "immunize" them from Socialist appeals. In contrast, Chicago's city hall was in the hands of a coalition of Republicans and municipal reformers who a year earlier had decisively defeated the People's Party. The two central organizers of the People's Party, Anton Hesing and Dan O'Hara, were at the end of their careers. In disarray, the city's machine politicians could not provide bold leadership. Meanwhile, the Republicans in city hall feared that any union or-ganizing or political initiative by labor would stymie needed political reforms and aid the Socialists. This antilabor stance contrasted with the reaction of the Republican administration during the eight-hour strike in 1867, when the mayor even voiced support for the goal of the strike and was reluctant to use the police against it. The inability of mainstream Chicago politicians to offer viable appeals to workers during the long depression of the 1870s created an opening for the Socialists to speak for working people.[2]

The weakness of labor unions added to the opportunity. Even at the height of the labor upsurge between 1864 and 1872, only two Chicago unions—the typographers and stonecutters—were powerful enough to control wages and working conditions in their trade. The membership and bargaining strength of other unions fluctuated wildly according to seasonal and business cycles. With the coming of the 1870s depression and consequent wage reductions, organized labor activity practically halted. At the same time, popular cultural activities thrived in working-class districts. Among German-speaking central Europeans—Germans, Swiss, and Austrians plus some Poles, Czechs, and Hungarians—the level of organization and morale remained particularly high. A thriving community-based movement culture emerged among Chicago Socialists that paralleled that of the Socialists in imperial Germany. It included a party press, periodic parades, picnics, meetings, militia drills, and yearly celebrations of the Paris Commune. The Socialist Lehr- und Wehr Verein was the main militia group among the Germans, and similar military companies existed among the Irish, Bohemians, and native-born. Privately funded, such militia groups had been common in the United States since the Revolution, but they took on new meanings amid the class conflict of the 1870s.

During and after the strike, the emergence of a large segment of politically mobilized workers with armed organizations presented a glaring exception to the state's claim to a monopoly on armed coercion. The fact that these militias were in the hands of people openly challenging the legitimacy of the new industrial capitalist order created the prospect of dual authority within one state, what one Socialist called "armed political competition." This looming crisis was only resolved when a voter realignment and a new political regime emerged beginning in 1879. The regime created a new constellation of power and redefined the formal and informal rules for governing that endured for decades.[3]

A RAILROAD STRIKE BECOMES AN UPRISING IN CHICAGO

The depression of the 1870s reached its depth shortly before the Great Strike began. Seeking to avoid insolvency, employers produced even more and thus exacerbated overproduction, wages fell to their lowest level, and unemployed workingmen tramped the country. In Chicago, as elsewhere, unemployed workers thronged city streets, creating the "tramp menace." On July 2, 1877, a new Illinois vagrant law went into effect that allowed police for the first time to arrest without warrant "any one who goes about begging; . . . persons who do not support themselves or their families; and those who take lodgings in the open air or unoccupied houses or barns and give no accounts of themselves." The police used the law to harass both vagrants and labor organizers.[4]

Desperate for business, railroads engaged in fratricidal rate cutting, pushing their industry to the brink of collapse. In the spring of 1877, the large railroads decided to pass along their losses to their employees in the form of wage cuts starting at 10 percent—on top of earlier cuts of approximately 20 percent. In April, the only viable railroad union, the Brotherhood of Locomotive Engineers, balked at the cuts but suffered defeat at the hands of the Philadelphia and Reading Railroad. On July 16 a spontaneous strike began among brakemen of the Baltimore and Ohio Railroad at Camden Junction, Maryland. The strike—marked by the stopping of trains, seizing and destruction of railroad property, and violent clashes with police and militia—spread rapidly along the dense railroad network in the industrializing Northeast and Midwest. In many cities, the rail strike quickly spread to workers in other industries, and the dispatch of the militia by authorities provoked widespread rioting and violence. In Pittsburgh on July 21, the militia sent from Philadelphia to protect strikebreakers fired into a crowd of railroaders, killing at least twenty workers and prompting a crowd to burn the rail yard. The Philadelphia militia had to be called in because the local Pittsburgh militia proved sympathetic to the strikers, even refusing to prevent them from blocking railroad traffic. Authorities began to fear that local governments might lack the means to contain the violence.[5]

In Chicago, authorities were worried about the aggressive role taken by the Socialists, now part of the Workingmen's Party of the United States (WPUS). Founded the previous year in Pittsburgh but headquartered in Chicago, the WPUS had forty-five hundred members nationally. It had also temporarily settled its internal division between Lassalleans, who stressed electoral politics, and Marxists, who prioritized organizing trade unions. Despite their differences, since the marches of the unemployed in late 1873, Chicago's Lassalleans and Marxists had worked to build a network of organizations among workers that could sustain both union organizing and political activity.[6]

A recent development aided this effort: New English-speaking leaders helped the WPUS's largely foreign-born and German-speaking constituency present a new face in public. Based in Chicago, the national president, Philip Van Patten, was native-born and an excellent speaker. Others included George Schilling, a bilingual German-born cooper, who would later become an influential leader of the Knights of Labor and a nonviolent anarchist; Thomas J. Morgan, a British-born machinist, poised to become the city's leading advocate of independent Socialist involvement in electoral politics; and the charismatic Albert Parsons, a tramping printer of old American stock, recently arrived with his African American wife Lucy from Texas, where they had been driven out for their Radical Republican organizing. The new English speakers were closer to the Lassallean wing of the party in their favoring of the ballot over trade union action, while Conrad Conzett's *Vorbote* was closer to the Marxists.[7]

On Saturday, July 21—six days after the strike began in Camden Junction, Maryland—all eyes were on Chicago's railroad workers. Talk of a strike against recent wage cuts circulated among employees of the Rock Island and Pacific, Lake Shore and Michigan Southern, and Illinois Central Railroads. That same Saturday, the Socialist Party's Chicago-based national executive committee met to ask its members to "render all possible moral and substantial assistance to our brethren" now on strike. It promulgated the party's program of nationalizing the railroads and telegraph lines and establishing the eight-hour workday as a solution to unemployment and falling wages. On Saturday night, the party held a packed solidarity rally on the Southwest Side in Sacks Hall. Portentous talk emanated from the audience of applying the "Pittsburgh solution" to the Chicago problem.[8]

Sunday was relatively calm despite another large meeting, but Monday, July 23, was another matter. Railroad workers from different lines gathered in small knots throughout the rail yards to discuss grievances and plan action. Meanwhile, fearing both the strike and property damage like that in Pittsburgh, many railroad officials in the city canceled their freight runs, leaving their rolling stock on tracks outside the city. The North Western and Chicago, Danville, and Vincennes Railroads restored the pay cut of some or all of their workers; other lines discussed doing the same. In secret conclave with Police Chief Michael Hickey and militia commanders, Mayor Monroe Heath decided to assemble the militia in readiness for action but reportedly decided not to have them board trains, escort strikebreakers, or "do anything to precipitate violence." Later reports indicated that the mayor instructed police either to use blanks in their pistols or fire over the heads of rioters if provoked, a decision widely questioned by leading citizens once the strikes and riots had begun in earnest.[9]

All day Monday, Socialists leafleted the working-class districts, advertising an evening mass meeting for the third consecutive day. The republican rhetoric of the leaflet reflected the influence of the new English-speaking leadership of the party. It asked workingmen, "Have You no Rights?—No Ambition? No Manhood?" This appeal to manhood resonated with the central experience of the Civil War: proving one's mettle in battle. Only now, labor leaders, not military officers, called on workingmen to demonstrate it in the arena of urban class conflict. In such conflicts, notions of manhood became ideological weapons, with labor leaders claiming true manhood for workers against a debauched, effete, duplicitous, and morally bankrupt elite.[10]

The circular argued further that, while employers combined to reduce wages, they used the new tramp ordinance and the state law against conspiracy to prevent workers from joining together for their own protection. "These aristocrats refuse to pay their taxes! HOW LONG WILL YOU BE MADE FOOLS OF?" The circular went on to accuse the dominant businessmen, to whom it referred as "money lords," of conspiring to restrict the vote to property holders and to bring back monarchy. This fear had originated in the agitation of the Chicago Citizens' Association for a restricted suffrage three years earlier and in widely reported discussions of limiting the vote in other states, particularly New York.[11]

That Monday night, one of the largest gatherings the city had known crowded into the intersection of Market and Madison streets on the Near West Side (map 4). The size of the gathering, somewhere between ten thousand and thirty thousand, made it necessary for six speaker rostrums to be erected.[12] In an ironic allusion to the Grand Army of the Republic—the post–Civil War veterans' organization and mainstay of the Republican Party—Albert Parsons addressed his listeners as the "Grand Army of Starvation":

> Fellow workers, let us recollect that in this Great Republic that has been handed down to us by our forefathers from 1776, that while we have the Republic, we still have hope. A mighty spirit is animating the hearts of the American people today. When I say the American people I mean the backbone of the country—the men who till the soil, guide the machine, who weave the material and cover the backs of civilized men. We are a portion of that people. Our brothers . . . have demanded of those in possession of the means of production . . . that they be permitted to live and that those men do not appropriate the life to themselves, and that they be not allowed to turn us upon the earth as vagrants and tramps. . . . We have come together this evening, if it is possible, to find the means by which

the great gloom that now hangs over our Republic can be lifted and once more the rays of happiness can be shed on the face of this broad land.[13]

As the throng swelled beyond the point where any single speaker could be heard, additional rostrums were improvised at different locations. At one rostrum, an Irish Union Army veteran, who had fought at Shiloh, told the crowd: "The Black man has been fought for; and we have given him the ballot; the people have shown an interest in him, and have done all they can to bring him up to the point where he could compete with the white man. Now why not do something for the workingman? . . . I was through the war. I fought for the big bugs—the capitalists—and many of you have done the same. And what is our reward now? What have the capitalists done for us?" The two themes—the corruption of the republic by an oligarchy of wealth and the veteran's complaint of betrayal and disinheritance—would echo in the actions of strikers and rioters in the days to come.[14]

Inaugurated formally on Monday by the railroaders, the strike spread on Tuesday, July 24. Mobile crowds—what the *Inter Ocean* called "roaming committees of strikers"—traveled from workplace to workplace calling out employees on strike. To the bulk of the press, these crowds of strikers were lawless mobs—"ragamuffins, vagrants, saloon bummers"—attracting sympathizers and hangers-on not directly interested in the strike, appropriating public streets as their theater of action, and coercing proprietors and other workers. A crowd on Tuesday led by a small group of Michigan Central switchmen belied this stereotype. The acknowledged chief was a discharged railroad hand named John Hanlon, a "dark complexioned man with chin whiskers and a pipe in his mouth." Carrying pine sticks, the men marched south along the tracks, stopping at the Baltimore and Ohio, Rock Island and Chicago, and Alton freight shops. The police offered no resistance. At each stop, Hanlon, attempting to persuade rather than intimidate, led a small delegation inside the shop. At one yard, employees did not want to quit, saying that their pay cut had been restored. Hanlon asked if the restoration applied to all employees on the line. When told that it did not, he responded that "they were working for the rights of all" and that work must cease until wages had been restored to all employees. Part of the crowd boarded a train to the South Side where it tried to spread the strike to the packinghouses. The men visited each establishment and, after securing a verbal agreement to restore wage cuts, raised a cheer for the employers.[15]

The method of striking was part of a long tradition. Early unions—before they were able to sustain membership loyalty, employ full-time leadership, and bargain with employers—were usually makeshift operations that assembled members only in times of strike, typically by resorting to crowd actions and the enthusiasm of the moment, often enhanced by brass bands—the band-wagon effect. This style of striking had deep roots among unskilled workers in America's preindustrial seaport cities and had been used during the 1867 eight-hour strike by crowds emerging from Bridgeport to enforce the shorter working day.[16]

Not traditional, however, was the effort of the strikers in 1877 to broaden the conflicts beyond their places of employment into wider strikes of the whole industry and even into a general strike. Beginning on Monday and Tuesday, July 23 and 24, general strikes in St. Louis and Kansas City may have served as models, but more important was the defeat of machine politicians by the Citizens' Association in the mid-1870s and consequent prominence of the Socialists, who took an early and significant part in the Chicago events. Even before the crowds took to the streets, the Socialists alone had advocated a program of the eight-hour workday that spoke to the interests of all workers, including the unemployed. Moreover, unlike English-speaking labor reform-ers, the Socialists still maintained an organizational base in Chicago's working class, mainly through the network of cultural and political organizations sustained by the city's German movement culture.[17]

By late Tuesday afternoon, the strike was no longer confined to the rail-roads. Concentrated on the Southwest Side, Bohemian lumbershovers com-menced a strike for the third year in a row. The strike had also spread to the heavily industrialized area just west of the Chicago River. Bands of workers and teenagers roamed up and down Canal, Clinton, and Jefferson streets shutting shops and factories. German and Bohemian furniture workers, many of whom were Socialists, joined the crowd. As yet there had been no interfer-ence by police, and the mood of the crowd was exuberant, like being "out on holiday," a disapproving reporter noted. Every instance of shutdown was lustily cheered and buoyed the crowd's enthusiasm.[18]

At least half of the crowds on Tuesday were composed of young men be-tween the ages of twelve and nineteen. "It seems strange, "remarked a *Tribune* reporter, "that full grown men should at the bidding of half-grown men and boys quit their work, but so it was." In fact, the phenomenon should not have seemed so strange. In an era before effective compulsory education, half-grown men and boys were important elements of the city's growing industrial workforce, laboring as apprentices, helpers, and more generally in the sweated trades. While, no doubt, many were attracted for thrills, others understood the crowd actions as being in their interest. Thus one boy, on being asked by

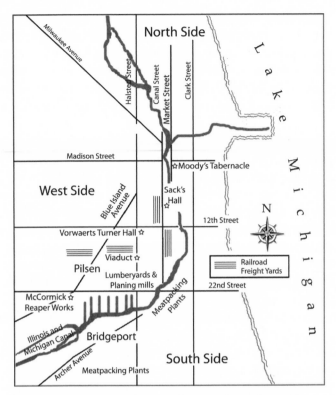

Map 4. The great railroad strike of 1877. Redrawn from *Atlas of Whiteside Co. and the State of Illinois to Which Is Added an Atlas of the United States, Maps of the Hemispheres, &c., &c., &c.* (Chicago: Warner and Beers, 1872), 13.

a reporter why he was striking, replied, "No man ought to work for less'n a dollar 'n a half" (a day)."[19]

The WPUS continued to try to organize a general strike for a 20 percent wage increase and the eight-hour workday. A Socialist circular called on workers to appoint delegates to a provisional strike committee. Though a minority of the committee wanted the party to support the crowd actions, the majority opinion, as expressed in the circular, urged strikers to "keep quiet" until an orderly strike could be planned. The city's business leaders, however, accused the Socialists of inciting the strikes and crowd actions. That afternoon, they took matters into their own hands. Albert Parsons, the most influential Socialist, found himself fired from his job as a printer at the *Times*, and detectives escorted him to the city hall. There, in the company of the police chief and over thirty aldermen and members of the Board of Trade, he and WPUS chairman Philip Van Patten were browbeaten and threatened with lynching. They were saved from arrest only because the authorities feared creating martyrs, and they released the men on the promise to absent themselves from strike activity for twenty-four hours. "Parsons, your life is in danger," said Police Chief Michael Hickey before Parsons was freed. "Everything you say or do is made known to me. . . . Do you know you are liable to be assassinated any moment on the street? Why, those board of trade men would as leave hang you to a lamp post as not." Meanwhile, the mayor issued a proclamation calling for citizen patrols in local neighborhoods and closing all saloons.[20]

In spite of the WPUS circular, a crowd of about three thousand gathered Tuesday evening at the spot of the previous night's rally. The Socialists, their leaders intimidated into silence and inaction, were absent, but the police were not. A police phalanx of one hundred fifty charged the peaceable gathering, clubbing indiscriminately, and firing over the heads of the panic-stricken crowd. This attack by the police was the first during the strike in which widespread clubbing and shooting had been used to disperse a peaceful crowd. It set a precedent for a pattern of police violence against working-class crowds that would transform the incidents into armed confrontations; it also further intimidated the Socialists and precluded them from organizing an effective general strike, such as those in Kansas City and St. Louis. An editorial in the *Illinois Staats-Zeitung* caught the confrontational mood: "From hour to hour the strikes and uprisings of the railroad workers take on the character of a revolution, if not to say a social war. . . . What originally began as an effort to reverse the lowering of the railroad workers' wages has become, in the course of a few days, a general vendetta between labor and capital."[21]

The next day, Wednesday, July 25, the center of the strike's gravity shifted to the city's main industrial areas. The composition of the crowds changed with the location of the strikes. Whereas teenagers composed a large portion of Tuesday's crowds, adult workingmen dominated on Wednesday. The *Illinois Staats-Zeitung*, for example, thought the crowd on Wednesday was composed largely of "real strikers, mainly wood workers."[22] At the same time, the policy of local authorities toward the strike changed, particularly as crowds of adult workers emerged at the center of it. The *Tribune* described a debate going on among city and business leaders. One faction, consisting of "the mayor and his advisors," counseled police restraint to avoid bloodshed and property damage. The other, led by the city's press and business leaders, wanted sterner action, arguing that "by allowing the crowds to run wild through the streets, the riot was but abetted." A delegation of businessmen from the Board of Trade asked the mayor to call a citizen's meeting Wednesday afternoon. The mayor complied and opened the gathering at the Moody and Sankey Tabernacle by issuing a proclamation calling on five thousand citizens, composed as much as possible of army veterans, to organize themselves as auxiliaries to the police. This proclamation was squarely within the long American tradition of an armed citizenry organizing to defend the republic.[23]

While the city authorities were regrouping, the strike continued. The action had resumed early on Wednesday as between six hundred and eight hundred Bohemian and some Polish lumbershovers gathered in the lumber district again. Armed with clubs taken from lumber scrap, they scattered the few employees remaining at work, closed the Union Rolling Stock Company, and advanced on the McCormick Reaper Works. Having grown to about fifteen hundred, the crowd was met by a squad of fifty police. The commander ordered the crowd to disperse, but his words were met with jeers and curses. The lumbershovers were the most combative group of workers in the city, and the Socialists had a strong constituency among their Bohemian members. When the police attempted to arrest their leaders, the lumbershovers responded with a shower of stones. The police fired into the crowd, wounding two and causing a wild retreat. When part of the crowd reassembled on the prairie west of the city, a few of the participants, apparently officers in the Bohemian militia company, talked of calling this unit out to protect their strike. News of such a possibility reached authorities, for that same day General Joseph T. Torrence, commander of the Illinois National Guard, signed an order disarming the "Bohemian Rifles." He may also have seen reports in the *Tribune* a few days earlier that the rioters in Pittsburgh had seized the arms of local militia groups.[24]

With so many discontented people lining the streets and excitement at such high pitch, any small group of workers with purpose and a target could get up a crowd. Conversely, a large crowd often would melt away just as quickly as it had formed. Many police literally bloodied their feet marching back and forth dispersing crowds that seemed to rise up, disappear, and reappear at random. One notable small crowd of unemployed dockworkers and laborers gathered near Lake Michigan. Finding nearly everything shut down, an Irish boat hand climbed up on an abandoned flatcar to make a speech: "'Look at me, . . . do I look like a loafer or a laboring man?' [in apparent response to press characterizations of the crowd] The crowd yelled and cheered and assured him that he was one of them. 'Of course I am,' he said; 'I am as honest a workingman as ever worked in a shop. Look at my hands. . . . These hands show what I am. We know what we're fighting for and what we're doing. We're fighting those God d—d capitalists. That is what we're doing. Ain't we? . . . Let us kill those damned aristocrats.' He had been a railroad worker himself once, he said, and knew what he was talking about. They had the thing started, and they were going to keep it going until those big bugs had been put down."[25]

The city was now preparing itself for a full-scale insurrection. For over an hour, the authorities raised the lift bridges and closed the tunnels to the West Side for fear that a crowd would gather there and attack city hall. Two companies of the U.S. Army arrived in the city at the request of the governor, who had responded to the mayor's request the day before. They had lately been battling Sioux in the Dakotas. In a revealing metaphor, the *Tribune* headlined "Red War" the next day, conjuring up at once images of insurrectionary communists, Indian savages, and the spilling of blood. While the bronzed and grizzled veterans won cheers from businessmen and clerks downtown, they fielded jeers and catcalls from Canal Street crowds as they marched west along Madison Street to the Exposition Building.[26]

In response to the mayor's proclamation, the city's propertied middle classes had begun to arm themselves. Field, Leiter and Company and J. V. Farwell dry goods stores organized companies of armed clerks, as did the Illinois Central Railroad. In the heavily Republican Fourth Ward, three hundred Civil War veterans organized. Citizen patrols formed in a host of wards, but reports of patrols were few in the wards of the foreign-born.[27] Despite the feeling conveyed by the press that the city was in the midst of civil war, with a few minor exceptions neither the armed citizen patrols, the special police, the state militia, nor the U.S. Army saw sustained action; only the Chicago police engaged in battle. Nonetheless, there was a real possibility for organized armed conflict, involving not only the coercive forces of the state but also groups of armed citizens, some of which were sympathetic to the strikers.

After dinner on Wednesday, a crowd of about fifteen hundred gathered at the Burlington yards. Upon satisfying themselves that the rail lines were not in use, they were about to disperse when a squad of sixteen policemen pulled up. Called "peelers" by Irish workers—after the hated Irish constabulary of Sir Robert Peel, manned by native-born Irishmen and viewed by the Irish as turncoats—the police rode headlong into a volley of stones and shouts of defiance. Though the police fired at the crowd with their revolvers, the crowd did not flee. According to a *Times* reporter, "They faltered not in the least but stood up under fire like war-scarred veterans or men resolved to perish for their cause rather than abandon it." Some of the crowd replied to the police fusillade with stones and sporadic fire from their own weapons. Shots were exchanged for fully two minutes until the police ran out of ammunition and fled for their lives. Part of the crowd followed in close pursuit. The roles of the past two days had been reversed, and for the first time the crowd had taken the offensive.[28]

On Thursday morning, the scene of crowd activity shifted into the residential communities. By 9 A.M., a crowd of three thousand men, women, and teenagers from surrounding neighborhoods had gathered along Halsted Street between Twelfth Street and a viaduct at Sixteenth Street. This area of Halsted was narrow, skirted with frame buildings, and could easily be blockaded.[29] The battle of Halsted Street began when a squad of police attempted to break up the crowd by chasing it south. At Sixteenth Street, confronted by an angry crowd of approximately five thousand, the police emptied their revolvers into the masses of humanity. "Although men were seen to drop away at every minute the mob dragged or carried them away at the instant." After they almost had expended their last round of ammunition, the police turned into headlong retreat north under the viaduct. They were closely followed by the crowd, which pelted them with stones. One officer later admitted, "I was never in such close quarters in my life before." One block later, the police picked up reinforcements and again turned on the crowd, firing and clubbing mercilessly. One member of the crowd fell mortally wounded; this had a "sobering effect," and the tide turned once again. But after the officers had chased the rioters across the river, a "gang of toughs" raised the bridge and isolated a small band of police on the south side. The police might have suffered grievously had not a small boy turned a lever to lower the bridge and allow a squad of volunteer cavalry to ride to their rescue.[30]

South Halsted Street, the scene of battle, straddled two working-class communities, one Bohemian, the other Irish, both of which were encompassed by the Fifth, Sixth, and Seventh wards. Well over half of the Sixth Ward's Fourth Precinct was Bohemian, and half its heads of household were laborers.[31] The precinct lay in the heart of the Bohemian community known as Pilsen, which had a strong community of freethinkers, recently alienated from the Catholic Church, as well as a significant Socialist constituency. During the 1877 strikes and riots, almost the entire Pilsen community rose up against the police. One disapproving Republican wrote in a letter to the *Tribune:* "I was perhaps the only Bohemian in Chicago who opposed the powerful current of the aroused public feeling of my countrymen."[32]

The other major source of crowd casualties was the Irish community of Bridgeport in the Fifth Ward. Bridgeport originated as a settlement of Irish and German canal laborers, but by the 1870s it was the site of three fast-growing industries: brick making, iron and steel, and slaughtering and meatpacking, the later employing upward of twenty thousand at its seasonal peak. At the same time, the district still thrived as a port for lake and canal shipping as well as for the dockworkers who serviced it. Thus, like the lumber district across the river, its workforce contained a volatile mixture of new industrial workers and traditional seaport laborers. In 1875, a reporter commented, "There is probably as much real poverty in Bridgeport as anywhere in the town. It is also the haunt of the roughest characters." A slight majority of all those arrested had Irish surnames, and teenagers with Irish names were two and a half times as likely to be killed as German and Bohemian teenagers.[33]

On Thursday in the midst of the "Battle of Halsted Street," a contingent of five hundred stockyard workers from Bridgeport set out along Archer Avenue to join the Bohemian lumbershovers on Halsted. Many of them were butchers, still wearing their aprons and carrying butcher knives and gambrels for clubs. The police drove the crowd back to Bridgeport after an hour-long pitched battle for the Halsted Street Bridge.[34]

When the crowd shifted to the neighborhoods, large numbers of women joined the fray. According to the *Times,* they constituted at least one-fifth of every gathering. On Halsted Street, Bohemian women brought stones in their aprons to the men, encouraging them to "clean out and kill the soldiers." Not only did they incite the men, but they also engaged in their own resistance. Police detectives roaming the crowd sought out women wearing one stocking on the assumption they had used the other to fill with stones for use as a swinging weapon. In Pilsen on Twenty-second Street between Fisk and May, Bohemian women gathered in the afternoon at a door and sash manufactory. The reporters' descriptions of the ensuing altercation reflected their dismay at behavior that blatantly violated the norms of middle-class womanhood. "Dresses were tucked up around the waists," and "brawny, sunburnt arms brandished clubs" torn from the fence surrounding the factory. When the police arrived to protect the factory from what the *Inter Ocean* styled an "Outbreak of Bohemian Amazons," the women remained firm and stoned the hated police till they left. The *Tribune* concluded that these immigrant working-class women were "a great deal worse than the men."[35]

Up until Thursday, the organized trade unions had largely stayed aloof from the crowds, although on Wednesday large meetings of tailors and cigar makers had met on the Southwest Side to organize strikes. On Thursday, more trades began to hold meetings to discuss striking. But by this time, the police were making no distinction between the proverbial "honest workingman" and the rioters. The coopers, cigar makers, stonecutters, and tailors all had their meetings proscribed or attacked by police. The most blatant abridgment of the right to free assembly occurred at the Vorwärts Turner Hall on Halsted near Twelfth Street, where three hundred journeymen cabinetmakers had gathered to negotiate with their employers. With no provocation, a band of police rushed into the hall, clubbing and shooting indiscriminately. One carpenter, Carl Tessman, was killed and dozens wounded. This incident became a defining moment for the German left in the city, heightening its sense of alienation not only from American governmental institutions but also from the leadership of Chicago Germans. The *Illinois Staats-Zeitung,* for example, justified the police action as understandable during a civil war, for "war knows no consideration." Two years later, the Harmonia Joiners Society won a suit against the policemen involved, the judge terming their actions a "criminal riot." Indicative of the incident's repercussions, Governor John Peter Altgeld referred to it in his pardon message justifying the freeing of the imprisoned Haymarket anarchists in 1893.[36]

As evening approached on Thursday, the Battle of Halsted Street subsided. Here and there, police exchanged shots with snipers and occasionally cleared out homes, but the high tide of the upheaval had passed. The city was an armed camp, and the formation of crowds was impossible without immediate opposition. Despite the police patrols and the decline in crowds, hitherto sporadic attempts of workers to call strikes began to produce results. The West Division Street railway stockmen, stonecutters, West Side gas workers, South Side glass workers, and lime-kiln workers all went on strike. Most railroads as well as the city's lumber district, rolling mills, and stockyards remained closed into the next week. By then, a significant minority of those involved, notably railroad workers, had won restoration of wage cuts.

Throughout the city's West and South sides, Irish, Bohemian, German, and Polish families mourned their dead relatives and neighbors, tended the wounded, or attempted to raise bond for the almost two hundred men who had been arrested. Approximately thirty men and boys had been killed—many buried anonymously in lime pits—and another two hundred wounded. Chicago's casualties exceeded that of any other city in the Great Strike of 1877. No police had been killed, and eighteen had been wounded, none seriously.[37]

THE GREAT STRIKE AND THE CHICAGO BOURGEOISIE

Just after the most violent day of the strike, Thursday, July 26, the *Tribune* argued that the strike posed a mortal threat: "The criminal class, the mob, the Communistic faction, have offered violence to everything which the American people hold dear and sacred." These three elements combined to create an enemy that threatened the whole social order, just as France had been challenged by the Commune in 1871. By Sunday, Joseph Medill argued that mass immigration, the Civil War, widespread tramping, and the rise of labor unions' intimidation had created something hitherto unknown in America: the "dangerous classes." The phrase *dangerous classes* had been used in the press, particularly in New York City, since the early 1870s to describe the wage-earning working class, especially when it took collective actions in riots, demonstrations, and strikes under political leadership to the left of the mainstream. A book published by Charles Loring Brace in 1872—*The Dangerous Classes of New York and Twenty Years' Work among Them*—made the phrase common coin outside the press, and the Great Strike awakened the nation to the social reality it denoted. By using the term *dangerous classes,* Medill was participating in a national discussion about a new class phenomenon.[38]

The strike confronted the Chicago bourgeoisie with the most fundamental questions about how to rule the city: Was armed force the only way to protect property and control the immigrant working class? If so, how much coercion was necessary? Would the city become an armed camp? On the other hand, on what basis might class peace be achieved? What place did workers have in the social order and how might they come to accept it? Was there a place in the social order for the working class at all? Would Chicago workers always remain the "dangerous classes"?

The new climate of public opinion after the strike posed a special threat to the Citizens' Association, which had no answer to the labor question. Its program was designed to produce an efficient, inexpensive, and incorruptible administration of the city's business, not find work for the unemployed, raise wages, or shorten the working day. Uncertain in the new political situation, the city's new upper class pursued three options at the same time: It built its own cultural world, armed the state in case repression was needed, and engaged in paternalistic reform.

Following the strike, men like Cyrus McCormick, George Pullman, and Marshall Field participated in building private social clubs and cultural activities that helped fashion a new and distinctive cultural world. In December 1877, Pullman and Field helped found the Commercial Club, which promoted "social intercourse" and the "prosperity and growth of this city." Similar clubs were founded soon afterward, including the Calumet Club (1878), which had a special interest in the early history of Chicago, as did the Old Settlers' Room (1879). The Union League Club (1879) advanced the social life and politics of the Republican Party, as did the Iroquois Club for the Democrats. Upper-class women were in advance of their male counterparts. Including the "ultra-fashionable society figures of the city," the Fortnightly Club (1873) spawned a whole set of sister societies, most prominently the Chicago Woman's Club (1876), which was interested in "social problems." This social and cultural work flowered in the 1880s and 1890s under the direction of an interlocking set of philanthropic businesspeople who founded and served on the boards of the city's major cultural institutions. A similar burst of institution building and cultural definition took place in major cities across the North as, according to Sven Beckert, bourgeois Americans built "an insular world of their own" that not only distinguished them culturally and socially from the working class and lower middle class but also linked them with compatriots across the North.[39]

As they enjoyed their own company and promoted the city, members of the Commercial Club actively advocated the use of the federal army as a police force in case of new uprisings by the lower orders, and they successfully lobbied for the building of Fort Sheridan on the North Shore of Lake Michigan to insure that adequate armed force was nearby. The club bought six hundred acres of land for the fort and donated it to the federal government. Private militia companies were no longer adequate to protect the social order; in fact, they had become a threat to it as the companies separated out by class, politics, and ethnicity. There was no longer a homogeneous citizenry that could be depended upon to mobilize and protect the city. Recognizing this problem earlier, the Citizens' Association had been trying since 1874 to reorganize the militia under the auspices of the state government, while at the same time it provided funds and organizational support for new regiments in Chicago composed primarily of reliable clerks and salespeople in major businesses. This support exemplified direct assistance in building the modern bureaucratic state, a central political goal of the America bourgeoisie in the last third of the nineteenth century.[40]

At the same time, many business leaders were also interested in reform as a means of pacifying the "dangerous classes." Though some leaders advocated arbitration of disputes on the railroads and government regulation of their rates (with some success at the state level), reform usually centered on the improvement of working-class character. The ideal workingman would strive for self-improvement and social mobility through hard work, refraining from alcohol and the saloon fraternity, and deferring immediate gratification in favor of industriousness and frugality. The result would be a worker who struggled to leave his class rather than unite with the rest of his fellows to fight for better working conditions and pay. Up through the 1870s, most reformers viewed Moody revivalism, public education, moral exhortation, and enforcement of the temperance laws as the means to inculcate such values in Chicago workers. In this vein, the Commercial Club sponsored the Chicago Manual Training School, which provided poor working-class youth a three-year training program to turn them into skilled mechanics. Following the Great Strike, Field, Pullman, and other leading businessmen formed the Citizens League to enforce the laws against selling liquor to minors, the same teenagers so prominent during the riots. Some upper-class reformers even moved beyond the prevalent individualistic morality, adopting a more overt social environmental approach to changing workers' behavior.[41]

The leader in the environmental shift was railroad car builder George Pullman. In 1879, Pullman followed closely the movement in New York to create model tenements that offered working-class families clean and ventilated space to reduce sickness and disease and promote good morals by inducing men to stay at home rather than escape to saloons. In return, investors would receive a reasonable 7 percent return. Pullman adopted the idea that improving workers' material conditions of life could be made compatible with the most efficient and economical business practices, and it lay at the heart of his plan in 1880 to build a model town south of Chicago. To Pullman, the town was neither philanthropy nor a utopian experiment. It was an attempt to demonstrate that reform and uplift could be a paying proposition, just as he had turned comfort, beauty, and luxury in railroad travel into a successful business enterprise. The subsequent violent history of his town illustrated the limits of his paternalistic ideas.[42]

Pulled in several directions at the same time in the late 1870s, Chicago's leading businessmen lacked anything like a consensus on a strategy for governing the city through persuasion, as distinguished from simply repressing uprisings. The history of the Citizens' Association illustrated that fact. In the year after the Great Strike, despite its previous reforms, the Citizens' Association was without a programmatic response to the municipal government's insolvency. Its main proposal to address the challenge of the "dangerous classes" was to increase the coercive force of the several levels of government while banning the formation of private armed organizations. In addition to its efforts to strengthen the state militia after the Great Strike, the Citizens' Association sought to expand the size of the police force and arm it with one thousand "improved Springfield rifles" as well as several howitzers, all for "use in the case of riot." The Association also strengthened the hand of the police by successfully lobbying the state legislature for a stricter vagrancy law. Otherwise, its successes were modest and its failures larger, especially its inability to completely capture the county government from the "bummers" or to eliminate the town governments, two of its longtime goals. The momentum of the municipal reformers, so strong in 1876, had waned by late 1877.[43]

Yet the greatest weakness of the Citizens' Association stemmed not from the strength of its enemies but rather from the refusal of its own constituency among native-born businessmen to take full responsibility for ruling the new social order. The most glaring instance of this was the refusal to pay taxes sufficient to support even the minimalist government it advocated. In the spring of 1878, an Illinois Supreme Court decision revealed the financial frailty of the city government by prohibiting the issuing of debt in anticipation of uncollected taxes. The city quickly ran out of any means to pay its employees or bills. The court decision was not the root of the problem, however. According to the executive committee of the Citizens' Association, "the present difficulty originates from disregard of the law in regard to the standard of valuation in making assessments."[44]

Three different parties did the disregarding: individuals, corporations, and tax assessors. Individuals lied about their wealth, particularly their personal property; corporations simply refused to state the value of their holdings; and the assessors cooperated in the corruption by undervaluing personal and corporate holdings, presumably for bribes. Thus, although state law called for assessment "at fair cash value," the assessed value was 30 percent of that, or lower, on personal property and land in Chicago. The undervaluing of corporations was even more egregious. In 1873, the value of the state's railroad corporations had been assessed at $85,507,532, whereas in 1877 that figure had fallen to $1,605,783. In 1877, over one hundred Chicago corporations were not assessed at all, including the Union Stock Yards and the Chamber of Commerce itself. The Citizens' Association succeeded in saving the city's finances by organizing a syndicate of wealthy Chicagoans, chaired by Marshall Field, which backed warrants issued by the city at a fixed discount rate of 8 percent. While the syndicate helped the city weather this crisis, "tax fighting" continued for decades, severely limiting the ability of the municipal government to address the city's problems.[45]

The fiscal crisis of the city in the late 1870s had deep roots in the class conflict that had erupted during the depression and culminated in the Great Strike. The depression increased competition and lowered profits, both of which made tax fraud and wage cuts attractive as methods to protect capital accumulation. The triumph of the People's Party in 1873 also made tax fraud attractive as a way to limit and undermine an administration the businessmen detested. These economic and political challenges accentuated the impact of the fires and labor unrest in the 1870s. Hermann Raster of the *Illinois Staats-Zeitung* summed up the complex crisis when, in the middle of the Great Strike, he tried to argue workers into staying off the streets: "The city of Chicago is perhaps less in a position than any other large city in the land to endure this unrest with its open disturbance of the peace and its threat to private property. For in the last six years no other has lived through such horrible afflictions as the two huge fires of 9 October 1871 and 14 July 1874. Every sensible worker knows that, through them and through the melee of 1873, the situation of capital holdings in Chicago has become very uncertain and unstable."[46]

The Great Strike's threat to capital accumulation was evident in its challenge to the prevailing business strategy of slashing wages as a response to declining revenue. Aware of its social and political costs, employers thought at least twice about reducing wages. Adolph Douai stated the message flamboyantly in 1877: "As with a magic stroke the working people awake across the whole country and cry: Up to this point, Mister Capital, and no farther! We workers also have a bit to say about this!" *Iron Age,* the premier trade journal of the iron and steel industry, stated it more matter-of-factly: "The reduction in the wages of labor has reached its lowest point. . . . It would be a bold step in a wrong direction to give notice of a decrease in wages." Some railroad leaders drew the same conclusion. The president of the Burlington Railroad noted, "that a reduction of pay to employes [*sic*] may be as expensive to the Co. as an increase of pay." According to historian David Lightner, managers of the Illinois Central Railroad remembered this message sixteen years later in 1893: "The strikes of 1877 tended to put a floor under the wages of American workingmen, so that the earnings of the industrial labor force displayed a remarkable stability throughout the remainder of the nineteenth century." This constraint on the ability to reduce wages was not universally detrimental to business. *Iron Age* thought this constraint also limited decreases in prices that had been the main weapon in the "cutthroat competition" that threatened profits.[47]

Wage reductions did not stop after 1877, of course, but they were not the ready answer to protecting capital that they had once been. And, as a consequence, the attractiveness of tax fraud and other means of reducing costs increased. In turn, the political influence and credibility of the Citizens' Association shrank, in part because the government it spent so much time reforming was practically bankrupt. The reformed municipal government was fiscally too weak to achieve the Association's vision of limited, inexpensive, and effective government led by the "best men." At the end of the decade, the Citizens' Association assumed a new role: Instead of leading a social movement to take over and reform the municipal government, as it had in the mid-1870s, it shrank into a good government interest group.

The most glaring leadership failure of the city's bourgeoisie was its inability to convince, incorporate, or marginalize the threat of the "dangerous classes." Masses of people from all national groups were willing to actively resist first the railroads, then employers more generally, and finally public authorities. The usual means of integrating them into the social, economic, and political order—elections, jobs, property ownership, and Protestant revivalism—had not worked, at least to the point of preventing such an upheaval. The Chicago bourgeoisie faced an enormous challenge to achieving consent to their rule from people and groups throughout the social order. To resolve its dilemma, it had to acknowledge and address energetic new political initiatives emerging from the city's working class.[48]

THE GREAT STRIKE INVIGORATES POPULAR POLITICS AMONG THE IRISH AND ANGLO AMERICANS

The Great Strike challenged the city's unions as well as the leading business-men. Afterward, Andrew Cameron wrote: "Our unions are isolated and con-sequently are weak and inefficient. They have no common ties, no sympathy in common with each other and are indifferent to each other's success and elevation."[49] The aggressive crowds and, even more, the myriad instances of unity across lines of skill, trade, ethnicity, religion, and sex made it clear to many labor leaders that they needed new and more inclusive forms of orga-nization. Clearly, they had to incorporate the unskilled laborers and factory hands whenever possible.

Anglo American labor reformers, Irish trade unionists and nationalists, and Socialists all responded with new initiatives that tried to channel the popular energy that outlived the strike. Quiescent in the 1870s, Anglo American and Irish trade unionists helped found the Knights of Labor in Chicago, which went on to become one of the city's strongest labor organizations in the 1880s. The same group also organized the city's small Greenback Party. Prominent among this group of English-speaking activists, Irish trade unionists started to build neighborhood-based labor organizations, which were able to include non-Irish ethnic groups. At the same time, Irish nationalists built a genuine social movement with ties to labor, ward politicians, and the Catholic Church, and by doing so they helped revive the Chicago Democratic Party. Finally, capitalizing on their strong organizational base, the German Socialists attracted new English-speaking leaders, who helped them lead the Chicago labor movement for the next two years. All such initiatives responded to the same new reality: The Great Strike of 1877 had enhanced and extended the popular agitation and democratic unrest that had originated in the sectional crisis of the 1850s, expanded during the Civil War, and then refueled during the depression of the 1870s.[50]

Three weeks after the end of the 1877 railroad strike, about fifty men founded Local Assembly 400 of the Knights of Labor in Chicago. Part of the attraction of the Knights of Labor was that it represented an alternative to typical trade unions, which had so obviously failed to provide leadership and protection to the city's workers during the depression and the Great Strike. Hoping to unite on a scale commensurate with the new national corporations, working people made "amalgamation" a rallying cry, and the Knights of Labor offered a model for such unity and power. The Knights "embraced all who earned an honest living without distinction of trade," and their basic units of organization—the mixed local assembly and mixed district assembly—embodied this principle by including a diversity of occupations and people of low-white-collar status, though a large majority of a Knights assembly had to be wage earners. Also, in contrast to unions, the Knights preferred arbitration to strikes, which had just proved both powerful and costly. In the late 1870s, however, the membership and influence of the Knights was circumscribed by their secrecy and fraternal rituals, which were opposed by some, most prominently the Catholic Church, and which proved to be liabilities in politics.[51]

Soon after the July strike, Irish workers formed or revived labor organizations based in Bridgeport. Notably, they were not simply Irish in ethnicity, nor were they confined to the local neighborhoods; rather, these organizations were initial attempts to transform the mass strike into more enduring forms of organization with links outside their geographic and ethnic origins. A new class solidarity had emerged among unskilled seamen, day laborers, packinghouse workers, and lumbershovers, which made them ripe for organization. In spring 1878, brick makers founded a protective organization, and sailors revived their union under the leadership of Richard Powers. According to Powers, the 1877 strikes, "although detrimental to some, gave stability and backbone to others. . . . It was then that many of the unions now existing . . . were organized." The most important union to emerge from the 1877 experience was the Butchers and Packinghouse Workers Benevolent Society, the city's first industrial union of the post-1877 era. Fearful that unemployed sailors would cross their picket lines, the skilled butchers decided to expand their organization to laborers with the help of Powers. Initially backed by the local Catholic Church and boasting five thousand members from several ethnic groups, the union mounted a large but ultimately unsuccessful strike of the packinghouses in 1879. When church support faltered, the union turned to Socialist-run labor institutions for support.[52]

The same multiethnic tendencies evident among Irish trade unionists were prominent among Irish nationalists. In late August 1877—one month after the strike—the Irish nationalists of Chicago held a parade and picnic at Ogden's Grove to raise money for the "Irish national fund." The event was so successful that it became an annual affair for Irish Chicagoans. After declaring devotion to the American republic as well as fealty to independence movements in Ireland, Cuba, Poland, and Hungary, the event's statement of principles lauded "aggressive organization," including "armed volunteers," such as the contemporary Fenians. The most important aspect of aggressive organization was that it assumed popular will had to be enforced from below by disciplined, organized collective power. Such power could take many forms, from the boycott that the Irish nationalists bequeathed to the American labor movement to fund-raising at the annual Irish nationalist picnics celebrated each August. The Great Strike of 1877 revived a broad swath of organized popular activities with political import, even when they were not directly related to electoral politics.[53]

THE SOCIALIST LEFT LEADS A SOCIAL MOVEMENT AFTER THE GREAT STRIKE

Chicago's Socialists were best situated to take advantage of the Great Strike of July 1877, given their strong institutional roots in the city's German-speaking population, their advocacy of militancy throughout the depression, and their ability to synthesize divergent Marxist and Lassallean strategies. They spoke through the *Vorbote,* which Conrad Conzett and his fellow Marxists had taken over in 1875 from the strong Chicago Lassallean group led by Carl Klings after their electoral defeats.

The most important left thinker to offer an intellectual framework for political action was Adolph Douai.[54] Immigrating to the United States in 1852, he had participated in the antislavery movement before the Civil War, including for a while in Texas, while working as a teacher and editor. To Douai, the strike reinforced the Marxist position that economic organization was the precondition for fundamental and lasting change. Without the organization of the railroad workers, there would have been no sustained resistance to the wage reductions, and it was this resistance that taught the masses of people that they could successfully defend themselves through their own collective actions. Thus to Douai the economic organization of the railroad workers had profound political consequences, certainly more so than any election, because collective organization and direct action transformed popular sentiment in a revolutionary direction.

Whereas most people were passive observers in an election campaign, a strike deeply engaged and empowered them, according to Douai. While subordinate in importance, political action was necessary to link economic organizations together, provide a means for consultation and decision making, and give a successful Socialist direction to the movement. To meet these objectives, a special type of political action was necessary:

> Election campaigning is not the only, is not even the best form of political activity. As is well known, one can be very effective politically through mass meetings, if care is taken for accurate reports of the speeches; one can be no less effective through all kinds of grand demonstrations, as for example marches, festivals, wearing badges with recognized meanings, collecting money for unfortunate comrades, petitions to legislatures and officials; finally one can do the best through the party press and pamphlets, as well as through congresses of party representatives and publishing their decisions. And all these means of agitation cost less money than one election campaign, while they have a wider effect.

For Douai, such political agitation was uniquely possible in the United States, in contrast to Europe, where it was legally hindered and in some cases banned.[55]

Douai's thinking closely paralleled that of the young New York cigar maker Samuel Gompers. Like Douai, Gompers feared that the workers' movement would be taken over by doctrinaires and sectarians who were more concerned with theoretical purity and passing resolutions than with the needs of the real workers' movement. Like Douai, Gompers believed that the labor movement, "pure and simple," was itself political. Following Ira Steward and other Anglo American eight-hour-workday advocates, Gompers believed that unions could raise the standard of living and open workers' minds to higher goals, including a version of Socialism.[56]

But, unlike Gompers's thinking on unionism, Douai's position also led in a revolutionary direction. Using the example of the Great Strike as evidence for the insurrectionary potential of "economic organization," Douai thought that unions could draw on, shape, and extend popular politics into revolutionary action. This position could lead the labor left in several directions. By stressing the radical possibilities of economic organization practically to the exclusion of electoral politics, one could find the origins of revolutionary unionism, a kind of syndicalism that among anarchists became known as the "Chicago idea." The Chicago idea guided local anarchists during the eight-hour upheaval of 1886. Alternatively, by emphasizing the priority of economic organization, minimizing radical political agitation, and participating in elections on the basis of trade union demands, one could arrive at the "pure and simple unionism" that prevailed in the American Federation of Labor under the leadership of Samuel Gompers. Finally, by giving both union organization and political agitation equal priority, Socialists could fashion a compromise solution. Chicago's Socialist left pursued this third option for the next year and a half before the spring municipal elections of 1879.[57]

The popular mobilization during and after the Great Strike emboldened both German Lassalleans and English-speaking Socialists to reenter electoral politics. As the campaign season opened in the fall of 1877, the Illinois section of the WPUS published a far-reaching platform that went well beyond their modest locally oriented program in the spring, which reflected the then prominent position of the Marxists who advocated economic organization first. In line with the national platform, the Illinois section called for the eight-hour workday, takeover of the transportation system by the national government, and the management of all industrial enterprises by cooperatives. It also added some planks of its own.[58]

In the fall 1877 election, the WPUS surprised even itself as well as the local political establishment. Emboldened by the strike, the WPUS fielded candidates for all thirteen open county offices, and its candidates received 14 percent of the total vote.[59] The Socialists drew their strength from huge immigrant working-class districts on the South, Southwest, and Northwest sides. Over 80 percent of the Socialist vote for Albert Parsons as county clerk came from seven wards out of eighteen in the whole city, and six of the seven were on the South and West sides.[60] The Sixth Ward's Bohemian precinct adjoining the lumberyards, the home of so many riot victims, delivered the highest percentage Socialist vote of any precinct in the city and continued to do so in two of the next three elections. The Socialists were particularly strong in the Sixth Ward and its immediate neighbors to the east and north, which encompassed not only the riot district during the Great Strike but also the traditional core of the Democratic Party's strength.[61]

Both success and internal divisions doomed the WPUS after its surprising electoral victory in the fall of 1877. Founded nationally on a compromise between Marxists and Lassalleans, the party was dedicated first of all to advancing the economic organization of workers, not to winning elections. The electoral success in the fall of 1877 emboldened the Lassalleans to reject this strategy. As a result, the WPUS broke apart in December at a meeting in Newark, New Jersey. The political wing of the WPUS became the Socialistic Labor Party (changed quickly to Socialist Labor Party [SLP]), put electoral action at the core of its program, and rejected the WPUS's official newspaper because it was too closely associated with the trade unions first faction. Chicagoans soon followed these national developments by creating their own local organization of the SLP in the winter and spring of 1878. The party effectively became the directing force of Chicago labor politics for the next year and a half, achieving this prominence through a tour de force of agitation that combined cultural and political activities appealing to numerous national groups.[62]

The SLP drew strength from its sister organization, the Trade and Labor Council, which helped produce the kind of economic power the Marxists advocated as the precondition for political success. Mirroring developments among political Socialists, Albert Parsons and Thomas Morgan called for a new central labor organization soon after the fall 1877 elections. They helped organize a pivotal meeting of trade unions on December 1, where Chicago labor delegates established the Trade and Labor Assembly (TLA) after narrowly defeating a motion to set up a local organization of the secret Knights of Labor. The meeting chose Parsons, politically the city's most prominent Socialist, as the organization's first president. The founding of the TLA was a revival of a tradition of central union organizations that had begun during the Civil War with the Trades Assembly. As unions revived in 1878 and 1879, most ended up joining the Socialist-led TLA, and Socialists won leadership positions in some of Chicago's most influential union organizations. Unlike the shadowy Knights of Labor, the TLA could offer concrete assistance by sponsoring citywide mass meetings and collecting strike support funds. Despite tactical and ideological differences, the TLA was heir to the same interethnic and international radical traditions as the SLP.[63]

These traditions were evident in a parade the TLA organized in support of Irish nationalism late in 1879. The marchers followed a symbolically charged route, beginning at Greif's Hall on 54 West Lake Street, a central Socialist meeting place. Organizations marching included the Seamen's Union, Lehr-und Wehr-Verein, Jaeger Verein, and the English, French, and German sections of the TLA. When the marchers arrived at the viaduct on Halsted Street, scene of the most violent confrontation in 1877, they were joined by three thousand members of the Butchers and Packinghouse Workers Benevolent

Society, which was led by Irish trade unionists. Then the combined group marched to the Vorwärts Turner Hall, scene of the attack on the German furniture workers union in 1877.[64]

Throughout the period studied in this book, the ability of German and Irish immigrant workers to build alliances determined the degree to which democratically grounded social change could garner political support. The ability of the Fenians and German forty-eighters to cooperate during the Civil War helped forestall in Chicago the antidraft riots that marred New York City's response to emancipation. The rise of interethnic unions by 1864 and the eight-hour-workday movement owed their successes to the willingness of Irish and German workers to transcend religious and ethnic differences. Municipal reform led by the upper class, though progressive in some respects, was defeated by an Irish-German coalition under the banner of the People's Party because it neglected the social needs of the city's immigrant working class. The 1877 strike and general uprising also owed its strength to the ability of Irish and German-speaking workers to fight in the streets against a common class enemy. Following the strike, the Socialists, now led by English speakers, took full advantage of this interethnic unity and the spread of labor and reform organizations in working-class civil society to fuel their electoral forays of 1878 and 1879.

By contrast, the city's upper class, having united behind the Citizens' Association and the anti-People's Party ticket in 1876, could not sustain its own reform impulses in the midst of the depression. Tax dodging, a deep fear of the "dangerous classes," the inability of evangelical religion to penetrate immigrant culture, and a ready resort to repression prevented the local bourgeoisie from developing through the Republican Party the kind of policies that would win workers' consent to the suddenly controversial new capitalist order. It would take a new regime emerging out of the Democratic Party to do that.

7 Regime Change

MORE THAN ANY SINGLE PERSON or institution, Democratic Mayor Carter Harrison pacified class relations in Chicago, freeing the city's capitalists to accumulate wealth without governing directly. Harrison was neither a native-born evangelical Protestant with roots in New England or New York, like most of Chicago's upper class, nor an immigrant machine politician. Rather, he was a one-term congressman who had been born in Kentucky and proudly displayed the southern political style of a popular aristocrat. Harrison arrived in Chicago politics at a critical moment when his outsider status gave him freedom to maneuver politically, when his cosmopolitan cultural style gave him cachet among immigrant workers, and when the city was critically in need of a new kind of political leadership.[1]

In 1879, Harrison initiated a party realignment in the city that endured for decades, ending the Republican dominance that had begun during the political crisis of the 1850s. From 1879 through 1897, Democrats won seven of the ten mayoral elections, and two of the three Republican victories were due to a split in the Democratic vote. Harrison's leadership also created a new "regime"—a set of formal and informal governing institutions linking state and civil society—that endured into the Progressive Era.

REPUBLICAN RULE SHATTERED

In the aftermath of the 1877 railroad strike, the Socialists extended their leadership over the labor movement in Chicago, aided in part by the arrival of experienced and energetic new leaders fleeing repression in Germany under Otto von Bismarck's Anti-Socialist Law. Passed in 1878, the law banned the Social Democratic Party and trade union organization until 1890, creating an "outlaw" culture and politics within the German working class. Among the exiles exported by Bismarck's repression was Paul Grottkau, an architect and mason who had been active in trade union affairs in Berlin and a leader in Ferdinand Lassalle's party. When Grottkau immigrated to the United States in January 1878, he was well-known in labor circles within and outside Germany, even at the relatively young age of thirty-two.[2]

In early March—just a few months after his arrival in Chicago—a crowd packed the sizeable Vorwärts Turner Hall to hear Grottkau speak. He ended his address by observing that, while the 1877 railroad strike was over "for the time being," it was "in no way forgotten": "Since then, in all cities, unions are being organized, Socialist organizations are being founded. The day is not far when . . . the men who once freed the black slaves from the yoke of serfdom will be men enough to gain freedom for the white slaves." By the summer, he had taken over editorship of the *Vorbote,* a weekly, and its sister paper, the *Chicagoer Arbeiter-Zeitung,* which appeared three times a week. Grottkau's seamless entry into the culture and politics of the Chicago left illuminated the transnational world of German labor and social reform, which was analogous to the Anglo American phenomenon represented in Chicago by such people as Andrew Cameron, the Scottish printer and editor of the *Workingman's Advocate.*[3]

A week after Grottkau's speech in early March, the Chicago chapter of the Socialist Labor Party (SLP) held its organizational meeting for the spring 1878 elections. In the locally oriented campaign, the SLP modestly increased its total vote to over seven thousand, compared to about sixty-three hundred in the fall of 1877, and elected Frank Stauber to the city council from the Fourteenth Ward on the Northwest Side. Around thirty years old and the owner of a hardware store, Stauber was German Swiss and had been in the United States about eleven years. For the next several years, sitting members of the Common Council engaged in repeated maneuvers and subterfuges to keep him from being seated and then to isolate him politically after he was. The chicanery employed against Stauber in this and subsequent elections by members of both major parties became a cause célèbre among the Socialists, signifying to many that electoral politics was a sham. Alderman James McGrath, a key ally of Anton Hesing's, was one of Stauber's main enemies.[4]

The success of the SLP in appealing to a Democratic constituency produced an immediate response. Carter Harrison, then a sitting U.S. congressman, started courting the Socialists during the summer, enthusiastically visiting their picnics. In anticipation of the fall 1878 elections, he gave a speech at the Aurora Turner Hall, the Socialists' main meeting place on the Northwest Side, in which he claimed credit for a menu of locally popular measures as well as for introducing a bill in Congress to institute a progressive income tax. Such a tax had been advocated by the national convention of the Workingmen's Party of the United States (WPUS) in December 1877 and subsequently supported by the Chicago SLP. The major English-language newspapers mocked Harrison for this speech while acknowledging the political reality he faced. According to the *Chicago Times* (hereafter *Times*), he believed that "no man can be elected on the West side without the communist vote."[5]

Despite limited voter turnout, the spring 1878 election aroused considerable excitement among working-class activists, stimulated not only by the Socialists' election of their first city councilman but also by a wider revival of working-class institutions. For the first time in nearly five years, the city's trade unions felt strong enough to organize a parade and picnic in late June, under the auspices of the Trade and Labor Council. About three thousand men in sixteen unions marched in a parade to the Ogden's Grove picnic grounds, led by a band, the Trade and Labor Council, and the Lehr- und Wehr-Verein, composed of about one hundred sixty men carrying their weapons. Their marching with their arms had been the most hotly contested question among the parade's organizers, and the issue remained central to public discussion about the left for several years.[6]

The main theme of the speakers at the labor picnic, and at an even larger meeting a few days later, was the imminent international revival of republicanism under the leadership of labor. The main speakers were New Englanders George E. McNeill and George Gunton, two prominent leaders of labor reform, who saw Socialism as an extension of abolitionism and as a fulfillment of republicanism. As McNeill argued, "our movement is republican, in the real sense of the word. We simply propose to perfect the principles of republican institutions." McNeill was the most prominent leader of the trade union faction that emerged on the East Coast after the split of the WPUS, and he was then president of the International Labor Union of America. Gunton emphasized labor's international character: "It was the intention of the labor movement to organize the men and women in one organization, so that in Europe and America they could demand the same thing at the same time." He even thought that "foreigners" would take the lead in labor's revival of republicanism in the United States because "foreigners had left a monarchy for a republic, and were, therefore, republicans of the best possible type." In keeping with that theme, it was appropriate that Paul Grottkau gave the closing speech in German. A few days later on July 3, 1878, these three speakers addressed the same themes before five thousand people in the Tabernacle, where Dwight Moody had led his evangelical revival in the fall and winter of 1876–77. In a challenging alternative to Moody, McNeill wanted to initiate "a revival of interest in the labor question and in republican institutions."[7]

The momentum built up in the summer of 1878 carried over into the fall elections, in which county and state offices were at stake. The SLP ran on a locally oriented platform geared to wage earners. On this platform, the SLP elected one state senator and three state representatives. Only one of these state legislators replaced a Republican, while the other three came from Democratic districts, leading the *Vorbote* to claim that "the socialist gain is a Democratic loss." The Republicans were the victors in the fall of 1878, winning in all three congressional districts that included parts of the city, while their slate did very well in county offices. The election featured low voter turnout, which in large part resulted from the separation of the county from the city elections. In the opinion of the *Times,* the city's leading Democratic paper, the Democratic Party had degenerated into "an assemblage of clans" without "recognized head or organization" that could hardly control its rank and file.[8]

The Socialists adeptly took advantage of their gains by having their newly elected officials present themselves as the public voice of Chicago's workers. As the municipal election approached on April 1, 1879, the Socialists initiated a special investigation by the state legislature into conditions of the working classes in Chicago and took an active part in an intense debate about increasing the state militia. Christian Meier, newly elected Socialist member of the state assembly, called for the special state investigation. In response to Meier, the legislature formed a seven-man committee headed by another recently elected Chicago Socialist, Charles Ehrhardt. On March 1, 1879, exactly a month before the municipal election, a group from the Trade and Labor Council guided this committee through the city's factories and the stockyards. Led by Thomas Morgan, numerous members of the Trade and Labor Council and the SLP testified. The *Vorbote* considered these hearings so important that it devoted more space to them than to the spring municipal elections. Similarly, four months later the Socialists acted as spokesmen for the wage-earning working class in hearings held in Chicago by a committee of the U.S. House of Representatives investigating the causes of the depression.[9]

The state's special legislative investigation produced a report and initiated the creation of a state Bureau of Labor Statistics. Both the report and the bureau were of considerable import because they helped broaden the public sphere by including organized labor as a distinct interest. The creation of the Bureau of Labor Statistics also gave labor a permanent beachhead within the government. The Trade and Labor Council's report to the state legislative committee was entitled "Changes in the Mode of Production," and it presented its findings and arguments not only in Marxist terms but also in the emerging language of social science, as used in reports of other bureaus of labor statistics, in the writings of thinkers such as John Stuart Mill and Louis Blanc, and in a pamphlet entitled "Our Labor Difficulties" by a committee appointed by the American Social Science Association. In such ways, the Socialists were part of a fundamental change in the public discourse Americans used to analyze their society in the late nineteenth century. Prominent in reports of investigatory commissions and bureaus of labor statistics, the new social discourse helped give wage earners a voice distinct from that of the artisans who had led urban labor movements through the Civil War. The Socialists were also using their new elected positions to make a convincing claim to be the main spokesmen for Chicago's working class in the public sphere, a role typically performed by political machines in American cities.[10]

In mid-March 1879—only two weeks before the municipal election and a few days after the party nominating conventions—the new Socialist legislators played a similar role in a heated debate in the Illinois legislature on a bill to reorganize and substantially increase the size of the state militia. The long shadow of the 1877 railroad strike loomed over the hearings, which attracted an excited crowd in the gallery. The majority of a special committee on the militia favored the proposed bill, while a minority strongly opposed it, fearing that the new military force would be the "entering wedge to the organization of a standing army" that would crush liberty. The leader of the minority, David H. Harts, caused a sensation when he said that "had he been a rioter [in 1877] he would have fired back had troops fired on him." Elijah B. Sherman of Cook County "whirled about toward Mr. Harts, and . . . charged upon him THE UTTERANCE OF TREASON in sanctioning the possible resistance of military force by rioters." Backing Sherman, Col. William H. Thompson, also of Cook County, noted that "less than three years ago an embargo was placed upon the entire traffic of the country, and its vast interests held for days and days in the grip of a mob whose organization stretched all over the land; and . . . that the same cause which led to that vast uprising existed to-day."[11]

George Scroggs of Champaign asserted that a well-organized military force was needed "to successfully confront and defeat the gaunt demon of modern socialism." Responding to Scroggs, Christian Meier, Socialist legislator from Chicago, "took up the gauntlet in behalf of the commune, . . . referring to the uprisings of Berlin and Paris, the armed hosts in Chicago, the Lehr und Wehr Verein, and the crimson flag." Thompson responded, "'you are one from among those OUTCASTS SPEWED FROM FOREIGN SHORES and sent here to vote as some secret and revolutionary council orders.'"[12]

The militia bill ultimately passed in altered form, including a ban on armed groups marching in public, a clear challenge to organizations such as the Lehr- und Wehr-Verein. In turn, Chicago Socialists made the militia law a litmus test dividing friends from foes. Carter Harrison used the opportunity to present himself as a friend of labor. Nonetheless, the passage of the militia bill was most significant as a chapter in the building of a modern state that claimed a monopoly on the legitimate use of physical force.[13]

SLP strength reached its zenith in spring 1879, a few weeks after the militia debate, when it nominated German Dr. Ernst Schmidt for mayor. His nomination was surprising, since he was not one of the prominent leaders of the party, such as T. J. Morgan, Albert Parsons, or George Schilling. Reminiscing on his life, Schmidt said that he "consented" to run for mayor as a means of electing Carter Harrison, whose "understanding and sympathy for the worker's plight" he respected. In contrast, he opposed the antilabor policies of the Republicans and their wealthy backers, and was particularly incensed by the Republican efforts to keep Frank Stauber from taking his seat on the Common Council. To help Harrison, "we of the Socialist Labor party hoped to get enough votes away from Wright [the Republican candidate] to enable Harrison to win, and this we did."[14]

Whatever the truth of Schmidt's claims from hindsight, he made a significant contribution to the election result. The key was that Schmidt could pull in new votes from German liberals who were outside the Socialists' core constituency but were restless within the Republican Party. They had periodically bolted the Republicans since the early 1870s, primarily because of ethnic and class issues. Like most German forty-eighters, Schmidt had advocated liberal and radical Republican causes since his arrival in 1857, and his continued prominence in those circles was symbolized by the fact that his medical offices were in the *Illinois Staats-Zeitung*'s building, a center of public life in German Chicago.[15]

It was not just Schmidt's prestige and connections that drew liberal Republican voters: In the spring of 1879, the SLP expanded its platform to appeal to the municipal reform movement. A new plank called for the elimination of the three town governments and the three park boards, a goal long advocated by the Citizens' Association as a means for destroying nests of patronage and corruption. Appealing to the municipal reformers' goal of centralizing responsibility in local government, the same plank opposed all multiperson administrative bodies lying outside the oversight of representatives elected by all the citizens. This was a direct attack on agencies such as the Board of Police and Fire Commissioners that had so frustrated reformers after the Great Fire.[16]

A wide-ranging section of the platform dealt with several liberal issues, while phrasing them in a way that appealed to the anger of small property owners resentful of concessions to the rich and powerful. After calling for public operation of the streetcars and gasworks and for restructuring of the city debt, the platform attacked the "tight-fistedness" of the city government in rejecting higher taxes for genuinely public purposes, calling it an abrogation of the city council's civic responsibility that coddled the rich. It went on to call taxes contributions to the good of the community analogous to financial support for one's family, and then it attacked avoiding taxes as a "political crime." While such sentiments likely appealed to German political values that affirmed a strong municipal authority, they also attracted liberals who wanted a financially sound and effective local government, something Chicago sorely lacked and which the Citizens' Association championed, while also opposing tax evasion. The planks on municipal issues were part of a broad platform of reforms that included the eight-hour workday, the city's provision of work for the unemployed, salaries for public officials, public baths, and sanitary inspection of factories and stores. Altogether, the planks amounted to one of the nation's first urban progressive platforms combining prolabor and municipal reform issues.[17]

Meanwhile, the Republicans exuded confidence that the current administration of Monroe Heath would find a worthy Republican successor in mayoral candidate Albert M. Wright, a commission merchant with strong ties to the temperance movement. A significant player in the city's grain trade, Wright later became president of the Chicago Board of Trade, and members of the board strongly supported his candidacy. In addition to the attraction of Wright as one of their own, the Board of Trade members were repelled by Harrison, whom they accused of "hobnobbing with the Communists." But, by nominating a temperance advocate, the Republicans created tensions with their German constituency, and they made matters worse by replacing the well-known political veteran Caspar Butz on their citywide ticket with the relatively unknown young German Peter Bushwah, an employee in the county clerk's office. The Republicans entered the spring campaign confidently, believing that the Heath administration remained popular, the Democrats were divided, and the "bloody shirt" still held currency. Thus the Republicans billed the election as a warm-up for the presidential contest of 1880.[18]

The Democrats were not as divided as the Republicans wished, because the party's elite had taken firm control after the defeat in the fall elections of 1877. That election had produced a Republican victory combined with surprising strength for the SLP, which was one sign that the Great Strike would create a political upheaval. The Democrats regrouped by fundamentally changing their party's structure, under the initiative of Perry H. Smith, the Democrats' losing candidate for mayor in 1877, and John Mattocks, a prominent lawyer originally from Vermont. The new structure for the party was patterned after changes in Tammany Hall in New York City, which led the Chicago press to refer to the Democratic reformers as the "Tammany Hall faction." Smith and Mattocks proposed that the party be run by a central council composed of one elected representative from each of the wards and townships in the county. These elected representatives would appoint the precinct workers within their wards and townships, and the central council itself would control all conventions and nominations and have ultimate authority over ward, township, and precinct organizations. Notably, these party officials would not be paid, but rather would be rewarded for their effectiveness with the spoils of victory. The upshot of the reorganization was a more centralized and hierarchical party with less influence by neighborhood politicians, who criticized the plan as undemocratic. Notwithstanding the Tammany Hall analogy, the Chicago Democratic Party never approached the degree of centralization achieved in New York City.[19]

With the new organizational scheme in place, attendance at the Democratic nominating convention was limited to sixty-four ticket holders. In contrast, the Republicans had 148 delegates at their convention, while the much smaller SLP had 300. No less than fourteen policemen enforced the restriction at the entrance to the Democratic convention, in the face of a dense crowd milling about outside. Clearly constituting the party's "better element," the Democratic delegates were primarily native-born Americans and Irish, plus a few Germans. Playing prominent roles in the proceedings were longtime leaders such as A. C. Storey, editor of the *Times,* Perry H. Smith, John Mattocks, and Francis A. Hoffmann Jr., a lawyer whose German-born father had been a Republican lieutenant governor of Illinois during the Civil War. These notable Chicago Democrats were similar to the "swallowtail" (frock-coated) faction of New York's Tammany Hall that had supported John Kelly's centralizing reforms in the 1870s.[20]

The *Times* considered Hoffmann the "presiding genius" among the leaders of the Democratic campaign because of his intimate knowledge of liberal German Republicans who might be detached from their party by Dr. Schmidt and by their antipathy to Wright and his temperance associations. The Democratic candidates for citywide office included one German, William Seipp, the son of one of Chicago's leading brewers. The *Times* was impressed with the candidates and with "the set of men who have immediate charge of the ticket. Hitherto the worst element in the party has always been largely represented in the makeup of the leading committee, but this year this class is obliged to take back seats. Some of the very best men to be found have been brought to the front."[21]

Chicago was still a Republican city, and mayoral candidate Harrison knew that his campaign had to minimize any association with issues and symbols that would revive Civil War era sentiment. Facing Republican attacks that he had been "raised among slaveholders," Harrison repeatedly gave lofty patriotic speeches, earning him the nickname "Our Eagle." He had a live pet eagle, which he sometimes brought to campaign events, evoking wild enthusiasm from the audience, especially when the bird flapped its wings and squawked. How could a man with a pet eagle be a Confederate traitor? His other weapon against "bloody-shirt" tactics was to strictly separate local from national issues, a tactic followed not only by Harrison but also by every Democratic candidate. Harrison was especially adept at speaking in political and moral platitudes about controversial issues while at the same time communicating through gestures and symbols that he understood and identified with his audience.[22]

A case in point was his finessing of the Germans on the interrelated issues of temperance and Sabbath-keeping, two of the campaign's most controversial questions. In an interview with the *Illinois Staats-Zeitung* before the election, the reporter—probably Hermann Raster, the editor—asked Harrison for a clear position on Sunday-closing laws. Avoiding clarity, Harrison replied that "a man can best be judged on the basis of his past and his character, and I have decidedly avoided saying more than that I will do my duty, as it is required of me." He did not come out strongly against the Sunday-closing laws, as the Germans wanted, because he hoped to attract moderate Republican votes. In the same interview, however, he also managed to say that if the reporter visited his house he would find German spoken around the dinner table, that he and his family had spent three summers in Germany, that he hired a German-speaking governess to raise his children after his wife died, that the governess taught the neighbor's children German, that his children spoke more fluent German than English since it was the neighborhood lingua franca, and that he had never found places more orderly than beer gardens in Germany. He did not bother to mention that he was running on a citywide ticket with the son of one of Chicago's biggest German brewers. Harrison also gave political speeches in German.[23]

The election was marked by unusual efforts to mobilize the voters, especially among the Democrats and Socialists. The Democrats were energized by the prospect of winning the mayor's office for the first time since before the Civil War, and their new structure allowed them to channel their resources into the wards where it did the most good. The Republicans knew how to mobilize voters as well, but this year the enthusiasm of their core constituency was dampened by their candidate's mistakes. Apparently assuming that temperance advocates had nowhere else to go, Wright made overt appeals to saloon keepers and Germans and thus raised doubts among the native-born evangelical Protestants about whether he would really enforce the temperance and Sunday-closing laws. Wright also did a poor job of presenting himself as a worthy successor to the popular Heath administration.[24]

The Socialists put extraordinary efforts into mobilizing their constituency. They built strong ward organizations from the precinct level up, especially in the working-class districts of the South and West sides. Their most prominent success was their Peoples' Spring Festival celebrating the popular uprisings of 1848 and 1871. Held nine days before the election, the celebration doubled as a fund-raiser for the Socialistic Publishing Society so that it could turn the *Chicagoer Arbeiter-Zeitung* into a daily, instead of publishing it three times a week. Upward of forty thousand people crowded around and into the Exposition Building, where they applauded marching armed groups numbering about six hundred men from three different nationalities: the Bohemian Sharpshooters, Irish Labor Guards, the German Jäger Verein, and Lehr- und Wehr-Verein. Beer flowed freely, tobacco smoke thickened the air, and bands competed with the SLP's key speakers. So popular was the event that it spilled over from Saturday into Sunday, provoking the churchgoing public, probably intentionally. The swirl of demonstrations, picnics, parades, concerts, plays, exhibitions, and rallies was part of the self-organization of the Chicago immigrant working class that dated back at least to the 1877 railroad strike.[25]

The political ferment in the working class extended to the naturalization of citizens. Chicago's immigrant working class was significantly underrepresented among eligible voters. Some states allowed aliens to vote simply by stating their intent to become citizens, but Illinois did not, like other states with large immigrant working-class populations. Thus a substantial proportion of alien males over age twenty-one could not participate effectively in the electoral process. In 1870, when the U.S. census asked Chicagoans if they were citizens, almost one-third of all males twenty-one and older said no. In other words, about a third of the potential electorate could not vote, and that amounted to 30,968 foreign-born men. (The native-born were citizens by law.) The total almost equaled all votes cast in the contest for Chicago's mayor the previous year: 31,236. Figure 9 analyzes the national origins of these foreign-born men

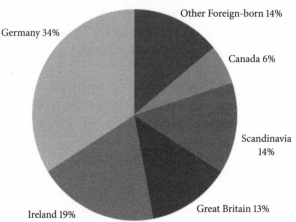

Figure 9
Males 21 Years and Older Who Were Not Citizens
by Place of Birth: Chicago 1870

Other Foreign-born 14%

Germany 34%

Canada 6%

Scandinavia
14%

Great Britain 13%

Ireland 19%

Source: Sample of male citizens with occupations in the 1870
manuscript population census for Chicago; N = 651.

who were not citizens in 1870. This pool of potential voters increased during the next decade, despite the depression, as the city's population increased by two-thirds to just over five hundred thousand. These immigrant aliens were overwhelmingly skilled or unskilled workers—85 percent in 1870—a fact that strengthened the hand of those on the left who argued that labor's participation in electoral campaigns was a sham. At the same time, these potential voters were an attraction to the major political parties and the Socialists. The key question was whether immigrants would get naturalized and then cast a ballot. The mobilizing effects of the Great Strike, the strenuous agitation of the Socialists, and the organizing efforts of the newly energized Democrats meant that this potential came to realization in the late 1870s.[26]

One *Times* reporter described the naturalization efforts when he visited the county court during special extended hours from 7:30 until 10:00 P.M. so that candidates for naturalization could come after work. The only requirement consisted of having two witnesses testify to the person's moral character, to their requisite length of stay in the country and the state, and to their intention for at least three years to become a citizen. The reporter estimated that the court officials could naturalize people at the rate of one a minute: "The Bohemians predominated last night, though various other nationalities were represented." Exhibiting the class and ethnic bias typical of the mainstream press, he thought they were likely "honest, hard-working men, for the most part useful subjects of czar and the kaiser" but incapable of exercising the judgment required of citizens in a democracy. Immigrants were "marched up in platoons to the county court" by party operatives, whose partisan affiliations went unnamed but were likely the Democrats and Socialists, since they had the most to gain from the immigrant vote.[27]

The election on April 1, 1879, produced extraordinary gains for the SLP and victory for the Democrats, amid an unusually high voter turnout. The Democrats won all the citywide offices, returning to power in the city for the first time since the 1850s, while Dr. Ernst Schmidt nearly doubled the SLP vote to almost twelve thousand, about 19 percent of the total. The *Illinois Staats-Zeitung* summed up the results by saying that "the socialists have succeeded in deciding the election, to be sure not to the advantage of their own candidates, but rather for the Democrats against the Republicans." Indeed, the increase in the SLP vote almost precisely equaled Harrison's margin of victory. Like most observers, and modern commentators, the paper attributed the Socialists' ability to attract German Republican votes to the popularity of Dr. Schmidt, whose reputation for incorruptibility attracted the liberal Germans. The correlation between Germans and the SLP vote was the highest for any of the city's national groups, followed by the Bohemians. That widely acknowledged fact led Dr. Schmidt and the *Illinois Staats-Zeitung* to claim that the movement of the German liberals from the Republicans to the SLP allowed Carter Harrison to win the mayor's seat. While accurate, this explanation of the Democratic victory needs to be complemented by an analysis of the voters' high turnout.[28]

The total vote in the municipal election of 1879 was the highest for any in Chicago since the presidential contest of 1876, and it surpassed all local elections beginning in that year. It even came close to the 1876 presidential contest, missing its total of over 61,100 by only 3,300. The *Illinois Staats-Zeitung* noted that previously one could expect to win a citywide office with eighteen thousand votes, but in this election it took from twenty-one thousand to twenty-three thousand. (In the previous several years, the presence of more than two parties, usually Greenbackers and Socialists, meant that citywide victory was possible without a majority.) Figure 10 compares the increase in vote by ward between the elections of November 1878 and April 1879, while also illustrating the geographical distribution of the high turnout. The short time span between the two elections makes population increase a minor explanatory factor.[29]

The increase in the votes in the spring compared to the previous fall amounted to 12,200, raising the total to almost 58,000. Just four of the eighteen

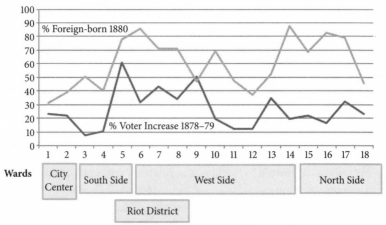

Figure 10

Increased Turnout in Chicago Local Elections from November 1878 to April 1879 Compared to Proportion of Foreign-born by Ward

Source: *Tribune,* April 3, 1879, and a sample of the manuscript schedules of the U.S. Census for 1880; N = 2,846.

Note: The percentage foreign-born is of males twenty-one and older with occupations listed in the manuscript census schedules.

wards—the Fifth, Sixth, Seventh, and Eighth—contributed over 40 percent of the increased vote (map 5). These were all on the South and Southwest sides and encompassed the "riot district" that provided the most support to the railroad strike of 1877, particularly the crowds that enforced it on the rest of the city. The Fifth Ward on the South Side, the base of Socialist leader Thomas J. Morgan, had an increased turnout of over 60 percent compared to 1878, the highest in the city. The average increase in the vote in these four wards amounted to over 42 percent, compared to 22 percent for the remaining fourteen. This increased turnout was not simply a factor of foreign birth. The wards on the Northwest and far North sides—the Fourteenth, Fifteenth, Sixteenth, and Seventeenth— had high proportions of foreign-born residents comparable to those of the riot district but not similarly high increases in turnout. The four riot wards contributed over 41 percent of the Socialist vote and 36 percent of the Democratic total. Looking at this evidence, one can reasonably conclude that the 1877 rebellion of immigrant workers had continued and taken political form.[30]

The high voter turnout helped the Democrats as much as the Socialists. The most striking example was the Ninth Ward on the West Side, a traditionally Republican area. The Ninth Ward had the second highest increase in its vote compared to November 1878: over 50 percent (fig. 10). It gave Harrison a solid

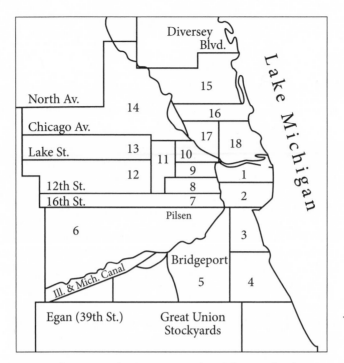

Map 5. Chicago wards in 1879. Reproduced from Richard Schneirov, *Labor and Urban Politics: Class Conflict and the Origins of Modern Liberalism in Chicago, 1864–97*, following p. 98. Copyright 1998 by the Board of Trustees of the University of Illinois. Used with permission of the University of Illinois Press.

majority, as did the Fifth Ward. Altogether, the Democrats won a plurality in seven of the eighteen wards, all but one of them on the South and West sides. The increased voter turnout in these seven wards averaged 37 percent. In contrast, the increase in voting in the Republican wards was modest. Eight wards gave the Republicans a plurality, and they were concentrated in the city center, the near North, and the central West sides. Their growth in voter turnout averaged 18 percent, well below the citywide average of 27 percent. The *Chicago Daily Tribune* (hereafter *Tribune*) drew the obvious conclusion from the election statistics: The Republicans did not turn out sufficiently in their strongholds, while the Democrats did in theirs. When the contrast in turnout is combined with the defection of German Republicans to Dr. Schmidt and the SLP, it is easy to explain the first Democratic sweep of the municipal election since the 1850s.[31]

The Democratic victory in the spring 1879 elections gave Harrison the opportunity to found a new regime in the city. The concept of regime follows from the insight that governance cannot be reduced to the succession of presidential, gubernatorial, or mayoral administrations. Like the idea of party realignment, the theory of regimes divides American political history into extended periods during which a set of interlocking institutions, regardless of party administration, govern state, politics, and society. These governing institutions, in addition to the constitutionally mandated branches of government, include public administration and regulatory agencies; politics broadly defined to include elections, parties, and candidate selection; public doctrines such as the dominant legal interpretations and party ideologies; and the politically effective institutions of civil society, including newspapers, churches, and voluntary associations. These institutions operate according to a set of formal and informal "working rules," which define "the application of public power." Political elites play a critical role by articulating these working rules and public doctrines in a way that becomes the "common sense" of the regime, providing it with both legitimacy and coherence.[32]

The process of class rule within modern capitalist societies requires a complex set of rewards, accommodations, and coercions that result in consent from most elements of the population to the rule of the class or coalition of class fractions dominant at the time. When the use of force is risky and when consent is especially difficult to achieve, it is likely that extralegal corruption will become a prevalent element in the brokering of class peace. In the 1870s and 1880s, the stalemate between the classes in Chicago made the use of force hazardous, and achieving consent was a profound challenge, not only because of the heterogeneous and politicized population but also because much of the upper class had a garrison mentality that viewed the working class as too alien to be part of the social order.[33]

As a result, toleration and corruption became the new common sense of Chicago politics, providing an important part of the language, attitudes, and values linking the state to the constituent elements of civil society sustaining it. Toleration assumed not only acceptance of cultural differences but also a limited state, one that would not intervene in the social life of the constituent elements of the population, most famously in the public consumption of alcoholic beverages. Toleration presupposed the political marginalization of evangelical Protestants, who wanted to use the state to enforce their cultural norms on the whole population. Their marginalization constituted the major negative of the new regime, that is, the dismantling of a formerly significant structure of power.[34]

Evangelical Protestants had been the core of the Republican Party, the city's predominant political force since the late 1850s, and Chicago's Protestant ministers and their churches had been one of the central components of civil society sustaining the previous regime. Allied with the evangelical churches had been powerful private reform and philanthropic organizations, such as the Chicago Relief and Aid Society and the Citizens' Association. The Arbeiterverein, the pro-Republican social and cultural society of the German forty-eighters, had given the Republicans a substantial voice among Germans in the Civil War era. Harrison isolated these groups from power, governing instead in alliance with a different set of institutions, including Irish nationalists, such as the Fenians, German ethnic organizations like the Turners, the Socialist Labor Party and its descendants, the revitalized trade unions, associations of businessmen in industries like brewing and distilling, and the Iroquois Club, an elite society of businessmen in favor of free trade. These groups constituted a historic bloc linking Chicago's religiously, ethnically, and politically variegated working class with elements of the bourgeoisie.

While toleration represented the genial face of the new regime, corruption permeated its daily operation. Corruption emerged from private interests bargaining with a weak municipal state over enforcement of the law. Immigrants liked the weak state because it had fewer resources to interfere in their lives, and businessmen liked it because they did not want to pay for an expensive government apparatus. They would rather take up private collections to fund militia regiments or give the federal government land for a nearby army base, in case another 1877 required brute force to protect them. The weak state combined with a stalemate between the classes required the use of corruption to win the consent of the governed. With little else to offer besides his considerable charisma, Harrison used law enforcement, or its lack, to build both allegiance and alliances. Toleration and corruption were not so much policies as informal methods of governance that made possible communication and cooperation between the state and its organized supporters in civil society.[35]

Harrison's Democrats changed the government as they had their own party—both would become more centralized and hierarchical—although in ways foreign to the Citizens' Association and its charter reforms. Harrison brought coordination and centralization to the disparate governments of the city and county, not through altering their formal structures, but through a disciplined political party. On the day of his inauguration, for example,

Harrison assumed the power to appoint the members of the Common Council's committees. True to his style, he presented this power grab as a favor to the council, which seemed to have difficulty accomplishing the task. His Democrats represented on the local level an updating of the antebellum party state, or "patronage democracy" in the terms of Theda Skocpol. Arising to full prominence in the 1840s, patronage democracy witnessed the rise of a new elite of professional politicians—not local notables prominent for their wealth or family status—who manned both the party apparatus and public administration within an electoral democracy and an industrializing economy. Loyal to their parties and celebrating political competition, these politicians ran the innumerable elections in a decentralized political system with an eye first of all to their organization's success, rather than to ideological consistency.[36]

Harrison also had to win the acceptance—in some cases active support—of key power centers in the city. First among them was the bourgeoisie, which was politically divided, despite holding the heights of the economy. Harrison proved masterful at both accommodating the Gilded Age upper class and exploiting its divisions. In the late 1870s, Chicago's bourgeoisie wanted four things politically: low taxes, efficient but limited municipal government, class peace, and the observance of temperance laws and the Sabbath. Harrison accommodated them on the first three, but not on alcoholic beverages and public behavior on Sunday. To enforce temperance and Sabbath-keeping on the whole population would have so jeopardized his relations with the foreign-born working class that his ability to deliver class peace would have been undermined. Instead, Harrison marginalized evangelical Protestants. Key elements of the bourgeoisie accepted this because, like Joseph Medill, they knew the enormous costs of evangelical political goals from firsthand experience in the 1870s. Many of these business leaders had in the meantime become prominent members and financial backers of the liberal Protestant church of David Swing, whose cool intellectual style and tolerant doctrines offended evangelicals. Politically marginalizing the evangelicals diluted the business leaders' core constituency and lessened the possibility of any political threats to Harrison from that quarter.

Other things were more important to businessmen than temperance and Sabbath-keeping. Harrison delivered low taxes by continuing the policies of fiscal retrenchment followed by the Republican Heath administration and by tolerating the evasion of taxes, as had his predecessors. The Heath administration had reduced the annual amounts raised by taxation from over $5.1 million in 1875, the last full year of rule by the People's Party, to about

$3.7 million in 1878, Heath's last full year. In his inaugural address, Harrison promised to maintain such fiscal retrenchment by recognizing "but one science in finance. That is to collect the revenues and live within them." In continuing fiscal retrenchment, Harrison followed a path similar to that of Tammany Hall's Kelly in New York City, who had to satisfy the prominent "swallowtails" among his backers. Harrison kept his word announced in his inaugural, although he had little room to maneuver. A new state law passed in the spring of 1879 limited the amount of money that could be levied annually in taxes by cities and villages to 2 percent of the assessed valuation of real and personal property. Anticipating this limit in the coming fiscal year, Mayor Harrison quickly ordered the city's departments to curtail their expenditures to 75 percent of the current tax levy.[37]

Actually, if the assessed valuation of the city's property had been remotely accurate, the 2 percent restriction would not have been draconian, but such was not the case. Tax evasion by individuals and corporations had become systematic and egregious in Chicago since the taxpayer revolt of the mid-1870s. Harrison tolerated tax evasion during his five administrations, and it survived his assassination in 1893 by a disgruntled office seeker. In 1896, the assessed valuation of real and personal property in Chicago was actually substantially less than it had been in 1873, even though in those years the city had expanded its territory by five times and its population by four and a half. The evasion of taxes was the most significant form of corruption during his administrations, although gambling, prostitution, and drinking were more notorious.[38]

Chicago lacked enlightened conservatives among its business leaders, who might have realized that they needed to help integrate the immigrant working class into society and that paying taxes for an effective municipal government was one means to that end. In the absence of such enlightened conservatism, Harrison had to use corruption to buy the bourgeoisie's acquiescence to his rule. However, both retrenchment in expenditures and acceptance of tax evasion severely constricted Harrison's ability to build the alliances necessary to sustain him in power. He had little ability, for example, to expand the regulatory capacity of the local state to arbitrate labor disputes or use city resources to deliver city services to working-class communities. Instead, he relied heavily on negotiations, accommodations, and understandings with key players about how, and the extent to which, municipal laws would be enforced.

Harrison went further than his opponents expected in providing efficient and limited government, as well as low taxes. By appointing honest professionals rather than patronage hacks to head the fire department, the departments of public works and health, and, most important, the post of city comptroller, Chicago's financial czar, Harrison furthered the growth of an administrative state apparatus within the confines of the existing party-state. Through the comptroller, the city's business elite obtained their own beachhead within the city government, which reassured them after they had so recently saved the city from bankruptcy in 1878 through a "syndicate" led by Marshall Field.[39]

While popular among the bourgeoisie, the goal of efficient, limited, and inexpensive government could also prove divisive, because it could be used against the projects of municipal reformers. An example mentioned in Harrison's inaugural was the municipal ordinance on curbing noxious fumes created by the packing and tanning industries, which had recently been upheld in the court. While pledging to "foster healthfulness," Harrison warned that he would do nothing to "destroy our great commercial interests. . . . [P]eople should remember that Chicago has no money in her treasury, is forbidden to borrow, and is forced to live on revenues not collectable for nearly a year." Here Harrison used the overriding concern of the business community for a limited and inexpensive government to trump a municipal reform issue supported by the reform-minded bourgeoisie, among others. In the process, he helped marginalize the once-mighty Citizens' Association, confirming its recently acquired status as a good government interest group instead of the leader of a social movement that took over the city government in 1876. At the same time, he took a large step toward institutionalizing the conditions in Chicago for the recurrent, even ritualized, conflict between professional politicians and reformers that came to characterize Gilded Age urban politics nationally.[40]

The bourgeoisie also wanted class peace, but to deliver it Harrison had to accommodate the working class in ways that often offended the city's upper class. This accommodation went well beyond "hobnobbing with the Communists" at their picnics. One example was his opposition to the Citizens' Association's solution to the threat of another 1877: an increase in the police force to be paid for by license fees on saloons. On this all-important issue, Harrison catered to the immigrant working class: There would be no new restrictions on its favorite leisure activity, much less one that would increase the coercive power of the state in case of another rebellious strike. In his inaugural, Harrison signaled his policy of toleration on cultural issues vital to immigrants: "Ours is a cosmopolitan people aggregated from many nationalities. . . . Each should study to accommodate itself as much as possible to the social life and prejudices of each of the others and of the whole. For anyone to attempt to make a Procrustean bed, to which the others should be forced to fit, would be both ungenerous and unwise." The last sentence was a clear rejection of the favorite political projects of native-born evangelical Protestants: temperance and Sabbatarianism. Instead, Harrison adopted a laissez-faire policy on the consumption of alcoholic beverages and Sabbath-keeping that essentially reinstated the one followed by the People's Party. In the immigrant districts, people could follow their customs on these matters without interference from the police. Harrison's tolerant policies on cultural differences and alcoholic beverages followed the tendencies of the Democrats nationally. Harrison accommodated the city's underworld elements in a similar way. The city's gambling king, Mike McDonald, had contributed funds to both the People's and the Democratic parties in the 1870s, and Harrison allowed him to continue his lucrative activities.[41]

Harrison used analogous strategies with the labor movement and the Socialists. The fact that he had to accommodate them at all was testimony to a new political era: The slavery question had been resolved, and the "labor question" was now part of the public sphere. Harrison's greatest concession to the labor movement came in his policies on the use of the police: They would not intervene in strikes on the side of employers by protecting strike breakers. Thus Harrison dealt with workers' strikes in the same way the machine politicians in the People's Party had dealt with the saloon and fire-limit issues: granting violators immunity from enforcement of the law by police. He also appointed several police officials sympathetic with local communities, particularly Bridgeport, where he needed to mend fences with the Irish, who felt neglected by his strenuous efforts to court the Germans during the election. Bridgeport was also part of the riot district and thus needed some watching. By 1885, the unwillingness of Harrison's police to protect strikebreakers had become notorious. A Citizens' Association report observed that politicians found it advantageous "to calculate the probable effect of a prompt, bold, and determined attitude against a large body of defiant rioters who have ballots to cast."[42]

Harrison's need to address the Socialists was more immediate and political. Given his narrow victory, Harrison recognized that maintaining his power required either bringing the Socialists directly into the Democratic Party or fostering a strong Socialist vote as a third force in upcoming elections. He also needed the support of four SLP aldermen in the closely divided city council. Thus from the very beginning of his administration, he courted Socialists, first of all by backing the SLP's opposition to the new militia law with its restrictions on armed groups parading in public with their weapons. In his inaugural, Harrison said that "some persons fear an organized resistance to authority in Chicago. I do not. I do not believe that there is in our midst any considerable body of men mad enough to attempt such folly." He went even further by defending the "right to keep and bear arms" while clearly denying any "right to use arms to threaten or to resist lawful authority," and he subsequently supported the Lehr- und Wehr-Verein in its campaign against the new militia law. He let them march without interference, for example, while arranging to have a preselected member arrested to set up a court test. When members of the Bohemian militia were arrested for firing at Irish toughs who had invaded their picnic, Harrison secured their immediate release and defused public clamor for retaliation.[43]

Harrison's Democrats also gave patronage jobs to the Socialists, selected other officials sympathetic to their causes, and bargained with unions. During his first term as mayor, Harrison appointed the defeated Ernst Schmidt to the Library Board, German Socialist politico Joe Gruenhut to the city's Health Department, and gave the city's German printing to the *Arbeiter Zeitung*, the SLP paper. Returning these favors in mid-1879, the SLP supported the reelection of Democratic Judge William McAllister, who had just declared the Vagrant Act unconstitutional. The police had used this act to harass and arrest workers during strikes. Finally, Harrison pioneered overt appeals to organized interest groups, including unions hitherto excluded from respectability and power. Thus, when multiethnic trade unions revived and grew during the 1880s prosperity, Harrison bargained with them. The results of these Democratic efforts were evident in the city elections of 1881, when large numbers of SLP voters split their tickets. In the party's Fourteenth Ward stronghold, the SLP aldermanic candidate received 837 votes, while its mayoral rival to Harrison won only 231 votes. This politics was not distinctive to Chicago. Analyzing the receptivity of the major parties to labor issues in the Gilded Age, David Montgomery found that "it was the socialist presence in German communities that accounted for the appeal of labor legislation to local Democrats."[44]

The migration of the Socialist voters to the Democrats contributed substantially to a local electoral realignment, and the Democrats dominated local elections between 1879 and 1897. In effect, the Democrats under Harrison reconstituted the Irish and German electoral alliance that had brought the People's Party to power, and they did it by broadening their appeal to all immigrant voters, including the SLP's central European working-class base mobilized by the 1877 strike. Much of their appeal derived from their reinstituting the policy of the People's Party on public drinking and the Sabbath, that is, toleration of the different practices of the city's various national groups on these issues.[45]

After the spring 1879 election, the SLP lost its dynamism and degenerated into debilitating factionalism. Politics was the main source of dispute, specifically the extent to which the party should make alliances with other political groups and more generally whether electoral politics was worth the cost of participation. In June 1879, Albert Parsons led a segment of the SLP's constituency into an alliance with Anglo American labor reformers and trade unionists to form an Eight Hour League. The SLP's core political leadership led by Thomas Morgan opposed the move, considering the eight-hour workday a minor demand that diverted resources from electoral politics. Morgan also detested the labor reformers' appetite for patronage jobs. In turn, Morgan's faction began to form alliances with a revived trade union movement and a resurgent Knights of Labor, both of which profited from the economy's rebound. To complete the circle, German elements of the SLP under Paul Grottkau revived their opposition to electoral politics and attacked the Morgan faction's leadership of the party, eventuating in the anarchist or revolutionary Socialist tendency so prominent in Chicago during the 1880s. The two wings—trade union–based reform and revolutionary Socialism—replaced the old Lassallean and Marxist division and correspond to the modern divisions lasting into the twentieth century within the Socialist movement.[46]

Amid all this infighting, it is easy to overlook two critical external factors contributing to the SLP's demise: the deft politics of Harrison's Democratic Party and the economic recovery, which helped revive trade unions as competitors to the SLP and the German unions it sponsored. The union revival began in the building trades, which profited from renewed construction, and resulted in an awakened city-central body, the Trade and Labor Council. The Trade and Labor Council chaffed under the efforts of Morgan's SLP to determine its politics and policies. Meanwhile, Harrison's Democratic Party not only enticed the SLP's constituency with patronage and labor-friendly policies, it also seized the role the SLP had played as the advocate for the immigrant working class in the public sphere. This advocacy role was more important to most immigrant workers than the SLP's platform, and Mayor Harrison played the advocate more effectively than the SLP. The decline of trade unions during the depression, the Democratic Party's weakness before 1879, and the defeat of machine politicians in the People's Party by the Citizens' Association had created a unique opportunity for the Socialists to speak for Chicago's workers from the mid-1870s into 1879. But that moment had passed.

CONCLUSION

In *Reconstruction: America's Unfinished Revolution, 1863–1877,* widely considered the standard interpretation of the period, Eric Foner included a long chapter entitled "The Reconstruction of the North." According to Foner, the North "experienced a social transformation after the Civil War," though unlike the South's it was not as revolutionary but "continued to accelerate in peacetime." Despite this insight, the history of Chicago and other Northern cities is normally written outside the context of Reconstruction, which is commonly viewed by historians as a Southern question. In contrast, this book argues that the economy, society, and politics of the North underwent profound changes rooted in the rise to national dominance of capitalism.[47]

Placing Chicago's history in that framework suggests a return to the issues raised by Barrington Moore Jr. In his *Social Origins of Dictatorship and Democracy,* Moore portrayed the era of the Civil War and Reconstruction as a "capitalist revolution," which also furthered democratization. Moore understood that the Civil War was not a revolution initiated and led by capitalists to further their ends, but rather one carried out by a historic bloc of business, agricultural, and labor interests in the Northeast and Midwest to extend the northern social order throughout the country. To accomplish this, they had to destroy the planters as a class and chattel slavery as a labor system. Their revolution cleared away obstacles that had prevented capitalism and democracy from fully developing.[48]

Our work on Chicago has documented how an emerging capitalist social order overturned, eclipsed, or merged in complex ways with precapitalist social formations and how that social order unleashed new democratic possibilities. Thus the Civil War shattered the segmented governmental regime of the antebellum era, which had empowered property owners in an economy dominated by real estate speculators and merchants. During the 1860s, this booster class quickly gave way to a new one of capital accumulators employing wage labor. Meanwhile, just as in the South, a subaltern class—in this case, wageworkers—entered the public sphere and underwent a transformation in consciousness as it struggled to make sense of life in an emerging industrial city. A politicized working class challenged the new bourgeoisie, which, by the 1870s, responded by flirting with antidemocratic ideology while relying on coercion to suppress organized threats. However, the "Liberal" response proved inadequate in Chicago, as highlighted by the Great Strike of 1877. By the end of Reconstruction, a durable political synthesis took root in the city in the form of a new regime, pioneered by Carter Harrison and the Democratic Party. This regime accommodated the politicized working class, in contrast to the subsequent suppression of the freedmen in the South.

Some historians, notably Nancy Cohen, have argued that during Reconstruction and the Gilded Age, American Liberals and Liberalism underwent a profound antidemocratic "reconstruction" in response to threats to private property emanating from politically empowered freedmen in the South and producers' and labor movements in the North. We think she overemphasizes the influence of antidemocratic tendencies in the era. This book has argued that mainstream politicians like Anton Hesing and Carter Harrison brokered compromises and accommodations with democratic movements resulting in important gains for democratic governance. This was evident in the new range of democratic options available in the German community. It was also evident in the four new democratic social movements that surfaced as recurring fixtures in the city: that of the trade unions, Socialists, urban populists, and municipal reformers. By appealing to powerful political ideologies, ethnic cultures, and religious traditions, these four movements, together with evangelical revivalism and a nascent feminist movement, extended and deepened democratic politics, even while reconciling it tenuously with the new social order.[49]

Led by Anglo Americans, the labor movement during the Civil War was the first to challenge the old order by bringing workers into it as a new public, primarily through its eight-hour campaign. Chicago's new bourgeoisie did not feel the need to politically mobilize until the Great Fire of 1871, though even then it did so under the aegis of the evangelical wing of the Republican Party. However, the attempt to enforce temperance proved so culturally divisive that it spawned the urban populist People's Party, the first social movement to successfully capture the local government. Only when another fire in 1874 created a capital accumulation crisis did the city's capitalists separate themselves from their evangelical allies and create their own municipal reform movement, led by the Citizens' Association. Successful in electing Monroe Heath in 1876, the reform politics of the Citizens' Association could not be sustained, as tax evasion by its own business constituency bankrupted the local government while its evangelical allies failed to convert the city with their Moody revival. Meanwhile, a Socialist movement led by German-speaking immigrants sloughed off Anglo American leadership and rode a wave of depression-related social unrest to politically mobilize its immigrant working-class constituency. But the Socialists could never fully unite Chicago's diverse working class, just as

Moody could not convert it. In that respect, the Socialists were analogous to the municipal reformers: Neither could sufficiently transcend their core constituencies to rule the city. Nonetheless, with the help of German middle-class liberals like Ernst Schmidt, the Socialists helped detach enough Germans from the Republican Party to decisively end Republican dominance during the era of the Civil War and Reconstruction.

The new regime of Carter Harrison incorporated some of the needs, demands, and politics of the four large social movements while politically marginalizing evangelical Protestants. Just as important, the Harrison regime updated the older party-state not only by incorporating new social groups but also by integrating administrative elements into its framework, exemplifying what Stephen Skowronek has called the Gilded Age's "patchwork" pattern of state building. These initiatives both pleased business leaders and marginalized the Citizens' Association. Yet the key to Harrison's success was not in any particular policy but rather in his recognition that a politicized immigrant working class had to be accommodated within the polity, something the Republicans were reluctant to acknowledge.[50]

Through the Harrison regime, Chicago's bourgeoisie achieved a tenuous hegemony in the city, something it had failed to attain through ruling directly. Harrison's regime accomplished in Chicago what, according to Martin Shefter, John Kelly brought to New York's Democratic Party from the mid-1870s to the mid-1880s: "Kelly's centralizing reforms were a means of reconciling, in the context of an industrializing city . . ., the security of wealth with a system of mass suffrage." Thus Harrison solved the conundrum of making democracy safe for property by setting limits to both. He set limits to the rule of property by acknowledging the legitimate interests of other sectors of the society besides the bourgeoisie, even granting them real but distinctly limited power over parts of the government while retaining fiscal control for leading capitalist interests. Jon C. Teaford summed up this urban system for American cities in the Gilded Age: "The patrician, the plutocrat, the plebeian, and the professional bureaucrat all had their place in late-nineteenth-century municipal government; each staked an informal but definite claim to a particular domain within the municipal structure." In Chicago, this system produced a regime of broker politics characterized by toleration and corruption, which together constituted the common sense of the new political era.[51]

Nonetheless, Harrison's solution and the resulting bourgeois hegemony were brittle. Brittle materials are hard, but they also shatter dramatically, and such was the case with the ability of the upper class to maintain its dominant social and political position in Chicago during the Gilded Age. In the uprising over the eight-hour workday in 1886–87, and again during the Pullman strike of 1894, open class warfare broke out in the city. If one counts the eight-hour strike of 1867 and the Great Strike of 1877, a major labor uprising occurred about every seven to ten years in the last third of the nineteenth century. While many factors contribute to explaining each upheaval, the limits on achieving consent to upper-class ascendancy in a city like Chicago help one understand their frequency and depth.

In his inaugural, Harrison said that the different peoples of Chicago "have one bond of union—devotion to republican institutions and energy in the pursuit of fortune."[52] Only republicanism and the market-driven pursuit of wealth—not a common language, religion, or ethnicity—bound Chicagoans together. In Chicago, cultural commonalities and the moral standing and authority that went with them were thin or nonexistent. The accommodations and compromises in civil society so central to hegemony had to be worked out within a narrow range of politics and a limited state. At the same time, the ability to accumulate wealth, which Harrison considered a central unifier, was constricted for large segments of the population by social inequality and the era's frequent economic downturns. As a consequence, consent to the class system frequently and dramatically broke down, and those in authority resorted to force to maintain social order. Standing on a brittle accommodation between the classes, Gilded Age Chicago remained haunted by nightmares of volcanic class conflict.

Notes

Introduction

1. James Madison as cited in Drew R. McCoy, *The Elusive Republic: Political Economy in Jeffersonian America* (Chapel Hill: University of North Carolina Press, 1980), 255 (quotes); see also John Ashworth, *Slavery, Capitalism, and Politics in the Antebellum Republic*, vol. 1, *Commerce and Compromise, 1820–1850* (Cambridge: Cambridge University Press, 1995), 10–12, 187–91, 307–9, 320–23.

2. Eric Hobsbawm, *The Age of Capital, 1848–1875* (New York: Vintage, 1989).

3. Jurgen Habermas, "The Public Sphere: An Encyclopedia Article (1964)," *New German Critique* 3 (Autumn 1974): 49–55; Michael Schudson, "The 'Public Sphere' and Its Problems: Bringing the State (Back) In," *Notre Dame Journal of Law, Ethics, and Public Policy* 8, no. 2 (1994): 529–46.

4. Coleen A. Sheehan, *James Madison and the Spirit of Republican Self-Government* (Cambridge: Cambridge University Press, 2009), 31–40, 59–62, 81–83, 100, 164–75.

5. Johann N. Neem, *Creating a Nation of Joiners: Democracy and Civil Society in Early National Massachusetts* (Cambridge, Mass.: Harvard University Press, 2008), 10–32, 172–80; Philip J. Ethington, *The Public City: The Political Construction of Urban Life in San Francisco, 1850–1900* (Cambridge: Cambridge University Press, 1994), 8–14.

6. On wage labor in relation to free labor in the Republican Party, see Eric Foner, "Free Labor and Nineteenth-Century Ideology," and John Ashworth, "Free Labor, Wage Labor, and the Slave Power: Republicanism and the Republican Party in the 1850s," in *The Market Revolution in America: Social, Political and Religious Expression, 1800–1880*, ed. Melvyn Stokes and Stephen Conway (Charlottesville: University of Virginia Press, 1996), 99–127, 128–46; James L. Huston, "A Political Response to Industrialism: The Republican Embrace of Protectionist Labor Doctrines," *Journal of American History* 70 (June 1983): 35–57; John Ashworth, *Slavery, Capitalism, and Politics in the Antebellum Republic*, vol. 2, *The Coming of the Civil War 1850–1861* (Cambridge: Cambridge University Press, 2007), 265–303.

7. E. L. Godkin, "The Labor Crisis," *The Nation* 216 (July 1867): 177–213.

8. On the national level, these changes are covered by David Montgomery, *Beyond Equality: Labor and the Radical Republicans, 1862–72* (New York: Vintage, 1967), 230–424.

9. *Illinois Staats-Zeitung* (Chicago), January 18, 1872.

10. Montgomery, *Beyond Equality*, x, 230–60.

11. *Chicago Tribune,* July 26, 1874.

12. Joseph A. Buttigieg, "The Contemporary Discourse on Civil Society: A Gramscian Critique," *boundary 2* 32, no. 1 (Spring 2005): 43–44.

13. Antonio Gramsci, *Selections from the Prison Notebooks of Antonio Gramsci,* ed. and trans. by Quintin Hoare and Geoffrey Nowell Smith (New York: International Publishers, 1971), 228–43; Buttigieg, "The Contemporary Discourse on Civil Society," 43–47; on active versus passive consent, see Perry Anderson, "The Antinomies of Antonio Gramsci," *New Left Review* 100 (1976–77): 5–78.

14. Charles A. Beard and Mary R. Beard, *The Rise of American Civilization,* vol. 2, *The Industrial Era,* new ed., two volumes in one, rev. and enl. (New York: McMillan, 1933), 52–121; Robert P. Sharkey, *Money, Class, and Party: An Economic Study of Civil War and Reconstruction* (Baltimore: Johns Hopkins University Press, 1959), 291–311; Stanley Coben, "Northeastern Business and Radical Reconstruction: A Re-examination," *Mississippi Valley Historical Review* 46 (June 1959): 67–90; Eric Foner, *Free Soil, Free Labor, Free Men: The Ideology of the Republican Party before the Civil War* (New York: Oxford University Press, 1970); for an updating of Foner's ideological interpretation, see Ashworth, *Slavery, Capitalism, and Politics in the Antebellum Republic,* vols. 1 and 2.

15. Barrington Moore Jr., *Social Origins of Dictatorship and Democracy: Lord and Peasant in the Making of the Modern World* (Boston: Beacon Press, 1966), 111–55, esp. 145–54; on Southern labor, see R. Tracy McKenzie, "Southern Labor and Reconstruction," in *A Companion to the Civil War and Reconstruction,* ed. Lacy K. Ford (Malden, Mass.: Blackwell, 2005), 366–85; Alex Lichtenstein, "Was the Emancipated Slave a Proletarian?: Sharecroppers and the Politics of Protest in the Rural South, 1880–1940," *Reviews in American History* 26 (March 1988): 124–45; and Scott P. Marler, "Fables of Reconstruction: Reconstruction of the Fables," *Journal of the Historical Society* 4 (Winter 2004): 113–37. For debate about Moore and his methodology, see George Ross, Theda Skocpol, Tony Smith, and Judith Eisenberg Vichniac, "Barrington Moore's Social Origins and Beyond: Historical Social Analysis since the 1960s," in *Democracy, Revolution, and History,* ed. Theda Skocpol (Ithaca, N.Y.: Cornell University Press, 1998), 1–21; and Edward Friedman, "Development, Revolution, Democracy, and Dictatorship: China Versus India?," in *Democracy, Revolution, and History,* ed. Theda Skocpol, 102–23 (Ithaca, N.Y.: Cornell University Press, 1998); Barrett L. McCormick, "Modernization, Democracy, and Morality: The Work of Barrington Moore, Jr.," *International Journal of Politics, Culture and Society* 13 (Summer 2000): 591–606 (quote 593). For two outstanding examples of the continuing relevance of Moore's large canvas methodology, see Steve Hahn, "Postemancipation Societies: Southern Planters in Comparative Perspective," *American Historical Review* 95 (February 1990): 75–98; and Alex Lichtenstein, *Twice the Work of Free Labor: The Political Economy of Convict Labor in the New South* (London: Verso Press, 1996), 1–16.

16. Theda Skocpol, "Did the Civil War Further American Democracy? A Reflection on the Expansion of Benefits for Union Veterans," in *Democracy, Revolution,*

and History, 73–101 (quote 101); Theda Skocpol, *Protecting Soldiers and Mothers: The Political Origins of Social Policy in the United States* (Cambridge, Mass.: Belknap Press of Harvard University Press, 1992); Dietrich Rueschemeyer, Evelyne Huber Stephens, and John D. Stephens, *Capitalist Development and Democracy* (Chicago: University of Chicago Press, 1992), 7 (quote). One exception to Reconstruction historiography is Eric Foner's chapter entitled "The Reconstruction of the North," in *Reconstruction: America's Unfinished Revolution, 1863–1877* (New York: Harper and Row, 1988), 460–511.

Chapter 1. The City

1. *Chicago Daily Tribune* (hereafter *Tribune*), November 3, 1869; Frederick Francis Cook, *Bygone Days in Chicago: Recollections of the "Garden City" of the Sixties* (Chicago: A. C. McClurg, 1910), 173.

2. Roy P. Basler, ed., *The Collected Works of Abraham Lincoln* (New Brunswick, N.J.: Rutgers University Press, 1953), 3:478–79.

3. John Ashworth, "The Republican Triumph," in *A Companion to the Civil War and Reconstruction,* ed. Lacy K. Ford, (Oxford: Blackwell, 2005), 176–80; John Ashworth, *Slavery, Capitalism, and Politics in the Antebellum Republic,* vol. 2, *The Coming of the Civil War, 1850–1861* (Cambridge: Cambridge University Press, 2007), 265–87.

4. Basler, *The Collected Works of Abraham Lincoln,* 3:478–79.

5. On the theoretical assumptions of the previous two paragraphs, see the political theorist C. B. McPherson, who distinguished between simple and possessive market societies, the latter being characterized by the "authoritative allocation of work" and by class differentiation; *The Political Theory of Possessive Individualism: Hobbes to Locke* (New York: Oxford, 1962), 51–61. Karl Polanyi made a similar distinction between a market society based on the commoditization of fabricated products and one that also commoditized labor and land; *The Great Transformation: The Political and Economic Origins of Our Time* (Boston: Beacon, 1957), chaps. 3–10. In a similar vein, Karl Marx distinguished between simple commodity production and capitalism; *Capital: A Critical Analysis of Capitalist Production,* vol. 1, ed. Frederick Engels (New York: International, 1967), 146–55. For an attempt to use the work of these theorists to understand the transition to the Gilded Age, see Richard Schneirov, "Thoughts on Periodizing the Gilded Age: Capital Accumulation, Society, and Politics, 1873–1898," *Journal of the Gilded Age and Progressive Era* 5 (July 2006): 189–224. For a review of similar changes in eastern cities, see Amy Bridges, "Becoming Americans: The Working Classes in the United States before the Civil War," in *Working-Class Formation: Nineteenth-Century Patterns in Western Europe and the United States,* ed. Ira Katznelson and Aristide R. Zolberg (Princeton, N.J.: Princeton University Press, 1986), 168–77.

6. Jeffrey S. Adler, *Yankee Merchants and the Making of the Urban West: The Rise and Fall of Antebellum St. Louis* (Cambridge: Cambridge University Press, 1991), 140–44; Carl Abbott, *Boosters and Businessmen: Popular Economic Thought and*

Urban Growth in the Antebellum Middle West, Contributions in American Studies, No. 53 (Westport, Conn.: Greenwood Press, 1981), 19–20, 24; William Cronon, *Chicago and the Great West* (New York: W. W. Norton, 1991), 263–309.

7. U.S. Bureau of the Census, *Tenth Census, 1880, Population* (Washington, DC: GPO, 1883), 538; Bessie Louise Pierce, *A History of Chicago*, vol. 3, *The Rise of a Modern City 1871–1893* (New York: Alfred A. Knopf, 1957), 533; Carl Smith, *Chicago and the American Literary Imagination* (Chicago: University of Chicago Press, 1984), 3; Harold L. Platt, *Shock Cities: The Environmental Transformation and Reform of Manchester and Chicago* (Chicago: University of Chicago Press, 2005), 3–23.

8. Jeremy Atack and Peter Passell, *A New Economic View of American History from Colonial Times to 1940*, 2nd ed. (New York: W. W. Norton, 1994), 276.

9. Douglass C. North, *The Economic Growth of the United States 1790–1860* (Englewood Cliffs, N.J.: Prentice-Hall, 1961), 150–53.

10. Jeremy Atack and Fred Bateman, *To Their Own Soil: Agriculture in the Antebellum North* (Ames: Iowa State University Press, 1987), 243; Atack and Passell, *A New Economic View of American History*, 281–82.

11. G. A. Cohen, *Karl Marx's Theory of History: A Defense* (Princeton, N.J.: Princeton University Press, 1978), 81; Allan Kulikoff, "Households and Markets: Toward a New Synthesis of American Agrarian History," *William and Mary Quarterly*, 3rd ser., 50 (April 1993): 349; Atack and Bateman, *To Their Own Soil*, 263; see also Jeremy Atack, Fred Bateman, and William N. Parker, "The Farm, the Farmer, and the Market," in *The Cambridge Economic History of the United States*, vol. 2, *The Long Nineteenth Century*, ed. Stanley L. Engerman and Robert E. Gallman (Cambridge: Cambridge University Press, 2000), 276–77, 283–84.

12. Daniel Nelson, *Farm and Factory: Workers in the Midwest 1880–1990* (Bloomington: Indiana University Press, 1995), vii; Kulikoff, "Households and Markets," 348; Christopher Clark, "The Consequences of the Market Revolution in the American North," in *The Market Revolution in America: Social, Political, and Religious Expressions, 1800–1880*, ed. Melvyn Stokes and Stephen Conway (Charlottesville: University Press of Virginia, 1996), 27.

13. Figures calculated from samples of the federal manuscript population censuses.

14. All figures in this paragraph were developed from the federal manuscript manufacturing schedules. For comparisons to other cities, see David R. Meyer, "Midwestern Industrialization and the American Manufacturing Belt in the Nineteenth Century," *Journal of Economic History* 49 (December 1989): 931.

15. The figure for the total employed in manufacturing in 1850 is an estimate based on our sample of the federal manuscript population census; the figure for 1880 is from Bessie Louise Pierce, *A History of Chicago*, 3:518. The analysis of the clothing industry was taken from the federal manuscript manufacturing censuses. The proportion of women working as servants was taken from samples of the federal manuscript population censuses (fig. 7, chap. 4).

16. *Illinois Staats-Zeitung*, April 2, 4, 1864; John B. Jentz, "Bread and Labor: Chi-

cago's German Bakers Organize," *Chicago History* 12 (Summer 1983): 24–35; Bruce Laurie, *Artisans into Workers: Labor in Nineteenth-Century America* (New York: Hill and Wang, 1989).

17. On the Chicago ordinance, see Murray F. Tuley, comp., *Laws and Ordinances Governing the City of Chicago* (published by authority of the Common Council of the City, Chicago: Bulletin Printing Company, 1873), http://quod.lib.umich.edu/ cgi/t/text/text-idx?c=moa;idno=AHM9766.0001.001 (accessed August 4, 2009), 68; Robert E. Bailey et al., *Chicago City Council Proceedings Files 1833–1871: An Inventory* (Springfield: Illinois State Archives, 1987), 896. Information on ordinances in other cities can be found in the same online source, Making of America, http:// quod.lib.umich.edu/m/moa/ (accessed June 14, 2011).

18. On boardinghouses for bakers, see Jentz, "Bread and Labor," 28–29. On the German Aid Society and Castle Garden, see Hartmut Keil and John B. Jentz, *German Workers in Chicago: A Documentary History of Working-Class Culture from 1850 to World War I* (Urbana: University of Illinois Press, 1988), 21, 35–36, 39–42; John Francis Maguire, *The Irish in America* (New York: D. and J. Sadlier, 1868), http://name.umdl.umich.edu/ABL3952.0001.001 (accessed July 11, 2002), 208.

19. Joshua L. Rosenbloom, "The Extent of the Labor Market in the United States, 1870–1914," *Social Science History* 22 (Fall 1998): 292–94, 297, 310–11. His findings are supported in part by Robert A. Margo and Georgia C. Villaflor, "The Growth of Wages in Antebellum America: New Evidence," *Journal of Economic History* 47 (December 1987): 129–31; Robert A. Margo, "The Labor Force in the Nineteenth Century," in *The Cambridge Economic History of the United States*, ed. Engerman and Gallman, 2:222–25; Robert A. Margo, *Wages and Labor Markets in the United States, 1820–1860* (Chicago: University of Chicago Press, 2000), 107–8; Jeffrey G. Williamson, "The Evolution of Global Labor Markets since 1830: Background Evidence and Hypotheses," *Explorations in Economic History* 32 (April 1995): 150–51, 156.

20. Philip R. P. Coelho and James F. Shepherd, "Differences in Regional Prices: The United States, 1851–1880," *Journal of Economic History* 34 (September 1974): 551, 568, 576, 578. For a battle against eastern conditions, see Anton Hesing as cited in John B. Jentz, "Class and Politics in an Emerging Industrial City: Chicago in the 1860s and 1870s," *Journal of Urban History* 17 (May 1991): 240.

21. Rima Lunin Schultz, "The Businessman's Role in Western Settlement: The Entrepreneurial Frontier, Chicago, 1833–1872" (PhD dissertation, Boston University, 1985), 17–34, 73; Adler, *Yankee Merchants*, 154.

22. Robin L. Einhorn, *Property Rules: Political Economy in Chicago, 1833–1872* (Chicago: University of Chicago Press, 1991), 28–60; A. T. Andreas, *History of Chicago from the Earliest Period to the Present Time*, vol. 1, *Ending with the Year 1857* (Chicago: A. T. Andreas, 1886), 133–34; Michael P. Conzen, "1848: The Birth of Modern Chicago," in *1848: Turning Point for Chicago, Turning Point for the Region*, Michael P. Conzen, Douglas Knox, and Dennis H. Cremin (Chicago: Newberry Library, 1998), 8–9, 19 (quote); Abbott, *Boosters and Businessmen*, 130–33, 136, 141–42.

23. On the role of merchants in the credit system, see Schultz, "The Businessmen's Role in Western Settlement," 65–97, 184–86; Glenn Porter and Harold C. Livesay, *Merchants and Manufacturers: Studies in the Changing Structure of Nineteenth-Century Marketing* (Baltimore: Johns Hopkins University Press, 1971), 7–8; Cronon, *Chicago and the Great West,* 322–24. On the attractions of real estate for investors and the difficulties of raising capital for manufacturing, see *Tribune,* March 13, 1854; Abbott, *Boosters and Businessmen,* 138; Allan R. Pred, *The Spatial Dynamics of Urban-Industrial Growth, 1800–1914* (Cambridge, Mass.: MIT Press, 1966), 143–76. Quote is from *Tribune,* June 13, 1871.

24. Frederic Cople Jaher, *The Urban Establishment: Upper Strata in Boston, New York, Charleston, Chicago, and Los Angeles* (Urbana: University of Illinois Press, 1982), 491–94, 503–5; Schultz, "The Businessman's Role in Western Settlement," 6–8, 243–66; Kathleen D. McCarthy, *Noblesse Oblige: Charity and Cultural Philanthropy in Chicago, 1849–1929* (Chicago: University of Chicago Press, 1982), 53–66.

25. Adler, *Yankee Merchants,* 150–55; Schultz, "The Businessman's Role in Western Settlement," 7–8, 186.

26. See the debate around Wesley C. Mitchell's thesis; Wesley C. Mitchell, "The Production and Consumption of Wealth," and "The Greenbacks and the Cost of the Civil War"; for a critique of this thesis, see Reuben A. Kessell and Armen Alchian, "Real Wages in the North during the Civil War: Mitchell's Data Reinterpreted"; all in *The Economic Impact of the Civil War,* ed. Ralph L. Andreano (Cambridge, Mass.: Schenkman, 1967). More recent work tends to reinstate the Mitchell and Beardian thesis that the Civil War was "The Second American Revolution," which was the title of chapter 18 in Charles A. Beard and Mary R. Beard, *The Rise of American Civilization,* vol. 2, *The Industrial Era* (New York: Macmillan, 1930), 52–121; see the critique of Kessell and Alchian by Stephen J. De Canio and Joel Makyr, "Inflation and the Wage Lag during the American Civil War," *Explorations in Economic History* 14 (July 1977): 311–36; influential in this interpretation has been the important study by Porter and Livesay, *Merchants and Manufacturers.* On the clothing industry, see Bessie Louise Pierce, *A History of Chicago,* vol. 2, *From Town to City, 1848–1871* (Chicago: Alfred A. Knopf, 1940), 110; *Chicago Times* (hereafter *Times*), February 3, 1864.

27. Porter and Livesay, *Merchants and Manufacturers,* 10, 116–19, 123–24, 127–29 (quote 128); Margaret Walsh, *The Rise of the Midwestern Meat Packing Industry* (Lexington: University Press of Kentucky, 1982), 57–59; Louise Carroll Wade, *Chicago's Pride: The Stockyards, Packington, and Environs in the Nineteenth Century* (Urbana: University of Illinois Press, 1987), 32–33.

28. Joseph C. Bigott, *From Cottage to Bungalow: Houses and the Working Class in Metropolitan Chicago, 1869–1929* (Chicago: University of Chicago Press, 2001), 30; David C. Klingaman, "The Nature of Midwest Manufacturing in 1890," in *Essays on the Economy of the Old Northwest,* ed. David C. Klingaman and Richard K. Vedder (Athens: Ohio University Press, 1987), 285–86; David R. Meyer, "Midwestern Industrialization and the American Manufacturing Belt in the Nineteenth Century,"

Journal of Economic History 49 (December 1989): 923–24, 929; figures on the growth of the Chicago manufacturing workforce in 1860 and 1870 taken from the federal manuscript manufacturing censuses for those years.

29. Porter and Livesay, *Merchants and Manufacturers,* 7–8; figures on capital investment per worker were calculated from the federal manuscript manufacturing census for 1860.

30. John R. Commons et al., *A Documentary History of American Industrial Society,* vol. 9, *Labor Movement* (Cleveland, Ohio: Arthur H. Clark, 1910), 20–22 (quote 22).

31. Harry N. Scheiber, "Granger Cases," in *Encyclopedia of the American Constitution,* ed. Leonard W. Levy et al., 4 vols. (New York: Macmillan, 1986), 2:862–63.

32. On the compact antebellum city, see Sam Bass Warner, *The Private City: Philadelphia in Three Periods of Its Growth* (Philadelphia: University of Pennsylvania Press, 1968), 49–62; Allan Pred, "Manufacturing in the American Mercantile City: 1800–1840," *Annals of the Association of American Geographers* 56 (June 1966): 325–38.

33. McCarthy, *Noblesse Oblige,* ix, 58.

34. Jaher, *The Urban Establishment,* 463 (quote), 503–5; Schultz, "The Businessman's Role in Western Settlement," 6–7, 192–94, 265–67; Einhorn, *Property Rules,* 28, 39–42; Edward Pessen, *Riches, Class, and Power before the Civil War* (Lexington, Mass.: D. C. Heath, 1973), 282–92.

35. The figures on length of stay in the city were calculated from a sample of Gager's *Chicago City Directory: for the Year Ending June 1st, 1857* (Chicago: John Gager, 1856). On institution building, see Pierce, *A History of Chicago,* 2:3–34, 166–67, 390–430.

36. Einhorn, *Property Rules,* 28–60, 107–46.

37. Ibid., 76, 83.

38. Ibid., 61 (quote), 196, 203–4; Richard L. McCormick, "The Party Period and Public Policy: An Exploratory Hypothesis," in *The Party Period and Public Policy: American Politics from the Age of Jackson to the Progressive Era* (New York: Oxford University Press, 1986), 204; Theodore J. Lowi, "American Business, Public Policy, Case-Studies, and Political Theory," *World Politics* 16 (July 1964): 690.

39. Lowi, "American Business," 691; Einhorn, *Property Rules,* 100, 195.

40. Einhorn, *Property Rules,* 104, 161–68, 186; Christine Meisner Rosen, *The Limits of Power: Great Fires and the Process of City Growth in America* (New York: Cambridge University Press, 1986), 126–27, 171–74; Richard Wilson Renner, "In a Perfect Ferment: Chicago, the Know-Nothings, and the Riot for Lager Beer," *Chicago History* 5 (1976): 161–69.

41. Nikolaus Schwenck as cited in Keil and Jentz, *German Workers in Chicago,* 28–29.

42. *Tribune,* November 13, 16, 17, 19, and December 2, 1857; *Times,* November 4, 1857; Amy Bridges, *A City in the Republic: Antebellum New York and the Origins of Machine Politics* (New York: Cambridge University Press, 1984), 110–12.

43. Pierce, *A History of Chicago*, 2:201–2, 437; *Times*, November 14, 1857; *Daily Democrat*, October 25, 1850; *Tribune*, November 13, 16, 19, and December 4, 1857.

44. *Times*, November 7, 8, 13, 14, 1857.

45. Einhorn, *Property Rules*, 61–103, 144–87; Bridges, *A City in the Republic*, 123.

46. *Tribune*, November 16, 1857 (quote); Emil Dietzsch, *Chicago's Deutsche Männer: Erinnerungs-Blätter auf Chicago's Fünfzigjaehriges Jubiläum Geschichte der Stadt Chicago* (Chicago: M. Stern, 1885), 27–30.

47. Bruce Levine, *The Spirit of 1848: German Immigrants, Labor Conflict, and the Coming of the Civil War* (Urbana: University of Illinois Press, 1992), 225–26; Chicago Relief and Aid Society, *Annual Report, 1858–59*, Chicago City Council Proceedings Files 0498A 08/02, Cook County, Illinois Regional Archives Depository System, Northeastern Illinois University.

48. Chicago Relief and Aid Society, *Annual Report, 1858–59*; *Tribune*, November 13, 1857; Einhorn, *Property Rules*, 15–16, 18 (quote); in 1860, 25.5 percent of the unskilled workers in the Tenth Ward—site of Throop's docks—owned real property, compared to 15.9 percent in the whole city.

49. On anticipated growth in land values and the financing of public improvements, see Einhorn, *Property Rules*, 16–17; Schultz, "The Businessman's Role in Western Settlement," 229–32.

50. Abbott, *Boosters and Businessmen*, 42–44; Louis P. Cain, "From Mud to Metropolis," *Research in Economic History* 10 (1986): 124.

51. *Chicago Magazine: The West as It Is* (Chicago: J. Gager for the Chicago Mechanics' Institute, 1857), 363; William Cronon, *Nature's Metropolis: Chicago and the Great West* (New York: W. W. Norton, 1991).

52. Bruce Laurie, *Artisans into Workers: Labor in Nineteenth-Century America* (New York: Hill and Wang, 1989), 15–46; James Livingston, *Pragmatism and the Political Economy of Cultural Revolution, 1850–1940* (Chapel Hill: University of North Carolina Press, 1994), 24–40.

53. Pierce, *A History of Chicago*, 2:93.

54. Ibid., 2:114; *Tribune*, December 4, 1852, March 16, 1854, and June 14, 1862.

55. On the Eagle Works, see *Chicago Republican*, November 7, 1866; Bruce Laurie and Mark Schmitz, "Manufacture and Productivity: The Making of an Industrial Base, Philadelphia, 1850–1880," in *Philadelphia: Work, Space, Family, and Group Experience in the Nineteenth Century: Essays toward an Interdisciplinary History of the City*, ed. Theodore Hershberg (New York: Oxford University Press, 1981), 52–64 (quote 52); David M. Gordon, Richard Edwards, and Michael Reich, *Segmented Work, Divided Workers: The Historical Transformation of Labor in the United States* (Cambridge: Cambridge University Press, 1982), 64–66.

56. The description of the car shops is taken from *Tribune*, March 15 1853, January 30 and March 16, 1854 (quote), and June 15, 1863; figures from the federal manuscript manufacturing censuses for Chicago.

57. Laurie and Schmitz, "Manufacture and Productivity," 58–60; Gordon, Edwards, and Reich, *Segmented Work, Divided Workers*, 64–66; Anthony F. C. Wallace, *Rock-*

dale: The Growth of an American Village in the Early Industrial Revolution (New York: Alfred A. Knopf, 1978), 211–26; Porter and Livesay, *Merchants and Manufacturers*, 9–10, 114–15.

58. Our figures are based on the birthplaces of 659 owners in the federal manuscript manufacturing census for 1870; see also Schultz, "The Businessman's Role in Western Settlement," 386–87.

59. Steven J. Ross, *Workers on the Edge: Work, Leisure, and Politics in Industrializing Cincinnati, 1788–1890* (New York: Columbia University Press, 1985), 95–118, 226–30, 217–90; *Tribune*, March 15, 1853, March 16, 1854, and April 22, 1861; figures on the national origins of machinists from a sample of the 1860 manuscript population census for Chicago.

60. Cronon, *Nature's Metropolis*, 230; *Tribune*, April 10, November 22, 1862; figures on capital investment from the 1870 manuscript federal manufacturing census for Chicago.

61. Walsh, *The Rise of the Midwestern Meat Packing Industry*, 63; Wade, *Chicago's Pride*, 30–34; *Tribune*, November 16, 1863, March 20, 1865.

62. *Tribune*, November 16, 1863 (quote); Ross, *Workers on the Edge*, 120–24; Cronon, *Nature's Metropolis*, 230; figures on steam power taken from the federal manuscript manufacturing census for Chicago in 1870.

63. This and the following description of Tobey and Booth's packinghouse are based on the *Tribune*, December 11, 1868.

64. In 1870, the plants in which these men worked were of substantial size: Over 80 percent of the workers in this Chicago industry labored in plants with more than twenty-five employees. Only the packing, apparel, and building materials industries could match that percentage; from the 1870 federal manuscript manufacturing census for Chicago. On labor in such plants, see Ross, *Workers on the Edge*, 124.

65. Figures computed from the 1870 manuscript federal manufacturing census.

66. Men listed in the census of 1860 as "day laborer" and "laborer" made up 23.4 percent of all those employed; from the sample of the federal manuscript population census for Chicago, 1860.

67. On urban casual labor, see David Montgomery, "The Working Classes of the Preindustrial American City, 1780–1830," *Labor History* 9 (Winter 1968): 3–32.

68. Ross, *Workers on the Edge*, 80–82; Jentz, "Bread and Labor," 26–29; Jeremy Atack, "Economies of Scale and Efficiency Gains in the Rise of the Factory in America, 1820–1900," in *Quantity and Quiddity: Essays in U.S. Economic History*, ed. Peter Kilby, Jeremy Atack, and Stanley Lebergott (Middletown, Conn.: Wesleyan University Press, 1987), 320–22.

69. Jentz, "Bread and Labor," 24–35; on C. L. Woodman, see *Tribune*, February 20, 1869; A. T. Andreas, *History of Chicago*, vol. 2, *From 1857 Until the Fire of 1871* (Chicago: A. T. Andreas, 1885), 49–50, 661; S. S. Schoff, *The Glory of Chicago—Her Manufactories* (Chicago: Knight and Leonard, 1873), 165.

70. Jentz, "Bread and Labor," 24–35; Sean Wilentz, *Chants Democratic: New York*

City and the Rise of the American Working Class, 1788–1850 (New York: Oxford University Press, 1984), 107–42; *New York Sun*, May 27, 1872.

71. *Illinois Staats-Zeitung*, June 6, 9, 13, 20, 1864; *Tribune*, June 8, 10, 20, 1864.

72. *Illinois Staats-Zeitung*, October 2, 1862; Ross, *Workers on the Edge*, 131–34.

73. Figures calculated from the manuscript federal manufacturing censuses for Chicago; *Tribune*, February 13, 1870.

74. A series on women workers appeared in the Sunday edition of the *Tribune* beginning on February 6, 1870.

75. On the new white-collar occupations required by new bureaucratic forms of organization, see Olivier Zunz, *Making America Corporate, 1870–1920* (Chicago: University of Chicago Press, 1990), 125–48. People in Chicago employed in the "low white-collar" category of the Philadelphia Social History Project increased from 15 percent in 1850 to 21 percent in 1880; figures based on samples of federal manuscript censuses for those years.

76. *Illinois Staats-Zeitung*, March 11, 1871; Platt, *Shock Cities*, 126–31; Hermann Schlüter, *The Brewing Industry and the Brewery Workers' Movement in America* (New York: Burt Franklin, 1970 [1910]), 56–59, 62–75.

77. McCarthy, *Noblesse Oblige*, 53–54, 64.

78. On the formation of a distinct upper class in this era, see Jaher, *The Urban Establishment*, 2–4; Sven Beckert, *The Monied Metropolis: New York City and the Consolidation of the American Bourgeoisie, 1850–1896* (New York: Cambridge University Press, 2001), 4–9.

79. Richard Schneirov, *Labor and Urban Politics: Class Conflict and the Origins of Modern Liberalism in Chicago, 1864–97* (Urbana: University of Illinois Press, 1998), 17–18, 32–33; Pierce, *A History of Chicago*, 2:150–74.

80. Einhorn, *Property Rules*, 207–8, 225–27; *Tribune*, March 14, October 25, 29, 1862, March 30, 1865.

81. Einhorn, *Property Rules*, 182–85, 204–30; Platt, *Shock Cities*, 132–34.

Chapter 2. The Internationale of the Citizen Workers

1. *Chicago Daily Tribune* (hereafter *Tribune*), July 1, 1865.

2. Martin Shefter, "Trade Unions and Political Machines: The Organization and Disorganization of the American Working Class," in *Political Parties and the State: The American Historical Experience,* Martin Shefter (Princeton, N.J.: Princeton University Press, 1994), 101–68.

3. The first two paragraphs derive their basic concepts from Bernard Bailyn, *The Ideological Origins of the American Revolution* (Cambridge, Mass.: Harvard University Press, 1967); Gordon S. Wood, *Creation of the American Republic, 1776–1787* (Charlotte: University of North Carolina Press, 1969); J. G. A. Pocock, *The Machiavellian Moment: Florentine Political Thought and the Atlantic Republican Tradition* (Princeton, N.J.: Princeton University Press, 1975); Gordon S. Wood, *The Radicalism of the American Revolution* (New York: Random House, 1993); Daniel T. Rodgers,

"Republicanism: Career of a Concept," *Journal of American History* 79 (June 1992): 11–38.

4. James L. Huston, "The American Revolutionaries, the Political Economy of Aristocracy, and the American Concept of the Distribution of Wealth, 1765–1900," *American Historical Review* 98 (October 1993): 1079–1105; James L. Huston, *Securing the Fruits of Labor: The American Concept of Wealth Distribution, 1765–1900* (Baton Rouge: Louisiana State University Press, 1998).

5. E. P. Thompson, *The Making of the English Working Class* (New York: Vintage, 1963); Alfred F. Young, *Liberty Tree: Ordinary People and the American Revolution* (New York: New York University Press, 2006); Eric Foner, *Tom Paine and Revolutionary America* (New York: Oxford University Press, 2004); Norman Ware, *The Industrial Worker, 1840–1860* (Chicago: Quadrangle, 1964); Sean Wilentz, *Chants Democratic: New York City and the Rise of the American Working Class, 1788–1850* (New York: Oxford University Press, 1984); David R. Roediger, *The Wages of Whiteness: Race and the Making of the American Working Class* (London: Verso, 1991).

6. On the nineteenth century "disembedding" of the market from society and the making of its autonomy, see Karl Polanyi, *The Great Transformation: The Political and Economic Origins of Our Time* (Boston: Beacon Press, 1944); William J. Novak, *The People's Welfare: Law and Regulation in Nineteenth-Century America* (Chapel Hill: University of North Carolina Press, 1996), 235–48; David Montgomery, *Citizen Worker: The Experience of Workers in the United States with Democracy and the Free Market during the Nineteenth Century* (Cambridge: Cambridge University Press, 1993); Herbert Hovenkamp, *Enterprise and American Law, 1836–1937* (Cambridge, Mass.: Harvard University Press, 1991), 67–78.

7. Marcel van der Linden, "Transnationalizing American Labor History," *Journal of American History* 86 (December 1999): 1078–92; Michael P. Hanagan, "An Agenda for Transnational Labor History," *International Review of Social History* 49 (Fall 2004): 455–74. On transnational social republicanism in this period, see Richard Schneirov, "Political Cultures and the Role of the State in Labor's Republic: The View from Chicago, 1848–1877," *Labor History* 32 (Summer 1991): 376–400; Stanley Nadel, "From the Barricades of Paris to the Sidewalks of New York: German Artisans and the European Roots of American Labor Radicalism," *Labor History* 30 (Winter 1989): 47–75; Thomas Bender, *A Nation among Nations: America's Place in World History* (New York: Hill and Wang, 2006), 246–95; David Montgomery, "Labor and the Republic in Industrial America: 1860–1920," *Le Mouvement Social* 111 (April–June 1980): 250–56; Bruce Levine, *The Spirit of 1848: German Immigrants, Labor Conflict, and the Coming of the Civil War* (Urbana: University of Illinois Press, 1992), 83–110.

8. Peter A. Coclanis and Scott Marler, "The Economics of Reconstruction," in *A Companion to the Civil War and Reconstruction*, ed. Lacy K. Ford (Malden, Mass.: Blackwell, 2005), 342–65; Jeffrey Rogers Hummel, "The Civil War and Reconstruction," in *Government and the American Economy: A New History*, Price Fishback et al. (Chicago: University of Chicago Press, 2007), 188–231; Jeffrey G. Williamson,

"Watersheds and Turning Points: Conjectures on the Long-Term Impact of Civil War Financing," *Journal of Economic History* 34 (September 1974): 636–61; Hovenkamp, *Enterprise and American Law*, 93–101, 125–30.

9. Robin Einhorn, *Property Rules: Political Economy in Chicago, 1833–1872* (Chicago: University of Chicago Press, 1991), 196–204.

10. Kevin H. O'Rourke and Jeffrey G. Williamson, *Globalization and History: The Evolution of a Nineteenth Century Atlantic Economy* (Cambridge, Mass.: MIT Press, 1999), 119–44; Dirk Hoerder, *Cultures in Contact: World Migrations in the Second Millennium* (Durham, N.C.: Duke University Press, 2002), 331–57; Bessie Louise Pierce, *A History of Chicago*, vol. 2, *From Town to City, 1848–1871* (New York: Alfred A. Knopf, 1940), 27–28; Robert Walter Johannsen, *Stephen A. Douglas* (New York: Oxford University Press, 1973), 344–46; Mark A. Lause, *Young America: Land, Labor, and the Republican Community* (Urbana: University of Illinois Press, 2005), 1–5.

11. Rowland Berthoff, "Peasants and Artisans, Puritans and Republicans: Personal Liberty and Communal Equality in American History," *Journal of American History* 69 (December 1982): 579–98; Schneirov, "Political Cultures and the Role of the State," 376–400.

12. Mark A. Noll, *America's God: From Jonathan Edwards to Abraham Lincoln* (New York: Oxford University Press, 2002), 53–92, 422–38; James Brewer Steward, *Holy Warriors: The Abolitionists and American Slavery* (New York: Hill and Wang, 1976), 33–45; Herbert G. Gutman, "Protestantism and the American Labor Movement: The Christian Spirit in the Gilded Age," in *Work, Culture, and Society in Industrializing America: Essays in American Working-Class and Social History*, Herbert G. Gutman (New York: Alfred A. Knopf, 1976), 79–117; William A. Mirola, "Asking for Bread, Receiving a Stone: The Rise and Fall of Religious Ideologies in Chicago's Eight-Hour Movement," *Social Problems* 50 (May 2003): 278–82. For examples of evangelical Protestantism mixed with social republicanism, see the speeches of Richard Trevellick and William Sylvis at the Fourth of July celebration organized by the Chicago Trades Assembly; *Tribune*, July 6, 1865.

13. Einhorn, *Property Rules*, 61–103, 188–230; the quote is from the preface to the 2001 edition of Einhorn's book, xii; see also Philip J. Ethington, *The Public City: The Political Construction of Urban Life in San Francisco, 1850–1900* (Cambridge: Cambridge University Press, 1994), 1–35; Richard Jensen, *Illinois: A History* (New York: W. W. Norton, 1978), 61–75.

14. *Tribune*, January 13, 1863; *Illinois Staats-Zeitung*, January 6, 1863 (quote).

15. Pierce, *A History of Chicago*, 2:420 (note 74); Einhorn, *Property Rules*, 253–56; founding documents of the Sozialer Arbeiterverein are reprinted in the *Illinois Staats-Zeitung*, March 13, 1862; for a description of its activities, see *Illinois Staats-Zeitung*, February 12, 1861.

16. Jörg Nagler, *Fremont contra Lincoln: Die deutsch-amerikanische Opposition in der Republikanischen Partei während des amerikanischen Buergerkrieges* (Frankfurt: Peter Lang, 1984), 153–54. For the "Address to the Liberal Germans in the Union,"

see *Der Demokrat* (weekly edition, Davenport, Iowa), October 29, 1863. For the Louisville platform, see John P. Sanderson, *Republican Landmarks. The Views and Opinions of American Statesmen on Foreign Immigration* (Philadelphia: J. B. Lippincott, 1856), 221–22.

17. John B. Jentz, "The 48ers and the Politics of the German Labor Movement in Chicago during the Civil War Era: Community Formation and the Rise of a Labor Press," in *The German-American Radical Press: The Shaping of a Left Political Culture, 1850–1940,* ed. Elliott Shore, Ken Fones-Wolf, and James P. Danky (Urbana: University of Illinois Press, 1992), 49–62; Levine, *The Spirit of 1848,* 114, 258–63.

18. Pierce, *A History of Chicago,* 2:258; Theodore J. Karamanski, *Rally 'Round the Flag: Chicago and the Civil War* (Chicago: Nelson-Hall, 1993), 77–82, 113; David Montgomery, *Beyond Equality: Labor and the Radical Republicans, 1862–1872* (New York: Alfred A. Knopf, 1967), 127–34; Lawrence McCaffrey, *The Irish Diaspora in America* (Bloomington: Indiana University Press, 1976), 117–18; William D'Arcy, *The Fenian Movement in the United States: 1858–1886* (New York: Russell and Russell, 1947), 33–35.

19. Roediger, *The Wages of Whiteness,* 59–60, 117–18, 122–27, 133–63; Eric Lott, *Love and Theft: Blackface Minstrelsy and the American Working Class* (New York: Oxford University Press, 1995); Alexander Saxton, *The Rise and Fall of the White Republic: Class Politics and Mass Culture in Nineteenth-Century America* (New York: Verso, 1990). We agree with critics of the concept of whiteness that the Irish and other immigrants were never considered nonwhite in America; we also dissent from the idea that whiteness was a social construction of white workers in isolation from the rest of society or that it can be used as an all-encompassing explanation for the lack of working-class consciousness. However, we think that the cultural identity of whiteness in the antebellum era helps explain the impact of emancipation on white workers; see the roundtable on Eric Arnesen's criticisms of the whiteness thesis in *International Labor and Working-Class History* 60 (Fall 2001): 3–92.

20. *Tribune,* July 15, 17, August 11, November 12, 1862, July 21, August 11, 1863; Eric Benjaminson, "A Regiment of Immigrants: The 82nd Illinois Volunteer Infantry and the Letters of Captain Rudolph Mueller," *Journal of the Illinois State Historical Society* 94, no. 2 (Summer 2001): 144; Karamanski, *Rally 'Round the Flag,* 178–79; on the 90th Illinois regiment, see Frank L. Klement, *Copperheads in the Middle West* (Chicago: University of Chicago Press, 1960), 50–51.

21. Montgomery, *Beyond Equality,* 129; Kerby A. Miller, *Emigrants and Exiles: Ireland and the Irish Exodus to North America* (New York: Oxford University Press, 1985), 360.

22. *Chicago Times* (hereafter *Times*), March 23, 1864; *Tribune,* March 24, 1864 (quote).

23. McCaffrey, *The Irish Diaspora in America,* 117–18.

24. D'Arcy, *The Fenian Movement in the United States,* 34–35 (quote); Montgomery, *Beyond Equality,* 127–34; Miller, *Emigrants and Exiles,* 438, 549–50; *Western Tablet,* February 28, April 17, May 15, December 4, 1852, September 17, 1853.

25. John B. Jentz and Richard Schneirov, "Chicago's Fenian Fair of 1864: A Window into the Civil War as a Popular Political Awakening," *Labor's Heritage* 6 (March 1995): 4–19.

26. Pierce, *A History of Chicago*, 2:276; Karamanski, *Rally 'Round the Flag*, 235; James M. McPherson, *Battle Cry of Freedom: The Civil War Era* (New York: Ballantine Books, 1988), 448–49. Estimates of Chicago's workforce were drawn from the federal manuscript population census for 1860 and the *Tribune*, January 14, 1864.

27. *Tribune*, October 8, 1863 (quote), June 14, 1864; Pierce, *A History of Chicago*, 2:157; Arthur C. Cole, *The Era of the Civil War, 1848–1870*, ed. Clarence W. Alvord (Springfield: Illinois Centennial Commission, 1919), 368, 373; David M. Gordon, Richard Edwards, and Michael Reich, *Segmented Work, Divided Workers: The Historical Transformation of Labor in the United States* (Cambridge: Cambridge University Press, 1982), 64–66.

28. On the carpenters strike, see *Tribune*, March 7, 9, 14, 1863; *Illinois Staats-Zeitung*, March 7, 18, 19, August 3, 1863, March 15, 22, 31, 1864. On female sales clerks, see *Times*, February 3, 1864.

29. J. Matthew Gallman, *Mastering Wartime: A Social History of Philadelphia during the Civil War* (New York: Cambridge University Press, 1990), 227–40; Pierce, *A History of Chicago*, 2:162–64, 501–3; John R. Commons et al., *History of Labour in the United States*, 4 vols. (New York: McMillan, 1918, 1946), 2:16 (quote), 19, 72.

30. On wages and the cost of living in the North, see Lawrence H. Officer, *Two Centuries of Compensation for U. S. Production Workers in Manufacturing* (New York: Palgrave Macmillan, 2009), table 7.2, 170. On the wartime decline in real wages in Chicago, see Pierce, *A History of Chicago*, 2:157–58, 500.

31. *Tribune*, January 14, 1864; *Times*, March 1, 1864 (quote).

32. *Tribune*, January 14, 1864; Eric Hobsbawm, "Wages, Custom, and Workload in the Nineteenth Century," in *Labouring Men*, Eric Hobsbawm (London: Wiedenfield and Nicolson, 1964), 409–10. The coopers were 61 percent German and Irish, the tailors 74 percent, and the bakers 50 percent; figures from combined systematic samples of the 1860 and 1870 federal manuscript population censuses for Chicago.

33. *Illinois Staats-Zeitung*, January 8, 12, 13, 1861, January, 6, 8, 13, 1864; *Tribune*, January 6, 8, 1864. In the 1860s, the Germans constituted about two-fifths of the coopers, making them the largest national group.

34. *Tribune*, March 23, May 1, 3, 1864; figures calculated from the manuscript federal manufacturing census for 1870.

35. *Illinois Staats-Zeitung*, March 3, 5, 10, May 7, 21, June 9, July 16, 1864; *Tribune*, March 21, 1864; John B. Jentz, "Bread and Labor: Chicago's German Bakers Organize," *Chicago History* 12 (Summer 1983): 24–35.

36. *Tribune*, April 10, May 26, June 8, 14, 20, 23, 1864; *Illinois Staats-Zeitung*, June 9, 13, 20, 1864.

37. The Cabinet Makers Society of Chicago was incorporated in 1855, probably based on the Schreiner-Verein; Pierce, *A History of Chicago*, 2:166; see also Richard

Schneirov and Thomas J. Suhrbur, *Union Brotherhood, Union Town: The History of the Carpenters' Union of Chicago, 1863–1987* (Carbondale: Southern Illinois University Press, 1988), 1–17.

38. *Tribune,* March 7, 1862, March 7, 1863, March 31, April 15, 1864; *Illinois Staats-Zeitung,* March 9, October 22, 1863, March 15, 22, 31, April 7, 1864; *Times,* May 19, 1864.

39. Ira Katznelson, "Working-Class Formation: Constructing Cases and Comparisons," in *Working-Class Formation: Nineteenth-Century Patterns in Western Europe and the United States,* ed. Ira Katznelson and Aristide R. Zolberg (Princeton, N.J.: Princeton University Press, 1986), 35–38; Amy Bridges, "Becoming American: The Working Classes in the United States before the Civil War," in *Working-Class Formation,* 162–82.

40. In the 1860s, the birthplaces of the Chicago machinists were 40 percent United States, 25 percent Great Britain, 12 percent Germany, 10 percent Ireland, 5 percent Scandinavia, 10 percent other; figures taken from combined samples of the 1860 and 1870 federal manuscript population censuses for Chicago.

41. *Tribune,* January 20, March 7, 15, 16, 18, 28, May 9, 11, 1864; Pierce, *A History of Chicago,* 2:165.

42. *Tribune,* August 21 (first quote), September 11 (second quote), 1864.

43. *Tribune,* April 27, 1864.

44. Montgomery, *Beyond Equality,* 129; Miller, *Emigrants and Exiles,* 360; D'Arcy, *The Fenian Movement in the United States,* 21–45, 61.

45. *Times,* February 3, 8, 28, April 7, 1864; *Tribune,* February 8 (quote), March 15, 17, 18, 1864.

46. *Times,* February 18, March 28, 29, 1864; *Tribune,* February 18, March 26, 28, 29, April 1, 1864; Beverly Gordon, "'A Furor of Benevolence,'" *Chicago History* 15 (Winter 1986–1987): 48–65; John B. Jentz and Richard Schneirov, "Chicago's Fenian Fair of 1864: A Window into the Civil War as a Popular Political Awakening," *Labor's Heritage* 6 (Winter 1995): 4–19; Nina Silber, "Northern Women during the Age of Emancipation," in *A Companion to the Civil War and Reconstruction,* ed. Lacy K. Ford (Oxford: Blackwell, 2005), 388.

47. Nagler, *Fremont contra Lincoln,* 154 (quote); Jentz, "The 48ers and the Politics of the German Labor Movement in Chicago," 50–53.

48. *Times,* April 27, 1864; *Tribune,* April 27, 1864.

49. *Times,* April 27, 1864 (quotes); Roediger, *The Wages of Whiteness,* 81, 87, 173–76; Eric Foner, "Abolitionism and the Labor Movement in Ante-bellum America," in *Politics and Ideology in the Age of the Civil War,* Eric Foner (New York: Oxford University Press, 1980), 74–76.

50. *Times,* April 27, 1864; *Workingman's Advocate,* September 17, 1864.

51. Pierce, *A History of Chicago,* 2:162–63; McPherson, *Battle Cry of Freedom,* 770–71; Bernard Mandel, *Labor, Free and Slave: Workingmen and the Anti-Slavery Movement in the United States* (New York: Associated Authors, 1955), 182–83.

52. *Tribune,* August 21, 1864 (quotes).

53. Ibid. (quotes).

54. Ibid. (quotes). On the racism of the Douglas Democracy, see Jean H. Baker, *Affairs of Party: The Political Culture of Northern Democrats in the Nineteenth Century* (Ithaca, N.Y.: Cornell University Press, 1983), 177–211.

55. *Tribune,* August 21, 1864 (quote); Huston, "The American Revolutionaries," 1079–1105; Peter Argersinger, "'A Place on the Ballot': Fusion Politics and Antifusion Laws," in *Structure, Process and Party: Essays in American Political History,* Peter Argersinger (New York: M. E. Sharpe, 1991), 150–71.

56. *Tribune,* August 2 (quote), 4, 1864.

57. Pierce, *A History of Chicago,* 2:501; *Workingman's Advocate,* September 17, 1864; *Tribune,* September 11, 12, 1864; *Times,* September 12, 1864; Karamanski, *Rally 'Round the Flag,* 177–78.

58. *Workingman's Advocate,* September 17, 1864 (quote); *Tribune,* September 11, 1864.

59. Karl Marx, *Capital,* vol. 1, *A Critical Analysis of Capitalist Production* (New York: International Publishers, 1974; orig. publ. 1867), 301.

Chapter 3. The Eight-Hour Day and the Legitimacy of Wage Labor

1. *Chicago Daily Tribune* (hereafter *Tribune*), May 2, 1867.

2. Ibid.

3. David Montgomery, *Citizen Worker: The Experience of Workers in the United States with Democracy and the Free Market during the Nineteenth Century* (Cambridge: Cambridge University Press, 1993), 13; Eric Foner, "The Idea of Free Labor in Nineteenth-Century America," in *Free Soil, Free Labor, Free Men: The Ideology of the Republican Party Before the Civil War,* Eric Foner (New York: Oxford University Press, 1995), xv–xvi; Eric Hobsbawm, *The Age of Capital, 1848–1875* (New York: Vintage, 1989).

4. George McNeill, quoted in Lawrence B. Glickman, *A Living Wage: American Workers and the Making of Consumer Society* (Ithaca, N.Y.: Cornell University Press, 1997), 99; David Brody, "Time and Work during Early American Industrialism," in *In Labor's Cause: Main Themes on the History of the American Worker,* David Brody (New York: Oxford University Press, 1993), 3–42 (quotes 34).

5. Amy Dru Stanley, *From Bondage to Contract: Wage Labor, Marriage, and the Market in the Age of Slave Emancipation* (Cambridge: Cambridge University Press, 1998), 89–90; Glickman, *A Living Wage,* 17–34; David Montgomery, "Labor and the Republic in Industrial America: 1860–1920," *Le Mouvement Social* 111 (April–June 1980): 250–56.

6. Stanley, *From Bondage to Contract,* 89–90 (quote 90).

7. Robert J. Steinfeld, *The Invention of Free Labor: The Employment Relation in English and American Law and Culture, 1350–1870* (Chapel Hill: University of North Carolina Press, 1991), 185–87.

8. *Workingman's Advocate* (Chicago), May 20, 1871 (quote); on Andrew Cameron's thought, see Richard Schneirov, "Political Cultures and the Role of the State in Labor's Republic: The View from Chicago, 1848–1877," *Labor History* 32 (Summer 1991): 376–400.

9. Ira Steward, "A Reduction of Hours, An Increase of Wages" was first published in *Fincher's Trades Review* (hereafter *Fincher's*), October 14, 1865, and reprinted in *A Documentary History of American Industrial Society,* ed. John R. Commons, Ulrich B. Phillips, Eugene A. Gilmore, Helen L. Sumner, and John B. Andrews (1910; reprint, New York: Russell and Russell, 1958), 284–301; David Montgomery, *Beyond Equality: Labor and the Radical Republicans* (New York: Vintage Books, 1967), 249–60; Lawrence R. Glickman, "Workers of the World Consume: Ira Steward and the Origins of Labor Consumerism," *International Labor and Working Class History* 52 (Fall 1997): 72–86.

10. Schneirov, "Political Cultures and the Role of the State in Labor's Republic," 376–400.

11. By 1865, *Fincher's* had a circulation of eleven thousand in thirty-one of thirty-six states and in five British cities; Gary M. Fink, *Biographical Dictionary of American Labor* (Westport, Conn.: Greenwood Press, 1984), 222; Anthony F. C. Wallace, *Rockdale: The Growth of an American Village in the Early Industrial Revolution* (New York: Alfred A. Knopf, 1978), 211–39.

12. *Fincher's,* June 6, October 3, 1863, March 26, 1864; David Randall Roediger, "The Movement for a Shorter Working Day in the United States Before 1866" (unpublished PhD diss., Northwestern University, 1980), 235, 241–43.

13. Roediger, "The Movement for a Shorter Working Day," 193, 241–42; *Chicago Republican* (hereafter *Republican*), December 21, 1865. For references to Great Britain, see *Workingman's Advocate* as reprinted in the *St. Louis Democratic Press,* January 4, March 9, 10, April 27, 1865.

14. Roediger, "The Movement for a Shorter Working Day," 226–29, 266–67; Montgomery, *Beyond Equality,* 123–24, 251–2.

15. Steven J. Ross, *Workers on the Edge: Work, Leisure, and Politics in Industrializing Cincinnati, 1788–1890* (New York: Columbia University Press, 1985), 96–10; David R. Roediger and Philip S. Foner, *Our Own Time: A History of American Labor and the Working Day* (New York: Greenwood Press, 1989), 82–83, 96–99; *Tribune,* September 15, 1865 (quote).

16. On the Arbeiterverein's activities, see Bessie Louise Pierce, *A History of Chicago,* vol. 2, *From Town to City 1848–1871* (Chicago: University of Chicago Press, 1940), 166–67; *Illinois Staats-Zeitung,* March 28, June 12, September 4, December 5, 1861. On the culture of German skilled workers, two collections of essays are particularly useful: Hartmut Keil, ed., *German Workers' Culture in the United States, 1850 to 1920* (Washington, DC: Smithsonian Institution Press, 1988); Ulrich Engelhardt, ed., *Handwerker in der Industrialisierung: Lage, Kultur und Politik von späten 18. Bis ins frühe 20. Jahrhundert* (Stuttgart: Klett-Cotta, 1984). On the Arbeiterverein and the eight-hour workday, see *Republican,* December 10, 1865; *Tribune,* February 6,

1866; the *Illinois Staats-Zeitung* sympathetically reported eight-hour agitation in New York and other states; *Illinois Staats-Zeitung,* March 1, June 5, 1866.

17. Roediger, "The Movement for a Shorter Working Day," 264–66; Montgomery, *Beyond Equality,* 236–37, 260.

18. Pierce, *A History of Chicago,* 2:162–63, 170–75; John B. Jentz, "The 48ers and the Politics of the German Labor Movement in Chicago during the Civil War Era: Community Formation and the Rise of a Labor Press," in *The German-American Radical Press: The Shaping of a Left Political Culture, 1850–1940,* Elliott Shore, Ken Foner-Wolf, and James P. Danky (Urbana: University of Illinois Press, 1992), 55–57.

19. *Tribune,* July 6, 1865.

20. *Tribune,* September 15, 1865 (quotes).

21. *Tribune,* September 18, 1865; Roediger and Foner, *Our Own Time,* 98–100; Montgomery, *Beyond Equality,* 254–56.

22. *Republican,* November 12, 1865; on unions, politics, and labor reform, see Montgomery, *Beyond Equality,* 135–40.

23. *Fincher's,* November 28, 1863 (quote), March 4, May 6, August 26, 1865, January 13, 20, 1866. On the abolitionists and public opinion, see Aileen S. Kraditor, *Means and Ends in American Abolitionism: Garrison and His Critics on Strategy and Tactics, 1834–1850* (New York: Pantheon Books, 1969), 28–32, 165–68; James Brewer Stewart, *Holy Warriors: The Abolitionists and American Slavery* (New York: Hill and Wang, 1976), 74–88.

24. *Republican,* December 10, 1865 (quote); on the unions in the Trades Assembly, see *Tribune,* September 15, 1865.

25. Chicago, Common Council, *Proceedings of the Common Council of the City of Chicago 1865/1866* (serial publication, annual; Chicago: The Council, 1866), 253, 273; *Workingman's Advocate,* April 21, 1866; *Republican,* April 17, 1866; *Tribune,* October 9, 1866.

26. *Republican,* April 17, 18, 1866; *Times,* April 18, 1866; *Workingman's Advocate,* April 21, 1866.

27. *Workingman's Advocate,* April 21, 1866 (first two quotes); *Workingman's Advocate,* May 11, 1866 (third quote).

28. Dale Baum, "The 'Irish Vote' and Party Politics in Massachusetts, 1860–1876," *Civil War History* 26 (June, 1980): 134.

29. *Republican,* October 31, 1866; Chicago, Common Council, *Proceedings, 1865/1866,* 253, 273; Chicago, Common Council, *Proceedings, 1866/1867,* 103; Pierce, *A History of Chicago,* 2:175; Baum, "The 'Irish Vote' and Party Politics," 130–33.

30. *Republican,* October 20 (quote), 24, 1866, March 8, April 16, 18, 1867; *Tribune,* October 9, 1866; James M. McPherson, *The Civil War Era* (New York: Ballantine Books, 1988), 195–201.

31. *Republican,* March 17, 1867.

32. The *Times* summarized its opposition to the law in its issue of May 1, 1867. For its position on the interrelated issues of the eight-hour workday, cooperation, and protection, see *Times,* April 1, 18, 19, 23, 26, 28, May 3, 4, 1867.

33. Montgomery, *Beyond Equality,* 247–48, 335, 383–84; Joseph Logsdon, *Horace White, Nineteenth Century Liberal* (Westport, Conn.: Greenwood, 1971), 3, 166–218, 327–561; Nancy Cohen, *The Reconstruction of American Liberalism, 1865–1914* (Chapel Hill: University of North Carolina Press, 2002), 38–43; however, we disagree with Cohen's evaluation of Gilded Age Liberalism as profoundly antidemocratic; see chap. 7.

34. On the special Massachusetts committee and its report, see Montgomery, *Beyond Equality,* 266–68; *Tribune,* March 26, April 4 (quotes), 1867.

35. *Tribune,* April 11 (quote), 27, 1867; on Godkin's support for cooperation, see E. L. Godkin, "The Labor Crisis," *North American Review* 105 (July 1867): 196–98.

36. James L. Huston, "A Political Response to Industrialism: The Republican Embrace of Protectionist Labor Doctrines," *Journal of American History* 70 (1983): 35–57; Jeffrey Sklansky, *The Soul's Economy: Market Society and Selfhood in American Thought, 1820–1920* (Chapel Hill: University of North Carolina Press, 2002), 77–93; on the prolabor character of Republican protectionism, see John R. Commons, "Horace Greeley and the Working Class Origins of the Republican Party," *Political Science Quarterly* 24 (September 1919): 468–88.

37. *Republican,* May 6, 1867. For a short history of the founding of the *Republican,* see its issue of May 6, 1867.

38. *Republican,* May 7, 1867 (quotes); James L. Huston, *Securing the Fruits of Labor: The American Concept of Wealth Distribution, 1765–1900* (Baton Rouge: Louisiana State University Press, 1998), 178–80. In emphasizing human creativity, Huston argues that Carey and his Radical Republican followers fully anticipated the modern theory of human capital.

39. *Republican,* May 7 (quote), 12, 1867; James Harrison Wilson, *The Life of Charles A. Dana* (New York: Harper, 1907), 33–60; Charles A. Dana and William B. Greene, *Proudhon's Solution of the Social Problem,* ed. Henry Cohen (New York: Vanguard Press, 1927).

40. *Illinois Staats-Zeitung,* June 5, 1866, February 24, April 22, 29, May 3, 6, 7, 8, 11, 17, 1867; *Republican,* April 20 (first quote), 27 (second quote), 1867. On theories of labor productivity and a rising standard of living, see Jonathan A. Glickstein, *Concepts of Free Labor in Antebellum America* (New Haven, Conn.: Yale University Press, 1991), 50–52; David Montgomery, "Workers' Control of Machine Production in the Nineteenth Century," *Labor History* 17 (Fall 1976): 485–509; David Montgomery, *The Fall of the House of Labor: The Workplace, the State, and American Labor Activism, 1865–1925* (Cambridge: Cambridge University Press, 1987), 9–57; Anthony F. C. Wallace, *Rockdale: The Growth of an American Village in the Early Industrial Revolution* (New York: Alfred A. Knopf, 1978), 211–29.

41. *Tribune,* January 17, 1866, April 9 (first quote), 21(second quote), 1867.

42. *Republican,* February 23, 1866; *Illinois Staats-Zeitung,* February 16, 1866.

43. Philip Scranton, "Varieties of Paternalism: Industrial Structures and the Social Relations of Production in American Textiles," *American Quarterly* 36 (Summer 1984): 238–51. The spokesman for German entrepreneurs was Anton Hesing; Joseph

Medill was president of the organization; *Republican,* February 23, 1866; *Tribune,* February1, 2 1866.

44. *Tribune,* March 17, 30, 1867; *Republican,* April 21 (quote), March 31, November 20, 1867. On the prolabor strain of the American radical reform tradition, see Montgomery, *Beyond Equality,* 387–424.

45. *Tribune,* May 28, 1867.

46. *Republican,* May 1, 1867 (quote); *Tribune,* April 25, May 1, 3, 4, 7, 1867.

47. Sean Wilentz, *Chants Democratic: New York City and the Rise of the American Working Class, 1788–1850* (New York: Oxford University Press, 1984), 93–95 (quote 94).

48. *Tribune,* May 1, 2, 1867; *Republican,* May 1, 1867.

49. *Republican,* March 31 (first quote), May 27, 1867; Montgomery, *Beyond Equality,* 305; Alexander Yard, "Coercive Government within a Minimal State: The Idea of Public Opinion in Gilded Age Labor Reform Culture," *Labor History* 34 (Fall 1993): 443–56.

50. *Republican,* May 1 (quote), 27, 1867.

51. *Tribune,* May 2, 1867; *Times,* May 2, 1867; *Illinois Staats-Zeitung,* May 2, 3, 1867. The *Tribune* estimated the marchers at five thousand, the *Times,* six thousand, the *Republican,* over five thousand.

52. *Times,* May 2, 1867 (quotes); *Tribune,* May 2, 1867.

53. *Tribune,* May 2, 1867. There is a considerable literature on the crowds of preindustrial cities; for an introduction, see Wilentz, *Chants Democratic,* 64–67; Eric Foner, *Tom Paine and Revolutionary America* (New York: Oxford University Press, 1976), 45–69; David Montgomery, "The Shuttle and the Cross: Weavers and Artisans in the Kensington Riots of 1844," *Journal of Social History* 5 (Summer 1972): 411–46.

54. *Tribune,* May 3, 1867; *Times,* May 3, 1867 (quotes).

55. *Republican,* June 2, 1867 (first quote); *Tribune,* May 3, 1867 (all subsequent quotes).

56. *Tribune,* May 3, 4 (all quotes), 1867. Statements about the national origins of the participants in the strike are based on an analysis of the names of those arrested and on the birthplaces of those from the Sixth and Seventh wards contained in our sample of the 1870 federal manuscript population census.

57. *Tribune,* May 8, 1867; *Times,* May 5, 1867.

58. *Times,* May 3, 4, 1867; *Tribune,* May 3, 4, 5, 1867.

59. *Republican,* May 9, 1867; *Illinois Staats-Zeitung,* May 7, 1867.

60. Pierce, *A History of Chicago,* 2:16; Hartmut Keil and John B. Jentz, *German Workers in Chicago: A Documentary History of Working-Class Culture from 1850 to World War I* (Urbana: University of Illinois Press, 1988), 160–69.

61. The Central Executive Committee that directed the strike had twenty-five members, three of whom had Germanic, or perhaps Scandinavian, names; the rest of the names were Anglo American; *Republican,* May 5, 1867. Of twenty-six metalworkers who were strike leaders and whose national origins could be identified,

twelve were born in Wales, Scotland, or England, one in British Canada, four in the United States, and nine in Ireland. The birthplaces of eighteen machinists, who were also leaders, could be identified, and eleven were British-born. On the Amalgamated Society of Engineers and English New Model Unionism, see Sidney Webb and Beatrice Webb, *The History of Trade Unionism,* rev. ed. (London: Longmans, Green, 1935), 206–26; Clifton K. Yearley, *Britons in American Labor: A History of the Influence of the United Kingdom Immigrants on American Labor, 1820–1914* (Baltimore: Johns Hopkins University Press, 1957), 46–83. Hayes and Ramsbottom were officers of the Amalgamated Society branch in Chicago; *Workingman's Advocate,* January 2, 1869.

62. *Republican,* May 10, 1867 (quotes). On William Cobbett, see E. P. Thompson, *The Making of the English Working Class* (New York: Vintage Books, 1963), 451–71.

63. *Tribune,* May 10 (first quote), 11 (third quote), 1867; *Republican,* May 11, 1867 (second quote).

64. *Tribune,* May 11, 1867 (quotes). On transatlantic radical movements stemming from the eighteenth century, see Edward Countryman, *The American Revolution,* rev. ed. (New York: Hill and Wang, 2003), 67–97; Foner, *Tom Paine and Revolutionary America,* 51–56; Sidney Tarrow, *Power in Movement: Social Movements and Contentious Politics,* 2nd ed. (Cambridge: Cambridge University Press, 1998), 43–53. On moral suasion and the Second Great Awakening, see Stewart, *Holy Warriors,* 54–55; Ronald G. Walters, *American Reformers 1815–1860* (New York: Hill and Wang, 1978), 77–100.

65. *Tribune,* May 2, 1867 (quote; emphases in the original); *Republican,* May 12, 14, 15, 16, 1867.

66. *Republican,* May 17, 1867; John Bright, as cited in Yearley, *Britons in American Labor,* 50.

67. The *Republican* of May 31, 1867, provides a good survey of the effects of the strike to that point.

68. *Workingman's Advocate,* May 23, August 22, 1868, June 5, 1869.

69. On the significance of construction for Irish labor and business in the whole country, see David Montgomery, "The Irish and the American Labor Movement," in *America and Ireland, 1776–1976: The American Identity and the Irish Connection,* ed. David Noel Doyle and Owen Dudley Edwards (Westport, Conn.: Greenwood, 1980), 211–12.

70. John B. Jentz, "Skilled Workers and Industrialization: Chicago's German Cabinetmakers and Machinists, 1880–1900," in *German Workers in Industrial Chicago, 1850–1910: A Comparative Perspective,* ed. Hartmut Keil and John B. Jentz (DeKalb: Northern Illinois University Press, 1983), 73–85; Bruce Laurie, Theodore Hershberg, and George Alter, "Immigrants and Industry: The Philadelphia Experience, 1850–1880," in *Philadelphia: Work, Space, Family, and Group Experience in the Nineteenth Century: Essays toward an Interdisciplinary History of the City,* ed. Theodore Hershberg (Oxford: Oxford University Press, 1981), 109–16; Montgomery, "The Irish and the American Labor Movement," 213.

71. Montgomery, *Beyond Equality*, 126–127; Montgomery, "The Irish and the American Labor Movement," 205–7, 211, 212 (quote).

72. Although the convention seated fourteen delegates from Chicago, none of them were Germans until Eduard Schläger's credentials as the representative of the Arbeiterverein were accepted, after a contentious debate, on the fourth day of the six-day meeting; *Republican*, August 22, 23, 1867. The German labor paper *Der Deutsche Arbeiter* was edited by Carl Klings, a Lassallean who emigrated in the mid-1860s.

73. *Tribune*, May 26, 30, June 13, 1867.

74. *Tribune*, May 11, 14, 1867; *Republican*, May 10, 1867; Jeffrey Haydu, *Citizen Employers: Business Communities and Labor in Cincinnati and San Francisco, 1870–1916* (Ithaca, N.Y.: Cornell University Press, 2008), 35–50.

75. *Tribune*, May 26, 1867; *Republican*, May 8, 18, 1867. For a discussion of the pro-working-class strain of the native radical reform tradition of which E. S. Warner and John Orvis were a part, see David Montgomery's discussion of the "sentimental reformers" in *Beyond Equality*, 387–424; for a contrasting interpretation, see Timothy Messer-Kruse, *The Yankee International: Marxism and the American Reform Tradition, 1848–1876* (Chapel Hill: University of North Carolina Press, 1998).

76. Richard Schneirov and Thomas J. Suhrbur, *Union Brotherhood, Union Town: The History of the Carpenters' Union of Chicago, 1863–1987* (Carbondale: Southern Illinois University Press, 1988), 12, 17–18; *Illinois Staats-Zeitung*, May 9, 18, 1867; *Tribune*, May 29, 1867; *Republican*, May 18, 31, 1867; *Workingman's Advocate*, December 7, 1867, January 25, May 23, 1868, February 20, November 6, 1869; see also Merchants Farmers and Mechanics Savings Bank, *The Labor Question* (Chicago: Warden, 1867), 42–43.

77. Leon Fink, *Workingmen's Democracy: The Knights of Labor and American Politics* (Urbana: University of Illinois Press, 1983), 6–15; Lawrence Goodwyn, *The Populist Moment: A Short History of the Agrarian Revolt in America* (New York: Oxford University Press, 1978), 55–93; Steve Leikin, *The Practical Utopians: American Workers and the Cooperative Movement in the Gilded Age* (Detroit: Wayne State University Press, 2005), 1–52; Richard Schneirov, *Labor and Urban Politics: Class Conflict and the Origins of Modern Liberalism in Chicago, 1864–97* (Urbana: University of Illinois Press, 1998), 148, 184–91.

78. Samuel Gompers, *Seventy Years of Life and Labor* (New York: E. P. Dutton, 1957), 64.

Chapter 4. Chicago's Immigrant Working Class and the Rise of Urban Populism, 1867–73

1. *Illinois Staats-Zeitung*, January 18, 1872.

2. David M. Gordon, Richard Edwards, and Michael Reich, *Segmented Work, Divided Workers: The Historical Transformation of Labor in the United States* (Cambridge: Cambridge University Press, 1982), 77–78, 119–20; Richard Schneirov, "Class

Conflict, Municipal Politics, and Governmental Reform in Gilded Age Chicago, 1871–75," in *German Workers in Industrial Chicago, 1850–1910: A Comparative Perspective*, ed. Hartmut Keil and John B. Jentz (De Kalb: Northern Illinois University Press, 1983), 183–205.

3. Charles W. Calhoun, *Conceiving a New Republic: The Republican Party and the Southern Question, 1869–1900* (Lawrence: University of Kansas Press, 2006), 47–89 (quote in title of chapter).

4. Paul Kleppner, *The Third Electoral System, 1853–1892: Parties, Voters, and Political Cultures* (Chapel Hill: University of North Carolina Press, 1979), 97–142; Joel H. Silbey, *The American Political Nation, 1838–1893* (Stanford, Calif.: Stanford University Press, 1991), 218–36.

5. *Chicago Daily Tribune* (hereafter *Tribune*), December 5, 1869 (quote); Chicago, *Laws and Ordinances Governing the City of Chicago, January 1, 1866* (Chicago: E. B. Myers and Chandler, 1866), http://name.umdl.umich.edu/AEY1821.0001.001 (accessed June 25, 2011), 271–72. On the character of immigration at this time, see Ulf Beijbom, *Swedes in Chicago: A Demographic and Social Study of the 1846–1880 Immigration* (Stockholm: Läromeldelsförlagen, 1971), 6, 68; Kevin Kenny, *The American Irish: A History* (Harlow, England: Longman, 2000), 137–39; John B. Jentz and Hartmut Keil, "From Immigrants to Urban Workers: Chicago's German Poor in the Gilded Age and Progressive Era, 1883–1908," *Vierteljahrschrift für Sozial- und Wirtschaftsgeschichte* 68, no. 1 (1981): 67–73. On the industrial working class and the labor markets, see Ira Katznelson, "Working-Class Formation: Constructing Cases and Comparisons," in *Working-Class Formation: Nineteenth-Century Patterns in Western Europe and the United States*, ed. Ira Katznelson and Aristide R. Zolberg (Princeton, N.J.: Princeton University Press, 1986), 4–5.

6. Stephen Thernstrom, *The Other Bostonians: Poverty and Progress in the American Metropolis, 1880–1970* (Cambridge, Mass.: Harvard University Press, 1973), 9–28.

7. Donald W. Griffin and Richard E. Preston, "A Restatement of the 'Transition Zone' Concept," *Annals of the Association of American Geographers* 56 (June 1966): 339–50; Richard E. Preston, "The Zone in Transition: A Study of Urban Land Use Patterns," *Economic Geography* 42 (July 1966): 236–60; Homer Hoyt, *One Hundred Years of Land Values in Chicago: The Relationship of the Growth of Chicago to the Rise in Its Land Values, 1830–1933* (Chicago: University of Chicago Press, 1933), 102.

8. Michael Kazin, *The Populist Persuasion: An American History* (New York: Basic Books, 1995), 5–6, 13–16; Robin L. Einhorn, *Property Rules: Political Economy in Chicago, 1833–1872* (Chicago: University of Chicago Press, 1991), 249–56.

9. Moving from squatter to home owner is well summarized by Beijbom, *Swedes in Chicago*, 79–81, 99–105.

10. *Workingman's Advocate*, September 14, 1867 (quotes).

11. Ibid.; Hoyt, *One Hundred Years of Land Values in Chicago*, 88; Einhorn, *Property Rules*, 249–52.

12. Einhorn, *Property Rules*, 250; *Workingman's Advocate*, July 30, 1870 (quote);

Tribune, July 19, 1869; Francis Frederick Cook, *Bygone Days in Chicago: Recollections of the "Garden City" of the Sixties* (Chicago: A. C. McClurg, 1910), 173.

13. The statistics were drawn from the 1870 federal manuscript population and manufacturing censuses. On women working in Chicago's large clothing shops, see *Tribune,* February 13, 1870.

14. Cook, *Bygone Days in Chicago,* 134–36; Alice Kessler-Harris, *Out to Work: A History of Wage-Earning Women in the United States* (Oxford: Oxford University Press, 1982), 45–72 (quote 49).

15. *Der Westen,* February 13, 1868; *Tribune,* February 6, November 13, 1870.

16. *Tribune,* February 6 (first quote), March 27, November 13, 1870; *Der Westen,* February 13, 1868; *Chicago Republican* (hereafter *Republican*), September 19, 1865 (second quote); see also *Workingman's Advocate,* August 13, 1870, July 15 1871.

17. Rima Lunin Schultz, "Women's Rights, Market Rules, and Reform Movements in Late-Nineteenth Century Chicago," paper delivered at the annual meeting of the Social Science History Association, November 15–18, 2007, Chicago; Reva B. Siegel, "Home as Work: The First Woman's Rights Claims Concerning Household Labor, 1850–1880," *Yale Law Journal* 103 (March 1993): 1073–1217; Amy Dru Stanley, *From Bondage to Contract: Wage Labor, Marriage, and the Market in the Age of Slave Emancipation* (Cambridge, Mass.: Harvard University Press, 1998), 175–217.

18. Ellen Carol DuBois, *Feminism and Suffrage* (Ithaca, N.Y.: Cornell University Press, 1978), 179–202; Steven M Buechler, *The Transformation of the Woman Suffrage Movement: The Case of Illinois, 1850–1920* (New Brunswick, N.J.: Rutgers University Press, 1986), 56–100; Rima Lunin Schultz, "Kate Newell Doggett," in *Women Building Chicago, 1790–1990: A Biographical Dictionary* (Bloomington: Indiana University Press, 2001), 224–29; Wendy Hamand Venet, *A Strong-Minded Woman: The Life of Mary Livermore* (Amherst, Mass.: University of Massachusetts Press, 2005), 179–80, 196, 203, 225, 248.

19. Marten Shefter, "Trade Unions and Political Machines: The Organization and Disorganization of the American Working Class in the Late Nineteenth Century," in *Working-Class Formation,* ed. Katznelson and Zolberg, 197–208, 240–43, 252–53, 269–73.

20. In 1870, the Irish constituted 37.4 percent of Chicago's laborers, by far the largest national group; the next highest proportion was Germans at 24.3 percent; U.S. Bureau of the Census, *Ninth Census 1870,* vol. 1, *Population* (Washington, DC: GPO, 1873), 782. On the significance of construction for Irish labor and business in the whole country, see David Montgomery, "The Irish and the American Labor Movement," in *America and Ireland, 1776–1976: The American Identity and the Irish Connection,* ed. David Noel Doyle and Owen Dudley Edwards (Westport, Conn.: Greenwood, 1980), 211–12. On union activity in the construction trades, see *Workingman's Advocate,* June 6, 14, July 11, August 1, 1868.

21. John B. Jentz, "Class and Politics in an Emerging Industrial City: Chicago in the 1860s and 1870s," *Journal of Urban History* 17 (May 1991): 227–35; Bruce Laurie, Theodore Hershberg, and George Alter, "Immigrants and Industry: The Phila-

delphia Experience, 1850–1880," in *Philadelphia: Work, Space, Family, and Group Experience in the Nineteenth Century: Essays toward an Interdisciplinary History of the City*, ed. Theodore Hershberg (New York: Oxford University Press, 1981), 109–16; David Montgomery, *Beyond Equality: Labor and the Radical Republicans, 1862–72* (New York: Vintage, 1967), 126–27; Montgomery, "Irish and the American Labor Movement," 205–7, 211, 212, 213; *Workingman's Advocate*, September 12, 1868 (quote).

22. For an introduction to the Allgemeiner Deutscher Arbeiterverein, see Helga Grebing, *Geschichte der deutschen Arbeiterbewegung: Ein Überblick* (Munich: Nymphenburger Verlagshandlung GmbH, 1966), 61–68; *Illinois Staats-Zeitung*, May 22, 27, 1867.

23. *Der Deutsche Arbeiter* (Chicago), June 18, 1870; Thomas Welskopp, *Das Banner der Brüderlichkeit: Die deutsche Sozialdemokratie vom Vormärz bis zum Sozilistengesetz* (Bonn, Germany: Verlag J. H. W. Dietz, 2000), 752–54.

24. John R. Commons et al., *History of Labour in the United States* (New York: Macmillan, 1918), 2:46–48, 223–24; Bruce Levine, *The Spirit of 1848: German Immigrants, Labor Conflict, and the Coming of the Civil War* (Urbana: University of Illinois Press, 1992), 111–45; *Workingman's Advocate*, January 30, June 19, 1869.

25. Grebing, *Geschichte der deutschen Arbeiterbewegung*, 50–61; John B. Jentz, "The 48ers and the Politics of the German Labor Movement in Chicago during the Civil War Era: Community Formation and the Rise of a Labor Press," in *The German-American Radical Press: The Shaping of a Left Political Culture, 1850–1940*, ed. Elliott Shore, Ken Fones-Wolf, and James P. Danky (Urbana: University of Illinois Press, 1992), 49–62; *Illinois Staats-Zeitung*, January 20, 1872.

26. Figures on the proportions of workers in industries employed by Germans are based on an analysis of the owners of businesses listed in the 1870 federal manuscript manufacturing census for Chicago. On ethnic neighborhoods, see Kathleen Neils Conzen, "Immigrants, Immigrant Neighborhoods, and Ethnic Identity: Historical Issues," *Journal of American History* 66 (December 1979): 603–15.

27. Grebing, *Geschichte der deutschen Arbeiterbewegung*, 40–47. On the interethnic reach of the German language, see Hartmut Keil and John B. Jentz, *German Workers in Chicago: A Documentary History of Working-Class Culture from 1850 to World War I* (Urbana: University of Illinois Press, 1988), 42.

28. When using the term *middle class*, we are speaking of governmental employees, such as policemen and inspectors of grain; of small proprietors, such as saloon keepers and grocery store owners; of low-status white-collar employees, such as clerks and teachers; and of skilled workers, some of whom became entrepreneurs, however small. In 1870, 17 percent of employed German males and 10 percent of employed Irish males held such middling types of occupations. In each case, this percentage was a modest increase in proportion of employed males over 1860. These figures are based on samples of the 1860 and 1870 federal manuscript population census for Chicago.

29. Figures based on a sample of the 1870 federal manuscript population census for Chicago.

30. William H. Sylvis, "What Is Money?" in *The Life, Speeches, Labors and Essays of William H. Sylvis,* ed. James C. Sylvis (Philadelphia: Claxton, Remsen Y. Haffelfinger, 1872), 351–86. On Cameron, Sylvis, Campbell, and currency reform, see Richard Schneirov, "Political Cultures and the Role of the State in Labor's Republic: The View from Chicago, 1848–1877," *Labor History* 32 (June 1991): 388–91; James L. Huston, "The American Revolutionaries, the Political Economy of Aristocracy, and the American Concept of the Distribution of Wealth, 1765–1900," *American Historical Review* 98 (October 1993): 1079–94; Montgomery, *Beyond Equality,* 426–34.

31. Earl R. Beckner, *A History of Labor Legislation in Illinois* (Chicago: University of Chicago Press, 1929), 10 (quote). For contrasting views on labor reformers and trade unionists, see Montgomery, *Beyond Equality,* 195–96; Victoria C. Hattam, *Labor Visions and State Power: The Origins of Business Unionism in the United States* (Princeton, N.J.: Princeton University Press, 1993), 112–79. On workers shaping the rules of the market through unionism, see David Montgomery, "Strikes in Nineteenth-Century America," *Social Science History* 4 (February 1980): 89; Richard Schneirov, *Labor and Urban Politics: Class Conflict and the Origins of Modern Liberalism in Chicago, 1864–1897* (Urbana: University of Illinois Press, 1998), 145–49, 187, 205, 298–322; Rosanne Currarino, "The Politics of 'More': The Labor Question and the Idea of Economic Liberty in Industrial America," *Journal of American History* 90 (June 2006): 17–36. On the 1868 platform, see *Workingman's Advocate,* September 19, 1868.

32. *Workingman's Advocate,* September 19, October 31, 1868, August 21, 1869.

33. *Workingman's Advocate,* October 9, 23, 30, 1869.

34. Peter H. Olden, "Anton C. Hesing: The Rise of a Chicago Boss," *Journal of the Illinois State Historical Society* 35 (September 1942): 260–87.

35. *Tribune,* September 6, October 23, 26, 1869; Joseph Logsdon, *Horace White, Nineteenth Century Liberal* (Westport, Conn.: Greenwood, 1971), 175–76.

36. On the politics of municipal reform, see David Montgomery, *Citizen Worker: The Experience of Workers in the United States with Democracy and the Free Market during the Nineteenth Century* (Cambridge: Cambridge University Press, 1993), 1–3, 8, 9, 58–59, 71–72; Schneirov, "Class Conflict, Municipal Politics, and Governmental Reform in Gilded Age Chicago," 192–200; Einhorn, *Property Rules,* 204–15.

37. Gary Lee Cardwell, "The Rise of the Stalwarts and the Transformation of Illinois Republican Politics, 1860–1880" (PhD diss., University of Virginia, 1976), 215–335; Schneirov, *Labor and Urban Politics,* 63; Montgomery, *Beyond Equality,* 356–60; Einhorn, *Property Rules,* 183–85; *Tribune,* September 6, 25, October 24, 26, November 3, 1869.

38. *Workingman's Advocate,* October 30, November 6, December 25, 1869, April 29, 1876.

39. Schneirov, *Labor and Urban Politics,* 38; Alison Clark Efford, "New Citizens: German Immigrants, African Americans, and the Reconstruction of Citizenship, 1865–1877" (unpublished PhD diss., Ohio State University, 2008), 186–88, 201–9, 215–23; *Der Deutsche Arbeiter,* July 16, 23, 1870.

40. Hoyt, *One Hundred Years of Land Values in Chicago*, 97, 101.

41. Schneirov, *Labor and Urban Politics*, 21–22; Harold G. Vatter, *The Drive to Industrial Maturity: The U.S. Economy 1860–1914* (Westport, Conn.: Greenwood Press, 1975), 57; see also Lance E. Davis and Robert E. Gallman, "Capital Formation in the United States during the Nineteenth Century," in *The Cambridge Economic History of Europe*, vol. 7, *The Industrial Economies: Capital, Labour, and Enterprise*, part 2, *The United States, Japan, and Russia*, ed. Peter Mathias and M. M. Postan (Cambridge: Cambridge University Press, 1978), 1–3, 65–69; Robert E. Gallman, "Investment Flows and Capital Stocks: U.S. Experience in the Nineteenth Century," in *Quantity and Quiddity: Essays in U.S. Economic History*, ed. Peter Kilby (Middletown, Conn.: Wesleyan University Press, 1987), 240–45; John A. James and Jonathan S. Skinner, "Sources of Savings in the Nineteenth Century United States," in *Quantity and Quiddity*, ed. Kilby, 255–59, 281–82.

42. Schneirov, *Labor and Urban Politics*, 49–50; Bessie Louise Pierce, *A History of Chicago*, vol. 3, *The Rise of a Modern City 1871–1893* (New York: Alfred A. Knopf, 1957), 7–8. On capital accumulation, see Edward J. Nell, "Accumulation of Capital," in *The New Palgrave: A Dictionary of Economics*, ed. John Eatwell, Murray Milgate, and Peter Newman (London: Macmillan, 1987), 1:14–18; Phillip Anthony O'Hara, "Reproduction Paradigm," in *Encyclopedia of Political Economy*, ed. Phillip Anthony O'Hara (London: Routledge, 1999), 22:977–80.

43. *Tribune*, October 14, 15, 18, 19, 22 (quotes), November 24, 28, 1871.

44. *Tribune*, October 23, 1871 (quote); A. T. Andreas, *History of Chicago: From the Earliest Period to the Present Time*, vol. 3, *From the Fire of 1871 until 1885* (Chicago: A. T. Andreas, 1886), 695. Medill did not obtain a controlling interest in the paper until November 1874.

45. *Tribune*, October, 23, 24, 26, 28, 29, November, 5, 15, 1871; Pierce, *A History of Chicago*, 3:11–15, 340–41; Samuel Sparling, *Municipal History and Present Organization of the City of Chicago* (Madison: Wisconsin Bulletin of the University of Wisconsin, No. 23., 1898), 81–83; Schneirov, "Class Conflict, Municipal Politics, and Governmental Reform in Gilded Age Chicago," 187–88.

46. Christine Meisner Rosen, *The Limits of Power: Great Fires and the Process of City Growth in America* (New York: Cambridge University Press, 1986), 99–100.

47. *Illinois Staats-Zeitung*, January 11, 1872 (quote); Einhorn, *Property Rules*, 238–39.

48. Small property owners on the North Side and the Ogdens submitted petitions to the Common Council against the fire limits. The two petitions are in the Chicago City Council Proceedings Files, Cook County, Illinois Regional Archives Depository System, Northeastern Illinois University, No. 71/72–0181B-02/05. On the composition of the marchers, see Anton Hesing's letter to the *Tribune*, January 18, 1872.

49. *Illinois Staats-Zeitung*, January 15, 1872; for a description of one of the barracks, see *Tribune*, November 14, 1871; Karen Sawislak, *Smoldering City: Chicagoans and the Great Fire, 1871–1874* (Chicago: University of Chicago Press, 1995), 148–51.

50. *Illinois Staats-Zeitung*, January 16, 1872; *Tribune*, January 16, 1872.

51. *Illinois Staats-Zeitung*, January 17, 18, 1872; *Tribune*, January 19 (Robert Collyer's letter), 21 (Anton Hesing's letter; emphases in the original), 1872. For a discussion of this debate, see Sawislak, *Smoldering City*, 154–58.

52. *Illinois Staats-Zeitung*, January 18, 29 (quote), 1872. This interpretation of the fire-limits controversy differs from those of Christine Rosen and Karen Sawislak, who too closely identify the protest with the working class, when it was a cross-class movement among immigrants. Compare Rosen, *The Limits of Power*, 100–2; Karen Sawislak, "Smoldering City," *Chicago History* 17 (Fall and Winter 1988–89): 88–89.

53. *Tribune*, January 21, 30, 1872; Rosen, *The Limits of Power*, 105–7; Hoyt, *One Hundred Years of Land Values in Chicago*, 104–7.

54. Pierce, *A History of Chicago*, 3:6; Sawislak, *Smoldering City*, 85–100; Chicago Relief and Aid Society, *Report of the Chicago Relief and Aid Society of Disbursement of Contributions for the Sufferers by the Chicago Fire* (Riverside, Mass.: Riverside Press, 1974), http://name.umdl.umich.edu/AAZ9846.0001.001 (accessed June 25, 2011), 184 (all quotes), 187–88, 196–202.

55. Ninety percent of the homes built with the support of the Relief and Aid society were constructed by the owners themselves or with their financial backing; Sawislak, *Smoldering City*, 75.

56. *Tribune*, March 18 (first quote), 24 (second quote), May 14, 1872; Sawislak, *Smoldering City*, 84–85. In 1870, the census counted 28,332 hands employed in manufacturing in Cook County, including women; U.S. Bureau of the Census, *Ninth Census of the United States, 1870*, vol. 3, *The Statistics of the Wealth and Industry of the United States* (Washington, DC: GPO, 1873), 649.

57. *Workingman's Advocate*, March 23, 1872 (all quotes).

58. *Tribune*, May 16, 1872; *Illinois Staats-Zeitung*, October 28, 1871 (quote).

59. *Tribune*, May 4, 8, 11, 15, 1872; *Illinois Staats-Zeitung*, May 15, 1872.

60. *Tribune*, May 4, 1872 (quote).

61. Stanley Nadel, "Those Who Would Be Free: The Eight-Hour Strikes of 1872," *Labor's Heritage* 2 (June 1990): 70–77; *Tribune*, May 14, 20 (quote), 1872; Sven Beckert, *The Monied Metropolis: New York City and the Consolidation of the American Bourgeoisie, 1850–1896* (Cambridge: Cambridge University Press, 2001), 192–95.

62. *Tribune*, May 15, 16, 1872; *Illinois Staats-Zeitung*, May 16, 1872.

63. *Tribune*, May 16, 1872 (quote).

64. *Tribune*, May 15, 16, 1872. The Knights of St. Crispin, a national shoemakers union, had founded several strong interethnic Chicago locals in the late 1860s and early 1870s; see *Workingman's Advocate*, February 20, May 1, December 11, 1869, April 9, 1870.

65. *Illinois Staats-Zeitung*, September 21, 24 (quote), 1872.

66. Richard Schneirov and Thomas J. Suhrbur, *Union Brotherhood, Union Town: The History of the Carpenters' Union of Chicago, 1863–1987* (Carbondale: Southern Illinois University Press, 1988), 6 (quote); Thomas J. Suhrbur, "Ethnicity in the

Formation of the Chicago Carpenters Union: 1855–1890," in *German Workers in Industrial Chicago, 1850–1910,* ed. Keil and Jentz, 86–103.

67. *Tribune,* October 14, 1872 (quote). For examples of crimes, see *Tribune,* October 22, 1871; *Illinois Staats-Zeitung,* September 25, October 7, 1872.

68. *Tribune,* September 10, 13 (quote), October 11, November 2, 1872; Sawislak, "Smoldering City," 97–99.

69. *Illinois Staats-Zeitung,* October 4, 1872 (quote). The electorate was about 59 percent foreign-born and 41 percent native-born. These figures were derived from a sample of males with listed occupations in the 1870 manuscript population census for Chicago who were over age twenty-one and either native-born or foreign-born and listed as citizens; n = 1,467.

70. *Illinois Staats-Zeitung,* October 24, 1872 (quote); *Tribune,* October 11, 14, 15, 1872; Andreas, *History of Chicago,* 3:855.

71. *Illinois Staats-Zeitung,* October 28, 29 (quote), 1872; on the Stalwarts, see Montgomery, *Beyond Equality,* 359–60, 371–74, 447.

72. *Illinois Staats-Zeitung,* October 9 (second quote), November 1 (first quote), 1872. The *Illinois Staats-Zeitung* of October 9, 1872, is a long special issue commemorating the first anniversary of the Great Fire. On the rebuilding of the North Side after the fire, see Sawislak, *Smoldering City,* 75; Rosen, *The Limits of Power,* 107–8; Eugen Seeger and Eduard Schläger, *Chicago. Entwickelung, Zerstörung und Wiederaufbau der Wunderstadt* (Chicago: M. Stern, 1872).

73. On politics and the creation of urban space, see Harold L. Platt, *Shock Cities: The Environmental Transformation and Reform of Manchester and Chicago* (Chicago: University of Chicago Press, 2005), 18–23.

74. *Tribune,* April 12, 25, 1873.

75. *Tribune,* April 12, 25, 1873; *Illinois Staats-Zeitung,* May 1, 1873; Pierce, *A History of Chicago,* 3:300–1, 303–4; A. T. Andreas, *History of Chicago: From the Earliest Period to the Present Time,* vol. 2, *From 1857 until the Fire of 1871* (Chicago: A. T. Andreas, 1885), 83–86.

76. Edwin G. Burrows and Mike Wallace, *Gotham: A History of New York City to 1898* (New York: Oxford University Press, 1999), 837–41.

77. Pierce, *A History of Chicago,* 3:303–4; Chicago Common Council, *Proceedings* (1872–73), 81; *Illinois Staats-Zeitung,* May 8, 10, 1873; M. L. Ahern, *The Great Revolution, A History of the Rise and Progress of the People's Party in the City of Chicago and County of Cook, with Sketches of the Elect in Office* (Chicago: Lakeside, 1872), 35–42, 139–44.

78. *Illinois Staats-Zeitung,* January 11, 1872, May 1, 2, 3, 9, 15, 21, 28, 30, 1873; Ahern, *The Great Revolution,* 65–67; Sawislak, *Smoldering City,* 98–101.

79. *Illinois Staats-Zeitung,* May 21, 30, August 29, 1873. On James J. McGrath, see *Tribune,* November 9, 1871; Fremont O. Bennett, *Politics and Politicians of Chicago, Cook County, and Illinois: Memorial Volume, 1787–1887* (Chicago: Blakely, 1886), 571–72.

80. *Illinois Staats-Zeitung,* September 2, 1873; Ahern, *The Great Revolution,* 79–80.

81. *Illinois Staats-Zeitung,* September 6, 13, October 6, 1873; Ahern, *The Great Revolution,* 92–93. On the currency issue, see Irwin Unger, *The Greenback Era: A Social and Political History of American Finance, 1865–1879* (Princeton, N.J.: Princeton University Press, 1964), 13–40; Gretchen Ritter, *Goldbugs and Greenbacks: The Antimonopoly Tradition and the Politics of Finance in America* (Cambridge: Cambridge University Press, 1997), 90–109, 123–35.

82. *Illinois Staats-Zeitung,* October 6, 1873 (first quote); *Tribune,* October 5, 1873 (second quote); Ahern, *The Great Revolution,* 94–99. On tax assessment, see Bennett Stark, "Political Economy of State Public Finance: Illinois, 1830–1970" (PhD diss., University of Wisconsin, Madison, 1982), 75–81, 95, 103, 113.

83. *Illinois Staats-Zeitung,* September 16, October 14, November 5, 1873; *Times,* September 2, October 18, 20, 1873; Ahern, *The Great Revolution,* 108–10; Lloyd Wendt, *Chicago Tribune: The Rise of a Great American Newspaper* (Chicago: Rand McNally, 1979), 243–44.

84. Ahern, *The Great Revolution,* 111–14; Bennett, *Politics and Politicians of Chicago, Cook County, and Illinois,* 155. With the thirteen victorious aldermen from the People's Party, the Common Council was 60 percent foreign-born. Among all of those arrested, the proportion of white native-born Americans increased from 31.9 percent to 41.4 percent; Chicago Board of Police Commissioners, annual reports for the years ending March 31, 1872, and March 31, 1874, Chicago City Council Proceedings Files, Cook County, Illinois Regional Archives Depository System, Northeastern Illinois University.

85. *Illinois Staats-Zeitung,* November 5, 1873 (quote).

86. Robert E. Gallman, "The Agricultural Sector and the Pace of Economic Growth: U.S. Experience in the Nineteenth Century," in *Essays in Nineteenth Century Economic History: The Old Northwest,* ed. David C. Klingaman and Richard K. Vedder (Athens: Ohio University Press, 1975), 37; James L. Huston, *Securing the Fruits of Labor: The American Concept of Wealth Distribution, 1765–1900* (Baton Rouge: Louisiana State University Press, 1998), 126–28; Rosanne Currarino "Meat vs. Rice: The Idea of Manly Labor and Anti-Chinese Hysteria," *Men and Masculinities* 9 (April 2007): 476–90.

Chapter 5. Class and Politics during the Depression of the 1870s

1. *Chicago Daily Tribune* (hereafter *Tribune*), January 1, 1874 (quote).

2. Figures are from the *Tribune's* annual review of the economy, January 1, 1877; Rendig Fels, *American Business Cycles, 1865–1897* (Chapel Hill: University of North Carolina Press, 1959), 98–102.

3. Karl Marx, *Capital,* vol. 1, *A Critical Analysis of Capitalist Production,* ed. Frederick Engels (New York: International Publishers, 1974 [1867]), 612–28. The neoclassical economic historian Jeffrey G. Williamson notes that the capital-labor ratio rose continuously in the late nineteenth century; see Jeffrey G. Williamson, *Late Nineteenth-Century American Development: A General Equilibrium History* (Cambridge: Cambridge University Press, 1974), 73.

4. U.S. House of Representatives, *Investigation by a Select Committee of the House of Representatives Relative to the Causes of the General Depression in Labor and Business; and as to Chinese Immigration,* 46th Cong., 2nd sess. (Washington, DC: GPO, 1879), 9 (Gage quote); Arthur T. Hadley, "Over-Production," in *Cyclopaedia of Political Science, Political Economy, and of the Political History of the United States,* ed. John J. Lalor (Chicago: Rand, McNally, 1884): 3:40–43 (quote on 41). On rigidities in businesses with high fixed costs, see Philip Scranton, *Proprietary Capitalism: The Textile Manufacture at Philadelphia, 1800–1885* (Cambridge: Cambridge University Press, 1983), 17–25.

5. For overviews of business practices and investment in this era, see Fels *American Business Cycles, 1865–1897,* 83–112; Williamson, *Late Nineteenth-Century American Development,* 93–163; Martin J. Sklar, *The Corporate Reconstruction of American Capitalism, 1890–1916: The Market, the Law, and Politics* (Cambridge: Cambridge University Press, 1988), 20–33, 43–47; David M. Gordon, Richard Edwards, and Michael Reich, *Segmented Work, Divided Workers: The Historical Transformations of Labor in the United States* (Cambridge: Cambridge University Press, 1982), 94–99, 101–3; James Livingston, "The Social Analysis of Economic History and Theory: Conjectures on Late-Nineteenth Century American Development," *American Historical Review* 92 (February 1987): 69–95; Rosanne Currarino, *The Labor Question in America: Economic Democracy in the Gilded Age* (Urbana: University of Illinois Press, 2011), 24–28. On Andrew Carnegie, see Alfred Dupont Chandler, *The Visible Hand: The Managerial Revolution in American Business* (Cambridge, Mass.: Belknap Press, 1977), 266–69. On trends in wages, see Lawrence H. Officer, *Two Centuries of Compensation for U.S. Production Workers in Manufacturing* (New York: Palgrave Macmillan, 2009), tables 7.1 and 7.2, 166, 170.

6. Antonio Gramsci, *Selections from the Prison Notebooks of Antonio Gramsci,* ed. and trans. Quintin Hoare and Geoffrey Nowell Smith (New York: International, 1971), 245–47, 252–53, 257–64; Joseph A Buttigeg, "The Contemporary Discourse on Civil Society: A Gramscian Critique," *Boundary* 32 (Spring 2005): 33–52.

7. *Workingman's Advocate,* December 27, 1873–January 3, 1874 (single issue); *Tribune,* December 23, 1873; John B. Jentz, "Artisan Culture and the Organization of Chicago's German Workers in the Gilded Age, 1860 to 1890," *Amerikastudien* 29 (Heft2/1984): 135–38. The two trades assemblies had been defunct since 1870, and the *Lakeside Annual Directory of the City of Chicago: 1874–75* listed only eighteen unions in the city, three of which had more than one lodge.

8. Hermann Schlüter, *Die Internationale in Amerika: Ein Beitrag zur Geschichte der Arbeiter-Bewegung in den Vereinigten Staaten* (Chicago: Deutsche Sprachgruppe der Sozialist. Partei der Ver. Staaten, 1918), 310–12; John R. Commons et al., *A Documentary History of American Industrial Society* (Cleveland: A. H. Clark, 1910–1911), 9:353. On the national origins of the Chicago electorate, see figure 8, chapter 4; the statistics on the electorate were calculated from a sample of citizens with occupations listed in the 1870 manuscript population census, n = 1466.

9. *Tribune,* December 22, 23 (quote), 1873. On the Grangers, see Ernest Ludlow

Bogart and Charles Manfred Thompson, *The Industrial State 1870–1893*, vol. 4, *The Centennial History of Illinois* (Springfield: Illinois Centennial Commission, 1920), 98–100.

10. *Tribune*, December 22, 25, 1873. On New York, see Friedrich A. Sorge, *Friedrich A. Sorge's Labor Movement in the United States: A History of the American Working Class from Colonial Times to 1890*, ed. Philip S. Foner and Brewster Chamberlin (Westport, Conn.: Greenwood, 1977), 152; Edwin G. Burrows and Mike Wallace, *Gotham: A History of New York City to 1898* (New York: Oxford University Press, 1999), 1020–27.

11. *Workingman's Advocate*, December 27, 1873–January 3, 1874 (single issue); *Illinois Staats-Zeitung*, December 23, 1873 (quotes); *Tribune*, December 23, 1873.

12. *Tribune*, December 23, 24, 1873, January 12, 1874; *Illinois Staats-Zeitung*, December 24, 1873, January 13, 1874. Eduard Schläger left the city in 1872 to return to Germany; *Illinois Staats-Zeitung*, January 20, 1872.

13. The other planks called for repeal of the contract system to build public works, speedy and just resolution of suits for the recovery of wages, abolition of prison labor, compulsory education for all children between the ages of seven and fourteen, direct payment of public servants, abolition of compensating public officials through fees, recall of officeholders by voters, and establishment of workingmen's associations; *Tribune*, January 12, 1874; *Illinois Staats-Zeitung*, January 13, 1874.

14. *Illinois Staats-Zeitung*, January 13, 1874.

15. Philip Kinsley, *The Chicago Tribune, Its First Hundred Years* (New York: Alfred A. Knopf, 1943), 2:225; Lloyd Wendt, *The Chicago Tribune: The Rise of a Great American Newspaper* (Chicago: Rand McNally, 1979), 262; Heather Cox Richardson, *The Greatest Nation of the Earth: Republican Economic Policies during the Civil War* (Cambridge, Mass.: Harvard University Press, 1997), 181–82, 202–3; Richard Franklin Bensel, *Yankee Leviathan: The Origins of Central State Authority in America, 1859–1877* (New York: Cambridge University Press, 1990), 150–51, 210–11.

16. Schlüter, *Die Internationale in Amerika*, 318–20 (quote 320); Bogart and Thompson, *The Industrial State 1870–1893*, 4:98–100.

17. *Tribune*, December 29, 1873; Bogart and Thompson, *The Industrial State 1870–1893*, 4:106; Schlüter, *Die International in Amerika*, 318–19.

18. Thomas Welskopp, *Das Banner der Brüderlichkeit: Die deutsche Sozialdemokratie vom Vormärz bis zum Sozialistengesetz* (Bonn; Verlag J. H. Dietz, 2000), 23–24, 48, 742–54; Volker R. Berghahn, *Imperial Germany, 1871–1918: Economy, Society, Culture, and Politics*, rev. and expanded ed. (New York: Berghahn Books, 2005), 27, 314 (table 25).

19. *Illinois Staats-Zeitung*, January 7, 19, 23, 1874; Renate Kiesewetter, "German-American Labor Press: The *Vorbote* and the *Chicagoer Arbeiter-Zeitung*," in *German Workers' Culture in the United States 1850 to 1920*, ed. Hartmut Heil (Washington, DC: Smithsonian Institution Press, 1988), 137–55.

20. *Illinois Staats-Zeitung*, January 8, 12, 1874. For other positions of Gottlieb Kellner, see *Illinois Staats-Zeitung*, December 30, 1873.

21. *Tribune,* March 30, 31, 1874; *Illinois Staats-Zeitung,* March 30, April 1, 9, 1874; Schlüter, *Die Internationale in Amerika,* 320.

22. *Vorbote,* May 23, June 6, 1874; *Tribune,* January 5, 1874; *Prairie Farmer* (Chicago), January 3, 1874 (quote); Schlüter, *Die Internationale in Amerika,* 319. On Grange ideology, see Thomas A. Woods, *Knights of the Plow: Oliver H. Kelley and the Origins of the Grange in Republican Ideology* (Ames: Iowa State University Press, 1991), 3–21, 165–208.

23. On Andrew Cameron's republicanism, see Richard Schneirov, "Political Cultures and the Role of the State in Labor's Republic: The View from Chicago, 1848–1877," *Labor History* 32 (June 1991): 376–400.

24. *Workingman's Advocate,* December 20, 1873.

25. *Workingman's Advocate,* January 24, 1874 (quote); Schneirov, "Political Cultures and the Role of the State in Labor's Republic," 376–400.

26. Jean H. Baker, *Affairs of Party: The Political Culture of Northern Democrats in the Mid-Nineteenth Century* (Ithaca, N.Y.: Cornell University Press, 1983), 143–76; Jean H. Baker, "From Belief into Culture: Republicanism in the Antebellum North," *American Quarterly* 37 (Fall 1985): 532–50; *Workingman's Advocate,* January 8, November 7, 1868, February 11, 1871, July 17, 1875.

27. *Workingman's Advocate,* November 6, 13, 27, 1869, September 27, 1873 (quote).

28. *Workingman's Advocate,* May 2, 16, 1874; *Tribune,* May 18 (first and second quotes), October 27 (third quote), 1874; *Vorbote,* May 23, 1874; Richard Schneirov, "The Knights of Labor in the Chicago Labor Movement and in Municipal Politics, 1877–1887" (unpublished PhD diss., Northern Illinois University, 1984), 60–68, 112–15, 564–75; Bruce C. Nelson, *Beyond the Martyrs: A Social History of Chicago's Anarchists, 1870–1900* (New Brunswick, N.J.: Rutgers University Press, 1988), 27–50.

29. Schlüter, *Die Internationale in Amerika,* 322; *Illinois Staats-Zeitung,* February 19, 1874; *Tribune,* November 5, 6, 1874; A. T. Andreas, *History of Chicago from the Earliest Period to the Present Time,* vol. 3, *From the Fire of 1871 until 1885* (Chicago: A. T. Andreas, 1886), 846.

30. Renate Kiesewetter, "Die Institution der deutsch-amerikanischen Arbeiterpresse in Chicago. Zur Geschichte des Vorboten und der Chicagoer Arbeiterzeitung, 1874–1886" (unpublished master's thesis, America Institute, University of Munich, 1982), 93–99; Schlüter, *Die Internationale in Amerika,* 325.

31. Hartmut Keil, "Immigrant Neighborhoods and American Society: German Immigrants on Chicago's Northwest Side in the Late Nineteenth Century," in *German Workers' Culture in the United States 1850 to 1920,* ed. Keil, 39–53; Kathleen Neils Conzen, "Germans," in *Harvard Encyclopedia of American Ethnic Groups,* ed. Stephan Thernstrom (Cambridge, Mass.: Belknap Press, 1980), 415–17; Kathleen Neils Conzen, *Immigrant Milwaukee, 1836–1860: Accommodation and Community in a Frontier City* (Cambridge, Mass.: Harvard University Press, 1976), 154–91; Stanley Nadel, *Little Germany: Ethnicity, Religion, and Class in New York City, 1845–80* (Urbana: University of Illinois Press, 1990), 104–21.

32. Hartmut Keil and John B. Jentz, eds., *German Workers in Chicago: A Documen-*

tary History of Working-Class Culture from 1850 to World War I (Urbana: University of Illinois Press, 1988), 151–405; Nelson, *Beyond the Martyrs*, 127–52; Kiesewetter, "German-American Labor Press,"137–55; Andrew Cameron as cited in Richard Schneirov, *Labor and Urban Politics: Class Conflict and the Origins of Modern Liberalism in Chicago, 1864–97* (Urbana: University of Illinois Press, 1998), 81.

33. Richard Schneirov, "Class Conflict, Municipal Politics, and Governmental Reform in Gilded Age Chicago, 1871–1875," in *German Workers in Industrial Chicago, 1850–1910: A Comparative Perspective*, ed. Hartmut Keil and John B. Jentz (DeKalb: Northern Illinois University Press, 1983), 198 (quote); Schneirov, *Labor and Urban Politics*, 59.

34. Christine Heiss, "German Radicals in Industrial America: The Lehr- und Wehr-Verein in Gilded Age Chicago," in *German Workers in Industrial Chicago, 1850–1910*, ed. Keil and Jentz, 206–23; Ralf Wagner, "Turner Societies in the Socialist Tradition," in *German Workers' Culture in the United States 1850 to 1920*, ed. Heil, 221–26, 229–34.

35. Welskopp, *Das Banner der Brüderlichkeit*, 23–24, 779–82.

36. Homer Hoyt, *One Hundred Years of Land Values in Chicago* (New York: Arno Press, 1970 [1933]), 117–27.

37. *Tribune*, April 14, 1876 (all quotes); Nancy Cohen, *The Reconstruction of American Liberalism, 1865–1914* (Chapel Hill: University of North Carolina Press, 2002), 121.

38. Carl Smith, *Urban Disorder and the Shape of Belief: The Great Chicago Fire, the Haymarket Bomb, and the Model Town of Pullman* (Chicago: University of Chicago Press, 1995), 49–51.

39. On the class and municipal reform, see Schneirov, "Class Conflict, Municipal Politics, and Governmental Reform in Gilded Age Chicago," 183–205; David Paul Nord, "The Paradox of Municipal Reform in the Late Nineteenth Century," *Wisconsin Magazine of History* 66 (Winter 1982–83): 128; Melvin Holli, *Reform in Detroit: Hazen S. Pingree and Urban Politics* (New York: Oxford University Press, 1969), 171–81. On the relation between a goal integrating elite and the larger class, see E. Digby Baltzell, *Philadelphia Gentlemen: The Making of a National Upper Class* (New York: Free Press, 1966), 36–48 (quote 40); Frederic Cople Jaher, *The Urban Establishment: Upper Strata in Boston, New York, Charleston, Chicago, and Los Angeles* (Urbana: University of Illinois Press, 1982), 2–3, 10; Sven Beckert, *The Monied Metropolis: New York City and the Consolidation of the American Bourgeoisie, 1850–1896* (Cambridge, Mass.: Harvard University Press, 2001), 8–9; Karen Sawislak, *Smoldering City: Chicagoans and the Great Fire, 1871–1874* (Chicago: University of Chicago Press, 1995), 88–93.

40. Buttigeg, "The Contemporary Discourse on Civil Society," 33–52; Nancy Fraser, *Justice Interruptus: Critical Reflections on the "Postsocialist" Condition* (New York: Routledge, 1997), 153.

41. Beckert, *The Monied Metropolis*, 207–10. On Horace White, Joseph Medill, and the *Tribune*, see *Tribune*, November 9, 1874; Kinsley, *The Chicago Tribune, Its*

First Hundred Years, 2:200, 207; Joseph Logsdon, *Horace White, Nineteenth Century Liberal* (Westport, Conn.: Greenwood, 1971), 268–69. On Franklin MacVeagh, see *Dictionary of American Biography,* vol. 11, suppl. 2, ed. Robert Livingston Schuyler and Edward T. James (New York: Charles Scribner's Sons, 1944), 535–36.

42. For examples of the *Tribune's* extended discussion of temperance, see its issues of April 5, December 21, 1874. For Medill's quote on religious affiliations of the electorate, see *Tribune,* June 24, 1877. As editor, Medill actively promoted the revival efforts of Dwight Moody; Kinsley, *The Chicago Tribune, Its First Hundred Years,* 2:224, 228, 230, 241.

43. *Tribune,* January 11 (quote), 25, 1874. Medill signed the articles with an "M."

44. *Tribune,* January 11, 1874 (quote).

45. Nord, "The Paradox of Municipal Reform in the Late Nineteenth Century," 128–30; Robert T. Handy, *A Christian America: Protestant Hopes and Historical Realities,* 2nd ed. (New York: Oxford University Press, 1984), 27–37.

46. Beckert, *The Monied Metropolis,* 210–19; Eric Foner, *Reconstruction: America's Unfinished Revolution, 1863–1877* (New York: Harper and Row, 1988), 488–94; David Montgomery, *Beyond Equality: Labor and the Radical Republicans, 1862–1872* (New York: Alfred A. Knopf, 1967), 379–86; *Tribune,* January 5, 1874 (quotes).

47. Horace White as cited in Logsdon, *Horace White,* 137; John G. Sproat, *The Best Men: Liberal Reformers in the Gilded Age* (New York: Oxford University Press, 1968), 3–110.

48. *Tribune,* December 23, 1873 (first two quotes), January 2, 1874 (third quote).

49. James L. Huston, *Securing the Fruits of Labor: The American Concept of Wealth Distribution 1765–1900* (Baton Rouge: Louisiana State University Press, 1998), 152–83; Montgomery, *Beyond Equality,* 21–25; *Chicago Republican,* May 6, 1867; *Inter Ocean* (Chicago), March 13, April 9, 1874.

50. *Tribune,* January 2, 1874 (quote).

51. Logsdon, *Horace White,* 262–67; Bogart and Thompson, *The Industrial State 1870–1893,* 4:84–85, 109; letter of Horace White to Hermann Raster, March 31, 1874, Raster papers, The Newberry Library; *Tribune,* April 9, 1874; Heather Cox Richardson, *West from Appomattox: The Reconstruction of America after the Civil War* (New Haven, Conn.: Yale University Press, 2007), 162–64, 171.

52. *Tribune,* April 18, 25, 1874 (all quotes); Logsdon, *Horace White,* 269–70. For the national context, see Michael Les Benedict, "Reform Republicans and the Retreat from Reconstruction," in *The Facts of Reconstruction: Essays in Honor of John Hope Franklin,* ed. Eric Anderson and Alfred A. Moss Jr. (Baton Rouge: Louisiana State University Press, 1991), 53–78; Richardson, *West from Appomattox,* 148–86.

53. *Tribune,* March 24, 1874; on Franklin MacVeagh, see Schneirov, "Class Conflict, Municipal Politics, and Governmental Reform in Gilded Age Chicago," 194–96.

54. *Tribune,* July 15 (first and second quotes), August 1 (third quote), 1874. On New York's elite 7th Regiment, see Beckert, *The Monied Metropolis,* 118, 233–34.

55. *Tribune,* July 16, 1874 (quote). On this periodization of capital flows between the East and the Midwest, see Williamson, *Late Nineteenth-Century American De-*

velopment, 132–33; Richard Franklin Bensel, *The Political Economy of American Industrialization, 1877–1900* (Cambridge: Cambridge University Press, 2000), 48–49. In Bensel's table 2.6, we interpret the relatively high interest rate in Cook County compared to Philadelphia, or to counties in Connecticut, as an indication of Chicago's continuing need for outside capital in 1890.

56. *Commercial Chronicle and Hunt's Merchants' Magazine* (New York), July 18, 1874; *New York Times,* July 26, 1874; Franklin MacVeagh, "To Extend the Fire Limits" (first quote), MacVeagh Papers, Library of Congress, container 44; *Tribune,* July 16 (second quote), 22, October 2, 1874. On the July fire, see Schneirov, *Labor and Urban Politics,* 56–58.

57. *Tribune,* July 18, 19, 21, 23, 28, 1874.

58. *Tribune,* July 18, 21, 27, August 17, 1874; Schneirov, *Labor and Urban Politics,* 57.

59. *Tribune,* July 26, 1874; Schneirov, *Labor and Urban Politics,* 56.

60. *Tribune,* July 28, August 1, 1874; Citizens' Association, *First Annual Report,* 6–7 (quotes), 11.

61. *Tribune,* July 28, 1874; Stephen Skowronek, *Building a New American State: The Expansion of National Administrative Capacities 1877–1920* (Cambridge: Cambridge University Press, 1982), 8–14, 42–45; Schneirov, "Class Conflict, Municipal Politics, and Governmental Reform in Gilded Age Chicago," 195 (quote). On Mugwumps and reform politics, see Robert H. Wiebe, *Businessmen and Reform: A Study of the Progressive Movement* (Cambridge, Mass.: Harvard University Press, 1962), 16–41; Geoffrey Blodgett, "The Mugwump Reputation, 1870 to the Present," *Journal of American History* 66 (March 1980): 867–87; Holli, *Reform in Detroit,* 157–81; Michael McGerr, *The Decline of Popular Politics: The American North, 1865–1928* (New York: Oxford University Press, 1986), 69–106; Michael McGerr, *A Fierce Discontent: The Rise and Fall of the Progressive Movement in America, 1870–1920* (New York: Free Press, 2003), 77–117.

62. *Times* as cited in Bessie Louise Pierce, *A History of Chicago,* vol. 3, *The Rise of the Modern City, 1871–1893* (New York: Alfred A. Knopf, 1957), 430.

63. David Swing, "A Plea for the Better Classes," in *Truths for To-Day: Second Series,* vol. 2, ed. David Swing (Chicago: Jansen, McClurg, 1876), 2:141–58 (quotes 144, 146, 156–58). The sermons in this volume were probably from 1875 or 1876. On doctrines judged by experience, see his "Christianity and Dogma," in *Truths for To-Day: Second Series,* vol. 1, ed. David Swing (Chicago: Jansen, McClurg, 1874), 69–83, especially 80. On other religions, see David Swing, "Our New Era," in *David Swing: A Memorial Volume: Ten Sermons, Selected and Prepared for Publication by Himself,* ed. David Swing (Chicago: F. Tennyson Neely, 1894), 214.

64. MacVeagh, "To Extend the Fire Limits," MacVeagh papers, Library of Congress, container 44. On the public interest and class interests, see Robin L. Einhorn, *Property Rules: Political Economy in Chicago, 1833–1872* (Chicago: University of Chicago Press, 1991), 188–244; Sawislak, *Smoldering City,* 261–64; Smith, *Urban Disorder and the Shape of Belief,* 70–73.

65. Citizens' Association, *First Annual Report,* 4 (first quote); Citizens' Associa-

tion, *Annual Report of the President (1875)*, 20 (second quote). This report is incorrectly labeled "1876."

66. *Tribune*, July 18, 24, 28, 29, August 6, September 8, 26, 1874; MacVeagh, "To Extend the Fire Limits," MacVeagh papers, Library of Congress, container 44.

67. *Tribune*, July 23, October 3, 6, 11, 23, 25, 30, 1874; Schneirov, "Class Conflict, Municipal Politics, and Governmental Reform in Gilded Age Chicago," 196–97.

68. *Tribune*, September 29, 1874.

69. Citizens' Association, Executive Committee, *Report for 1876*, 34; *Tribune*, November 4, 1874; Schneirov, "Class Conflict, Municipal Politics, and Governmental Reform in Gilded Age Chicago," 184–87; Samuel P. Hays, "The Politics of Reform in Municipal Government in the Progressive Era," *Pacific Northwest Quarterly* 55 (October 1964): 157–69; James Weinstein, *The Corporate Ideal in the Liberal State, 1900–1918* (Boston: Beacon Press, 1968), 92–116.

70. *Tribune*, September 1, November 4, 1874; Wendt, *The Chicago Tribune*, 250; Isaac E. Adams, *Life of Emery A. Storrs: His Wit and Eloquence, as Shown in a Notable Literary, Political and Forensic Career* (Chicago: G. L. Howe, 1886), 319–20.

71. Foner, *Reconstruction*, 517–35; Michael Perman, *The Road to Redemption: Southern Politics, 1869–1879* (Chapel Hill: University of North Carolina Press, 1984), 213–20; *Tribune*, November 4, 1874; Adams, *Life of Emery A. Storrs*, 319–20; Kinsley, *The Chicago Tribune, Its First Hundred Years*, 2:200, 207; Logsdon, *Horace White*, 268–29.

72. Paul Kleppner, *The Third Electoral System, 1853–1892: Parties, Voters, and Political Cultures* (Chapel Hill: University of North Carolina Press, 1979), 32–40, 121–42 (quote in title of chap. 4); *Tribune*, October 20, November 5, 1874.

73. *Tribune*, February 9, 1874 (quote); Schneirov, *Labor and Urban Politics*, 62. Prominent tax evaders are listed in the *Tribune*, July 26, 1876.

74. Bennett S. Stark, "The Political Economy of State Public Finance: A Model of the Determinants of Revenue Policy: The Illinois Case 1850–1970" (unpublished PhD diss., University of Wisconsin, Madison, 1982), 75–81, 95, 103, 113; Schneirov, *Labor and Urban Politics*, 61.

75. *Tribune*, November 2, 1874.

76. *Tribune*, October 17, 27, November 2, 1874.

77. Pierce, *A History of Chicago*, 3:344–45.

78. *Tribune*, March 11, 1876; quote from a handwritten "sequel" to Thomas Hoyne's inaugural address on July 9, 1875, delivered to the newly formed Jefferson Club, a Democratic reform group, in the "Thomas Hoyne Scrapbook, 1873–1882," Chicago Historical Society.

79. Darrel M. Robertson, *The Chicago Revival, 1876: Society and Revivalism in a Nineteenth-Century City* (Metuchen, N.J.: Scarecrow Press, 1989), 33–34; Pierce, *A History of Chicago*, 3:348–49.

80. *Tribune*, October 29, 1875; Schneirov, *Labor and Urban Politics*, 61.

81. Schneirov, *Labor and Urban Politics*, 61; Pierce, *A History of Chicago*, 3:345–46, 351, 539; Robertson, *The Chicago Revival, 1876*, 34–35, 37–38, 40.

82. Edwin G. Burrows and Mike Wallace, *Gotham: A History of New York City to 1898* (New York: Oxford University Press, 1999), 1008–12 (quote 1010).

83. *Inter Ocean,* July 25, 1876 (quote).

84. *Inter Ocean,* September 19, November 2, 1876 (quote).

85. Robertson, *The Chicago Revival, 1876,* 1, 20–42, 47–50. On the support of businessmen for Dwight Moody's revivalism, see Charles E. Hambrick-Stowe, "'Sanctified Business': Historical Perspectives on Financing Revivals of Religion," in *More Money, More Ministry: Money and Evangelicals in Recent North American History,* ed. Larry Eskridge and Mark A. Noll (Grand Rapids, Mich.: Eerdmans, 2000), 89–93; Marion L. Bell, *Crusade in the City: Revivalism in Nineteenth-Century Philadelphia* (Lewisburg, Penn.: Ducknell University Press, 1977), 211–13, 237–42.

86. Robertson, *The Chicago Revival, 1876,* 86–109, 116–23, 139–41.

87. Ibid., 158 (quote). On the class and ethnic dimensions of Protestantism in this era, see Bell, *Crusade in the City,* 19–20, 230–43, 246–50; Martin E. Marty, *Righteous Empire: The Protestant Experience in America* (New York: Dial Press, 1970), 101–10.

88. We think that the theory of hegemony is a more accurate model for the process of rule than that of social control, which tends to make those being controlled into passive objects. Hegemony allows those ruled to be active subjects in a larger political process that involves negotiation and compromise; for the social control approach, see Sawislak, *Smoldering City,* 80–106; Smith, *Urban Disorder and the Shape of Belief,* 64–87. Antonio Gramsci understood that with the advent of capitalism and modern civil society in the last third of the nineteenth century, state coercion and direct class domination played a declining part in achieving class rule; the result was a transition from what he called "war of maneuver," in which the state was to be taken by storm (insurrection), to a "war of position," in which workers and their representatives struggle to achieve power and inclusion through conflicts and accommodations within the institutions of civil society; Gramsci, *Selections from the Prison Notebooks of Antonio Gramsci,* 228–43.

Chapter 6. Combat in the Streets

1. George A. Schilling, "A History of the Labor Movement in Chicago," in *Life of Albert R. Parsons with Brief History of the Labor Movement in America, Also Sketches of the Lives of A. Spies, Geo. Engel, A. Fischer and Louis Lingg,* ed. Lucy E. Parsons (Chicago: Lucy E. Parsons, 1903), xxv; *New York Times,* July 27, 1877, as cited in Robert V. Bruce, *1877: Year of Violence* (Indianapolis: Bobbs-Merrill, 1959), 301.

2. Martin Shefter, "Regional Receptivity to Reform: The Legacy of the Progressive Era," *Political Science Quarterly* 98 (Autumn 1983): 459–83; Philip S. Foner, *The Great Labor Uprising of 1877* (New York: Monad Press, 1977), 12–32, 116–19; Albert Bernhardt Faust, *The German Element in the United States* (New York: Steuben Society of America, 1927), 1:580, 587–89. In 1876, Hesing had been convicted in the Whiskey Scandals and spent a short time in prison. He never regained his

former political power. Dan O'Hara died in the fall of 1877, while Mark Sheridan, a well-established Irish politician friendly to labor, had died early in the same year; *Chicago Daily Tribune* (hereafter *Tribune*), January 9, October 13, 1877.

3. Quote of John McAuliffe in *Inter Ocean* (Chicago), July 25, 1879.

4. *Tribune,* July 1, 1877 (quote).

5. Bruce, *1877: Year of Violence,* 33–42; Foner, *The Great Labor Uprising of 1877,* prologue.

6. Conrad Conzett, "Unsere Partei und die Gewerkschaften," *Vorbote,* March 31, 1877; Hartmut Keil, "German Working-Class Immigration and the Social Democratic Tradition of Germany," in *German Workers' Culture in the United States 1850 to 1920,* Hartmut Keil (Washington, DC: Smithsonian Institution Press, 1988), 13; Renate Kiesewetter, "German-American Labor Press: The *Vorbote* and the *Chicagoer Arbeiter-Zeitung,*" in *German Workers' Culture in the United States 1850 to 1920,* ed. Keil, 140–41.

7. Foner, *The Great Labor Uprising of 1877,* 106–14; Schilling, "A History of the Labor Movement in Chicago," xxii; *Vorbote,* March 31, 1877.

8. *Vorbote,* July 23, 1877 (first quote); *Tribune,* July 22, 1877 (second quote).

9. *Tribune,* July 24, 1874.

10. *Tribune,* July 24, 1877 (quote); Lorien Foote, *The Gentlemen and the Roughs: Manhood, Honor, and Violence in the Union Army* (New York: New York University Press, 2010), 174–78.

11. *Tribune,* July 24, 1877 (quote); *Illinois Staats-Zeitung,* July 24, 1877, has the German version of the circular. *Vorbote,* March 24, 1877, railed against efforts to restrict universal suffrage; see also Sven Beckert, *The Monied Metropolis: New York City and the Consolidation of the American Bourgeoisie, 1850–1896* (Cambridge: Cambridge University Press, 2001), 218–24.

12. John J. Flinn, *History of the Chicago Police from the Settlement of the Community to the Present Time* (Chicago: Police Book Fund, 1887), 162. There were widely varying estimates of the crowd: *Tribune,* July 24, 1877, mentioned six thousand; *Illinois Staats-Zeitung,* July 24, 1877, estimated six thousand to eight thousand; *Inter Ocean,* July 24, 1877, claimed thirty thousand; Schilling, "A History of the Labor Movement in Chicago," xxvi, claimed forty thousand.

13. *Illinois Staats-Zeitung,* July 24, 1877 (first quote); *Inter Ocean,* July 26, 1877 (Parsons quote); see also Foner, *The Great Labor Uprising of 1877,* 143–44.

14. *Illinois Staats-Zeitung,* July 24, 1877; *Tribune,* July 24, 1877 (quote).

15. Unless otherwise noted, the descriptions of the crowd on this day are composites based on the July 25, 1877, editions of the *Tribune, Inter Ocean, Chicago Times, Chicago Evening Journal,* and *Illinois Staats-Zeitung;* see also Bessie Louise Pierce, *A History of Chicago,* vol. 3, *The Rise of a Modern City, 1871–1893* (New York: Alfred A. Knopf, 1957), 248.

16. Richard Schneirov, *Labor and Urban Politics: Class Conflict and the Origins of Modern Liberalism in Chicago, 1864–1897* (Urbana: University of Illinois Press, 1998), 32–33, 38–39; Richard Schneirov and Thomas J. Suhrbur, *Union Brother-*

hood, *Union Town: The History of the Carpenters' Union of Chicago, 1863–1987* (Carbondale: Southern Illinois University Press, 1988), 9–10, 13–14, 15, 16, 17.

17. Foner, *The Great Labor Uprising of 1877,* 157–87.

18. *Tribune,* July 25, 1877.

19. *Tribune,* July 25, 1877 (first quote); *Chicago Times* (hereafter *Times*), July 25, 1877 (second quote).

20. *Tribune,* July 25, 1877; Albert Parsons, "Autobiography of Albert Parsons," in *Life of Albert R. Parsons,* ed. Parsons, 18–19 (quote).

21. *Illinois Staats-Zeitung,* July 25, 1877.

22. *Illinois Staats-Zeitung,* July 26, 1877.

23. *Tribune,* July 26, 1877 (quote).

24. *Tribune,* July 23, 25, 26, 27, 1877.

25. *Tribune,* July 26, 1877.

26. *Illinois Staats-Zeitung,* July 26, 1877; *Tribune,* July 26, 1877.

27. *Illinois Staats-Zeitung,* July 27, 1877, reported that three wards with substantial German populations, the Fifteenth, Sixteenth, and Eighteenth, had formed patrols as well.

28. *Times,* July 26, 1877.

29. Unless otherwise noted, the descriptions of the crowd on this day are composites based on the July 27, 1877, editions of the *Tribune, Inter Ocean, Times, Chicago Evening Journal,* and *Illinois Staats-Zeitung;* the quotations are from that issue of the *Illinois Staats-Zeitung.*

30. *Times,* July 27, 1877.

31. Federal manuscript population census schedules, Chicago, Sixth Ward, Roll 89.

32. Of the eighty-eight casualties reported in the press, 45 percent were boys age nineteen and under. Virtually all those whose addresses were listed lived in the Fifth, Sixth, and Seventh wards. The letter from J. Oliverius, editor of the Bohemian newspaper *Vestnck,* was published in *Inter Ocean,* July 28, 1877; see also Richard Schneirov, "Free Thought and Socialism in the Czech Community in Chicago, 1875–1887," in *"Struggle a Hard Battle": Essays on Working-Class Immigrants,* ed. Dirk Hoerder (De Kalb: Northern Illinois University Press, 1986), 121–42.

33. *Tribune,* Feb. 14, 1875 (quote); Schneirov, *Labor and Urban Politics,* 99–118.

34. *Tribune,* July 27, 29, 1877.

35. *Tribune,* July 27, 29, 1877; *Times,* July 27, 1877.

36. *Vorbote,* August 4, 11, 1877; *Illinois Staats-Zeitung,* July 27, 1877 (quote), April 25, 26, 1879; *Tribune,* July 27, 29, 1877; *Inter Ocean,* May 6, 1879; John Peter Altgeld, "Reasons for Pardoning Fielden, Neebe, and Schwab, the So-Called Anarchists," in *The Mind and Spirit of John Peter Altgeld, Selected Writings and Addresses,* ed. Henry M. Christman (Urbana: University of Illinois Press, 1965), 58–59.

37. A figure of twenty-eight deaths was compiled from lists in the *Tribune, Times,* and *Inter Ocean;* John J. Flinn, *History of the Chicago Police,* 199, listed thirty-five dead; the figure of two hundred wounded is from Howard Myers, "The Policing

of Labor Disputes in Chicago: A Case Study" (PhD diss., University of Chicago, 1929), 117–18.

38. *Tribune,* July 27 (first quote), 29 (second quote), 1877; Charles Loring Brace, *The Dangerous Classes of New York and Twenty Years' Work among Them* (New York: Wynkoop and Hallenbeck, 1872); Beckert, *Monied Metropolis,* 183–92, 211–36; Larry Isaac, "To Counter 'The Very Devil' and More: The Making of Independent Capitalist Militia in the Gilded Age," *American Journal of Sociology* 108 (September 2002): 364–68.

39. Charter of the Commercial Club as cited in Stanley Buder, *Pullman: An Experiment in Industrial Order and Community Planning 1880–1930* (New York: Oxford University Press, 1967), 32; Pierce, *A History of Chicago,* 3:483–86 (second and third quotes 485); Helen Lefkowitz Horowitz, *Culture and the City: Cultural Philanthropy in Chicago from the 1880s to 1917* (Lexington: University of Kentucky Press, 1976), x, 27–125; Sven Beckert, "Propertied of a Different Kind: Bourgeoisie and Lower Middle Class in the Nineteenth-Century United States," in *The Middling Sorts: Explorations in the History of the American Middle Class,* ed. Burton J. Bledstein and Robert D. Johnston (New York: Routledge, 2001), 290–91 (quote 290); see also Edward Chase Kirkland, *Dream and Thought in the Business Community, 1860–1900* (Ithaca, N.Y.: Cornell University Press, 1956), 29–49; Isaac, "To Counter 'The Very Devil' and More," 370–73; Stephen Skowronek, *Building a New American State: The Expansion of National Administrative Capacities, 1877–1920* (Cambridge: Cambridge University Press, 1982), 10–14, 42–45.

40. Skowronek, *Building a New American State,* 3–18; Max Weber, "Politics as a Vocation," in *From Max Weber: Essays in Sociology,* trans. and ed. H. H. Gerth and C. Wright Mills (New York: Oxford University Press, 1958), 82–83, 107–11. On the militia and Fort Sheridan, see Schneirov, "Class Conflict, Municipal Politics, and Governmental Reform in Gilded Age Chicago, 1871–1875," 196–98; Nina B. Smith, "'This Bleak Situation': The Founding of Fort Sheridan, Illinois," *Illinois Historical Journal* 80 (Spring 1987): 13–14; Beckert, "Properties of a Different Kind," 292.

41. Bruce, *1877: Year of Violence,* 314–15; Kirkland, *Dream and Thought in the Business Community, 1860–1900,* 56–72, 101–13; Edward C. Kirkland, *Industry Comes of Age: Business, Labor, and Public Policy 1860–1897* (Chicago: Quadrangle Books, 1967 [1961]), 338–41; Pierce, *A History of Chicago,* 3:459–60, note 76.

42. Buder, *Pullman,* 28–37; Carl Smith, *Urban Disorder and the Shape of Belief: The Great Chicago Fire, the Haymarket Bomb and the Model Town of Pullman* (Chicago: University of Chicago Press, 1995), 209–31.

43. William T. Hutchinson, *Cyrus Hall McCormick,* vol. 2, *Harvest, 1856–1884* (New York: D. Appleton-Century, 1935), 617; *Inter Ocean,* October 19, 1877 (first quote), June 1, 1878 (second quote).

44. *Inter Ocean,* March 27, 1878 (quote).

45. *Inter Ocean,* March 28, April 24, May 16, 1878; Robert H. Whitten, "The Assessment of Taxes in Chicago," *Journal of Political Economy* 5 (March 1897): 175–82.

46. *Illinois Staats-Zeitung,* July 25, 1877 (quote).

47. Adolf Douai, "Was der grosse Strike lehrt," *Vorbote*, August 4, 1877; *Iron Age* and president of the Burlington Railroad as cited in Bruce, *1877: Year of Violence*, 302; David L. Lightner, *Labor on the Illinois Central Railroad 1852–1900: The Evolution of an Industrial Environment* (New York: Arno Press, 1977), 204.

48. Joseph A. Buttigieg, "The Contemporary Discourse on Civil Society: A Gramscian Critique," *boundary 2* 32 (Spring 2005): 37–39, 43–44; Christine Buci-Glucksmann, "Hegemony and Consent: A Political Strategy," in *Approaches to Gramsci*, ed. Anne Showstack Sassoon (London: Writers and Readers Publishing Cooperative Society, 1982), 118–22.

49. *Workingman's Advocate*, October 13, 1877.

50. Barrington Moore Jr., *Social Origins of Dictatorship and Democracy: Lord and Peasant in the Making of the Modern World* (Boston: Beacon Press, 1966), 152–55; Eric Hobsbawm, *The Age of Capital: 1848–1875* (New York: Vintage Books, 1996 [1975]), 9–26, 98–115, 155–69; Bruce Levine, *The Spirit of 1848: German Immigrants, Labor Conflict, and the Coming of the Civil War* (Urbana: University of Illinois Press, 1992), 15–50.

51. Richard Schneirov, "The Knights of Labor in the Chicago Labor Movement and in Municipal Politics, 1877–1887" (unpublished PhD diss., Northern Illinois University, 1984), 80–98 (quote 87).

52. *Irish World and American Industrial Liberator*, October 4, 1879; *Progressive Age*, October 18, 1879, January 3, 1880, November 12, 1881 (quote); Schneirov, *Labor and Urban Politics*, 106–13.

53. *Inter Ocean*, August 27, 1877 (quote); Levine, *The Spirit of 1848*, 5–8; John B. Jentz and Richard Schneirov, "Chicago's Fenian Fair of 1864: A Window into the Civil War as a Popular Political Awakening," *Labor's Heritage* 6 (Winter 1995): 4–19; Schneirov, *Labor and Urban Politics*, 119–38.

54. The following analysis of Adolf Douai's position is based on his article "Was der grosse Strike lehrt," *Vorbote*, August 4, 11, 1877. This four-part article appeared in two issues. For more on Douai, see Justine Davis Randers-Pehrson, *Adolf Douai, 1819–1888: The Turbulent Life of a German Forty-Eighter in the Homeland and in the United States* (New York: Peter Lang, 2000).

55. *Vorbote*, August 11, 1877 (quote).

56. Stuart Bruce Kaufman, *Samuel Gompers and the Origins of the American Federation of Labor 1848–1896* (Westport, Conn.: Greenwood Press, 1973), 73–76, 81–100.

57. Paul Avrich, *The Haymarket Tragedy* (Princeton, N.J.: Princeton University Press, 1984), 79–176; James Green, *Death in the Haymarket: A Story of Chicago, the First Labor Movement and the Bombing That Divided Gilded Age America* (New York: Pantheon Books, 2006), 128–32, 156–58, 163; Kaufman, *Samuel Gompers*, 79–100.

58. For the spring platform, see *Vorbote*, March 24, 1877. The platform of the national party appears in German in *Vorbote*, September 1, 1877, and in English in Kaufman, *Samuel Gompers*, 64–65. The Chicago left advocated as well the payment

of wages in legal tender within a week, abolition of the "tramp law" allowing arrest for vagrancy, the replacement of all private banks by a national one, the election of all public officials, and an income tax to replace all indirect ones.

59. Vote percentages calculated using the election returns in the *Illinois Staats-Zeitung*, November 7, 1877.

60. The seven wards were Fifth, Sixth, Seventh, Eighth, Fourteenth, Fifteenth, and Sixteenth. These same seven wards contributed 28 percent of the total vote for the winning Republican candidate for county clerk and 48 percent of the vote for the Democratic candidate; *Illinois Staats-Zeitung*, November 7, 1877.

61. Schneirov, *Labor and Urban Politics*, 81–84; Schneirov, "The Knights of Labor in the Chicago Labor Movement and in Municipal Politics, 1877–1887," 99–103; *Tribune*, November 24 (quote), December 2, 1877.

62. *Illinois Staats-Zeitung*, November 12, 1877; *Vorbote*, November 17, 1877; *Tribune*, February 16, March 2, 11, June 17, 1878; Kaufman, *Samuel Gompers*, 88–89.

63. *Tribune*, November 19, December 2, 1877; Schneirov, *Labor and Urban Politics*, 81–88; Schneirov, "The Knights of Labor in the Chicago Labor Movement and in Municipal Politics, 1877–1887," 109–12; Kaufman, *Samuel Gompers*, 89–90; Nelson, *Beyond the Martyrs*, 55–66.

64. *Inter Ocean*, December 29, 1879; Schneirov, *Labor and Urban Politics*, 119–38.

Chapter 7. Regime Change

1. Bessie Louise Pierce, *A History of Chicago*, vol. 3, *The Rise of a Modern City 1871–1893* (New York: Alfred A. Knopf, 1957), 61, 355–56.

2. Hartmut Keil, "The German Immigrant Working Class of Chicago, 1875–90: Workers, Labor Leaders, and the Labor Movement," in *American Labor and Immigration History, 1877–1920s: Recent European Research,* ed. Dirk Hoerder (Urbana: University of Illinois Press, 1983), 165–70.

3. *Illinois Staats-Zeitung*, March 4, 1878 (quotes); Beate Hinrichs, *Deutschamerikanische Presse zwischen Tradition und Anpassung: Die Illinois Staatszeitung und Chicagoer Arbeiterzeitung 1879–1890* (Frankfurt am Main: Peter Lang, 1989), 76–77.

4. On the SLP platform, see *Vorbote* (Chicago), March 23, 1878; *Chicago Daily Tribune* (hereafter *Tribune*), March 11, 1878. James McGrath had helped Anton Hesing spread the movement against the fire limits to the Northwest Side. For biographical information on Frank Stauber, see *Illinois Staats-Zeitung*, April 4, 1878.

5. Ralph William Scharnau, "Thomas J. Morgan and the Chicago Socialist Movement, 1876–1901" (PhD diss., Northern Illinois University, 1970), 46–47; *Chicago Times* (hereafter *Times*), August 5, 1878 (quote); *Tribune,* August 5, 1878; *Inter Ocean* (Chicago), August 5, 1878.

6. *Times,* June 24, 1878; *Tribune,* June 30, July 1, 1878.

7. *Tribune,* June 30 (first quote), July 1 (second and third quotes), July 4, 1878; *Inter Ocean,* July 4, 1878 (fourth quote).

8. *Vorbote,* March 23, October 19, November 16 (quote), 1878; *Times,* November 6, 7, 1878.

9. *Vorbote,* March 8, 15, 1879; Illinois General Assembly, House of Representatives, *Report of Special Committee on Labor,* 31st General Assembly, 1879, 4; U.S. Congress, House Select Committee on Depression in Labor and Business, *Causes of General Depression in Labor and Business. Chinese Immigration,* 46th Cong., 2nd sess., H. Misc. Doc., 1879, 46-5.

10. Illinois General Assembly, House of Representatives, *Report of Special Committee on Labor;* Scharnau, "Thomas J. Morgan and the Chicago Socialist Movement, 1876–1901," 55–58; William Godwin Moody et al., *Our Labor Difficulties: The Cause, and the Way Out; Including the Paper on the Displacement of Labor by Improvements in Machinery, by a Committee Appointed by the American Social Science Association, Composed of Lorin Blodget, Rev. Edward E. Hale, W. Godwin Moody [and others] . . . Read Before the Association at Their Annual Meeting in Cincinnati, May 24, 1878* (Boston: A. William, 1878), 4–5, 8–11; Mary O. Furner, "The Republican Tradition and the New Liberalism: Social Investigation, State Building, and Social Learning in the Gilded Age," in *The State and Social Investigation in Britain and the United States,* ed. Michael J. Lacey and Mary O. Furner (New York: Woodrow Wilson Center Press and the Press Syndicate of the University of Cambridge, 1993), 198–205.

11. *Times,* March 19, 1879 (all quotes).

12. Ibid. (all quotes)

13. Ibid. (all quotes); Max Weber, "Politics as a Vocation," in *From Max Weber: Essays in Sociology,* ed. H. H. Gerth and C. Wright Mills (New York: Oxford University Press, 1958), 82–83.

14. Dr. Ernst Schmidt as cited in Frederick R. Schmidt and Richard E. Schmidt, *He Chose; the Other was a Treadmill Thing* (Santa Fe, N.M.: Frederick R. Schmidt, 1968), 122–23 (quote); *Times,* March 20, 27, 1879; Axel W.-O. Schmidt, *Der rothe Doktor von Chicago—ein deutsch-amerikanisches Auswandererschicksal: Biographie des Dr. Ernst Schmidt 1830–1900, Arzt und Soziularovolutionär* (Frankfurt am Main: Peter Lang, 2003), 131–32, 326–27.

15. Richard Schneirov, *Labor and Urban Politics: Class Conflict and the Origins of Modern Liberalism in Chicago, 1864–97* (Urbana: University of Illinois Press, 1998), 87–88; Bruce C. Nelson, *Beyond the Martyrs: A Social History of Chicago's Anarchists, 1870–1900* (New Brunswick, N.J.: Rutgers University Press, 1988).

16. *Illinois Staats-Zeitung,* February 6, 13, 1879; Socialist platform in the *Vorbote,* March 22, 1879, as reproduced in Schmidt, *Der rothe Doktor von Chicago,* 297–98.

17. Socialist platform in the *Vorbote,* March 22, 1879, as reproduced in Schmidt, *Der rothe Doktor von Chicago,* 297–98.

18. *Tribune,* February 16, March 12, 16 (quote), 23, 1879.

19. *Times,* December 3, 1877; *Tribune,* November 24, December 2, 1877; *Illinois Staats-Zeitung,* April 3, 1879. On divisions among Democrats over the organizational plan, see *Times,* January 17, 1878. On Tammany Hall as a model for Chicago, see

Inter Ocean, January 4, February 21, 1878. For an earlier analogous restructuring plan, see *Inter Ocean,* March 8, 1877. On the Tammany Hall reforms, see Martin Shefter, "The Emergence of the Political Machine: An Alternative View," in *Theoretical Perspectives on Urban Politics,* ed., Willis D. Hawley (Englewood Cliffs, N.J.: Prentice-Hall, 1976), 25–26.

20. *Times,* March 16, 1879; Shefter, "The Emergence of the Political Machine," 27–30.

21. *Times,* March 18, 20, 21 (quote), 1879; *Tribune,* March 16, 1879.

22. *Times,* March 29, April 1, 1879. See the Democrats' election-eve speeches in the *Times,* April 1, 1879.

23. *Illinois Staats-Zeitung,* March 26, 1879 (quote); Pierce, *A History of Chicago,* 3:353–54; Willis J. Abbot, *Carter Henry Harrison: A Memoir* (New York: Dodd, Mead, 1895), 50–51.

24. *Times,* March 27, 28, 1879; *Illinois Staats-Zeitung,* March 27, 1879.

25. *Vorbote,* March 29, 1879; *Der Westen* (Sunday edition of the *Illinois Staats-Zeitung*), March 23, 1879; *Times,* March 23, 29, 1879.

26. Figures on male citizens were calculated from our sample of the 1870 federal manuscript population census, supplemented by the "Historical Census Browser," University of Virginia Library, http://fisher.lib.virginia.edu/collections/stats/histcensus/ (accessed June 10, 2009); see also Paul Kleppner, *Who Voted?: The Dynamics of Electoral Turnout, 1870–1980* (New York: Praeger, 1982), 163–65; Leon E. Aylsworth, "The Passing of Alien Suffrage," *American Political Science Review* 25 (February 1931): 114–16.

27. *Times,* March 27, 1879.

28. *Illinois Staats-Zeitung,* April 2, 1879 (quote); *Tribune,* April 3, 1879; Schneirov, *Labor and Urban Politics,* 87–88; Nelson, *Beyond the Martyrs,* 63–64. Nelson's ecological regression between Socialist voting and national origin found the correlation between German origins and SLP voting to be (Pearson's r) +.931, followed by Bohemians at +.423 and Poles at +.411.

29. The total vote is calculated by adding the results for all candidates from all parties for the most prominent office in the election. The presidential vote in 1876 amounted to 61,216, while the mayoral vote in 1879 totaled 57,951. The previous high in a local election since 1876 was the April 1876 mayoral contest in which the People's Party fought desperately against a Republican-dominated reform coalition; see *Illinois Staats-Zeitung,* April 3, 4, 1879.

30. These figures were calculated from voting statistics in the *Tribune,* April 3, 1879.

31. Ibid.

32. Morton Keller, *America's Three Regimes: A New Political History* (New York: Oxford University Press, 2007), 1–6, 133–50 (quote 2.); Eldon J. Eisenach, *The Lost Promise of Progressivism* (Lawrence: University Press of Kansas, 1994), 8–47; Karen Orren and Stephen Skowronek, "Regimes and Regime Building in American Government: A Review of Literature on the 1940s," *Political Science Quarterly* 113 (Winter 1998–99): 693–702.

33. Antonio Gramsci, *Quaderni del Carcere* (Turin, Italy: G. Einaudi, 1975), 3:1638; Perry Anderson, "Force and Consent," *New Left Review* 17 (September–October 2002), http://www.newleftreview.org/?view=2407 (accessed June 25, 2011); Keller, *America's Three Regimes,* 1–6, 133–50.

34. Orren and Skowronek, "Regimes and Regime Building in American Government," 698–701.

35. *Tribune,* April 29, 1879.

36. Theda Skocpol, *Protecting Soldiers and Mothers: The Political Origins of Social Policy in the United States* (Cambridge, Mass.: Belknap Press, 1992), 71–76.

37. *Tribune,* April 29 (quote), June 7, 19, 1879; Robert H. Whitten, "The Assessment of Taxes in Chicago," *Journal of Political Economy* 5 (March 1897): 175–78; Shefter, "The Emergence of the Political Machine," 28. The 2 percent limit did not apply to taxes levied to pay bonded debt.

38. Whitten, "The Assessment of Taxes in Chicago," 177.

39. *Inter Ocean,* March 28, April 24, May 16, 1878.

40. Stephen Skowronek has called this Gilded Age hybrid process "state-building as patchwork"; Stephen Skowronek, *Building a New American State: The Expansion of National Administrative Capacities, 1877–1920* (Cambridge: Cambridge University Press, 1982), 16, 45–46; see also Jon C. Teaford, *Unheralded Triumph: City Government in America, 1870–1900* (Baltimore, Md.: Johns Hopkins University Press, 1984). On Harrison, the comptroller, and the appointment of competent professionals, see Schneirov, *Labor and Urban Politics,* 88–89, 142–43; Shefter, "The Emergence of the Political Machine," 27–30. All quotes from Harrison's inaugural are from *Tribune,* April 29, 1879.

41. *Tribune,* April 29, 1879 (quote); Schneirov, *Labor and Urban Politics,* 87–94; Skocpol, *Protecting Soldiers and Mothers,* 79–80.

42. Schneirov, *Labor and Urban Politics,* 110–13; Citizens' Association of Chicago, *Annual Reports,* 1885, 21.

43. *Tribune,* April 29 (quote), May 14, 1879, April 5, 1883; Pierce, *A History of Chicago,* 3:360; Teaford, *Unheralded Triumph,* 56, 60–64; Schneirov, *Labor and Urban Politics,* 60–63, 89, 162–68.

44. Claudius O. Johnson, *Carter Harrison I: A Political Leader* (Chicago: University of Chicago Press, 1928), 150; Schmidt and Schmidt, *He Chose,* 122–23; *Tribune,* April 18, June 7, 25, July 7, October 28, 1879, September 3, 1880, April 5, 6, 7, 1881, September 8, 1885; *Times,* August 28, 1884; Pierce, *A History of Chicago,* 3:352–54, 356, 379–80, 539; Schneirov, *Labor and Urban Politics,* 88–89; David Montgomery, *Citizen Worker: The Experience of Workers in the United State with Democracy and the Free Market during the Nineteenth Century* (Cambridge: Cambridge University Press, 1993), 152–53.

45. Schneirov, *Labor and Urban Politics,* 88–89, 142–44.

46. Ibid., 87–94; Daniel Bell, *Marxian Socialism in the United States* (Ithaca, N.Y.: Cornell University Press, 1994 [1952]), distinguishes between a Socialist politics of "responsibility" and one of "conscience."

47. Eric Foner, *Reconstruction: America's Unfinished Revolution, 1863–1877* (New York: Harper and Row, 1988), 460. For surveys of recent historical literature on Reconstruction, see Lacy K. Ford, ed., *A Companion to the Civil War and Reconstruction* (Malden, Mass.: Blackwell, 2005).

48. Barrington Moore Jr., *Social Origins of Dictatorship and Democracy: Lord and Peasant in the Making of the Modern World* (Boston: Beacon Press, 1966), 110–55.

49. Nancy Cohen, *The Reconstruction of American Liberalism, 1865–1914* (Chapel Hill: University of North Carolina Press, 2002), 1–60. While we agree with Cohen that Reconstruction-era liberals were not doctrinaire laissez-faire thinkers and sanctioned an expanded state, in our view her study overemphasizes the antidemocratic nature of liberal thinking in at least three ways: (1) by contrasting Reconstruction-era liberalism with Civil War Republican radicalism rather than antebellum liberalism (in Chicago, the segmented regime), she makes postwar development appear to be a degeneration rather than an advance; (2) by focusing on the theoretical writings of a small number of reform intellectuals rather than on practical politicians forced to balance and reconcile competing social classes, interests, and movements, she narrows the definition of Reconstruction-era liberalism; and (3) by slighting the contested character of the public sphere during Reconstruction and the mutual accommodations that occurred there between democratic movements and the imperatives of class rule, she misses the give-and-take of politics. For an interpretation of this period that also emphasizes the decline of democracy, see Sven Beckert, *The Monied Metropolis: New York City and the Consolidation of the American Bourgeoisie, 1850–1896* (Cambridge: Cambridge University Press, 2001).

50. Skowronek, *Building a New American State*, 16, 45–46. For two recent books that argue that the post–Civil War labor movement had a major impact on urban politics, see John Enyeart, *The Quest for "Just and Pure Law": Rocky Mountain Workers and American Social Democracy, 1870–1924* (Palo Alto, Calif.: Stanford University Press, 2009); and George Du Bois Jr., *Cross-Class Alliances and the Birth of Modern Liberalism: Maryland's Workers, 1865–1916* (Baltimore: Chesapeake, 2008).

51. Shefter, "The Emergence of the Political Machine," 28 (quote); Teaford, *Unheralded Triumph*, 6–9 (quote 6).

52. *Tribune*, April 29, 1879.

Index

Chicago Astronomical Society, 29

Chicago Board of Insurance Underwriters, 180

Chicago Board of Trade, 24, 45, 69, 180, 201–2, 226

Chicago Citizens' Association, 7; acts as "goal-integrating elite," 172, 192; charter reform, 184–85, 188, 235; credibility shrinks, 212–13; criticizes businessmen for tax fighting (fraud), 211–12, 213; fire marshal, 183–84; funds businessmen's militias, 169, 184, 209; influence on Heath administration, 190; lobbies for state law banning military parades, 169; MacVeagh and, 173, 178–79, 182–83; origins, 179; police, 238, 239; program of, 171–72, 225; purposes of, 180–81; relation to Central Church of David Swing, 182; Republican regime, 235; response to railroad strike of 1877, 210–11, 238; saloon license fee policy, 238; shrinks into good government interest group, 212–13, 219, 238; suffrage position, 183, 198; tax assessment, 226; vagrancy law, 210. *See also* MacVeagh, Franklin

Chicago Common Council, 30–33, 91, 92–93, 135–36, 183, 187–88, 189, 190

Chicago Daily Inter-Ocean, 176, 199

Chicagoer Arbeiter Zeitung, 168–69, 221, 229, 240

Chicago idea, 217

Chicago Manual Training School, 210

Chicago Mechanical Bakery, 46

Chicago Post, 75

Chicago Relief and Aid Society: acts as private government, 184; control of by city's capitalists, 135–36; depression of 1857 and, 35, 36; fear of dangerous classes, 7; labor market policies after 1871 fire, 136; model

for Citizens Reform, 133; origins and founding of, 49; Republican regime and, 10, 235; Socialists, 6–7, 159; subsidizes housing for stable working-class after 1871 fire, 140; Throop's employment plan, 36; urges unemployed to move to countryside, 124

Chicago Republican, 96–98, 109, 115, 176

Chicago River, 50, 51

Chicago Times, 34–35, 78, 94, 105–6, 109, 222, 227–28

Chicago Tribune, 5; advocates laissez-faire liberalism, 89; Civil War interpreted, 53; editors of, 5, 94–95; eight-hour day strike, 94–85, 105–6, 109; election of 1879, 233; fear of dangerous classes, 177–78; fire of 1874, 179; free trade, 132; Medill replaces White, 185; need to attract Eastern capital, 136; opposes machine politicians, 171; opposes Socialists, 175; railroad strike of 1877, 207–8; relation to Socialist program, 161; supports *Chicago Times* during strike, 78

Chicago Union, 150

Chicago Woman's Club, 209

cigarmakers, 206

Cincinnati, 15–16, 26–27, 42, 46–47, 114

Citizens reform movement, 132–34, 136

civil society, 8, 30, 51, 125–26, 129, 234, 245

Civil War-Reconstruction: democracy and 10–12, 53, 60, 66, 242, 243; federal financing of capital accumulation, 25–26, 56–57, 161; interpretation of, 10–11, 53, 56–57, 242, 293n49; labor and, 53, 60, 66, 79–80, 102. *See also* Reconstruction

class consciousness: distance between classes, 48–49; upper class, 7, 9,

and, 86, 108–10; skilled workers, 97; state law, 5, 93, 100–102; strike, 100–10; strike leadership, 106–7, 266–67n61; theory, 84; unskilled workers and, 103; wage-labor and, 82–85, 98

Einhorn, Robin, 30, 32, 60

Electorate, 146, 151–52, 158, 173, 229–31

Emancipation Proclamation, 2–3, 60–64

England. *See* Great Britain

Evangelical Protestants, 59; British dissenting tradition, 59, 85; eight-hour day movement and, 108–9; election of 1879, 229; marginalized, 9, 234–35; Methodism, 86–87; ministers support charter reform, 188; remedy for tyranny of the majority, 174; revival of 1876, 190–92, 243–44. *See also* temperance and Sabbath-keeping issue

Fackel, 168–69

Farwell, John, 191

Fenian National Fair, 73–74

Fenians, 58, 63, 64, 65–66, 73, 78, 92, 93, 215, 235

Feodore, Charles, 48

Field, Henry, 191

Field, Leiter and Company, 204

Field, Marshall, 25, 180, 191, 208, 210, 211, 238

Fincher, Jonathan C., 85, 87, 90, 109

Fincher's Trade Review, 85

fire insurance crisis, 179–80, 183–84

fire limits controversy, 137–40, 149, 180. *See also* Great Chicago Fire

Foner, Eric, 10, 242

Foran, Martin A., 116

foreign born: civil society, 129; entrepreneurs, 40–41, 130; local government, 129; middling stratum, 129; by nationality, 152; share of electorate,

151, 158, 173, 229–31; in trades, 70–71; workers, 18, 58

Fortnightly Club, 209

Fort Sheridan, 209

France, 11

Franco-Prussian War, 1871, 134

free-labor ideology, 14, 33–34, 94–96

free trade, 95, 96

Frémont, John, 61, 74, 88

French Revolution, 175

furniture workers union, 158, 207, 219

Gage, Lyman, 156

Galena and Chicago Union Railroad, 29, 72

garment workers, 46–47. *See also* women

Gates, P. W., 34, 39–40, 98, 99, 101, 113

General Trades Assembly: celebration of July 4, 88; cooperates with Arbeiter-Central-Verein, 126–27; disbanded, 110; founded, 53 67–68, 72; inter-ethnic unity, 72, 75, 129; labor convention organized (1868), 126; political platform (1868), 131; relation to public sphere and political parties, 73, 74–77, 79, 134; size, 127–28; support for eight-hour day, 102–3, 109; support for strikes, 69–70, 75–76, 102–3, 109; unions composing, 67–68, 90–91. *See also* Arbeiter-Central-Verein; trade unions

German Aid society, 23

German artisan entrepreneurs, 98–99

German district, Northside, 138, 140, 147; subculture, 168

German forty-eighters, 25, 35, 36, 60–62, 65–66, 74, 108, 127, 128, 159–60, 235

German Lutherans, 191

German Turners, 106–7; Democratic regime, 235; militia role, 170

tee of 25, 145, 146; convicted in Whiskey scandal, 188; democratic governance, 243; dual authority, 195; election of 1874, 187; founds and leads People's Party, 149, 151–52; idealizes stable working-class, 140, 142, 146–47; intertwining of politics and business, 130; leads march against fire limits, 117, 138–39; opposes Socialists, 163; purchases *Illinois Staats Zeitung*, 61; supports civil rights of black teamster during Civil War, 64; supports fire limits extension, 180; supports Lincoln, 61; target of Socialists, 160. See also *Illinois Staats Zeitung*

Hickey, Michael, 197, 202
Hielscher, Theodore, 62, 74
Hobsbawm, Eric, 1, 68, 82
Hoffmann, Jr., Francis A., 159–60, 227
Holden, Charles C. P., 136
home ownership, 7, 121, 138, 140. *See also* fire limits controversy
Howe, George, 180
Hoyne, Thomas, 188, 189
Hurlbut Bros. and Company, 69

Illinois and Michigan Canal, 15, 24, 36, 39
Illinois Bureau of Labor Statistics, 223
Illinois Central Car Works, 39, 91
Illinois Central Railroad, 72, 75, 76, 106, 197
Illinois 82nd Regiment, 61, 64
Illinois Grange, 163
Illinois National Guard, 197, 204
Illinois 90th Regiment, 64–65
Illinois Staats Zeitung: attacks Medill over saloon closing, 149; condemns Marxist influence, 159; cooperative movement, 163; election of 1879, 231; Ernst Schmidt, 225; founded, 35, 60–61; Hermann Raster and, 177;

opposes fire limits, 137, 139; railroad strike of 1877, 202, 207, 212; relation to Socialists, 160–61, 163, 164; supports eight-hour demand, 97. *See also* Hesing, Anton
Illinois 23rd Regiment, 62
immigrant workers, 17–18, 24, 58, 129. *See also* foreign born
immigration, 18, 23–24, 57–59, 119–20, 229–30
Industrial Congress, 166
Ingersoll, Robert G., 101
interconvertible bond system, 130. *See also* currency reform
International Association of Ship Carpenters and Caulkers, 86
International Labor Union, 222
International Workingmen's Association, 131–32
Ireland, 64
Irish Brigade, 62
Irish nationalists: builds genuine movement, 213; Catholic Church and, 62–63; forty-eighters, 62; Irish community and, 62–63; Irish national fund, 215; origins, 65; picnics, 215; ties to Socialists, 215; transnational republicanism, 65. *See also* Fenians
Irish workers: brick makers, 214; butchers and packinghouse workers, 306, 214–15; concentration in construction and metal working, 111, 126, 147; integration into labor movement, 111–12, 126, 214–15; laborers, 270n20; railroad strike of 1877, 204, 205–6; rebuilding after fire, 147; whiteness and racism, 63, 64
Iron Age, 212
Iroquois Club, 208

Jackson, Thomas "Stonewall," 64
Jaher, Frederic, 29

during railroad strike of 1877, 198; farmers, 18; German version of, 162; politicizes and empowers immigrant working-class, 117–18, 149–52; relation to producers' social order, 121. *See also* Hesing, Anton; People's Party

Porter, Glenn, 26

Powers, Richard, 214

Prairie Farmer, 163

Presbyterian Church, 181–82

Presbyterian Theological Seminar, 29

producers' cooperation: alternative to wage-labor, 82, 84, 163; *Chicago Republican*'s views on, 96–97; *Chicago Tribune*'s views on, 95; constituency of, 84; defined, 83, 99; following eight-hour strike, 113–15; Medill views on, 174. *See also* producers' cooperatives; profit-sharing

producers' cooperatives, 83, 97, 114–15; carpenters, 70; German carpenters, 70; iron molders, 115; machinists, 115; masons, 115; metalworkers, 114–15

producers' republicanism. *See* republicanism

producers' social order, 9, 14, 17, 28, 32, 117, 120, 121, 124, 130–31, 135, 137, 138, 153; republicanism, 28, 63, 82, 84, 165. *See also* populism

profit-sharing, 83, 95, 99, 113–15

protective tariff, 3, 7, 26, 94–98

public sphere, 1–2, 6, 8, 58, 60, 79–80, 90, 109, 117–18, 223, 243, 293n49

Pullman, George, 25, 208, 210

pure and simple unionism, 131, 216–17

railroad car shops, 37, 38–39, 67, 70–71, 91, 101, 106, 110–11

railroad strike of 1877: Battle of Halsted Street, 205–7; Bohemian lumbershovers, 203; Bohemian militia disarmed, 203; boy's role, 100–101; Bridgeport, 205–6; business leaders in, 201–3; butchers and stockyard workers, 206; casualties, 207; *Chicago Tribune* on, 207–8; economic origins, 196; furniture workers, 200; gas workers, 207; glass workers, 207; Hanlon speech, 199; *Illinois Staats Zeitung*, 202, 207; inspires fear, 224; Irish boat hand speech, 203–4; Irish workers, 204–5; map of, 201; Monday events, 198–99; origins of in contrast to East, 194; Parsons speech, 198–99; Philadelphia, 196; Pilsen community, 205; Pittsburgh, 196; police, 203, 204; political impact, 231–33; restoration of wage cuts following, 207; revives union activity, 215, 221; Schilling on, 194; Socialists in, 194–202 passim; spreads from East, 196; threat to capital accumulation, 212; Thursday events, 205–7; Tuesday events, 199–202; Union Army veteran's speech, 199; unions organize, 206; U.S. Army, 204; wage cutting policy reversed, 212; Wednesday's events, 202–4; women, 206

railroad workers, 72. *See also* railroad strike of 1877

Ramsbottom, Jabez, 107

Rapp, Wilhelm, 139

Raster, Hermann, 177, 212, 228

real estate: Gilded Age upper class investments of, 170–71; importance for booster elite, 24, 36–37, 135

Reconstruction: constitutional amendments, 118; dangerous classes, 177–78; democracy and, 11–12, 60, 242, 243, 293n49; disillusionment with, 183; issues of, 92; North, 242; radical republicans, 92–93; restoration of Democratic voting strength in 1874, 186; under siege, 118; social movements, 243–44; suffrage of freedmen, 175, 177–78, 184; support for redistributing rebel estates, 76. *See also* Civil War-Reconstruction regimes, 9–10, 27–33, 51, 195, 234–35. *See also* Harrison, Carter; segmented regime

Reno, C. A., 152

republicanism, 54, 153; artisan, 55; compared to European version, 56, 57–58, 161–62, 166, 170; distribution of wealth, 54–55; during railroad strike of 1877, 198–99; Jacksonian, 165; Jacobin, 58; producers', 28, 63, 77, 120, 130, 153; relation to liberalism, 54; theory of state, 165; transnational, 4, 56, 58, 62, 109; two transnational labor traditions, 166–67, 192, 221. *See also* free-labor ideology

Republican party: administration of Monroe Heath, 189–90; attitude toward wage-labor, 3–4, 14; Barnacles, 132, 136; *Chicago Tribune*, 94–95; conservative turn, 110; depression of 1857 and, 36; depression of 1873 and, 6; economic program, 161; eight-hour day, 93, 96, 101, 105, 194–95; election of 1866, 91; election of 1879, 226–33; emancipation proclamation, 2–3, 60–64; Frémont campaign, 88; German manufacturers in, 88; Germans leave, 6, 118, 167, 225–28, 231, 233; Grant elected president, 110; immigrants and, 130; inability to win workers' consent, 219; Irish, 64; Liberals, 5, 74, 95, 118, 132–33; Liberals vote Socialist, 225, 231–33; national, 2; party realignment, 1879–97, 220; protective tariff and free trade, 3, 26, 95–97, 132; radicals, 4, 6, 92, 93, 99–100, 110, 172,

181; Reconstruction, 118; regime, 51, 234–35; response to economic theory predicting impoverishment, 176; special mayoral election of 1876, 189; Stalwarts, 5, 133; suffrage, 175; taint of corruption, 187; temperance issue, 173, 181, 187. *See also* Lincoln administration; Medill, Joseph; Reconstruction

Ricardo, David, 96, 176

Rice, John B., 81, 91, 103, 143, 194–95

Richmond, VA, 76

Robertson, Darrel M., 191

Rochdale cooperative stores, 86

Rock Island and Chicago Railroad, 199

Rock Island and Pacific Railroad, 197

Roediger, David, 63, 86

Rosen, Christine, 274n52

Rosenbloom, Joshua, 23

Ross, Steven, J., 40

Rush Medical College, 29

Sawislak, Karen, 274n52

Saxton, Alexander, 63

Scheller, Martin, 48

Schilling, George, 194, 197

Schindler, Georg, 144

Schläger, Eduard, 58, 72, 75, 76, 108, 113, 128

Schmidt, Ernst, 225, 227, 231, 240, 244

Schmitz, Mark, 39

Schulze-Delitzsch, Franz Hermann, 173–74

Schwenck, Nikolaus, 33, 34, 39–40

Scranton, Philip, 98

Scroggs, George, 224

Seaman's Union, 218

segmented regime, 27–33, 36–37, 50–52, 60, 137, 242. *See also* regimes

Seipp, William, 227

Shaler, Alexander, 183–84

Shefter, Martin, 244

Shephard, Henry, M., 101

Shepherd, James, 23–24
Sheridan, Mark, 148–49, 184
Sheridan, Philip, 136
Sherman, Elijah B., 224
Sherman, William Tecumseh, 76
ship carpenters, 86
skilled workers, 40–41, 58, 68, 70–72, 128; bakers, 69–70; British, 86–87, 110–11; compared to Jacksonian era and contemporary European journeymen, 70; coopers, 68–69; craftsmen, 45–47; factory artisans, 40, 87, 112; home ownership, 122; by industry and nationality, 71, 112; Irish, 111, 126
Skocpol, Theda, 11, 236
Skowronek, Stephen, 244
Smith, Perry, 227
socialism. *See* Socialists
Socialistic Publishing Company, 229
Socialist Labor Party (SLP), 218; declines, 241–42; Democratic regime, 235; election of 1877, 221; election of 1878, 223; election of 1879, 225–33; income tax, 221; increased membership, 221; platform, 225–26. *See also* Socialists; Workingmen's Party of the United States
Socialists, 9; *Chicago Tribune*'s evaluation of, 175; claim to represent workers, 224; decline after 1874 debate over state militia bill, 224; elections, 167–68, 170, 217, 229–33; English-speaking leadership, 196–97, 213–14; Harrison woos, 9, 221–22, 238–41; immunity against in East, 194; inability to unite workers, 243–44; international character, 162, 168; "Internationals" and depression of 1873, 158–65; Marxists and Lassalleans, 35, 158, 168, 196–97, 215–16, 217–18, 220, 241; naturalization efforts, 230–31; program,

160–61, 278n13; railroad strike of 1877, 194–202 passim, 205, 217; reform and revolutionary wings of socialism, 241; Scandinavians, 168; socialism as extension of republicanism, 222; state investigation of workers' conditions, 223–24; subculture, 168–69, 195; transnational character of, 221. *See also* Socialist Labor Party; Workingmen's Party of Illinois; Workingmen's Party of the United States
Sons of Erin, 64
Sozial Demokratische Arbeiterpartei (Germany), 159
Sozial-Demokratische Arbeiterverein (formerly Sozial-Politischer Arbeiterverein), 159
Sozialer Arbeiterverein, 149
Sozial-Politischer Arbeiterverein, 158
Stalwarts, 5, 133. *See also* Republican Party
Stanley, Amy Dru, 82
Stauber, Frank, 221
Stephens, James, 65
Steward, Ira, 84, 89, 115–16, 216
St. Georges Hall, 106–7
St. Louis, 15–16, 24, 86 188, 202
Stonecutters Union, 195, 206
Storey, Wilbur, 78, 227
Storrs, E. A., 180
Strehlow, Albert, 127
strikes: against Illinois Central Railroad, 76; bakers, 66, 69; butchers and packinghouse workers, 214–15; carpenters, 66–67, 144; coopers, 66; Harrison's policy toward, 239; Joseph Medill, 141; labor uprisings during strikes, 245; New York eight-hour day, 142–43; painters, 66; political action and, 216; printers, 67, 75, 78; railroad workers, 67, 72, 76; reasons for Civil War strike

surge, 73; reliance on crowd actions, 103, 199–200; tailors, 66; wage inflation during Civil War, 68. *See also* eight-hour day movement; railroad strike of 1877

Swedes, 23, 147

Swedish Emigrant Society, 23

Swing, Rev. David, 181–82, 236

Sylvis, William, 88–89, 91, 116, 130, 160

tailors union, 46–47, 206

tax assessment: businessmen's revolt (tax fighting or tax fraud), 188–90, 211, 226, 237; decline in assessed values in city, 186, 211, 237; Harrison, 236–37; Illinois Supreme Court decision of 1787, 211; immunity of wealthy from taxation, 151; platform of Socialists, 226; relation to capital accumulation, 171

Taylor, William D., 107

Teaford, Jon C., 244

temperance and Sabbath-keeping issue: alienates Germans, 118, 149; Carter Harrison, 228, 236, 238–39; failure of politically, 174; Lager Beer Riot, 33, 137, 149; Medill administration enforces Sunday closing, 148; Moody revival and, 191; People's Party opposes temperance forces, 150–53; resolution of, 151–52, 181, 187; support for enforcement, 145–56. *See also* People's Party

Tenth Ward Sozialer Arbeiterverein, 61, 64

Thompson, William H., 224

Throop, A. G., 34, 37, 49, 61, 104

Tobey and Booth, 42–44

Tracy, James, 75

Trade and Labor Council, 218, 222, 223, 241

trade unions: butchers and packing-house workers, 42–44, 214–15, 218–19; Cameron on need for cooperation among unions, 213; carpenters, 66–67, 70, 82, 115, 143, 207; Catholic Church, 214–15; civil society and, 126; coopers, 68, 69, 206; depression of 1873, 195; furniture workers, 158, 207, 219; German unions, 128–29; Harrison's policy toward, 239, 240; home ownership and, 121–22; interethnic cooperation, 58, 59, 67, 71–72, 75, 79–80, 105, 144, 213–14, 218–19; Irish and, 111–12, 126; leadership, 58; locomotive engineers, 72, 196; Marxists in, 215–16; metalworkers, 75, 85, 106–7, 114–15; national, 128; in North, 67, 70, 85; populism, 154; printers, 68, 75, 100, 167, 195; pure and simple, 131, 216–17; railroad strike of 1877 revives, 214–15, 221; rebuilding after Fire, 142–43; reliance on crowd actions, 199–200; revive after depression, 241; seamen, 218; Socialists and, 166–67, 241; syndicalism, 217; tailors, 46–47, 206; transition from mutual benefit societies, 66. *See also* General Trades Assembly; *specific unions*

transient workers: crime fear, 141, 145; hostility to, 120; immigrant background, 119; mobility of, 120, 140; rebuilding after 1871 fire, 140–41, 145; socialist constituency, 170; strangers, 122, 141, 157; "tramp menace," 157, 196; vagrancy law, 196

transnational social republicanism, 4, 56, 157, 166–67, 221, 222. *See also* republicanism

Trevellick, Richard, 86–89, 91, 97, 102, 107, 160

Turners, 106–7; Democratic regime, 235; militia role, 170

Typographical Union, 68, 75, 100, 167, 195

unemployed march of 1873, 155, 158, 159

Union Fireproof Ticket, 136, 172

Union League Club, 208

Union Rolling Stock Company, 203

Union Stockyards, 211

unskilled workers: boardinghouses, 22–23; carpenters, 144; categories of laborer "works in," 21–22; depression of 1873, 157; eight-hour day strike, 85, 103–6; general labor market, 22–24, 68, 119–20, 141; home ownership and, 122; in industry, 21–24, 37, 42–44, 103; outdoor work, 44–45, 103, 199–200; railroad laborers, 71, 72; women, 122–24. *See also* transient workers

upper class (bourgeoisie): absence of enlightened conservatives, 237; businessmen's tax revolt, 186–87; clubs formed, 208; comptroller, 238; corruption, 237; dangerous classes, 177–78, 213, 219, 235; depression of 1873, 170; desire for class peace, 238–39; during crisis of 1874, 180, 181–82; during railroad strike of 1877, 201–3; emerges from segmented regime, 49–50; government, 50; Harrison integrates into regime, 10, 236–37; hegemony, 154, 191–93, 244–45; institutions, 48–49; lack of unity on response to railroad strike of 1877, 210–11, 219; philanthropy, 209; real estate investments of, 24, 170–71; Reconstruction, 242–43; reform of working-class character, 209–10; relation to Citizens Association, 172, 181; relation to Relief and Aid Society, 49–50; relation to temperance issue, 181; response to railroad strike of 1877, 9, 208–13, 238; self-awareness, 7, 49–50, 157, 181–82, 158; strategies, 7; tax fight-

ing, 211; transition from booster to capitalist leadership, 24–26, 49–50; united by David Swing, 181–82; urban establishment (1837–68), 29; wage cutting policy, 212. *See also* boosters; class consciousness; hegemony

Vagrant Act, 196, 240

Van Patten, Philip, 197

Vicksburg, 64

Vorbote, 160, 162, 168, 197, 215, 221, 223

wage-labor: acceptance of vs. resistance to, 1, 3, 14–15, 34, 55, 68, 82–85, 100–101, 115–16; citizenship and, 83; Lincoln on, 14; Madison on, 1; property ownership and, 14; Republican Party response to, 3–4, 14–15; rules of game, 68; unskilled, 21–24; vs. self-employment, 82, 84, 85, 115; wage-slavery, 55, 82, 98; women and, 124–25. *See also* eight-hour day movement

wages: depression of 1873, 155, 156–57; inflated value of during Civil War, 68; Malthus' theory of, 176; real wages in Midwest, 23–24

Ward, E. B., 38

Warner, E. S., 114

Washburne, Elihu, 148, 149

Wentworth, John, 79, 187

Westen, 124

Western Union Company, 161

White, Horace: anti-statism, 175–79; career of, 172; despairs of integrating urban masses into society, 177–78; free trade supporter, 132, 176; limiting suffrage, 175, 184; national workshops, 175–76; opposition to and fear of Socialists, 175, 177; opposition to inflation, 177; rethinking agenda of Republican Party, 94–95,

174–75; supports profit-sharing, 114; temperance issue, 173. *See also* liberalism

whiteness, 63, 65, 74, 79, 259n19

Wilentz, Sean, 46

Williamson, Jeffrey G., 23, 276n3

Wisconsin, 91

Woman's Christian Temperance Union, 125

women: challenge to society posed by new roles, 67, 123–24; civil rights in Illinois, 125; clubs formed, 209; during railroad strike of 1877, 206–7; employment of, 13, 20–22; feminism, 124–25; in Fenian National Fair, 74; garment workers (sewing girls), 122–23, 125; Great Fire, 136; prostitution, 49, 123; servants, 123–24, 136; war widow problem, 123

Woodman, C. L., 45

Workingman's Advocate, 68, 75, 79, 98, 106, 110, 121–22, 130–31, 142, 166. *See also* Cameron, Andrew

Workingmen's Party of Illinois: election of fall 1874, 163, 167; election of spring 1874, 163; fire limits position, 180; foreign language groups, 162; founded, 159–60; reform program, 160–62; relation to English-speaking organizations, 164; relation to Grangers, 162; *Vorbote* founded, 162. *See also* Klings, Carl

Workingmen's Party of the United States (WPUS): English-speaking leaders in, 196–97; founded, 196; income tax, 221–22; Lassalleans and Marxists in, 196, 197, 217–18

Wright, Albert W., 226, 227, 229

JOHN B. JENTZ is research and outreach librarian at Marquette University and the editor of *German Workers in Industrial Chicago, 1850–1910: A Comparative Perspective.*

RICHARD SCHNEIROV is professor of history at Indiana State University and the coeditor of *The Pullman Strike and the Crisis of the 1890s: Essays on Labor and Politics.*

THE WORKING CLASS IN AMERICAN HISTORY

German Workers in Chicago: A Documentary History of Working-Class
   Culture from 1850 to World War I   *Edited by Hartmut Keil and John B. Jentz*

On the Line: Essays in the History of Auto Work   *Edited by Nelson Lichtenstein
   and Stephen Meyer III*

Labor's Flaming Youth: Telephone Operators and Worker Militancy,
   1878–1923   *Stephen H. Norwood*

Another Civil War: Labor, Capital, and the State in the Anthracite Regions
   of Pennsylvania, 1840–68   *Grace Palladino*

Coal, Class, and Color: Blacks in Southern West Virginia, 1915–32
   Joe William Trotter Jr.

For Democracy, Workers, and God: Labor Song-Poems and Labor Protest,
   1865–95   *Clark D. Halker*

Dishing It Out: Waitresses and Their Unions in the Twentieth Century
   Dorothy Sue Cobble

The Spirit of 1848: German Immigrants, Labor Conflict, and the Coming
   of the Civil War   *Bruce Levine*

Working Women of Collar City: Gender, Class, and Community in Troy, New
   York, 1864–86   *Carole Turbin*

Southern Labor and Black Civil Rights: Organizing Memphis Workers
   Michael K. Honey

Radicals of the Worst Sort: Laboring Women in Lawrence, Massachusetts,
   1860–1912   *Ardis Cameron*

Producers, Proletarians, and Politicians: Workers and Party Politics
   in Evansville and New Albany, Indiana, 1850–87   *Lawrence M. Lipin*

The New Left and Labor in the 1960s   *Peter B. Levy*

The Making of Western Labor Radicalism: Denver's Organized Workers,
   1878–1905   *David Brundage*

In Search of the Working Class: Essays in American Labor History
   and Political Culture   *Leon Fink*

Lawyers against Labor: From Individual Rights to Corporate Liberalism
   Daniel R. Ernst

"We Are All Leaders": The Alternative Unionism of the Early 1930s
   Edited by Staughton Lynd

The Female Economy: The Millinery and Dressmaking Trades, 1860–
   1930   *Wendy Gamber*

"Negro and White, Unite and Fight!": A Social History of Industrial
   Unionism in Meatpacking, 1930–90   *Roger Horowitz*

Power at Odds: The 1922 National Railroad Shopmen's Strike   *Colin J. Davis*

The Common Ground of Womanhood: Class, Gender, and Working Girls'
   Clubs, 1884–1928   *Priscilla Murolo*

Marching Together: Women of the Brotherhood of Sleeping Car
   Porters   *Melinda Chateauvert*

Down on the Killing Floor: Black and White Workers in Chicago's
   Packinghouses, 1904–54   *Rick Halpern*

Labor and Urban Politics: Class Conflict and the Origins of Modern Liberalism
   in Chicago, 1864–97   *Richard Schneirov*

James P. Cannon and the Origins of the American Revolutionary Left,
    1890–1928   *Bryan D. Palmer*
Glass Towns: Industry, Labor, and Political Economy in Appalachia,
    1890–1930s   *Ken Fones-Wolf*
Workers and the Wild: Conservation, Consumerism, and Labor in Oregon,
    1910–30   *Lawrence M. Lipin*
Wobblies on the Waterfront: Interracial Unionism in Progressive-Era
    Philadelphia   *Peter Cole*
Red Chicago: American Communism at Its Grassroots, 1928–35   *Randi Storch*
Labor's Cold War: Local Politics in a Global Context   *Edited by
    Shelton Stromquist*
Bessie Abramowitz Hillman and the Making of the Amalgamated Clothing
    Workers of America   *Karen Pastorello*
The Great Strikes of 1877   *Edited by David O. Stowell*
Union-Free America: Workers and Antiunion Culture   *Lawrence Richards*
Race against Liberalism: Black Workers and the UAW in Detroit
    David M. Lewis-Colman
Teachers and Reform: Chicago Public Education, 1929–70   *John F. Lyons*
Upheaval in the Quiet Zone: 1199/SEIU and the Politics of Healthcare
    Unionism   *Leon Fink and Brian Greenberg*
Shadow of the Racketeer: Scandal in Organized Labor   *David Witwer*
Sweet Tyranny: Migrant Labor, Industrial Agriculture, and Imperial
    Politics   *Kathleen Mapes*
Staley: The Fight for a New American Labor Movement   *Steven K. Ashby
    and C. J. Hawking*
On the Ground: Labor Struggles in the American Airline Industry
    Liesl Miller Orenic
NAFTA and Labor in North America   *Norman Caulfield*
Making Capitalism Safe: Work Safety and Health Regulation in America,
    1880–1940   *Donald W. Rogers*
Good, Reliable, White Men: Railroad Brotherhoods, 1877–1917
    Paul Michel Taillon
Spirit of Rebellion: Labor and Religion in the New Cotton South
    Jarod Roll
The Labor Question in America: Economic Democracy in the
    Gilded Age   *Rosanne Currarino*
Banded Together: Economic Democratization in the Brass Valley
    Jeremy Brecher
The Gospel of the Working Class: Labor's Southern Prophets in New Deal
    America   *Erik Gellman and Jarod Roll*
Guest Workers and Resistance to U.S. Corporate Despotism   *Immanuel Ness*
Gleanings of Freedom: Free and Slave Labor along the Mason-Dixon Line,
    1790–1860   *Max Grivno*
Chicago in the Age of Capital: Class, Politics, and Democracy during
    the Civil War and Reconstruction   *John B. Jentz and Richard Schneirov*

The University of Illinois Press
is a founding member of the
Association of American University Presses.

University of Illinois Press
1325 South Oak Street
Champaign, IL 61820-6903
www.press.uillinois.edu